MGB
Owners Workshop Manual

J H Haynes OBE
Member of the Guild of Motoring Writers

Models covered

All models of the MGB Roadster and GT Coupé with 1798 cc (110 cu in) engine
Does not cover MGB GT V8

(111 - 3T4 - 240)

© Haynes Publishing 2010

A book in the **Haynes Service and Repair Manual Series**

All rights reserved. No part of this book may be reproduced or transmitted in any form or by any means, electronic or mechanical, including photocopying, recording or by any information storage or retrieval system, without permission in writing from the copyright holder.

ISBN **978 0 85733 707 8**

British Library Cataloguing in Publication Data
A catalogue record for this book is available from the British Library

ABCDE
FGHIJ
KLMNO
PQRS
4

Printed in Malaysia

Haynes Publishing
Sparkford, Yeovil, Somerset BA22 7JJ, England

Haynes North America, Inc
859 Lawrence Drive, Newbury Park, California 91320, USA

Printed using NORBRITE BOOK 48.8gsm (CODE: 40N6533) from NORPAC; procurement system certified under Sustainable Forestry Initiative standard.
Paper produced is certified to the SFI Certified Fiber Sourcing Standard (CERT - 0094271)

Contents

About this manual

Its aim

The aim of this manual is to help you get the best value from your car. It can do so in several ways. It can help you decide what work must be done (even should you choose to get it done by a garage), provide information on routine maintenance and servicing, and give a logical course of action and diagnosis when random faults occur. However, it is hoped that you will use the manual by tackling the work yourself. On simpler jobs it may even be quicker than booking the car into a garage and going there twice to leave and collect it. Perhaps most important, a lot of money can be saved by avoiding the costs the garage must charge to cover its labour and overheads.

The manual has drawings and descriptions to show the function of the various components so that their layout can be understood. Then the tasks are described and photographed in a step-by-step sequence so that even a novice can do the work.

Its arrangement

The manual is divided into twelve Chapters, each covering a logical sub-division of the vehicle. The Chapters are each divided into Sections, numbered with single figures, eg 5; and the Sections into paragraphs (or sub-sections), with decimal numbers following on from the Section they are in, eg 5.1, 5.2, 5.3 etc.

It is freely illustrated, especially in those parts where there is a detailed sequence of operations to be carried out. There are two forms of illustration: figures and photographs. The figures are numbered in sequence with decimal numbers, according to their position in the Chapter – eg Fig. 6.4 is the fourth drawing/illustration in Chapter 6. Photographs carry the same number (either individually or in related groups) as the Section or sub-section to which they relate.

There is an alphabetical index at the back of the manual as well as a contents list.

References to the 'left' or 'right' of the vehicle are in the sense of a person in the driver's seat facing forwards.

Unless otherwise stated, nuts and bolts are removed by turning anti-clockwise, and tightened by turning clockwise.

Vehicle manufacturers continually make changes to specifications and recommendations, and these when notified are incorporated into our manuals at the earliest opportunity.

Acknowledgements

Thanks are due to Marleen Toomer for supplying the 1979 model used in the photographs, *Mike Rolls Services for MGs* (www.mikerolls4mgs.co.uk) and all those people at Sparkford who helped in the production of this manual.

We take great pride in the accuracy of information given in this manual, but vehicle manufacturers make alterations and design changes during the production run of a particular vehicle of which they do not inform us. No liability can be accepted by the authors or publishers for loss, damage or injury caused by any errors in, or omissions from, the information given.

Introduction

The MG name had already become almost synonymous with the term sports car by the time that the famous Abingdon-on-Thames factory began building the first examples of its new MGB in the summer of 1962. The small and in to some extent quaintly old-fashioned plant had already set new factory production records with the previous MGA model, 101,081 examples of which were built in the seven years from launch in 1955 – which happened to be the year before John Haynes published his first manual – but surely nobody anticipated that the new model would be built for 18 years nor in nearly five times as many specimens as its predecessor.

The creation of the MGB was in many ways a work of genius; Chief Designer Syd Enever wanted to make a strong and rigid open sports car without a separate chassis, and the new MG was one of the earliest and best in the field. When MG Managing Director John Thornley saw the estimates for the tooling costs for the new car from body-maker Pressed Steel, he knew that he would have a hard job trying to convince BMC management to foot the bill, so he brokered a clever deal whereby Pressed Steel would shoulder some of the tooling costs in return for a royalty of £2 on every MGB built. It was a clever ruse and it worked.

Modest in size, mechanically simple, fun to drive, slightly over-engineered and great to look at, the pretty MGB was a marketing man's delight and a fabulous introduction to genuine sports car ownership. The all-important North American market was clearly going to be a key focus for sales efforts soon after the launch in September 1962, the first

export cars were not in the hands of US customers until the following spring. A high press profile at launch was given to the Iris Blue colour scheme, and indeed some of the first cars sold in the USA were finished in this colour, many with chrome wire wheels and white-wall tyres.

The MGB was the first car in the British Motor Corporation family to feature a new larger 1,798 c.c. version of the conveniently and coincidentally named 'B-Series' engine; to an extent the MG even served as an engine test bed for the subsequent BMC ADO17 '1800' saloon range, launched in Austin guise in September 1964. However, in anticipation of the 1800, the B-series was further developed to receive five main bearings in place of the original three in the interests of greater refinement, and so in October 1964, the MGB received the new smoother engine as the first of a great many modest enhancements that it would see over its lifetime.

Right from the outset, Thornley and Enever were determined to see a fixed-head coupé version of the MGB, and following the clever ministrations of internationally renowned stylist Pininfarina, the result was the MGB GT of September 1965. The Italian maestro cleverly married the classic curves of the MGB main bodyshell with his

characteristic sharp edged roof lines, with the added innovation of a generous opening tailgate, presaging the much later 'sports hatchback' concept.

By the late summer of 1966, BMC had acquired Pressed Steel, merged with Jaguar and launched the GT version of the MGB in the USA as the 'MGB/GT'. To the public, business looked good but bubbling below the surface of the motoring industry behemoth were growing financial, managerial and technical woes which before long would drive BMC into an ill-starred union with the much smaller but feistier Leyland Corporation, which happened to own MG's dreaded Triumph rival. Profit levels on BMC's bigger-selling models were not what they should have been, and, as the decade wore on, decisions were made which showed significant errors of judgement.

BMC had always offered a large six-cylinder engine saloon car and in order to satisfy this commitment, decided to re-engineered the old BMC six from the Austin-Healey and shoehorn the result into a body closely based on that of the ADO17. At the same time, it was decided that this engine would also be used for a new Austin-Healey and a closely related MG, both to be based on the structure of the MGB. Early into development of what would become the MGC, the Healey family told BMC management that they wanted nothing to do with it, and when the new six-cylinder MG was launched in September 1967, it was obvious that many engineering and budget compromises had been foisted on it which would haunt it throughout its short production life and for many years afterwards.

As if the genesis of the MGC was not enough of a headache, MG was having to wrestle with the growing raft of safety and emissions legislation in the North American market, which meant that many of BMC's important export currency earners had to be overhauled at considerable expense so that they could remain on sale. Before long, the specifications of US-market versions of the MG sports car family began to diverge more than ever before from their European counterparts, and American MGB owners would soon become familiar with the so-called 'Abingdon pillow' padded facia and other eccentricities.

In the midst of all this, Abingdon's own plans for an MGB replacement were sidelined, and with the MGC being seen by many pundits at the time as a blot on MG's otherwise almost impeccable copybook, the merger of BMC and Leyland in 1968 could hardly have come at a more awkward time. The supremacy of Triumph within Leyland's dowry meant that there were ominous signs for MG sports cars, although happily the continuing sales success of the MG Midget

and MGB and the primacy of the brand name helped sustain the case for keeping MG in the family. Even so, the logic of somehow rationalising TR and MG ranges seemed almost inescapable.

The MGC was an early victim of the rationalisation purge, giving a clear path for the TR6, but just as the three-litre MG went out of production, at the same time a modernisation programme saw dramatic facelifts for the Midget and MGB in September 1969 for the 1970 Model Year. In tandem with a cost-reduction exercise, the urge to modernise saw the sports cars lose their classic chrome radiator grilles in favour of recessed matt-black alloy fixtures with thin polished rims, loosely modelled on the style of Ford's 1967-68 Mustang. New colours, cheaper seat facings and declining performance levels were countered by racy 'Rostyle' steel wheels and, from 1970, a much-improved new folding roof for the MGB roadster courtesy of the Italian designer Michelotti.

Most enthusiasts mourned the loss of the traditional grille style, and for many years afterwards some owners would retrofit their cars with the older style grille; however, tastes and moreover attitudes to originality have changed, and the 1969-71 MGB nowadays has a dedicated band of followers. For North American MGB customers, yet more changes appeared which set their cars further apart from those sold in other markets; for a short time, the rear bumper was split either side of the number plate, side reflectors (later changed to lamps) appeared on the wings and to cope with new laws about the clear area of windscreens, there was the curious but clever solution of three wiper blades.

Resistance to the recessed grille was undoubtedly one of the factors behind the decision for the 1973 Model Year to backtrack to a more familiar MG grille style, although in a nod to both modernity and tradition, the grille openings were now graced with injection-moulded plastic cross-hatched grilles rather than vertical chrome slats. By this stage, the whole British sports car family was like Lazarus, back from the dead: US legislation that had threatened to kill off the open sports car had failed to materialise. British Leyland had already formulated its plans for the next generation of sports cars – what would become the Triumph TR7 and the Jaguar XJ-S – and both had been designed as fixed-head coupés. Despite the fact that the traditional British sports cars were being left behind by their younger international opposition, sales held up well in a market where few of the alternatives – in particular the Datsun 240Z – came in convertible form.

In late 1973, MG dabbled once again with the concept of a larger-engined MGB, but this time they used the 3.5-litre alloy V8 unit from

Rover – which in turn had started life as a Buick engine that predated the MGB itself. Inspiration had come from a privateer – Ken Costello – who had built up good business converting MGBs to V8 power for a discerning clientele. This time there were even fewer engineering and styling changes allowed, and the V8 model was limited to a GT version alone. One of the few obvious external clues was the use of special Dunlop alloy wheels with plated steel rims, and slighter larger section tyres. Performance and handling were terrific – the powerful and light weight engine transformed the MGB – but not enough customers were interested, the promised export sales never happened, and then when a Middle Eastern conflict in October 1973 caused fuel prices to spiral. MGB GT V8 sales began to plummet and just 2,591 production cars were built before the model was discontinued in the summer of 1976.

Sitting alongside the US emissions and safety lobbies was the equally powerful insurance industry, and from the early 1970s changes in legislation saw car manufacturers forced to re-design their products so that they would suffer minimal damage in minor collisions, with a major focus expensive breakages of peripheral components such as head and tail lamps. For British Leyland, investing heavily in the TR7

because of the launch in January 1975 of the Triumph TR7 Coupé. In 1975, British Leyland fell into public ownership, but this did not stop a final push for investment in the ageing MG line, and from the summer of 1976 some of the problems which had been caused by raising the suspension to meet bumper height regulations and the weight of those bumpers were partially redressed with what would prove to be the MGB's final facelift.

By now, for many people the MGB was beginning to resemble an ageing rockstar who everyone fondly remembered but was overdue retirement; even so, popularity, exclusivity and superb marketing helped the MGB to its best ever sales figures in 1977. However the world had not stood still, and with an increasingly troubled British Leyland wrestling with financial and production woes, management favoured creation of an open version of the TR7 and allowing the MGB to coast towards oblivion. Investment in further developments such as the new O-Series engine were abandoned, and quietly plans were put in place to terminate Abingdon's sports cars.

1979 saw the fiftieth anniversary of the MG factory at Abingdon, and British Leyland – or BL Cars as it had become the previous year – famously timed their announcement that the factory was to be closed with the closing day of a week of international festivities. Despite valiant efforts to save both car and factory, the die had been cast and – for the time being – the MG sports car line came to an end after a production total of 512,112 including a short run of limited editions at the end. It was a sad end for Abingdon, but not quite the end for the MGB; for not only did the car live on in hearts, minds and the garages of a legion of dedicated owners, enthusiasts, and MG club members, but it even formed the basis of a lucrative business selling complete new bodyshells and even a limited production sports car, the MG RV8, which heralded the rebirth of the MG sports car in the 1990s.

The MGB has grown up alongside Haynes – indeed the company was just two years old when Abingdon's new sports car was born – and both have earned a warm place in enthusiasts' hearts in those five momentous decades. As MG is synonymous with sports cars, Haynes is synonymous with workshop manuals. This special edition of the MGB Workshop manual – a long time staple of the Haynes portfolio – is effectively a joint celebration of two great classic British institutions, and they both deserve to be cherished with equal affection.

David Knowles
Ruislip, 2010

and XJ-S and other domestic ranges, this meant modifying the ageing sports cars with a make-do-and-mend approach which was a credit to the talents of the engineers and designers involved but yet another demonstration of parsimonious under-investment.

For the 1974 Model Year, the most obvious consequence of this for North American market customers concerned the so-called 'Sabrina' over-riders, named after a well-endowed minor starlet, which were mounted where the previous over-riders had been but projected so that they lengthened the car considerably and added heavy pendulum-like weights front and rear. This was just the beginning of a peculiar phase, for half way through the 1974 Model Year, the MGB family was facelifted with massive polyurethane covered steel bumpers which had been cleverly styled to blend with the bodywork, but resulted in the complete abandonment of the traditional MG grille. To the present day, this move divides opinion more than any other aspect of MGB evolution, although as with the recessed grille of 1969, the passage of time and changes in taste have lessened resistance.

This so-called '1974 ½' Model Year also heralded by year end the discontinuation of the 'MGB/GT' from export markets, partly because of certification costs and falling performance figures but more significantly

Buying spare parts

Spare parts are available from many sources, for example: the MG Owners' Club (www.mgownersclub.co.uk), accessory shops and motor factors. Our advice regarding spare parts is as follows:

MG Owners' Club. This is the best source of parts which are peculiar to your car and not generally available elsewhere, which in practice means most spares apart from the most basic service requirements. To be sure of getting the correct parts it will usually be necessary to quote one or more of the identification numbers described on this page.

Accessory shops. These are good places to buy material and components needed for routine maintenance (fluids, filters, spark plugs, bulbs, drivebelts, touch-up paint, etc). They also sell general accessories, usually have convenient opening hours and can often be found not far from home.

Motor factors. Good factors will stock all the more important components which wear out comparatively quickly, and can sometimes supply individual components needed for the overhaul of a larger assembly (eg, brake seals and hydraulic parts, bearing shells, pistons, valves). They may also handle work such as cylinder block reboring, crankshaft regrinding, etc.

ISBN 978 1 85960 607 0

Vehicle identification numbers

Modifications are a continuing and unpublished process in vehicle manufacture quite apart from major model changes. Spare parts manuals and lists are compiled upon a numerical basis, the individual vehicle numbers being essential to correct identification of the component required. The position of the numbers concerned has varied, but the following list gives some guidance.

The car will have an *identification plate*, normally found on the inside of one of the wing panels, under the bonnet.

The car number is preceded by three letters and one figure:

(a) The letter G standing for MG
(b) The letter H for the Leyland type of engine
(c) Either N for two-seater Tourer or D for the GT Coupe
(d) A type serial number, eg 3, 4, or 5

Thus, in 1972 the Tourer was GHN5, and the GT GHD5.

The car *commission number* will probably be found on the bonnet lock platform.

The *engine number* is stamped on a plate secured to the right-hand side of the engine block, or alternatively may be stamped directly upon the block.

The engine number starts with the figures 18. This signifies the 1798 cc engine. This used to be followed by the letter G for MG and a second letter for the type serial. Thus the 18GB followed the 18GA when five main bearings were introduced. This series went through to 18GH. This group of the number had after it a second group giving the type of gearbox:

(a) U for standard
(b) RU for overdrive
(c) We – All synchromesh box
(d) Rwe – All synchromesh with overdrive
(e) Rc – Automatic gearbox

The engine number/first group is now always 18V and the second group a three figure and one or two letter serial. Thus in October 1972 the home market was 18V/582F, Europe 18V/581Y and North America 18V/672Z.

The engine prefix is followed by one letter, H for high compression ratio and L for low, and then the serial number.

The *gearbox number* is stamped on the casing of the unit, as is the rear axle number.

Tools and working facilities

Introduction

A selection of good tools is a fundamental requirement for anyone contemplating the maintenance and repair of a motor vehicle. For the owner who does not possess any, their purchase will prove a considerable expense, offsetting some of the savings made by doing-it-yourself. However, provided that the tools purchased meet the relevant national safety standards and are of good quality, they will last for many years and prove an extremely worthwhile investment.

The help the average owner to decide which tools are needed to carry out the various tasks detailed in this manual, we have compiled three lists of tools under the following headings: *Maintenance and minor repair*, *Repair and overhaul*, and *Special*. The newcomer to practical mechanics should start off with the *Maintenance and minor repair* tool kit and confine himself to the simpler jobs around the vehicle. Then, as his confidence and experience grow, he can undertake more difficult tasks, buying extra tools as, and when, they are needed. In this way, a *Maintenance and minor repair* tool kit can be built-up into a *Repair and overhaul* tool kit over a considerable period of time without any major cash outlays. The experienced do-it-yourselfer will have a tool kit good enough to most repair and overhaul procedures and will add tools from the *Special* category when he feels the expense is justified by the amount of use these tools will be put to.

Maintenance and minor repair tool kit

The tools given in this list should be considered as a minimum requirement if routine maintenance, servicing and minor repair operations are to be undertaken. We recommend the purchase of combination spanners (ring one end, open-ended the other); although more expensive than open-ended ones, they do give the advantages of both types of spanner. Note that Imperial, metric or a mixture of thread types may be encountered, depending on production date.

Combination spanners – 1/4, 5/16, 3/8, 7/16, 9/16, 5/8, 11/16
7, 8, 9, 10, 11, 12, 13, 17, 19 mm
Adjustable spanner – 9 inch
Engine sump/gearbox/rear axle drain plug key
Spark plug spanner (with rubber insert)
Spark plug gap adjustment tool
Set of feeler gauges
Brake adjuster spanner
Brake bleed nipple spanner
Screwdriver – 4 in long x 1/4 in dia (flat blade)
Screwdriver – 4 in long x 1/4 in dia (cross blade)
Combination pliers
Hacksaw (junior)
Tyre pump
Tyre pressure gauge
Grease gun
Oil can
Fine emery cloth (1 sheet)
Wire brush (small)
Funnel (medium size)
Light with extension lead

Repair and overhaul tool kit

These tools are virtually essential for anyone undertaking any major repairs to a motor vehicle, and are additional to those given in the *Maintenance and minor repair* list. Included in this list is a comprehensive set of sockets. Although these are expensive they will be found invaluable as they are so versatile – particularly if various drives are included in the set. We recommend the 1/2 in square-drive type, as this can be used with most proprietary torque spanners. If you cannot afford a socket set, even bought piecemeal, then inexpensive tubular box wrenches are a useful alternative.

The tools in this list will occasionally need to be supplemented by tools in the *Special* list.

Sockets (or box spanners) to cover range in previous list
Reversible ratchet drive (for use with sockets)
Extension piece, 10 inch (for use with sockets)
Universal joint (for use with sockets)
Torque wrench (for use with sockets)
Mole wrench – 8 inch
Ball pein hammer
Soft-faced hammer, plastic or rubber
Screwdriver – 6 in long x 5/16 in dia (flat blade)
Screwdriver – 2 in long x 6/16 in square (flat blade)
Screwdriver – 1½ in long x 1/4 in dia (cross blade)
Screwdriver – 3 in long x 1/8 in dia (electricians)
Pliers – electricians side cutters
Pliers – needle nosed
Pliers – circlip (internal and external)
Cold chisel – 1/2 inch
Scriber
Scraper
Centre punch
Pin punch
Hacksaw
Valve grinding tool
Steel rule/straight-edge
Allen keys
Selection of files
Wire brush (large)
Axle-stands
Jack (strong scissor or hydraulic type)

Special tools

The tools in this list are those which are not used regularly, are expensive to buy, or which need to be used in accordance with their manufacturers' instructions. Unless relatively difficult mechanical jobs are undertaken frequently, it will not be economic to buy many of these tools. Where this is the case, you could consider clubbing together with friends (or joining a motorists' club) to make a joint purchase, or borrowing the tools against a deposit from a local garage or tool hire specialist.

The following list contains only those tools and instruments freely available to the public, and not those special tools produced by the vehicle manufacturer specifically for its dealer network. You will find occasional references to these manufacturers' special tools in the text of this manual. Generally, an alternative method of doing the job without the vehicle manufacturers' special tool is given. However, sometimes, there is no alternative to using them. Where this is the case and the relevant tool cannot be bought or borrowed you will have to entrust the work to a franchised garage.

Valve spring compressor
Piston ring compressor
Balljoint separator
Universal hub/bearing puller
Impact screwdriver
Micrometer and/or vernier gauge
Dial gauge
Stroboscopic timing light
Dwell angle meter/tachometer
Universal electrical multi-meter
Cylinder compression gauge
Lifting tackle
Trolley jack

Buying tools

For practically all tools, a tool factor is the best source since he will have a very comprehensive range compared with the average garage or accessory shop. Having said that, accessory shops often offer excellent quality tools at discount prices, so it pays to shop around.

There are plenty of good tools around at reasonable prices, but always aim to purchase items which meet the relevant national safety standards. If in doubt, ask the proprietor or manager of the shop for advice before making a purchase.

Care and maintenance of tools

Having purchased a reasonable tool kit, it is necessary to keep the tools in a clean serviceable condition. After use, always wipe off any dirt, grease and metal particles using a clean, dry cloth, before putting the tools away. Never leave them lying around after they have been used. A simple tool rack on the garage or workshop wall, for items such as screwdrivers and pliers is a good idea. Store all normal spanners and sockets in a metal box. Any measuring instruments, gauges, meters, etc, must be carefully stored where they cannot be damaged or become rusty.

Take a little care when tools are used. Hammer heads inevitably become marked and screwdrivers lose the keen edge on their blades from time to time. A little timely attention with emery cloth or a file will soon restore items like this to a good serviceable finish.

Working facilities

Not to be forgotten when discussing tools is the workshop itself. If anything more than routine maintenance is to be carried out, some form of suitable working area becomes essential.

It is appreciated that many an owner mechanic is forced by circumstances to remove an engine or similar item without the benefit of a garage or workshop. Having done this, any repairs should always be done under the cover of a roof.

Wherever possible, any dismantling should be done on a clean flat workbench or table at a suitable working height.

Any workbench needs a vice: one with a jaw opening of 4 in (100 mm) is suitable for most jobs. As mentioned previously, some clean dry storage space is also required for tools, as well as the lubricants, cleaning fluids, touch-up paints and so on which become necessary.

Another item which may be required, and which has a much more general usage, is an electric drill with a chuck capacity of at least 5/16 in (8 mm). This, together with a good range of twist drills, is virtually essential for fitting accessories such as wing mirrors and reversing lights.

Last, but not least, always keep a supply of old newspapers and clean, lint-free rags available, and try to keep any working area as clean as possible.

Spanner jaw gap comparison table

Jaw gap (in)	Spanner size
0.250	1/4 in AF
0.276	7 mm
0.313	5/16 in AF
0.315	8 mm
0.344	11/32 in AF, 1/8 in Whitworth
0.354	9 mm
0.375	3/8 in AF
0.394	10 mm
0.433	11 mm
0.438	7/16 in AF
0.445	3/16 in Whitworth, 1/4 in BSF
0.472	12 mm
0.500	1/2 in AF
0.512	13 mm
0.525	1/4 in Whitworth, 5/16 in BSF
0.551	14 mm
0.563	9/16 in AF
0.591	15 mm
0.600	5/16 in Whitworth, 3/8 in BSF
0.625	5/8 in AF
0.630	16 mm
0.669	17 mm
0.686	11/16 in AF
0.709	18 mm
0.710	3/8 in Whitworth, 7/16 in BSF
0.748	19 mm
0.750	3/4 in AF
0.813	13/16 in AF
0.820	7/16 in Whitworth, 1/2 in BSF
0.866	22 mm
0.875	7/8 in AF
0.920	1/2 in Whitworth, 9/16 in BSF
0.938	15/16 in AF
0.945	24 mm
1.000	1 in AF
1.010	9/16 in Whitworth, 5/8 in BSF
1.024	26 mm
1.063	1 1/16 in AF, 27 mm
1.100	5/8 in Whitworth, 11/16 in BSF
1.125	1 1/8 in AF
1.181	30 mm
1.200	11/16 in Whitworth, 3/4 in BSF
1.250	1 1/4 in AF
1.260	32 mm
1.300	3/4 in Whitworth, 7/8 in BSF
1.313	1 5/16 in AF
1.390	13/16 in Whitworth, 15/16 in BSF
1.417	36 mm
1.438	1 7/16 in AF
1.480	7/8 in Whitworth, 1 in BSF
1.500	1 1/2 in AF
1.575	40 mm, 15/16 in Whitworth
1.614	41 mm
1.625	1 5/8 in AF
1.670	1 in Whitworth, 1 1/8 in BSF
1.688	1 11/16 in AF
1.811	46 mm
1.813	1 13/16 in AF
1.860	1 1/8 in Whitworth, 1 1/4 in BSF
1.875	1 7/8 in AF
1.969	50 mm
2.000	2 in AF
2.050	1 1/4 in Whitworth, 1 3/8 in BSF
2.165	55 mm
2.362	60 mm

Jacking and towing

Jacking points

The jack supplied with the vehicle must only be used at the locations provided. Ensure that it is pushed fully home, and that the base of the jack is on firm ground, with the jack leaning slightly outwards at the top, to allow for radial movement of the vehicle as it is lifted. Do not work under a vehicle which is supported solely by the jack, but employ suitable additional supports under the side members or rear axle.

Jacks other than that supplied with the vehicle should be located either under the front crossmember, or under the axle casing. When jacking, a wheel should always be chocked on the opposite side of the car.

Towing points

If the vehicle has to be towed, the rope or cable should be secured round the front body crossmember (**not** the steering rack). Ensure that the towing line is clear of any items which may become damaged, and that when the line tightens under load it does not come against the body panels, causing damage.

If it is necessary to have an automatic transmission vehicle towed add an extra 3 pints (3.5 US pints, 1.7 litres) of fluid to the transmission, place the selector lever to N, and tow for no more than 40 miles (64 km) at a maximum speed of 30 mph (48 kmph). If the transmission is inoperative, or the maximum towing distance has to be exceeded, remove the propeller shaft or raise the rear of the vehicle. Tow-starting on an automatic transmission vehicle is not possible.

If another vehicle is to be towed, the towing line may be connected to the rear leaf spring shackle, tacking care that when the line goes taut it does not damage the bodywork or other parts of the vehicle.

The standard jack, in position

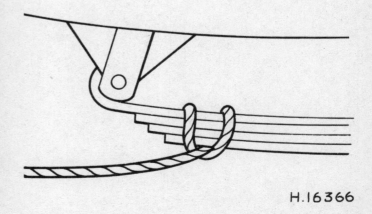

H.16366

Towing another vehicle, with the tow-line looped round a leaf spring shackle

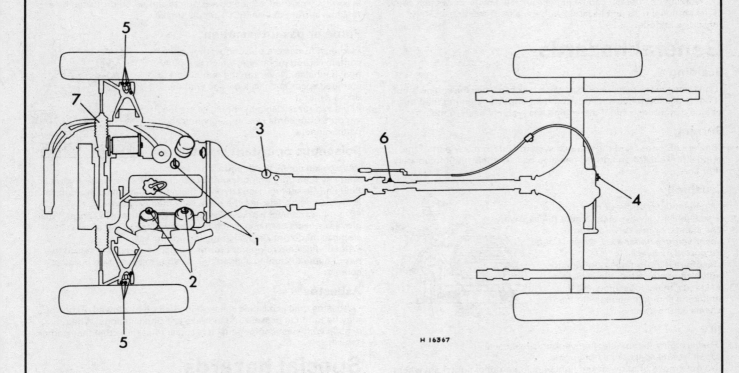

H 16367

Recommended lubricants and fluids

Component or system	Lubricant type/specification
1 **Engine**	Multigrade engine oil, viscosity SAE 20W/50
2 **Carburettor piston dampers**	Multigrade engine oil, viscosity SAE 20W/50
3 **Gearbox and overdrive**	Multigrade engine oil, viscosity SAE 20W/50
Automatic transmission	ATF to BLMC type F
4 **Rear axle**	Hypoid gear oil, viscosity SAE 90EP
5 **Front suspension**	Multi-purpose lithium based grease
6 **Propeller shaft**	Multi-purpose lithium based grease
7 **Steering rack**	Hypoid gear oil, viscosity SAE 90EP
Hydraulic systems	Hydraulic fluid to SAE J1703
Shock absorber damping fluid	Armstrong Super (Thin) Shock Absorber Fluid No 624 or any good-quality mineral oil to specification SAE 20W (this alternative is not suitable for low temperature operation)

Safety first!

Working on your car can be dangerous. This page shows just some of the potential risks and hazards, with the aim of creating a safety-conscious attitude.

General hazards

Scalding

• Don't remove the radiator or expansion tank cap while the engine is hot.
• Engine oil, automatic transmission fluid or power steering fluid may also be dangerously hot if the engine has recently been running.

Burning

• Beware of burns from the exhaust system and from any part of the engine. Brake discs and drums can also be extremely hot immediately after use.

Crushing

• When working under or near raised vehicle, always supplement the jack with axle stands, or use drive-on ramps.
Never venture under a car which is only supported by a jack.
• Take care if loosening or tightening high-torque nuts when the vehicle is on stands. Initial loosening and final tightening should be done with the wheels on the ground.

Fire

• Fuel is highly flammable; fuel vapour is explosive.
• Don't let fuel spill onto a hot engine.
• Do not smoke or allow naked lights (including pilot lights) anywhere near a vehicle being worked on. Also beware of creating sparks (electrically or by use of tools).
• Fuel vapour is heavier than air, so don't work on the fuel system with the vehicle over an inspection pit.
• Another cause of fire is an electrical overload or short-circuit. Take care when repairing or modifying the vehicle wiring.
• Keep a fire extinguisher handy, of a type suitable for use on fuel and electrical fires.

Electric shock

• Ignition HT voltage can be dangerous, especially to people with heart problems or a pacemaker. Don't work on or near the ignition system with the engine running or the ignition switched on.
• Mains voltage is also dangerous. Make sure that any mains-operated equipment

is correctly earthed. Mains power points should be protected by a residual current device (RCD) circuit breaker.

Fume or gas intoxication

• Exhaust fumes are poisonous; they often contain carbon monoxide, which is rapidly fatal if inhaled. Never run the engine in a confined space such as a garage with the doors shut.
• Fuel vapour is also poisonous, as are the vapours from some cleaning solvents and paint thinners.

Poisonous or irritant substances

• Avoid skin contact with battery acid and with any fuel, fluid or lubricant, especially antifreeze, brake hydraulic fluid and Diesel fuel. Don't syphon them by mouth. If such a substance is swallowed or gets into the eyes, seek medical advice.
• Prolonged contact with used engine oil can cause skin cancer. Wear gloves or use a barrier cream if necessary. Change out of oil-soaked clothes and do not keep oily rags in your pocket.
• Air conditioning refrigerant forms a poisonous gas if exposed to a naked flame (including a cigarette). It can also cause skin burns on contact.

Asbestos

• Asbestos dust can cause cancer if inhaled or swallowed. Asbestos may be found in gaskets and in brake and clutch linings. When dealing with such components it is safest to assume that they contain asbestos.

Special hazards

Hydrofluoric acid

• This extremely corrosive acid is formed when certain types of synthetic rubber, found in some O-rings, oil seals, fuel hoses etc, are exposed to temperatures above 400°C. The rubber changes into a charred or sticky substance containing the acid. *Once formed, the acid remains dangerous for years. If it gets onto the skin, it may be necessary to amputate the limb concerned.*
• When dealing with a vehicle which has suffered a fire, or with components salvaged from such a vehicle, wear protective gloves and discard them after use.

The battery

• Batteries contain sulphuric acid, which attacks clothing, eyes and skin. Take care when topping-up or carrying the battery.
• The hydrogen gas given off by the battery is highly explosive. Never cause a spark or allow a naked light nearby. Be careful when connecting and disconnecting battery chargers or jump leads.

Remember...

DO

• Do use eye protection when using power tools, and when working under the vehicle.

• Do wear gloves or use barrier cream to protect your hands when necessary.

• Do get someone to check periodically that all is well when working alone on the vehicle.

• Do keep loose clothing and long hair well out of the way of moving mechanical parts.

• Do remove rings, wristwatch etc, before working on the vehicle – especially the electrical system.

• Do ensure that any lifting or jacking equipment has a safe working load rating adequate for the job.

DON'T

• Don't attempt to lift a heavy component which may be beyond your capability – get assistance.

• Don't rush to finish a job, or take unverified short cuts.

• Don't use ill-fitting tools which may slip and cause injury.

• Don't leave tools or parts lying around where someone can trip over them. Mop up oil and fuel spills at once.

• Don't allow children or pets to play in or near a vehicle being worked on.

Routine Maintenance

Maintenance is essential for ensuring safety and reliability, coupled with maximum performance and economy. Over the years the need for periodic lubrication has been reduced considerably, but where this is still required, or where visual examination is necessary for certain items, it is important that the recommended tasks be carried out at the proper intervals.

The information given in this Section is not of a detailed nature, and where necessary reference should be made to the appropriate Chapter for full information.

Every 250 miles (400 km) or weekly

Check the tyre pressures and inflate if necessary.
Check the tyres for tread depth, cuts, exposure of the structure, and bulges.
Check the security of the wheel nuts.
Check the engine oil level, and top up if necessary.
Check the fluid level in the brake master cylinder.
Check the cooling system level.
Check the screen-washer water level, adding a good quality screen wash.
Check the operation of all equipment such as lights, wipers and indicators.
Check the battery electrolyte level.

Every 3000 miles (5000 km) or 3-monthly

Change engine oil if desired (advisable in arduous operating conditions).
Check the carburettor damper oil levels.
Check the screen washer operation.
Check the fanbelt adjustment and condition.
Check the fluid level in the clutch master cylinder.
Check the operation of the foot and hand brakes, and adjust if necessary.
Check visually all brake pipes for corrosion, abrasion and leaks.
Check the steering joints and gaiters, for security and leaks.
Check the steering rack for oil leaks.
Check the shock absorbers for leaks.
Check the headlamp alignment.
Check the windscreen wiper blade condition.
Check the security and condition of the seat belts.
Check the rear view mirror for defects.
Check visually all fuel and clutch hydraulic pipes and unions for corrosion, abrasion and leaks.
Check the exhaust system for security and leaks.
Check the fuel filter pipe to tank connections.
Lubricate all grease points, excluding hubs.
Lubricate all the door hinges and catches.

Topping-up engine oil level

Topping-up coolant level

Topping-up brake fluid level

The lubrication points on the front swivel pins

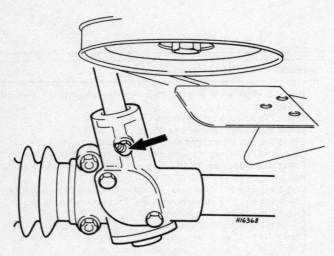

The lubrication point on early steering racks

The lubrication point on early water pumps

The sump drain plug

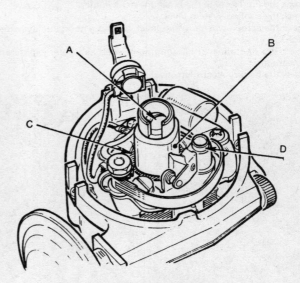

Distributor lubrication

A   *Access to automatic mechanism*
B   *Bearing lubrication point*
C   *Cam*
D   *Contact breaker pivot*

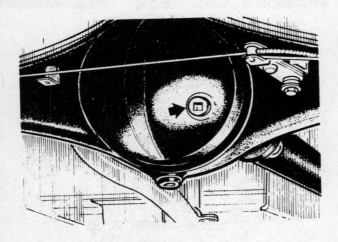

Rear axle oil level/filler plug

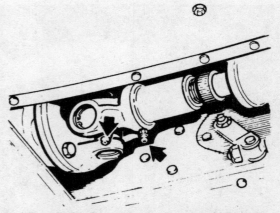

Propeller shaft grease points – early vehicles only

Lubricate the dynamo rear bearing (early models).
Lubricate the water pump (early models).
Check the condition and pressure of the spare tyre.
Carry out the items listed under 250 mile (400 km) service interval.

Every 6000 miles (10 000 km) or 6-monthly

Renew the engine oil and filter.
Check valve clearances and adjust if necessary.
Check the cooling and heating systems for leaks and general condition of hoses.
Lubricate the accelerator control linkage and pedal pivot.
Clean and adjust the spark plugs.
Check, and adjust or renew, the contact points (if applicable).
Lubricate the distributor.
Check and adjust the ignition timing.
Check the centrifugal and vacuum advance characteristics, using electronic equipment.

Handbrake cable grease point, when fitted

Check the gearbox oil level.
Check the rear axle oil level.
Lubricate the propeller shaft (if applicable).
Check the automatic transmission fluid level (if applicable).
Inspect the brake pads and brake discs.
Lubricate the handbrake and cables.
Smear some petroleum jelly on the battery connections.
Adjust the carburettors.
Check exhaust emission at idle speed (N America).
Check all steering and suspension fixings for security.
Change wheels over to equalise wear, if considered desirable.
Carry out the items listed under the 250 miles (400 km) and 3000 mile (5000 km) services.

Every 12 000 miles (20 000 km) or annually

Renew the carburettor air cleaner element(s).
Renew the fuel filter, where fitted.
Clean and check the crankcase breather.
Renew the engine oil filter cap.
Renew the spark plugs.
Renew the contact breaker points (if applicable).
Check the brake shoes and drums for wear.
Clean the brake servo filter element.
Check the front wheel alignment.
Carry out a compression check on the engine.
Renew air cleaner on air pump (N America).
Check gulp valve and renew if necessary (N America).
Check fuel filler cap seal.
Carry out the items listed under the 250 miles (400 km), 3000 mile (5000 km) and 6000 mile (10 000 km) services.

Every 24 000 miles (40 000 km) or 24 months

Renew all drivebelts.
Flush cooling system and renew antifreeze.
Check the air pump, and service or renew as necessary (N America).
Fit a new distributor cap and spark plug leads.
Fit a new absorption canister (N America).
Renew gearbox oil and (if applicable) clean the overdrive filter.
Renew rear axle oil.
Carry out the items specified in the previous schedules.

Every 36 000 miles (60 000 km) or 36 months

Renew all rubber hoses and seals in the brake hydraulic system.
Carry out the items specified in the previous schedules (as applicable).

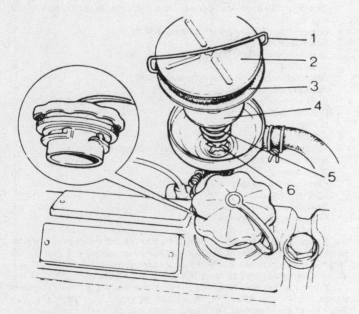

Crankcase breather valve

1	*Spring clip*	4	*Metering needle*
2	*Cover*	5	*Spring*
3	*Diaphragm*	6	*Cruciform guides*

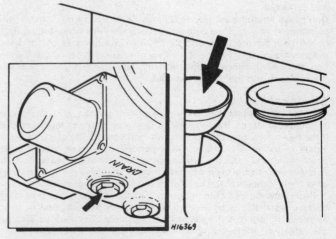

The overdrive drain plug (inset). The upper arrow shows a funnel in the dipstick hole, to assist with refilling

Fault Diagnosis

Introduction

The car owner who does his or her own maintenance according to the recommended schedules should not have to use this section of the manual very often. Modern component reliability is such that, provided those items subject to wear or deterioration are inspected or renewed at the specified intervals, sudden failure is comparatively rare. Faults do not usually just happen as a result of sudden failure, but develop over a period of time. Major mechanical failures in particular are usually preceded by characteristic symptoms over hundreds or even thousands of miles. Those components which do occasionally fail without warning are often small and easily carried in the car.

With any fault finding, the first step is to decide where to begin investigations. Sometimes this is obvious, but on other occasions a little detective work will be necessary. The owner who makes half a dozen haphazard adjustments or replacements may be successful in curing a fault (or its symptoms), but he will be none the wiser if the fault recurs and he may well have spent more time and money than was necessary. A calm and logical approach will be found to be more satisfactory in the long run. Always take into account any warning signs or abnormalities that may have been noticed in the period preceding the fault – power loss, high or low gauge readings, unusual noises or smells, etc – and remember that failure of components such as fuses or spark plugs may only be pointers to some underlying fault.

The pages which follow here are intended to help in cases of failure to start or breakdown on the road. There is also a Fault Diagnosis Section at the end of each Chapter which should be consulted if the preliminary checks prove unfruitful. Whatever the fault, certain basic principles apply. These are as follows:

Verify the fault. This is simply a matter of being sure that you know what the symptoms are before starting work. This is particularly important if you are investigating a fault for someone else who may not have described it very accurately.

Don't overlook the obvious. For example, if the car won't start, is there petrol in the tank? (Don't take anyone else's word on this particular point, and trust the fuel gauge either!) If an electrical fault is indicated, look for loose or broken wires before digging out the test gear.

Cure the disease, not the symptom. Substituting a flat battery with a fully charged one will get you off the hard shoulder, but if the underlying cause is not attended to, the new battery will go the same way. Similarly, changing oil-fouled spark plugs for a new set will get you moving again, but remember that the reason for the fouling (if it wasn't simply an incorrect grade of plug) will have to be established and corrected.

Don't take anything for granted. Particularly, don't forget that a 'new' component may itself be defective (especially if it's been rattling round in the boot for months), and don't leave components out of a fault diagnosis sequence just because they are new or recently fitted. When you do finally diagnose a difficult fault, you'll probably realise that all the evidence was there from the start.

Electrical Faults

Electrical faults can be more puzzling than straightforward mechanical failures, but they are no less susceptible to logical analysis if the basic principles of operation are understood. Car electrical wiring exists in extremely unfavourable conditions – heat, vibration and chemical attack – and the first things to look for are loose or corroded connections, and broken or chafed wires, especially where the wires pass through holes in the bodywork or are subject to vibration.

All metal-bodied cars in current production have one pole of the battery 'earthed', ie connected to the car bodywork, and in nearly all modern cars it is the negative (-) terminal. The various electrical components – motors, bulb holders etc – are also connected to earth, either by means of a lead or directly by their mountings. Electric current flows through the component and then back to the battery via the car bodywork. If the component mounting is loose or corroded, or if a good path back to the battery is not available, the circuit ill be incomplete and malfunction will result. The engine and/or gearbox are also earthed by means of flexible metal straps to the body or subframe; if these straps are loose or missing, starter motor, generator and ignition trouble may result.

Assuming the earth return to be satisfactory, electrical faults will be due either to component malfunction or to defects in the current supply. Individual components are dealt with in Chapter 10. If supply wires are broken or cracked internally this results in an open-circuit, and the easiest way to check for this is to bypass the suspect wire temporarily with a length of wire having a crocodile clip or suitable connector at each end. Alternatively, a 12V test lamp can be used to verify the presence of supply voltage at various points along the wire and the break can be thus isolated.

If a bare portion of a live wire touches the car bodywork or other earthed metal part the electricity will take the low-resistance path thus formed back to the battery: this is known as a short-circuit. Hopefully a short-circuit will blow a fuse, but otherwise it may cause burning of the insulation (and possibly further short-circuits) or even a fire. This is why it is inadvisable to bypass persistently blowing fuses with silver foil or wire.

Spares and tool kit

Most cars are only supplied with sufficient tools for wheel changing; the *Maintenance and minor repair tool kit* detailed in *Tools and working facilities,* with the addition of a hammer, is probably sufficient for those repairs that most motorists would consider attempting at the roadside. In addition a few items which can be fitted without too much trouble in the event of breakdown should be carried. Experience and available space will modify the list below, but the following may save having to call on professional assistance:

Spark plugs, clean and correctly gapped
HT leads and plug cap – long enough to reach the plug furthest from the distributor
Distributor rotor, condenser and contact breaker points (if applicable)
Drivebelt(s) – emergency type may suffice
Spare fuses
Set of principal light bulbs
Hose clips
Tin of radiator sealer and hose bandage
Tube of filler paste
Exhaust bandage
Roll of insulating tape
Length of soft iron wire
Length of electrical flex
Torch or inspection lamp (can double as test lamp)
Battery jump leads
Tow-rope
Ignition water dispersant aerosol
Litre of engine oil
Sealed can of hydraulic fluid
Emergency windscreen
Tyre valve core

If spare fuel is carried, a can designed for the purpose should be used to minimise risks of leakage and collision damage. A first aid kit and a warning triangle, whilst not at present compulsory in the UK, are obvious sensible items to carry in addition to the above.

When touring abroad it may be advisable to carry additional spares which, even if you cannot fit them yourself, could save having to wait while parts are obtained. The items below may be worth considering:

Cylinder head gasket
Dynamo or alternator brushes
Fuel pump repair kit

One of the motoring organisations will be able to advise on availability of fuel etc in foreign countries.

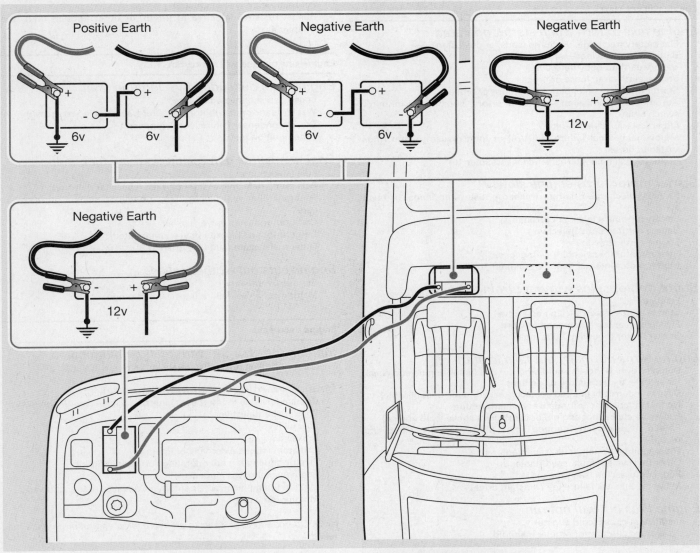

Positive Earth

6v 6v

Negative Earth

6v 6v

Negative Earth

12v

Negative Earth

12v

Correct way to connect jump leads. Do not allow car bodies to touch!

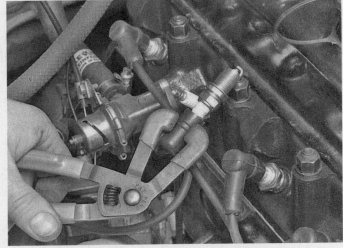

Crank engine and check for a spark. Note use of insulated pliers – dry cloth or rubber glove will suffice

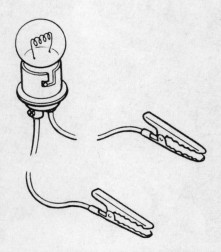

A simple test lamp is useful for investigating electrical faults

Engine will not start

Engine fails to turn when starter operated

Flat battery (recharge, use jump leads, or push start)
Battery terminals loose or corroded
Battery earth to body defective
Engine earth strap loose or broken
Starter motor (or solenoid) wiring loose or broken
Automatic transmission selector in wrong position, or inhibitor switch faulty
Ignition/starter switch faulty
Major mechanical failure (seizure) or long disuse (piston rings rusted to bores)
Starter or solenoid internal fault (see Chapter 10)

Starter motor turns engine slowly

Partially discharged battery (recharge, use jump leads, or push start)
Battery terminals loose or corroded
Battery earth to body defective
Engine earth strap loose
Starter motor (or solenoid) wiring loose
Starter motor internal fault (see Chapter 10)

Starter motor spins without turning engine

Flat battery
Starter motor pinion sticking on sleeve
Flywheel gear teeth damaged or worn
Starter motor mounting bolts loose

Engine turns normally but fails to start

Damp or dirty HT leads and distributor cap (crank engine and check for spark) – try a moisture dispersant
Dirty or incorrectly gapped contact breaker points (if applicable)
No fuel in tank (check for delivery at carburettor)
Excessive choke (hot engine) or insufficient choke (cold engine)
Fouled or incorrectly gapped spark plugs (remove, clean and regap)
Other ignition system fault (see Chapter 4)
Other fuel system fault (see Chapter 3)
Poor compression (see Chapter 1)
Major mechanical failure (eg camshaft drive)

Engine fires but will not run

Insufficient choke (cold engine)
Air leaks at carburettor or inlet manifold

Fuel starvation (see Chapter 3)
Ballast resistor defective (if fitted), or other ignition fault (see Chapter 4)

Engine cuts out and will not restart

Engine cuts out suddenly – ignition fault

Loose or disconnected LT wires
Wet HT leads or distributor cap (after traversing water splash)
Coil or condenser failure (check for spark)
Other ignition fault (see Chapter 4)

Engine misfires before cutting out – fuel fault

Fuel tank empty
Fuel pump defective or filter blocked (check for delivery)
Fuel tank filler vent blocked (suction will be evident on releasing cap)
Carburettor needle valve sticking
Carburettor jets blocked (fuel contaminated)
Other fuel system fault (see Chapter 3)

Engine cuts out – other causes

Serious overheating
Major mechanical failure (eg camshaft drive)

Engine overheats

Ignition (no charge) warning light illuminated

Slack or broken drivebelt – retension or renew (Chapter 2)

Ignition warning light not illuminated

Coolant loss due to internal or external leakage (see Chapter 2)
Thermostat defective
Low oil level
Brakes binding
Radiator clogged externally or internally
Electric cooling fan not operating correctly (if fitted)
Engine waterways clogged
Ignition timing incorrect or automatic advance malfunctioning
Mixture too weak

Note: *Do not add cold water to an overheated engine or damage may result*

Remove fuel pipe from carburettor and check that fuel is being delivered

A slack drivebelt may cause overheating and battery charging problems. Slacken bolts (arrowed) to adjust

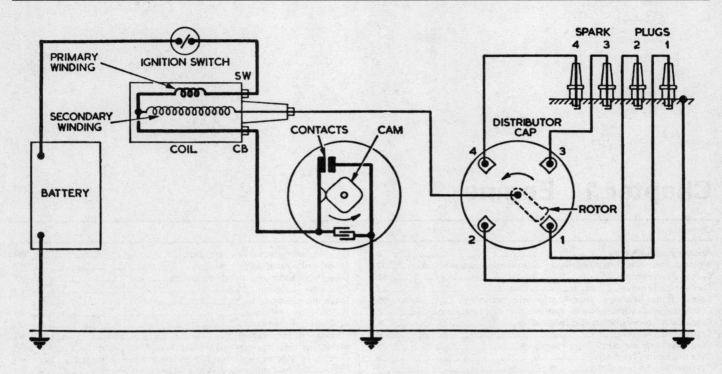

Ignition system schematic diagram. Some later models have a 6V coil and ballast resistor

Low engine oil pressure

Gauge reads low or warning light illuminates with engine running

Oil level low or incorrect grade
Defective gauge or sender unit
Wire to sender unit earthed
Engine overheating
Oil filter clogged or bypass valve defective
Oil pressure relief valve defective
Oil pick-up strainer clogged
Oil pump worn or mountings loose
Worn main or big-end bearings

Note: *Low oil pressure in a high-mileage engine at tickover is not necessarily a cause for concern. Sudden pressure loss at speed is far more significant. In any event, check the gauge or warning light sender before condemning the engine!*

Engine noises

Pre-ignition (pinking) on acceleration

Incorrect grade of fuel

Ignition timing incorrect
Distributor faulty or worn
Worn or maladjusted carburettor
Excessive carbon build-up in engine

Whistling or wheezing noises

Leaking vacuum hose
Leaking carburettor or manifold gasket
Blowing head gasket

Tapping or rattling

Incorrect valve clearances
Worn valve gear
Worn timing chain
Broken piston ring (ticking noise)

Knocking or thumping

Unintentional mechanical contact (eg fan blades)
Worn fanbelt
Peripheral component fault (generator, water pump etc)
Worn big-end bearings (regular heavy knocking, perhaps less under load)
Worn main bearings (rumbling and knocking, perhaps worsening under load)
Piston slap (most noticeable when cold)

Chapter 1 Engine

Contents

Specifications

These specifications are necessarily lengthy because of the various models of the MGB which have been produced. When looking for information for later models, the preceding Specifications have got to be taken into account as well.

Note that the following are additional features

Engine Nos		Key	
18GD – EEC	18V 585 Z – EEC, ELC, O	A	Automatic transmission
18GF – EEC	18V 672 Z – EEC, ELC	CC	Catalytic converter
18GG – EEC	18V 673 Z – EEC, ELC, O	CCV	Carburettor crankcase ventilation
18GH – EEC, CCV	18V 798 AE – O	EEC	Exhaust emission control
18GJ – EEC, ELC, CCV	18V 801 AE – CC	ELC	Evaporative loss control
18GK – EEC, ELC	18V 802 AE – O, CC	O	Overdrive
18V 581 F – S	18V 846 F – S	S	Synchromesh gearbox
18V 581 Y – S	18V 847 F – S, O	SO	Synchromesh overdrive
18V 582 F – S, O	18V 883 AE – S, CC		
18V 582 Y – S, O	18V 884 AE – CC, O		
18V 583 F – A	18V 890 AE – CC, S		
18V 583 Y – A	18V 891 AE – CC, O		
18V 584 Z – EEC, ELC	18V 892 AE – S		
	18V 893 AE – O		

Engine Nos 18G and 18GA

Engine – general

Type	Four cylinder, in-line, overhead valve, pushrod operated
Bore	3.16 in (80.26 mm)
Stroke	3.50 in (88.9 mm)
Capacity	1798 cc (109.8 cu in)
Compression ratio:	
High compression	8.8:1
Low compression	8.0:1
Compression pressure:	
High compression	160 lbf/in² (11.25 kgf/cm²)
Low compression	130 lbf/in² (9.15 kgf/cm²)
Firing order	1 – 3 – 4 – 2 (No 1 cylinder next to the radiator)
Engine mountings	3 (one at each side of the engine and one under the gearbox)

Crankshaft and main bearings

Main journal diameter	2.1262 to 2.1270 in (54.01 to 54.02 mm)
Crankpin journal diameter	1.8579 to 1.8764 in (47.648 to 47.661 mm)
Crankshaft endthrust	Taken on thrust washers at centre main bearing
Endfloat	0.004 to 0.005 in (0.10 to 0.13 mm)
Main bearings	3, shell type
Bearing length	1.125 in (28.5 mm)
Diametrical clearance	0.001 to 0.0027 in (0.0254 to 0.068 mm)
Available undersizes	-0.010, -0.020, -0.030 and -0.040 in (-0.254, -0.508, -0.762 and -1.016 mm)

Camshaft and bearings

Drive	Roller chain from the crankshaft
Bearings	3 replaceable-type liners
Journal diameter:	
Front	1.78875 to 1.78925 in (45.424 to 45.437 mm)
Centre	1.72875 to 1.72925 in (43.910 to 43.923 mm)
Rear	1.62275 to 1.62325 in (41.218 to 41.230 mm)
Bearing internal diameter after reaming in position:	
Front	1.79025 to 1.79075 in (45.472 to 45.485 mm)
Centre	1.73025 to 1.73075 in (43.948 to 43.961 mm)
Rear	1.62425 to 1.62475 in (41.256 to 41.269 mm)
Diametrical clearance	0.001 to 0.002 in (0.0254 to 0.0508 mm)
Endfloat	0.003 to 0.007 in (0.076 to 0.178 mm)

Pistons

Type	Aluminium with solid skirt
Clearance in cylinder:	
Top	0.0036 to 0.0045 in (0.091 to 0.121 mm)
Bottom	0.0018 to 0.0024 in (0.045 to 0.060 mm)
Oversize pistons available	+0.010, +0.020, +0.030 and +0.040 in (+0.254, +0.508, +0.762 and +1.020 mm)

Piston rings

Top	Parallel, cast iron, molybdenum filled
2nd and 3rd	Tapered, cast iron, molybdenum filled
Oil control	Slotted scraper
Fitted gap:	
Top, 2nd and 3rd	0.012 to 0.017 in (0.304 to 0.431 mm)
Oil control ring	0.0015 to 0.0035 in (0.038 to 0.088mm)
Grove clearance:	
Top, 2nd and 3rd	0.012 to 0.017 in (0.304 to 0.431 mm)
Oil control ring	0.0016 to 0.0036 in (0.04 to 0.09 mm)

Gudgeon pin

Type	Semi-floating, held by clamp bolt
Fit in piston	Free push fit at 20ºC (68ºF)
Outside diameter	0.7499 to 0.7501 in (19.04 to 19.05 mm)

Connecting rods and bearings

Type	Angular split big-end. Split clamp small-end
Length between centres	6.5 in (165.1 mm)
Endfloat on crankpin	0.008 to 0.012 in (0.2 to 0.3 mm)
Big-end bearings:	
Type	Shell
Length	0.995 to 1.005 in (25.20 to 25.52 mm)
Clearance	0.001 to 0.0027 in (0.0254 to 0.068 mm)
Undersize bearings available	-0.010, -0.020, -0.030 and -0.040 in (-0.254, -0.508, -0.762 and -1.016 mm)

Valves

	Inlet	Exhaust
Head diameter	1.562 to 1.567 in (38.67 to 38.80 mm)	1.343 to 1.348 in (34.11 to 34.23 mm)
Valve seat angle	45½°	45½°
Stem diameter	0.3422 to 0.3427 in (8.69 to 8.71 mm)	0.3417 to 0.3422 in (8.68 to 8.69 mm)
Stem-to-guide clearance	0.0015 to 0.0025 in (0.0381 to 0.0635 mm)	0.002 to 0.003 in (0.0508 to 0.0762 mm)
Valve lift	0.3645 in (9.25 mm)	0.3645 in (9.25 mm)
Valve stem-to-rocker clearance	0.015 in (0.38 mm) cold	0.015 in (0.38 mm) cold

Valve guides

	Inlet	Exhaust
Length:		
Early cars	1.625 in (41.275mm)	2.203 in (55.95mm)
Later cars	1.875 in (47.63 mm)	2.203 in (55.95 mm)
Outside diameter	0.5635 to 0.5640 in (14.30 to 14.32 mm)	As inlet
Inside diameter	0.3442 to 0.3447 in (8.73 to 8.74 mm)	As inlet
Fitted height above head surface:		
Early cars	0.625 in (15.875 mm)	As inlet
Later cars	0.750 in (19 mm)	0.625 in (15.875 mm)

Valve timing

	Inlet	Exhaust
Opens	16° BTDC	51° BBDC
Closes	56° ABDC	21° ATDC
Timing marks	Dimples on camshaft and crankshaft sprockets	

Valve springs

Type	Double coil
Free length:	
Inner	1.969 in (50.0 mm)
Outer	2.141 in (54.4 mm)

Rocker gear

Shaft:	
Length	14.031 in (356.0 mm)
Diameter	0.624 to 0.625 in (15.85 to 15.87 mm)
Rocker arm bush, inside diameter	0.6255 to 0.6260 in (15.80 to 15.90 mm)
Rocker arm ratio	1.4 : 1

Tappets

Type	Barrel, with flat base
Outside diameter	0.812 in (20.64 mm)
Length	2.293 to 2.303 in (58.25 to 58.50 mm)

Lubrication system

Type	Pressure and splash
Oil filter:	
Type	Full flow, renewable element
Capacity	1.0 Imp pt (0.57 litres, 1.2 US pt)
Oil type/specification	Multigrade engine oil, viscosity SAE 20W/50
Sump capacity	7.5 Imp pt (4.26 litres, 9 US pt)
Oil cooler capacity	0.75 Imp pt (0.42 litres, 0.9 US pt)
Oil pump:	
Type	Hobourn – Eaton or eccentric rotor
Capacity	3.25 gal/minute at 2000 rpm
Oil pressure:	
Idling	10 to 25 lbf/in^2 (0.7 to 1.7 kgf/cm^2)
At 3000 rpm	50 to 80 lbf/in^2 (3.5 to 5.6 kgf/cm^2)
Bypass valve opens	13 to 17 lbf/in^2 (0.9 to 1.1 kgf/cm^2)
Oil pressure relief valve:	
Opens	70 lbf/in^2 (4.9 kgf/cm^2)
Spring free length	3.0 in (76.2 mm)

Engine No 18GB
The Specifications above apply except where modified by those below

Main bearings

Number	5
Length:	
Front, centre and rear	1.125 in (28.5 mm)
Intermediate	0.875 in (22.23 mm)

Pistons

Skirt clearance in cylinder:
Top .... 0.0006 to 0.0012 in (0.015 to 0.030 mm)
Bottom .... 0.0021 to 0.0033 in (0.050 to 0.080 mm)

Gudgen pin

Type .... Fully floating
Fit in piston .... 0.0001 to 0.00035 in (0.0025 to 0.007 mm)
Outer diameter .... 0.8124 to 0.8127 in (20.608 to 20.615 mm)

Connecting rods and bearings

Type .... Angular split big-end, with bushed small-end
Big-end bearings, length .... 0.775 to 0.785 in (19.68 to 19.94 mm)

Engine Nos 18GD, 18GF, 18GG, 18GH, 18GJ, 18GK, 18V 584 Z, 18V 585 Z, 18V 672 Z and 18V 673 Z
The information provided for earlier models is applicable, except where either superseded or added to by that below

Pistons

Skirt clearance in cylinder:
Top .... 0.0021 to 0.0033 in (0.053 to 0.084 mm)
Bottom .... 0.006 to 0.0012 in (0.015 to 0.030 mm)

Piston rings

Number 3
Top .... Plain, sintered alloy
2nd .... Tapered, sintered alloy marked TOP
Oil control .... Two chrome-faced rings with apex expander
Fitted gaps:
Compression rings .... 0.012 to 0.022 in (0.305 to 0.600 mm)
Oil control ring .... 0.015 to 0.045 in (0.38 to 1.14 mm)

Gudgeon pin

Type .... Press fit in connecting rod
Fit in piston .... Hand push at 16°C (60°F)
Fit in small-end .... 12 lbf ft (16.3 Nm) minimum, using Leyland tool 18G 1150 and adaptor
type C

Connecting rods

Type .... Horizontal split big-end
Big-end locking method .... Multi-sided nut

Lubrication system

Oil filter type .... Full flow. Renewable element or inverted canister

Engine Nos 18V 797 AE, 18V 798 AE, 18V 801 AE and 18V 802 AE
The information provided for earlier models is applicable, except where either superceded or added to by that below

Engine – general

Compression ratio .... 8.0 : 1

Valve springs

Type .... Single coil
Free length .... 1.92 in (48.77 mm)

Valves

	Inlet	Exhaust
Stem diameter	0.3429 to 0.3434 in (8.70 to 8.72 mm)	0.3423 to 0.3428 in (8.69 to 8.70 mm)
Stem-to-guide clearance	0.0007 to 0.0019 in (0.020 to 0.045 mm)	0.0013 to 0.0025 in (0.03 to 0.06 mm)
Valve stem-to-rocker clearance	0.013 in (0.33 mm) warm	0.013 (0.33 mm) warm

Engine Nos 18V 846 F and 18V 847 F
The information provided for earlier models is applicable except where either superseded or added to by that below

Valves

Valve stem-to-rocker clearance:
Hot .... 0.013 in (0.33 mm)
Cold .... 0.015 in (0.38 mm)

Engine Nos 18V 581 F and Y, 18V 582 F and Y, 18V 583 F and Y, 18V 779 F and 18V 780 F
The information provided for earlier models is applicable except where either superseded or added to by that below

Engine – general
Compression ratio:
   High compression .... 9.0 : 1
   Low compression .... 8.0 : 1
Compression pressure .... 170 lbf/in^2 (11.9 kgf/cm^2) at 275 rpm

Valves
Inlet valve head diameter (early cars) .... 1.625 to 1.630 in (41.27 to 41.40 mm)

Engine Nos 18V 883 AE, 18V 884 AE, 18V 890 AE, 18V 891 AE, 18V 892 AE and 18V 893 AE
The information provided for earlier models is applicable except where either superseded or added to by that below

Main bearings
Intermediate bearing length .... 0.760 to 0.770 in (19.30 to 19.55 mm)

Valve timing

	Inlet	Exhaust
Opens	8° BTDC	54° BBDC
Closes	42° ABDC	18° ATDC

Tappets

Type		Bucket
Length	1.495 to 1.505 in (37.97 to 38.23 mm)	

Lubrication system
Oil pump type .... Hobourn-Eaton rotor type
Oil filter type.. Full flow, hanging canister

Engine No 18V 847 F
The information provided for earlier models is applicable except where either superseded or added to by that below

Engine – general
Compression ratio .... 9.0 : 1

Valve timing

	Inlet	Exhaust
Opens	20° BTDC	55° BBDC
Closes	52° ABDC	17° ATDC

All models

Torque wrench settings

	lbf ft	Nm
Big-end bolts (early models)...	35 to 40	48 to 54
Big-end nuts (later models)	33	45
Camshaft sprocket nut	60 to 70	81 to 95
Crankshaft pulley nut	70	95
Clutch-to-flywheel bolts	25 to 30	34 to 41
Cylinder head nuts..	45 to 50	61 to 68
Engine mounting bolt, rear..	38 to 40	52 to 54
Flywheel securing bolts	40	54
Front plate, 5/16 in screws	20	27
Gudgeon pin clamp bolts (early models only)	25	34
Main bearing nuts..	70	95
Manifold nuts..	15 to 16	20 to 22
Oil filter centre bolt (early models only	15	20
Oil pump-to-crankcase	14	19
Oil pump banjo unions...	37 (max)	50 (max)
Oil pressure relief valve domed nut:		
Early models (pre-1978)	43	58
Later models	40	54
Rear plate:		
5/16 in screws	20	27
3/8 in screws	30	41
Rocker bracket nuts	25	34
Sump bolts	6	8
Water pump-to-crankcase:		
Early models	25	34
Later models	17	23

1 General description

The engine is a four-cylinder in-line design, with overhead valves operated by a camshaft via pushrods and overhead rockers. The cylinder block has integral cylinders and waterways.

The crankshaft is supported in either three or five renewable bearings, and has drilled oilways for the essential lubrication functions. Endfloat is controlled by centrally-situated thrust washers.

Aluminium alloy pistons are fitted to H-section forged steel connecting rods.

The camshaft is driven by an automatically-adjusted chain. The drive for the distributor, oil pump and (on early models) the revolution counter are taken from the camshaft.

The cylinder head is of cast iron, with valves running in pressed-in guides.

2 Lubrication system – oil and oil filter maintenance

Checking the oil level

1 The dipstick is on the right-hand side of the engine, and is marked to indicate the correct oil level. Top up via the filler cap on the front of the rocker cover.

Changing the engine oil

2 This is best carried out when the engine is hot. Remove the drain plug, and allow the oil to drain for a suitable period. Refit the plug.
3 Refill with the correct grade of engine oil. Recheck the oil level after a few minutes running.

2.4 Later type filter with disposable cartridge

Changing the oil filter

4 Three types of filters may be fitted. That on early cars has a renewable element, whilst the later type is of the disposable cartridge type. The early type may be found mounted either above or below the filter head (photo).

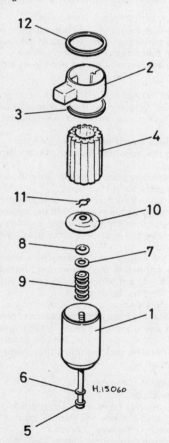

Fig 1.1 Oil filter, early type (Sec 2)

1	Case	7	Steel washer
2	Filter head	8	Seal
3	Seal	9	Spring
4	Element	10	Plate
5	Bolt	11	Clip
6	Seal	12	Seal

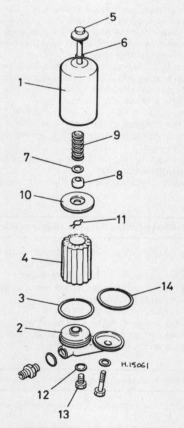

Fig 1.2 Oil filter, intermediate type (Sec 2)

1	Case	8	Seal
2	Filter head	9	Spring
3	Seal	10	Plate
4	Element	11	Clip
5	Bolt	12	Washer
6	Seal	13	Plug
7	Steel washer	14	Seal

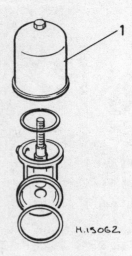

Fig 1.3 Oil filter, later type (Sec 2)
1 Renewable element

5   To change the element on the earlier engines, drain the filter by removing the plug, where appropriate. Remove the long centre bolt, lift off the body, and discard the element.

6   Wash out the casing with fuel, and clean the other parts. Check the sealing rings.

7   Reassemble all parts with a new element.

8   Remove the old sealing ring from the groove in the filter head, taking care not to damage the groove. Fit a new ring.

9   Where the filter assembly is of the type hanging below the filter bowl, refill the assembly with engine oil.

10   Offer up the assembly to the filter head, start the centre bolt, and check that the lip of the bowl is properly in the groove all round, before tightening the bolt to the specified torque.

11   Run the engine and check for leaks.

12   Check the oil level.

13   To change the element in the later type filter assembly, unscrew the complete cartridge and discard it. If it proves difficult to remove, employ a chain wrench.

14   Lubricate the sealing ring on the new cartridge with oil, and screw it into position using hands only.

15   Run the engine, check for leaks, and after a short period check the oil level.

3   Major operations possible with the engine in place

The following operations can be carried out with the engine in the vehicle:

    (a) Removing and refitting the cylinder head
    (b) Removing and refitting the timing chain and gears
    (c) Removing and refitting the sump
    (d) Removing and refitting the oil pump
    (e) Removing and refitting big-end bearings
    (f) Removing and refitting the pistons and connecting rods
    (g) Removing and refitting the camshaft

4   Major operations necessitating removal of the engine

The engine must be removed from the vehicle for the following operations:

    (a) Removing and refitting the main bearings
    (b) Removing and refitting the crankshaft
    (c) Removing and refitting the flywheel

5   Methods of engine removal

1   It is recommended that the engine and transmission be removed together, so that the possibility of damage to the clutch which may occur when manoeuvering the unit in the confined engine compartment, is obviated.

2   It is also possible to remove the engine alone, thus making the unit more easily handled.

3   Both methods of removal are described.

6   Engine – removal

1   Remove the battery connections (photo).

2   Drain the coolant (see Chapter 2).

3   Drain the engine oil (see Section 2).

4   Remove the bonnet (see Chapter 12) and the acoustic board where fitted.

5   Remove the oil cooler pipes at the engine. Remove the oil cooler fixing bolts, and take away the cooler complete with the radiator and surround (see Chapter 2). Disconnect the oil pressure gauge pipe at the engine (photo).

6   Remove the distributor cap and spark plug leads (see Chapter 4).

7   Remove the wiring from the generator and distributor (see Chapter 10).

8   Disconnect the thermal transmitter at the engine.

9   Disconnect the heater control cable and hoses (see Chapter 12).

10   Disconnect the starter wiring (see Chapter 10).

11   Disconnect the choke (when fitted) and throttle cables.

12   Disconnect the fuel pipe and remove the air cleaners (see Chapter 3). Detach the brake servo vacuum pipe from the inlet manifold.

13   Disconnect drive-type tachometer at the knurled nut (photo).

14   Disconnect the exhaust pipes at the manifold and at the gearbox clip (photos), or at the catalytic converter, where fitted.

North American models

15   Disconnect the wire from the induction manifold heater.

16   Disconnect the purge pipe from the top of the rocker cover, and the manifold pipe from the running-on control valve.

17   Disconnect the absorption canister hose from the rocker cover and carburettor.

Engine only removal (all models)

18   Place a chain or rope around the engine and take the weight on lifting tackle. Position a jack under the gearbox just behind its union with the engine.

19   Remove the bolts which hold the engine front mountings to the frame. Note the earth lead which is attached to the front top bolt on the left-hand mounting.

20   Withdraw the packing plate (if fitted) from the left-hand mounting and put it in a safe place for reassembly.

21   Undo the two bolts which hold the starter motor in place. It will not be possible to remove the starter until the engine has been drawn forward a few inches, unless the distributor is removed.

22   Undo and remove the nuts and bolts holding the engine to the gearbox bellhousing.

23   Slightly raise the engine, at the same time raising the jack under the gearbox. *It is important that no undue strain be placed on the gearbox input shaft* – do not allow the engine to hang on the shaft, nor the gearbox to be lifted by the engine.

24   Draw the engine forwards until it is clear of the bellhousing, then tilt it upwards to clear the front crossmember and hoist it out of the car. Depending on the space available and the technique adopted, it may be easier if the oil filter, the generator, the coil and the carburettors are removed. Do not remove the manifolds: they make good handles for manipulating the engine.

Engine removal with gearbox
Manual gearbox versions

25   Remove the gear lever by removing the screws from the surround. Lift the surround away. Raise the rubber boot. Remove the lever retaining bolts, and then the lever (photo).

26   Remove the screws from the clutch slave cylinder, and lay the cylinder aside (photo).

27   Disconnect the overdrive (when fitted) and reverse light switch wiring.

Automatic gearbox versions

28   Disconnect the manual control lever at the gearbox shaft, and the wires from the inhibitor and reverse light switch.

29   Disconnect the downshift cable at the carburettor.

6.1 Disconnecting the battery

6.5 Disconnecting the oil pressure gauge pipe (arrowed)

6.13 Disconnecting the cable drive type speedometer

6.14a Removing the nuts at an exhaust-pipe-to-manifold clamp

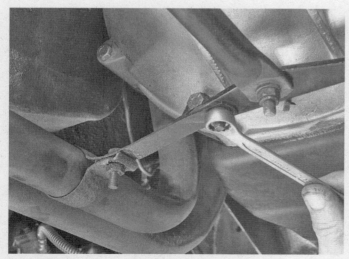

6.14b Disconnect the exhaust pipe clip

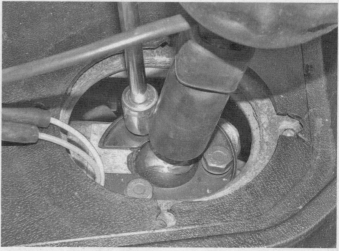

6.25 Removing the gear lever retaining bolts

6.26 Removing the clutch slave cylinder

6.32 Disconnect the engine earth strap

6.33 Remove the bolts from the rear crossmember

All vehicles

30   Disconnect the speedometer cable at the gearbox.

31   Disconnect and remove the propeller shaft as described in Chapter 7.

32   Support the gearbox, take the engine weight using a suitable hoist or crane, and remove the bolts which retain the engine front mountings to the frame. Disconnect the earth strap (photo).

On early vehicles

33   Remove the bolts from the rear crossmember, thereby allowing the gearbox to rest on the fixed crossmember (photo).

34   Detach the stay rod from the gearbox.

35   Remove the crossmember and stay rod, by taking out the bolts securing the rear mountings.

On later vehicles

36   Remove the engine restraint rod where fitted, by loosening the nuts at the rear and removing the rearmost nut, followed by the plate and buffer. Take the front nut and bolt out, and remove the rod.

37   Take out the four bolts holding the crossmember to the chassis frame, and the two bolts holding the lower tie bracket to the crossmember.

38   Lower the gearbox on to the crossmember, remove the nuts securing the rear mounting, and remove the crossmember.

All vehicles

39   Bring the unit forward to clear the crossmember. Tilt, and lift out (photo).

---

7   Engine – separation from transmission

Manual gearbox vehicles

1   To remove the gearbox, remove the starter motor, remove the screws holding the gearbox to the engine mounting plate, and draw the gearbox away squarely (photo).

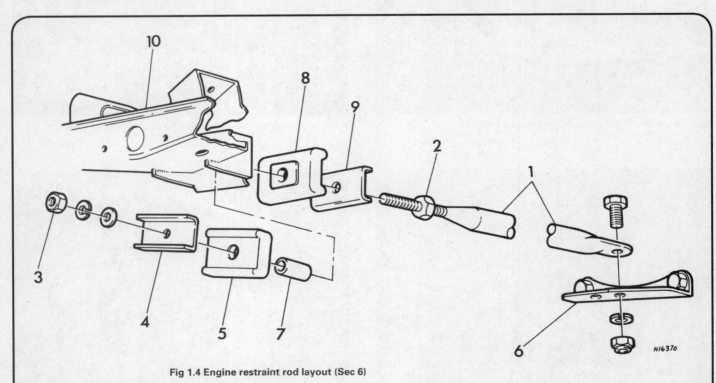

Fig 1.4 Engine restraint rod layout (Sec 6)

1	Engine restraint rod	5	Rear buffer	9	Front plate
2	Front nut	6	Gearbox bracket	10	Engine mounting rear
3	Rear nut	7	Distance tube		cross-member bracket
4	Rear plate	8	Front buffer		

H16370

6.39 Lifting out the engine and transmission

7.1 Draw the gearbox from the engine

Automatic transmission vehicles

2   Remove the bolts holding the gearbox to the converter housing, and remove the gearbox.
3   Remove the bolts securing the converter housing to the engine, and remove the housing.
4   Remove the bolts securing the converter to the driveplate. Remove the converter.

8   Engine dismantling – general

1   The engine is best mounted on a dismantling stand. If, however, this is not available, employ a strong bench to provide the correct working height. Failing this, dismantle the unit on the floor.
2   During dismantling, keep everything free from dirt. To aid this, thoroughly clean the engine exterior before beginning work.
3   Clean using paraffin or a grease solvent, working it well into any thickly embedded dirt with a wire brush. If a solvent is used, allow it to stand for a time, before washing off with a hose.
4   Finally wipe down the exterior of the engine with a rag and only then, when it is quite clean, should dismantling begin. As the engine is stripped, clean each part in paraffin.
5   Do not immerse parts with oilways, such as the crankshaft, in paraffin. Instead, clean them with a petrol-moistened rag, and clean the oilways with wire. If an air line is available, blow through the oilways.

10.7 Lift off the rocker assembly

6   To re-use old engine gaskets is false economy. It can give rise to oil and water leaks, or worse, and new gaskets should be used throughout.
7   Do not throw the old gaskets away. If an immediate replacement cannot be found, the old gasket is then useful as a template. Hang up the old gaskets as they are removed.
8   When dismantling, work from the top down. The sump provides a firm base on which the engine can be supported in an upright position. When the point is reached where the sump is to be removed, turn the engine on its side and carry out the remaining work with it in this position.
9   Where possible, refit nuts, bolts and washers, finger tight, to prevent loss or confusion. If this is not possible, lay them out in a systematic way to assist reassembly.
10 Whether or not the engine is to be fully dismantled, it is suggested that advantage be taken of the opportunity to clean it whilst it is out of the vehicle.

9   Ancillary components

1   If a reconditioned engine unit is to be fitted, establish which components will be supplied with it. It will then be necessary to remove and retain those which are not to be supplied.
2   If the unit is to be completely dismantled and reconditioned, all components should be removed as described in the relevant Chapters and Sections of this manual.

10   Rocker assembly – removal

1   If the engine is still in the car, drain the cooling system (see Chapter 2). This is essential because of the need to slacken the cylinder head nuts, which in turn is necessary because of the distortion that can occur if the rocker bracket fixing nuts only are released.
2   Disconnect the breather pipe or purge hose where relevant, from the rocker cover. Detach the vapour pipe where fitted.
3   Release the heater pipe from the rocker studs (where relevant) and move it clear.
4   Release the rocker cover front breather pipe.
5   Disconnect the throttle cable at the carburettor.
6   Remove the two nuts and then the rocker cover, noting the gasket, washers and rubber seals.
7   Slacken the cylinder head nuts in the order given in Fig. 1.5. Continue removing the eight rocker bracket nuts evenly, a turn at a time, until the load is released. Remove the eight nuts completely, and lift off the rocker assembly (photo).

10.8 Take out the pushrods

13.1 The collets, ready to be removed

8   Take out the pushrods and identify them for location (photo).
9   Note the locking plate under the nut on the rear rocker bracket.
10   Note the shims fitted under the two centre rocker brackets on later engines. These shims, 0.005 in (0.13 mm) thick, should be fitted to early engines also, when reassembling.
11   Note that later engines have longer pushrods and rocker adjusting screws, used in conjunction with bucket-type tappets. The whole is interchangeable, as a complete set, with the first type.

11 Rocker assembly – dismantling

1   Release the rocker shaft locating screw, remove the split pins, flat washers, and spring washers from each end of the shaft, and slide off the pedestals, rocker arms, and rocker spacing springs.
2   Undo the shaft end plug screw. Clean the shaft oilways.

12 Cylinder head – removal

Vehicles not fitted with exhaust emission control
1   This section fully covers removal of the cylinder head with the engine in the vehicle. If the unit is on the bench, certain operations can obviously be ignored.
2   Disconnect the batteries.
3   Drain the cooling system (see Chapter 2).
4   Disconnect the top hose, remove the nuts and washers, and remove the thermostat housing and thermostat.
5   Disconnect the control cable and hose from the water valve.

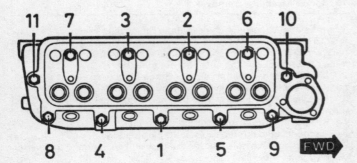
Fig 1.5 Cylinder head nuts – loosening and tightening sequence (Sec 12)

6   Unscrew the thermal transmitter from the cylinder head, or disconnect the electrical lead.
7   Remove the HT leads and spark plugs.
8   Remove the air cleaners and carburettors (see Chapter 3). Remove the throttle bracket from the inlet manifold on later models.
9   Slacken the inlet and exhaust manifold fixings (Section 15) but leave them in position as an aid to lifting off the cylinder head. Disconnect the exhaust downpipes from the manifold.
10   Remove the rocker assembly (Section 10) and also the external cylinder head nuts (see Fig. 1.5). Remove the heat shield where fitted.
11   Release the vacuum pipe from the rear cylinder head stud and distributor. Disconnect the vacuum pipe from the inlet manifold.
12   Disconnect the hoses from the cylinder head water pipe. Remove the pipe.
13   Break the cylinder head joint by careful levering at one end (do not touch the joint faces with the lever). Alternatively, rock the head with the manifold, or strike it with a soft-faced hammer. Lift off the head.
14   Remove the manifolds.

Vehicles fitted with exhaust emission control
15   Proceed largely as described in the preceding paragraphs. However, disconnect additional pipes relating to the emission system, as necessary.
16   Disconnect the automatic choke water hose from the cylinder head.
17   Remove the air pump (see Chapter 3).
18   Disconnect the bottom hose from the water pump.
19   Remove the hot air duct (see Chapter 3).
20   Remove the air manifold rail (see Chapter 3).
21   When removing the head nuts, note the position of the special nut for the air manifold rail.

13 Valves – removal

1   Remove the spring clips where fitted. Using a suitable valve spring compressor, compress each spring in turn and remove the collets (photo) followed by the remaining parts (see Fig. 1.9). Drop the valve out through the combustion chamber.
2   If, when the compressor is tightened down, the cap refuses to free from the collet, do not continue screwing down as damage may occur. Instead, hold the compressor in position, and tap the tool with a hammer to cause the cap to free.
3   If the valves are to be re-used, identify them by placing them in a piece of cardboard with eight holes, suitably numbered.
4   Certain valve gear is of single spring design, as in Fig. 1.10. Dismantling and reassembly are fundamentally the same.

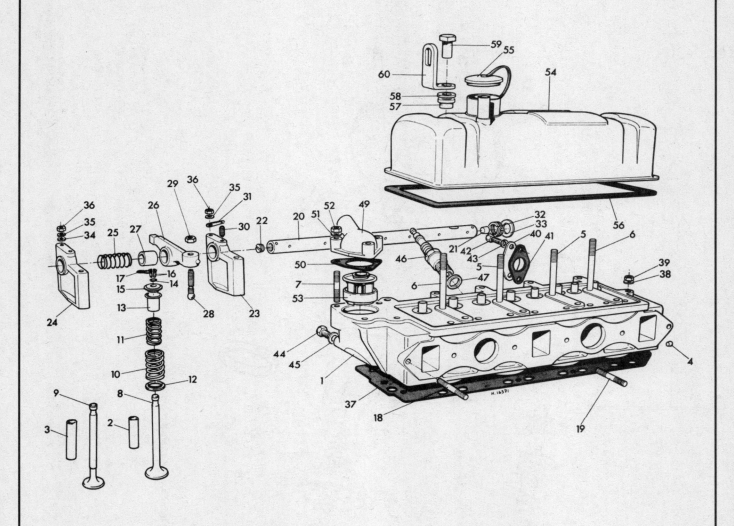

Fig 1.6 Cylinder head – exploded view (Sec 12)

1	Cylinder head assembly	15	Cap	30	Locating screw	45	Washer
2	Inlet valve guide	16	Collets	31	Lockplate	46	Spark plug
3	Exhaust valve guide	17	Circlip	32	Washer	47	Gasket
4	Plug	18	Stud	33	Washer	49	Elbow
5	Short stud	19	Stud	34	Washer	50	Gasket
6	Long stud	20	Valve rocker shaft	35	Washer	51	Plain washer
7	Stud	21	Plain plug	36	Nut	52	Nut
8	Inlet valve	22	Screwed plug	37	Gasket	53	Thermostat
9	Exhaust valve	23	Rocker shaft bracket	38	Washer	54	Cover
10	Outer valve spring	24	Rocker shaft bracket	39	Nut	55	Cap and cable
11	Inner valve spring	25	Spring	40	Blanking plate	56	Bush
12	Collar	26	Rocker	41	Gasket	58	Washer
13	Shroud (up to Engine No 4385 and L2815)	27	Bush	42	Screw	59	Nut
14	Ring	28	Adjusting screw	43	Spring washer	60	Bracket
		29	Nut	44	Plug		

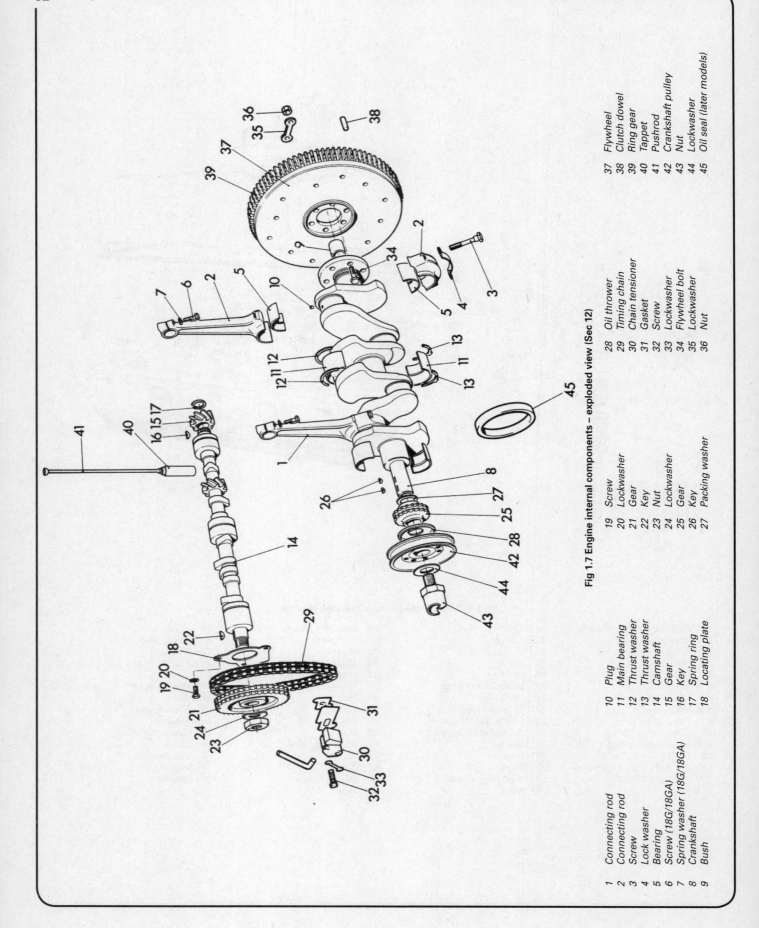

Fig 1.7 Engine internal components – exploded view (Sec 12)

1 Connecting rod
2 Connecting rod
3 Screw
4 Lock washer
5 Bearing
6 Screw (18G/18GA)
7 Spring washer (18G/18GA)
8 Crankshaft
9 Bush

10 Plug
11 Main bearing
12 Thrust washer
13 Thrust washer
14 Camshaft
15 Gear
16 Key
17 Spring ring
18 Locating plate

19 Screw
20 Lockwasher
21 Gear
22 Key
23 Nut
24 Lockwasher
25 Gear
26 Key
27 Packing washer

28 Oil thrower
29 Timing chain
30 Chain tensioner
31 Gasket
32 Screw
33 Lockwasher
34 Flywheel bolt
35 Lockwasher
36 Nut

37 Flywheel
38 Clutch dowel
39 Ring gear
40 Tappet
41 Pushrod
42 Crankshaft pulley
43 Nut
44 Lockwasher
45 Oil seal (later models)

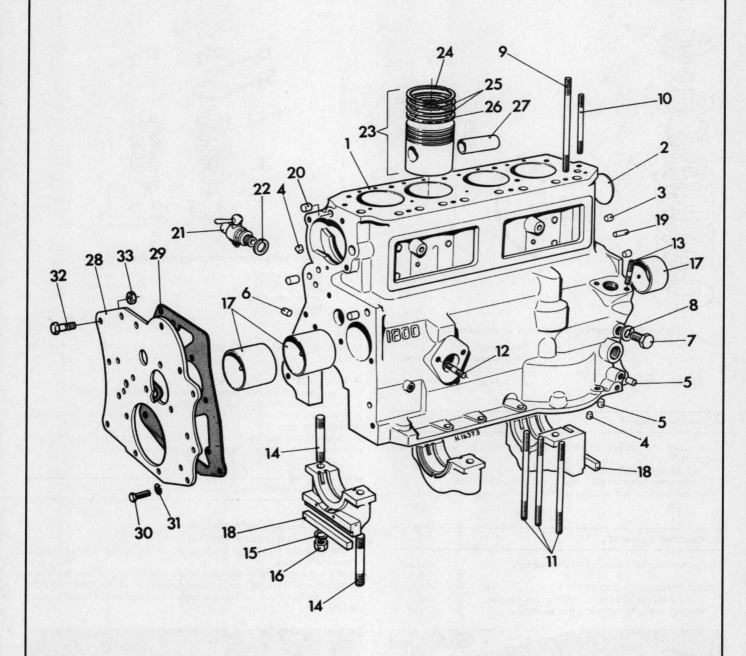

Fig 1.8 Cylinder block components – exploded view (Sec 12)

1	Cylinder block assembly	10	Stud	19	Dowel	26	Scraper piston ring
2	Plug	11	Stud	20	Dowel	27	Gudgeon pin
3	Plug	12	Stud	21	Drain tap	28	Plate
4	Plug	13	Stud	22	Washer	29	Gasket
5	Plug	14	Stud	23	Piston assembly –	30	Screw
6	Plug	15	Plain washer		standard HC	31	Spring washer
7	Plug	16	Nut	24	Piston ring	32	Bolt – RH top
8	Washer	17	Camshaft bearing	25	2nd and 3rd Piston ring	33	Nut
9	Stud	18	Gasket				

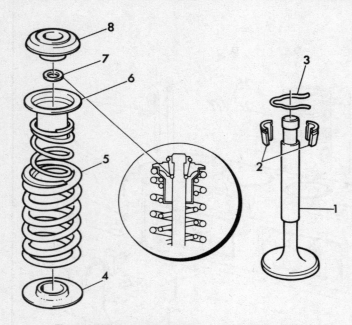

Fig 1.9 Valve assembly, double coil springs (Sec 13)

1	Valve	5	Double sprints
2	Collets	6	Shroud (early engines only)
3	Clip	7	Packing ring seal
4	Bottom collar	8	Spring cap

14 Tappets – removal

1 Remove the rocker assembly (see Section 10) and then the pushrods.
2 Remove the manifolds (see Section 15).
3 Remove the breather pipe and tappet covers (if fitted).
4 Lift out each tappet and identify for refitting purposes (photo).

15 Manifolds – removal

1 Remove the air cleaners and carburettors.

North American models
2 Disconnect the running-on control valve hose.
3 Remove the gulp valve and hot air shroud.

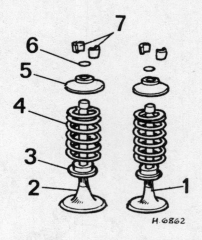

Fig 1.10 Valve assembly, single coil spring (Sec 13)

1	Exhaust valve	5	Valve spring collar
2	Inlet valve	6	Packing ring
3	Valve spring cup	7	Valve collets
4	Valve spring		

4 Disconnect the exhaust pipe from the catalytic converter where fitted.

All models
5 Disconnect the heater pipe at the manifold (early vehicles).
6 Remove the vacuum pipe at the manifold.
7 Remove the fixings at the exhaust pipe manifold connection, releasing the pipe.
8 Remove the four centre nuts and large washers, and the two end nuts with small washers. Remove the manifolds and gasket.

16 Distributor drive – removal

18G/18GA-engined vehicles
1 Remove the distributor (see Chapter 4).
2 Remove the distributor housing, by removing the single retaining screw and washer.
3 If the sump is still in position screw into the end of the distributor driveshaft a 5/16 in UNF bolt (a tappet cover bolt will do). The driveshaft can then be lifted out, turning it slightly in the process to free the gears (photo).

14.4 Lifting out a tappet

16.3 Lifting out the distributor driveshaft

17.3 The oil pressure relief valve components

18.2 Moving the tensioner back to the retracted position

4   If the sump is removed, simply push the driveshaft out from inside the crankcase.

18GB and later-engined vehicles
5   Proceed as in paragraphs 1 and 2.
6   Position the pistons halfway up the cylinder bores.
7   Proceed as in paragraphs 3 and 4.

17   Oil pressure relief valve – removal

1   The valve is identified externally by the large domed hexagonal nut at the left-hand rear of the engine.
2   To dismantle the valve, remove the domed nut with the two fibre or one copper sealing ring(s).
3   Extract the spring and cup (photo).
4   Check the spring length against the Specifications, and renew if too short.
5   Examine the cup, and renew it if the seat appears flawed.

18   Timing chain tensioner – removal

Double roller chain type
1   Remove the timing cover (Section 19).
2   Lock the tensioner in the retracted position (Section 19, paragraph 10) (photo).
3   Knock back the lockwasher tabs, remove the two retaining bolts and remove the tensioner.
4   Pull the rubber slipper together with the spring and plunger from the tensioner body. Fit the Alien key to its socket in the cylinder and, holding the slipper and plunger firmly, turn the key clockwise to free the cylinder and spring from the plunger.

Single roller chain type
5   Remove the timing cover (see Section 19).
6   Remove the tensioner by taking out the securing screws, prising the assembly out of the front plate whilst holding the slipper head, and removing the tensioner with the backplate and gasket.
7   Relax the tensioner spring and dismantle the assembly.

19   Timing cover, chain and chain wheels – removal

Double-roller chain type
1   This operation can be carried out with the engine in the vehicle. If the engine is on the bench, certain operations described will obviously be omitted.
2   Remove the radiator, as described in Chapter 2.

3   Remove the fanbelt (see Chapter 2).
4   On 18GB or later-engined vehicles, remove the bolts which hold the steering rack to the body. Ease the rack assembly forward, to permit the crankshaft pulley to come away.
5   Bend back the locking tab on the crankshaft pulley bolt. Remove the bolt.
6   Remove the pulley. Either use an extractor, or two levers. Take care not to damage the pulley or cover when using levers.
7   Remove the Woodruff key and store it safely.
8   Remove the timing cover bolts, noting the different sizes and where they fit. Pull off the cover and gasket.
9   Remove the oil thrower.
10   Remove the chain tensioner bottom plug. Insert a 1/8 in (3.18 mm) Allen key, and turn clockwise until the slipper head is right back and locked behind the limit head. Unbolt and remove the chain tensioner.
11   Bend back the lockwasher tag on the camshaft nut. Remove the nut.
12   Remove the two wheels complete with the chain. Ease each wheel forward a little at a time, using two levers.
13   If the wheels are locked solid, a proper extractor tool will be necessary.

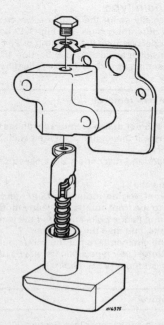

Fig 1.11 Timing chain tensioner (double row roller chain) – exploded view (Sec 18)

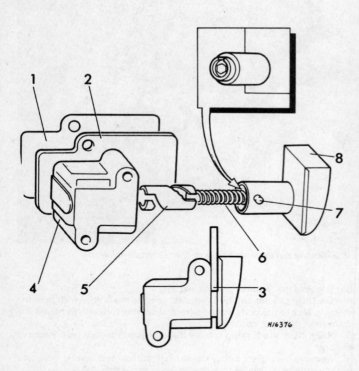

22.4 The flywheel bolts and locking (nuts may be employed)

Fig 1.12 Timing chain tensioner (single row roller chain) – exploded view (Sec 18)

1	Gasket	5	Inner cylinder
2	Backplate	6	Spring
3	Spacer to prevent	7	Peg
	disengagement	8	Slipper head
4	Tensioner body		

14   Remove the Woodruff keys and store them safely.
15   Retain the packing washers behind the crankshaft chain wheel.

Single roller chain type

16   Removal is basically as for the double roller chain type. However, the tensioner is of different design (see Fig. 1.12 and Section 18). On North American models remove the air pump drive belt where fitted.
17   Remove the tensioner as described in Section 18.
18   Continue dismantling as for the double roller chain design.

20   Sump and strainer – removal

1   The sump and strainer may be removed with the engine in or out of the vehicle. Obviously, if the engine is on the bench, certain operations will not be necessary.
2   Drain the coolant and disconnect the hoses to the radiator (early models).
3   Drain the engine oil.
4   Remove the front engine mounting bolts, and lift the unit until access is obtained to the front sump bolts (early models).
5   Take out the sump flange bolts and lower the sump.
6   Remove the bolts, and then the oil strainer.
7   To dismantle the strainer, take out the centre nut and bolt, and the pipe-flange bolts. **Note:** *Later type strainers maybe of one-piece design, and dismantling is not therefore possible.*

21   Oil pump – removal

1   Remove the sump and strainer (see Section 20).
2   Remove the three nuts, and lift away the pump, driveshaft and gasket.

22   Flywheel and engine endplate – removal

1   The power unit must be removed from the vehicle.
2   Remove the clutch (see Chapter 5).
3   Bend back the locking tabs on the nuts or bolts securing the flywheel.
4   Remove the nuts or bolts securing the flywheel (photo), and withdraw the flywheel. If difficulty is experienced, hold the flywheel either by placing a wooden block between the crankshaft and the inside of the crankcase (sump removed) or alternatively, and with due care, jamming a lever in the flywheel teeth via the starter motor hole in the endplate.
5   Remove the bolts, and remove the engine endplate. **Note:** *The fixings are of varying sizes, and a record should therefore be kept of their respective locations.*

23   Camshaft – removal

1   Camshaft removal is practicable with the engine either in or out of the vehicle. If the engine is on the bench, certain operations can obviously be ignored.
2   Disconnect the battery.
3   Remove the radiator and surround (see Chapter 2).
4   Remove the inlet and exhaust manifold (see Section 15).
5   Remove the tappets (see Section 14).
6   Remove the timing gear (see Section 19).
7   Remove the distributor drive (see Section 16).
8   Remove the oil pump (see Section 21).
9   Remove the drive if a drive-type tachometer is fitted, by removing the nuts and washers and withdrawing the drivegear.
10   Remove the three bolts and spring washers which hold the camshaft locating plate to the block. Remove the plate.
11   Withdraw the camshaft, taking care that the cam peaks do not damage the bearings as the shaft is pulled forward.

24   Pistons, connecting rods and big-end bearings – removal

1   Remove the cylinder head (see Section 12).
2   Remove the sump and oil strainer (see Section 20).
3   On 18G and 18GA engines knock back with a cold chisel the locking tabs on the big-end retaining bolts and remove the bolts and tabs. On 18GB engines unscrew the big-end nuts.
4   The big-end caps and connecting rods are sometimes marked for identification purposes, but not always. If necessary, they should be marked to ensure correct reassembly. If the bearings are not to be renewed, these should also be kept with the original cap and rod.

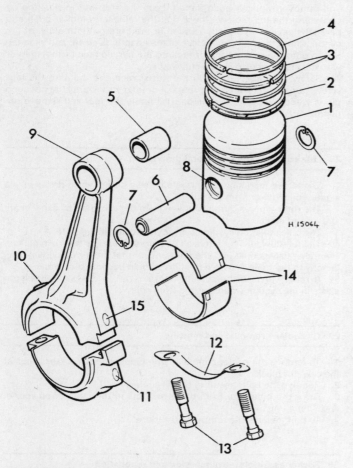

Fig 1.13 Piston and connecting rod assembly (fully floating gudgeon pin) – exploded view (Sec 24)

1	Piston	9	Connecting rod
2	Piston rings – scraper	10	Cylinder wall lubricating jet
3	Piston rings – taper	11	Connecting rod cap
4	Piston ring – parallel	12	Lockwasher
5	Small-end bush	13	Bolts
6	Gudgeon pin	14	Connecting rod bearings
7	Circlip	15	Connecting rod and cap
8	Gudgeon pin lubricating hole		marking

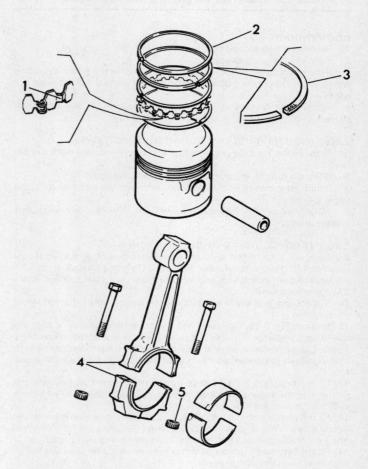

Fig 1.14 Piston and connecting rod assembly (press fit gudgeon pin) – exploded view (Sec 24)

1 Note that expander rail ends must butt
2 Compression ring
3 Compression ring
4 Identification marks on rod and cap
5 Multi-sided nut

5   Remove the big-end caps. If they are tight, gently tap them with a soft hammer. Retrieve the bearings.

6   Withdraw the piston and connecting rods upwards, identifying them as necessary, and refitting the cap and bearings to each one to avoid confusion.

25 Crankshaft and main bearings – removal

1   The power unit must be removed from the vehicle.

2   Remove the flywheel and engine endplate (see Section 22).

3   Remove the timing gear (see Section 19).

4   Remove the sump and oil strainer (see Section 20).

5   Remove the bolts and locking plate, which secure the front bearing cap to the engine bearer plate. Unbolt and remove the camshaft locating plate and engine front plate. Remove the gasket.

6   Evenly release the main bearing nuts, noting that some designs employ plain nuts with locking plates, and others use self-locking nuts and plain washers.

7   Lift away the bearing caps together with the half bearings and, in the case of the centre cap, with the thrust washer lower halves. If the bearings are to be re-used, keep them identified with their respective caps.

8   Check the endplay by pushing and pulling on the crankshaft, and measuring the gap between one of the thrust washers and the adjacent thrust face on the shaft. Compare with the Specifications, and order new thrust washers if necessary. Oversize thrust washers are available.

9   Lift out the crankshaft. Recover the remaining bearings, keeping them identified if they are to be re-used.

26 Piston rings – removal

1   Slide the piston rings carefully over the top of the piston, taking care not to scratch the aluminium alloy. Never slide them from the bottom of the piston skirt. It is very easy to break the rings if they are pulled off roughly.

2   It can be helpful to use an aid such as a 0.020 in (0.5 mm) feeler gauge. Lift one end of the piston ring to be removed from the groove, and insert the end of the feeler under it.

3   Turn the feeler gauge slowly round the piston and as the ring comes out of its groove apply slight upward pressure so that it rests on the land above. It can then be eased off the piston with the feeler stopping it from slipping into any empty grooves.

27 Pistons, connecting rods and gudgeon pins – dismantling

Early models

1   Remove the small-end bolt and washer.
2   Push out the gudgeon pin.
3   If the pin is tight, do not use force, but immerse the piston in boiling water. Expansion of the piston material should allow the pin to slide out easily.
4   Identify the respective pistons, rods and pins, if they are to be reused.

Later models (circlip-retained gudgeon pins)

5   Remove the locating circlip at one end of the pin, and push the pin out.
6   If the pin is tight, proceed as described in paragraph 3.
7   Identify the pins to enable refitting them into the same pistons, the same way round.
8   Identify all parts if they are to be re-used. Always use new circlips on reassembly.

Later models (press-fit gudgeon pins)

9   Gudgeon pins of this type are an interference fit, and special tool number 18G 1150 and adaptor 18G 1150 D must be used. It may be possible to borrow this tool and adaptor from your local Leyland agent or engineering firm.
10   If the tools are available proceed as described in the following paragraphs.
11   Refer to Fig. 1.15, securely hold the hexagonal body in a vice and screw back the large nut until it is flush with the end of the main centre screw. Lubricate the screw and large nut as they have to withstand high loading. Push the centre screw in until the nut just touches the thrust race.
12   Fit the adaptors (18G 1150 D) on the main centre screw, with the piston ring cutaway positioned uppermost. Slide the parallel sleeve with the groove end first onto the centre screw.
13   Fit the piston with the FRONT or A mark towards the adaptor on the centre screw. This is important because the gudgeon pin bore is offset and irreparable damage will result if fitted the wrong way round.
14   Fit the remover/replacer bush on the centre screw with the flange end away from the gudgeon pin.
15   Screw the stop nut onto the main centre screw and adjust it so that there is approximately 0.04 in (1 mm) endplay between the nut

and remover/replacer bush flange. Lock the stop nut in position by tightening the lock screw. Check that the replacer/remover bush and parallel sleeve are correctly located in the bore on both sides of the piston. Check that the curved face of the adaptor is clean, and slide the piston onto the tool, so that it fits into the curved face of the adaptor with the piston rings over the cutaway.
16   Screw the large nut up to the thrust race and, holding the lock screw, turn the nut with a ring spanner or long socket until the gudgeon pin is withdrawn from the piston. Dismantle the tool and remove the piston, rod and pin.

28 Lubrication system – general description

1   The forced feed lubrication system has a pump which draws oil via a gauze oil strainer from the sump.
2   The rotor-type oil pump is driven from the camshaft by skew gears and a short shaft.
3   The oil circulation system is clearly indicated in Fig. 1.16.
4   The full-flow oil filter filters all oil before it reaches the main gallery. Two relief valves built into the filter ensure that unfiltered oil will pass directly to the main gallery if the filter should become blocked.
5   A relief valve in the system operates when excessive pressure exists in the system when starting from cold.

29 Oil cooler – removal and refitting

1   To remove the cooler complete with pipes, disconnect the pipes at the cylinder block.
2   Remove the bolts securing the oil cooler.
3   Draw the pipes out from the grommets in the radiator surround, and lift the unit away.
4   To refit, reverse the removal procedure.

30 Rocker assembly – examination and renovation

1   Check the shaft for straightness by rolling it on a flat surface. Examine for obvious wear, and renew if defects are found. Ensure that all oilways are clear.
2   Check for wear of the rocker arm bushes by placing them on the shaft and testing for lateral shake. Leyland tool 18G 226 is required for bush renewal work, which will probably have to be entrusted to a local agent.
3   Examine the rocker pad and the ball end screw for wear, and renew if necessary.

31 Valves and valve seats – examination and renovation

Examination

1   Clean each valve thoroughly and examine for pitting and burning on the sealing face. Small marks can be removed by grinding, but larger defects will mean that the valve should be refaced on a proper machine, or renewed if necessary.
2   Pass a piece of clean rag through each valve guide, and test each valve in turn for excessive slackness in its guide. Renew if worn.

Renovations

3   Pitted or burnt valve seats should be recut by an engineering shop. If the defects are severe, or the seats have been cut before, it may be necessary to have inserts fitted to the head by a specialist.
4   When the basic condition of valves and seats is adequate, grind them together using medium and fine grinding paste, and a suction tool (obtainable at any accessory shop). A light coil spring under the valve head can help considerably when grinding. Use a semi-rotary motion, and lift and turn the valve occasionally.
5   When a smooth, unbroken, matt grey ring is obtained on the valve and seat, clean away all traces of grinding compound.

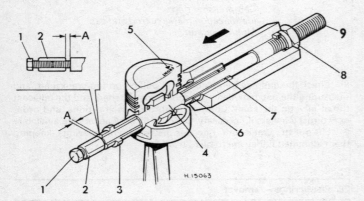

Fig 1.15 Press fit gudgeon pin removal, showing service tool 18G 1150 and adaptor set 18G 1150D in use (Sec 27)

A = 0.040 in (1 mm) endfloat	5 Piston front mark
1 Lockscrew	6 Adaptor
2 Stop nut	7 Groove in sleeve away from
3 Remover/replacer bush –	gudgeon pin
flange away from gudgeon	8 Nut
pin	9 Centre screw
4 Gudgeon pin	

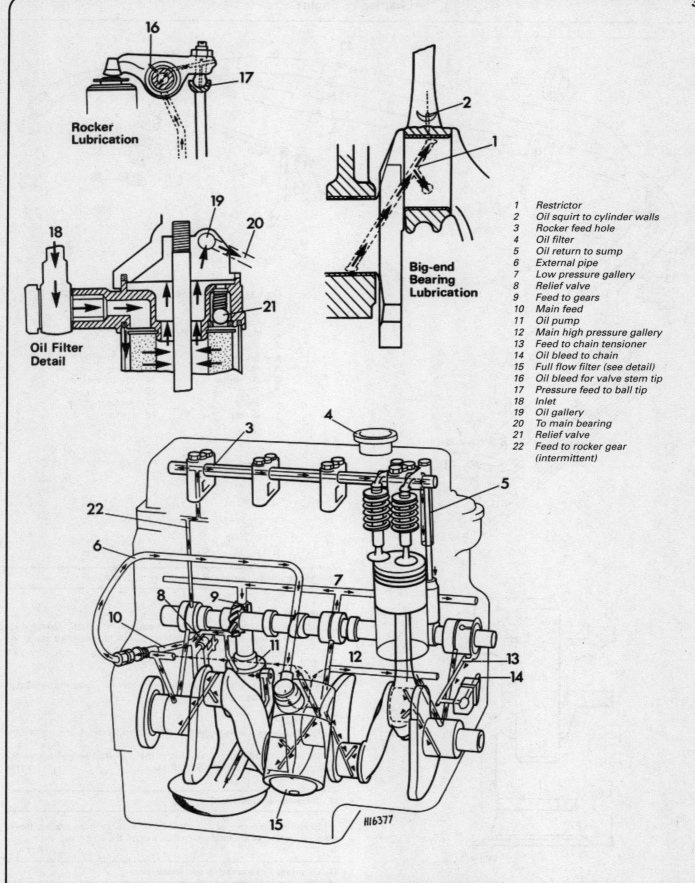

Rocker Lubrication

Big-end Bearing Lubrication

Oil Filter Detail

1 Restrictor
2 Oil squirt to cylinder walls
3 Rocker feed hole
4 Oil filter
5 Oil return to sump
6 External pipe
7 Low pressure gallery
8 Relief valve
9 Feed to gears
10 Main feed
11 Oil pump
12 Main high pressure gallery
13 Feed to chain tensioner
14 Oil bleed to chain
15 Full flow filter (see detail)
16 Oil bleed for valve stem tip
17 Pressure feed to ball tip
18 Inlet
19 Oil gallery
20 To main bearing
21 Relief valve
22 Feed to rocker gear
    (intermittent)

HI6377

Fig 1.16 Lubrication system – schematic view (Sec 28)

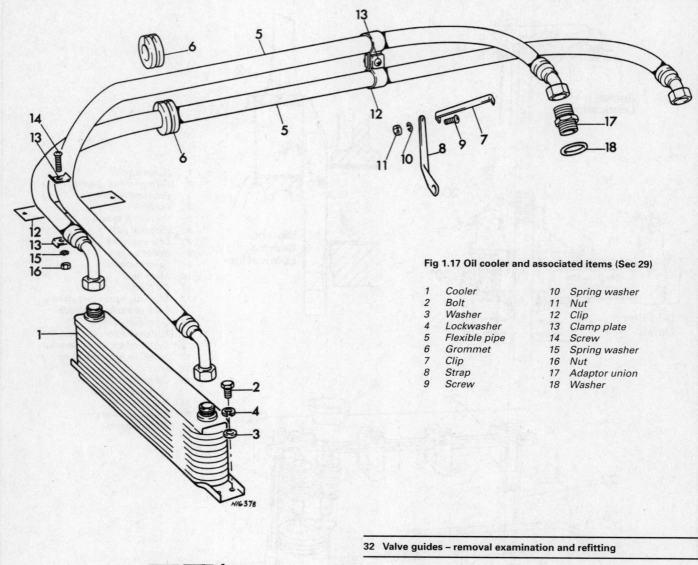

Fig 1.17 Oil cooler and associated items (Sec 29)

1	Cooler	10	Spring washer
2	Bolt	11	Nut
3	Washer	12	Clip
4	Lockwasher	13	Clamp plate
5	Flexible pipe	14	Screw
6	Grommet	15	Spring washer
7	Clip	16	Nut
8	Strap	17	Adaptor union
9	Screw	18	Washer

32   Valve guides – removal examination and refitting

Removal
1   To remove a guide, place the head on a bench, gasket face downwards. Use a suitable shouldered punch of hardened steel, and drive the guide down and out.

Examination
2   If there is any sign of lateral rocking of a new valve in the guides, then they should be replaced.

Refitting
3   Fit the new guide from the top of the cylinder head. Ensure that the large chamfer is at the top.
4   Drive the guide home, until it is the required height above the spring seat (see the relevant Specification).

33   Tappets – examination

Examine each tappet for obvious defects such as cracks, heavy wear, or crazing of the face which bears upon the camshaft.

34   Oil pump – examination and renovation

1   Clean all parts thoroughly in fuel.
2   With the rotors in place, put a straight-edge across the joint face of

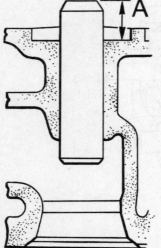

Fig 1.18 Valve guide fitting height A, measured from the spring seat machined surface to the end of the guide. Consult the Specifications for the relevant figures (Sec 32)

the pump body. Measure the clearance between rotors and straightedge (Fig. 1.19) which should not exceed 0.005 in (0.127 mm).

3   If the end clearance is excessive, lap in the pump body on a sheet of plate glass.

4   Check the lobe clearances (Fig. 1.20). Renew the rotors if this exceeds 0.006 in (0.152 mm).

5   Measure the gap between the outer rotor and the rotor pocket in the body. If this is in excess of 0.010 in (0.254 mm), put right by renewing the body or rotors.

6   If any doubts exist about the pump condition, or if wear is considerable, fit a new pump.

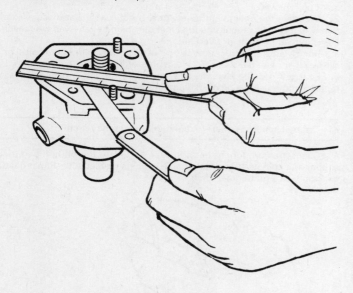

Fig 1.19 Measuring oil pump rotor endfloat (Sec 34)

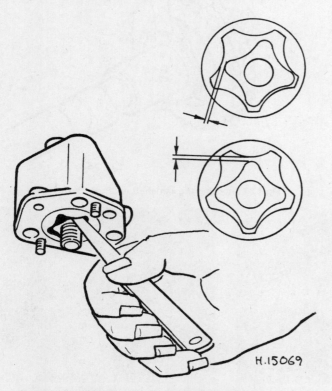

Fig 1.20 Measuring the oil pump rotor lobe clearances (in two positions) (Sec 34)

7   Before refitting a pump, check the following points:
   (a) Lubricate all parts with engine oil
   (b) Check that the chamfered end of the outer rotor is at the driving end of the pocket in the body
   (c) Check the pump for freedom of action

35 Crankshaft – examination and renovation

1   Examine the shaft for obvious visual defects.
2   Have the journals measured for ovality.
3   If reconditioning is considered necessary, the work should be entrusted to a specialist engineer.
4   On highly tuned engines the centre main bearing has been known to break up. This is not always immediately apparent, but slight vibration in an otherwise normally smooth engine and a very slight drop in oil pressure under normal conditions are clues. If this condition is suspected, immediately investigate by dropping the sump and removing the centre main bearing cap, or a badly scored crankshaft centre journal may be the result.
5   If the first motion shaft bush (ie the spigot bush) in the end of the shaft is in poor condition, this should be renewed by an engineering firm possessing the necessary tools.

36 Pistons and piston rings – examination and renovation

1   If the old pistons are to be refitted, remove the piston rings and clean the pistons, particularly the ring grooves. Do not scratch the aluminium. Take care if using a fragment of an old piston ring to clean the grooves – the edges of the ring may be sharp.
2   When fitting new rings to old pistons, the top ring must be of stepped design. This ensures that the ring will not strike the existing wear edge in the cylinder, causing ring breakage.
3   Before fitting the rings to the pistons the gaps must be checked in an unworn part of the cylinder bore. Place the ring in the bore, press it down (using the piston to keep it square) until it is about 3 in (76 mm) from the top, and check the gap against the Specifications. If the gap is too small, use a fine file to remove metal from the ends, and check the gap again (photo).
4   When a rebore has been carried out and new pistons are being fitted, check the ring gaps as in paragraph 3, except that in this case the measurements can be taken at any part of the bore.
5   When special oil control ring sets are being fitted to used pistons, pay particular attention to the fitting instructions which will be supplied by the manufacturer.
6   Oversize pistons have an ellipse marked on them enclosing the oversize.

36.3 Checking a piston ring gap

37 Big-end, main and thrust bearings – examination and renovation

1   Big-end wear is evidenced by a knocking from the crankcase. whilst wear in the main bearings gives rise to vibration and rumbling which increases as engine speed increases. A drop in oil pressure will be present in both cases.
2   Inspect the big-end, main and thrust bearings for signs of obvious wear. They should be matt grey in colour, and any sign of copper colour is clearly indicative of wear. Unless the bearing shells are virtually new it is false economy not to renew them.
3   Bearing sets are marked to correspond with the corresponding crankshaft size, ie if the crankshaft is ground to 0.010 in (0.254 mm) undersize, the bearing set will be similarly identified.
4   Experience has indicated that long engine life can be obtained by changing big-end bearings at 30 000 mile intervals, and main bearings at 50 000 mile intervals, irrespective of obvious bearing condition. Considerable mileage can thereby be achieved before crankshaft regrinding is required.

38 Crankcase and cylinder block – examination and renovation

1   Examine the crankcase jointly with the cylinder bores. Obviously, reboring is a waste of money if any other defects exist. Repairing cast iron items is a specialist job, and a new assembly, or alternatively one from a car breaker, may be more economical.
2   The ridge at the top of the cylinder gives an indication of the amount of wear which has occurred in the cylinders. This will confirm any indications which the owner may have already had, such as excessive oil consumption and blue smoke from the exhaust.
3   In case of doubt about the extent of reconditioning necessary, the owner is advised to seek specialist advice from an establishment possessing accurate measuring equipment. It is sometimes possible to adequately renovate marginally worn cylinders by using one of the sets of special oil control rings currently marketed for that purpose.
4   If reboring is necessary, a specialist engineering firm will undertake this, and also supply pistons to fit the new cylinder size.
5   In certain cases, where the cylinders are too badly worn to be rebored, cylinder liners can be fitted. This work will have to be undertaken by a Leyland agent, or specialist engineer.
6   Any defective threads should be put right by having inserts fitted. This requires special tools normally only possessed by an engineering shop.
7   Check all oilways and waterways for obstructions, and clear as necessary.

39 Camshaft and bearings – examination and renovation

1   The camshaft should show no signs of wear, and if wear is apparent it must be renewed.
2   If the bearings are worn or pitted, or the metal backing is visible, they must be renewed. This operation requires special tools, and the local agent should be consulted.
3   Fit the retaining plate and the chainwheel to the camshaft whilst it is on the bench, and check the clearance (ie endfloat) between the thrust face of the camshaft front journal, and the retaining plate. If outside the specified dimension, renew the retaining plate.

40 Timing cover, chain and chainwheels – examination and renovation

1   Examine the teeth on both chainwheels. If one side of the gearteeth is slightly concave when compared with the other, the chainwheels must be renewed.
2   Compare the chain with a new one. If noticeable slackness exists, renew it. It is in fact recommended that the chain be renewed whenever it is removed for a major overhaul.
3   Remove the old seal by knocking it out carefully with a cold chisel or screwdriver of suitable size. Take care not to distort the cover (photo).
4   Fit a new seal, lip inwards, by pressing in with the fingers and then tapping home using a block of wood (photos).

41 Timing chain tensioner – examination and renovation

1   Clean the component parts in fuel, and clear the oil holes in the slipper and spigot. After considerable mileages, renew the slipper head assembly as a matter of course.

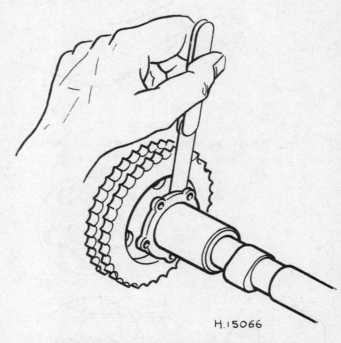

H.15066

Fig 1.21 Checking the camshaft endfloat (Sec 39)

40.3 Knocking out a timing cover seal

40.4a Starting a new seal in the timing cover

40.4b Tapping the new timing cover seal home, using a block of wood

42.6a A new engine endplate seal

42.6b Tapping the new engine endplate seal home, using a block of wood

2   Check the bore of the adjuster body for ovality. If the diameter is more than 0.003 in (0.076 mm) out of round at the mouth, fit a new unit.

42 Flywheel and engine endplate – examination and renovation

Flywheel
1   In view of the heating requirements necessary when renewing the ring gear, it is probably best for the average owner to entrust the work to a competent engineering works.
2   If the teeth of the flywheel are obviously in poor condition, remove the ring gear by splitting it with a cold chisel. Take care not to damage the flywheel, and protect yourself as far as possible, particularly the eyes.
3   Fit the new ring by first heating it to a temperature of 300 to 400°C (572 to 752°F), indicated by a light-blue colour. Do not exceed this temperature or the temper of the material will be lost.
4   Heating is best achieved in a properly controlled furnace. Alternatively, even heating using an oxy-acetylene flame may be used.
5   Fit the heated ring to the flywheel with the front of the teeth facing the flywheel register. Tap gently until fully home, and allow to cool.

Engine endplate
6   Check the condition of the oil seal which is fitted to the centre of later engine endplates only. Renew if necessary by knocking it out and tapping in a replacement, using a block of wood. Ensure that the seal is fitted the right way round (photos).

43 Cylinder head – servicing

1   With the head removed, use a blunt scraper to remove all traces of carbon from the combustion spaces and ports. Scrape the head face free of old gasket and other deposits.
2   Ensure that all dirt is removed from the ports, valve guides, bolt holes and other cavities, using pieces of rag, an air line if available and by thorough washing. If any dirt is allowed to remain, it may drop on to the cylinder head gasket when the head is refitted.
3   Check the head for distortion, by placing a straight-edge across the mating surface. If any daylight is visible, consult the local agent about the possibility of having the surface machined.
4   Refer to Section 31 for the procedure concerning renovation of the valve seats.

44 Pistons – decarbonising

1   If the pistons are still in the block, great care should be taken to ensure that no carbon gets into the cylinder bores as this could scratch the cylinder walls or cause damage to the piston and rings. To prevent this, turn the crankshaft so that two of the pistons are at the top of their bores, and pack pieces of rag into the other two, or seal them with paper and tape. Cover the waterways with small pieces of tape to prevent carbon entering the cooling system and damaging the water pump.
2   Press a little grease into the gap between the cylinder walls and the two pistons which are to be worked on. With a blunt scraper carefully scrape away the carbon from the piston crown, taking great care not to scratch the aluminium, and leaving a ring of carbon on the piston crown periphery, this last step being made easier if an old piston ring is inserted in the top of the bore to rest on the piston and ensure that carbon is not accidentally removed.
3   Leave the rim of carbon in place around the rim of the cylinder bore.
4   Clean away all traces of the carbon particles and contaminated grease.
5   Remove the masking tape and rag from the other two cylinders, bring their pistons to TDC, and clean them in similar fashion whilst masking the first two bores.
6   A final polish of the piston crowns with metal polish will assist in delaying carbon build-up.
7   Ensure complete cleanliness of the whole area upon completion.

45 Engine reassembly – general

1   Have available the necessary new gaskets, a can of clean engine oil, a supply of clean rag and a torque wrench.
2   Observe absolute cleanliness, blow through all oilways, and lubricate all moving parts as they are fitted.
3   Do not use excessive force when fitting any item. unless a force fit is actually specified. Instead, check the sizes and suitability of the parts involved.
4   Always use new lockwashers and seals, and tighten all fittings to the specified torque.
5   Reassemble most items before the engine is refitted to the vehicle. However, the dynamo or alternator and carburettor should be left until the unit is in place.
6   Fit the clutch and gearbox as described in the relevant Chapters.

46 Crankshaft – refitting

1   Ensure that the crankcase is clean, and that all the oilways are clear. Preferably blow them out with compressed air.
2   Inject oil into the oilways.
3   If the old main bearing shells are being used again (false economy unless they are as new), refit them to their former locations, which should first be wiped clean. Ensure correct location of the tabs.
4   If new bearings are being fitted, wipe away the protective coating before fitting as described in paragraph 3 (photo).

5   Lubricate the crankshaft journals and the half bearings, and place the crankshaft in position (photo).
6   Introduce the upper halves of the thrust washers (the halves without tabs) into the grooves on either side of the centre main bearing, whilst rotating the crankshaft a little to assist in feeding the thrust washers into their locations (photo). Ensure that the oil grooves face outwards from the thrust washers and are facing the crank bearing surface. Do not allow the main bearing halves to be rotated out of place.
7   Fit the remaining half bearings into the main bearing caps, and the remaining half thrust washers into their positions in the recesses on the centre cap with the tabs properly located in the slots (photos).
8   Apply jointing compound to the horizontal joint surfaces of the rear cap to ensure a perfect oil seal.
9   Refit the caps to their proper locations, checking that the thrust washers are properly in place with the oil grooves facing outwards and against the crank bearing surface. Ensure that all bearing surfaces are well lubricated during assembly (photo).

10 Fit the main bearing nuts (and locking plates, where relevant) and lightly pinch them up. Test the crankshaft to ensure that it is not excessively stiff.
11 Tighten the nuts to the specified torque and retest for excessive stiffness (photo).

47 Pistons, connecting rods and gudgeon pins – reassembly

Early models
1   To refit, reverse the dismantling procedure given in Section 27, noting the following details.
2   Carry out selective fitting of the gudgeon pins if new ones are being used. The pin should slide in under thumb pressure for three-quarters of the distance, and be tapped in finally with a rawhide mallet. Try each pin to each piston to obtain the best fit (photo).

46.4 The upper half main bearings, fitted and lubricated

46.5 Positioning the crankshaft

46.6 Fitting the thrust washer upper halves

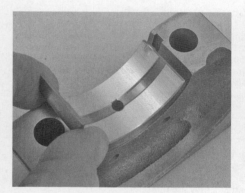
46.7a Fitting the half main bearings to the caps

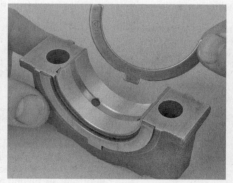
46.7b Locating the lower half thrust washers in the main bearing centre cap, with oilways facing outwards from the cap

46.9 Fitting a main bearing cap

46.11 Tightening the main bearing caps

47.2 Pressing home a gudgeon pin

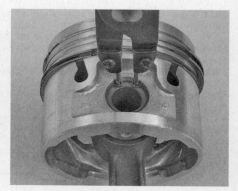
47.9 Fitting a piston circlip

3 Ensure that the piston is fitted to the connecting rod the right way round. Note the word FRONT on the piston crown, and that the connecting rod small-end clamp screw is on the camshaft side.
4 Position the gudgeon pin groove in line with the clamp screw hole.
5 Ensure that the clamp screw will pass freely into the hole and on into the thread. Check that the spring washer is in good condition, or fit a new one.
6 The piston may be warmed in hot water, as an aid to easy fitting of the pin.

Later models

7 Fit a new circlip in the piston gudgeon pin hole.
8 Correctly locate the piston on the connecting rod, with the marking FRONT on the crown towards the front of the engine, and the connecting rod caps towards the camshaft.
9 Push the gudgeon pin home, and fit the remaining circlip (photo).

Later models (press-fit gudgeon pins)

10 When refitting, ensure that the same piston, rod and gudgeon pin are being fitted together. If new pistons are to be used, they can be fitted to any connecting rod but the gudgeon pins must not be interchanged. Use Leyland tool number 18G 1150 and adaptor number 18G 1150D (see Fig. 1.22).
11 Unscrew the large nut and withdraw the centre screw from the body a few inches. Lubricate the nut and screw, and locate the piston support adaptor.
12 Slide the parallel sleeve carefully onto the centre screw up to the shoulder, groove end last. Lubricate the gudgeon pin, and piston and rod bores, with a graphited oil.
13 Fit the connecting rod and piston with the side marked FRONT or A towards the main part of the tool, with the rod entered on the sleeve up to the groove.
14 Fit the gudgeon pin into the bore up to connecting rod, and fit the remover/replacer bush, flange end towards the gudgeon pin.
15 Screw the stop nut on to the centre screw, and adjust to give 0.04 in (1 mm) endplay between the stop nut and remover/replacer bush. Lock the nut securely with the lock screw, ensure that the curved face of the adaptor is clean, and slide the piston on the tool so that it fits into the curved face of the adaptor with the piston rings over the adaptor cutaway.
16 Screw the large nut up to the thrust race.
17 Using a torque wrench set to 12 lbf ft (1.64 kgf m), and with a ring spanner on the lock screw, pull the gudgeon pin into the piston until the flange of the replacer/removal bush is the correct distance from the piston skirt (dimension B). It is critically important that the flange is not allowed to contact the piston.
18 Withdraw the tool.
19 If the torque wrench does not reach the specified torque, then the fit of the pin in the rod is not acceptable and renewals must be made.
20 With the tool removed, check that the piston pivots freely on the gudgeon pin and is able to slide sideways. Should stiffness exist, wash the assembly in paraffin, lubricate the gudgeon pin with graphited oil and recheck. If it remains stiff, dismantle and check for dirt or damage.
21 The complete assembly of rod and piston will fit earlier engines.

48 Piston rings – refitting

1 Check that the ring grooves are clean, and that the oil holes are clear.
2 Always fit the rings over the top of the piston.
3 The feeler gauge method (see Section 26, paragraphs 2 and 3) may be employed to fit the rings. Alternatively, spread the ring slightly with the thumbs and fingers, and place over the piston. Whichever method is employed, great care is needed to avoid breakage.
4 Where a press-fit gudgeon pin type piston assembly is fitted, the piston ring design also varies (see Fig. 1.14).
5 To refit rings to this later type, fit the bottom rail of the oil control ring, positioned initially below the bottom groove.
6 Fit the oil control expander to the bottom groove. Move the bottom rail into the bottom groove, and fit the top rail
7 Ensure that the expander ends are not overlapping. Set the gaps at 90° to each other.
8 Fit the thin compression ring in the second groove. Note the face marked TOP.
9 Fit the top ring.

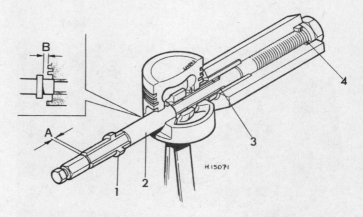

Fig 1.22 Press fit gudgeon pin refitting, showing service tool 18G 1150 and adaptor set 18G 115010 in use (Sec 47)

A = 0.040 in (1 mm)
B = 0.080 in (2 mm) from piston
1 Remover/replacer bush flange – towards the gudgeon pin
2 Gudgeon pin
3 Sleeve groove towards gudgeon pin
4 Note thrust race and screw thread must be lubricated

10 Position the gaps at 90° to each other and away from the piston thrust side.
11 Note that if new piston rings are to be fitted in worn bores, the top piston ring must be stepped. This is because the old ring will have worn in unison with the wear ridge at the top of the bore; a new, unstepped, ring may hit the ridge and break.
12 If special oil control rings are fitted, follow the manufacturer's instructions carefully.

49 Pistons, connecting rods and big-end bearings – refitting

1 The refitting procedure is largely a reversal of dismantling, as described in Section 24, but the following points should be noted.
2 Wipe the cylinder bores clean, and oil them (photo).
3 Ensure that the correct piston assembly is fitted to the correct bore, and that it is the right way round. Fit from the top.
4 When the piston is in the bore as far as the oil control ring, check that the ring gaps are at 90° to each other. Apply a proper piston ring clamp (obtainable from any motor accessory store) to the rings, and

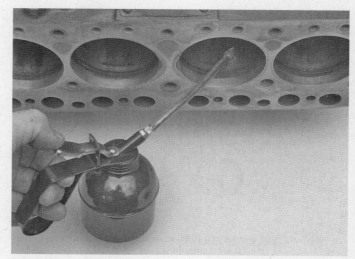

49.2 Oiling a cylinder bore

49.4 A piston ring clamp, applied to the rings

gently tap the piston down through the clamp using a hammer handle (photo). Take great care when carrying out any work relating to the piston rings, which are extremely brittle.

5   With the piston assembly in place, and ensuring complete cleanliness, fit the half bearings in each connecting rod with the locating tongue in the corresponding groove in the rod. If old bearings are being refitted, ensure that they are refitted in their original positions.

6   Lubricate the crankpins on the crankshaft with engine oil.

7   Draw the connecting rod onto the crankpin, turning the crank as necessary. Take care not to jam any rods against the crank webs.

8   Ensure that the connecting rod end caps are clean, and fit the remaining half bearings in each cap. Check that the locating tongue is correctly positioned.

9   Lubricate the bearing and fit to the connecting rod (photo).

10 Fit the end cap nuts or bolts and locking tabs if fitted (photo). Tighten to the specified torque, and knock up the tabs where fitted.

11 Check for freedom of rotation of the shaft.

50 Camshaft – refitting

1   To refit the shaft, reverse the removal procedure given in Section 23.

2   Before fitting the shaft, lubricate it and the bearings with engine oil.

3   When inserting the shaft, take care not to strike the cams on the bearings, thereby causing damage (photo).

4   Refit the engine front plate with a new gasket (photo). Refer to Section 53.

5   Refit the camshaft locating plate, and secure with the three bolts and washers (photo).

51 Timing cover, chain and chainwheels – refitting

Double-roller chain type

1   Refit the packing washers on the crankshaft nose (see paragraph 7, if new chainwheels have been fitted).

2   Ensure that the Woodruff keys are in place.

3   Place the chainwheels on a clean surface with the timing dots adjacent to each other. Place the chain over the wheels and into mesh, still keeping the timing marks adjacent to each other (photo).

4   Rotate the crankshaft so that the key is at TDC. (The engine should be upright on the sump.)

5   Rotate the camshaft so that when viewed from the front the key is at the one o'clock position.

6   Fit the timing chain and gearwheel assembly to the camshaft and crankshaft, keeping the timing marks adjacent. It may be necessary to rotate the camshaft a fraction to ensure accurate lining-up of the camshaft gearwheel.

7   Press the gearwheels on to the crankshaft and camshaft as far as they will go. Note that if new chainwheels are being fitted they should be checked for alignment. Place the wheels in position without the chain and place a straight-edge across them (photo). If a gap exists, modify the number of packing washers behind the crankshaft chainwheel to bring both wheels into the same plane.

8   Refit the tensioner, if this has been removed (see Section 52) (photo).

9   Refit the oil thrower to the crankshaft nose, concave side forward or letter F forward (ie away from the engine), depending upon the model. **Note:** *A later oil thrower must not be used with an early cover, or vice-versa.*

10 Refit the camshaft lockwasher, with the lcoating tab in the keyway. Fit and tighten the nut. Bend the locktab over the nut (photo).

11 Oil the chain and wheels.

12 Position a new timing cover gasket on the engine, lubricate the oil seal in the cover, and fit the cover (photo). Refit two or three of the cover bolts, finger tight.

13 Place the crankshaft pulley in position, to centralise the timing cover. Nip up the bolts securing the cover, and remove the pulley again.

14 Fit all the timing cover bolts and tighten to the specified torque.

15 Oil the pulley, where it passes through the oil seal. Fit the lockwasher and pulley retaining bolt. Tighten to the specified torque, and secure the locking washer (photo).

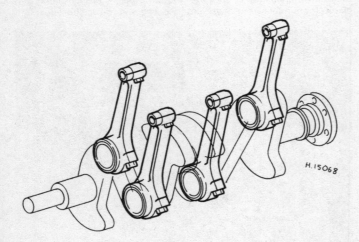

Fig 1.23 Early type connecting rods, assembled with the offsets in the correct positions (Sec 49)

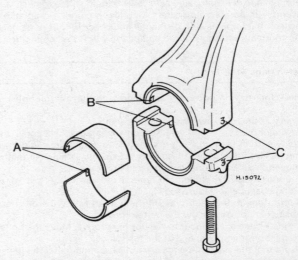

Fig 1.24 Connecting rod big-end. Ensure that the bearing tabs A fit in the rod gooves B, and that the rod and cap numbers at C correspond (Sec 49)

49.9 Lubricating a big-end cap, before fitting

49.10 The big-end locking nuts

50.3 Inserting the camshaft

50.4 Refitting the engine front plate

50.5 Refitting the camshaft securing plate

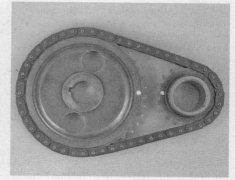

51.3 The timing chain and chainwheels, correctly assembled and ready for fitting

51.7 Checking the chainwheel alignment

51.8 The tensioner assembly, refitted

51.10 The camshaft nut, and lockwasher

51.12 The timing cover gasket and cover

51.15 The crankshaft pulley bolt and lockwasher

Single roller chain type

16 Proceed mainly as for the double-roller type, noting the following paragraphs.

17 When fitting the chainwheels and chain, assemble them together with the timing dots adjacent to each other on a line through the centre of the wheels. Have the crankshaft keyway at TDC and the camshaft keyway at two o'clock.

18 Fit the chain and wheels, moving the camshaft slightly if necessary, to permit engagement of the keys in the keyways.

19 Refit the timing chain tensioner as described in Section 52.

20 Continue as for the double roller chain type.

52 Timing chain tensioner – refitting

Double roller chain type

1 Insert one end of the spring in the plunger, and the other end in the cylinder.

2 Compress the spring until the cylinder enters the plunger bore, ensuring that the peg in the plunger engages the helical slot. Insert and turn the Allen key clockwise until the end of the cylinder is below the peg and the spring is held compressed.

3 Fit the backplate and secure the assembly to the cylinder block with the two bolts. Turn up the tabs of the lockwasher.

4 With the chain in position, insert the Allen key and turn it clockwise, so allowing the slipper head to move forward under spring pressure against the chain. Do not under any circumstances turn the key anti-clockwise or force the slipper head into the chain.

Single roller chain type

5 Fit the inner cylinder and spring into the slipper head, engaging the helical slot with the peg, and turn the cylinder clockwise until the peg and lower serration engage, retaining the inner cylinder.

6 Fit the slipper assembly in the body. Place a spacer, 0.06 in (1.6 mm) thick between the head and body, to prevent disengagement, and fit the tensioner, backplate and gasket to the front plate

7 Take out the spacer. Press the tensioner head into the body, and release it, when the inner cylinder will disengage.

53 Flywheel and engine endplate – refitting

Engine endplate

1 Fit the square-section cork seal into place in the rear bearing cap (photo).

2 Fit a new endplate paper gasket, retaining it with jointing compound.

3 Refit the endplate, and the oil seal retaining plate or locking tabs (depending upon the model). Fit the bolts, tightening to the specified torque, and bend up the locking tabs as appropriate (photo).

Flywheel

4 When refitting the flywheel (photo), ensure that the 1/4 timing mark on the periphery is at the top, when the numbers 1 and 4 pistons are at TDC. **Note:** *The depression in the crankshaft flange face has a mark like the one on the flywheel periphery, and these marks should be in line.*

5 Proceed in reverse of the removal procedure (Section 22, paragraphs 1-4).

54 Oil pump – refitting

1 To refit, reverse the removal procedure, noting the paragraphs which follow.

2 Lubricate all parts thoroughly, and fill the pump with oil.

3 Use new gaskets (photo).

55 Sump and strainer – refitting

1 Clean the strainer and sump, and remove all traces of the old gasket from the sump and crankcase flanges.

2 Refit the strainer by reversing the dismantling procedure (photo). See Section 20.

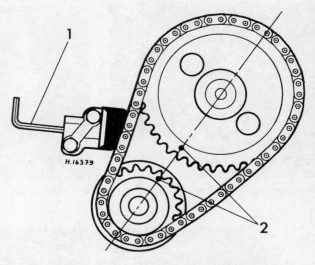

Fig 1.25 The timing gear and chain tensioner (Sec 52)

1   *Turn the Allen key clockwise to release the tension*
2   *The two dimples should be in line when the engine timing is set*

3 Fit new main bearing cap oil seals if necessary (photo).

4 Grease the crankcase flange, and position the new gasket (photo).

5 Place the sump in position, and fit the bolts. Tighten to the specified torque.

6 Reverse the procedure given in Section 20, paragraphs 2, 3 and 4.

56 Valves – refitting

1 Ensure that the valves, valve guides and cylinder head are completely clean.

2 Oil the valve stem and guide, and fit a valve into its guide (photo).

3 Fit the bottom collar, inner and outer spring, shroud (on early engines) and cap.

4 Compress the spring. Place a new oil seal ring over the valve and locate it at the base of the collet groove.

5 Refit the valve collets, remove the compressor, and refit the clip (on early engines).

6 Always use new sealing rings when reassembling the valves, otherwise excessive oil consumption may occur. Count the number of new rings in the packet – sometimes there are one or two spares.

7 Where valve gear of single spring design is fitted, proceed as for the double spring type. Always use a new packing ring, dipped in oil and pushed down the valve stem to just below the collet groove (photo). Note that no clip is fitted.

57 Tappets – refitting

1 Refit the tappets into their original locations, oiling them well both inside and out.

2 Refit the tappet covers, using new gaskets. Do not overtighten the securing bolts or the covers will distort.

58 Cylinder head – refitting

1 Ensure that the mating surfaces of the cylinder head and block are completely clean.

2 Lubricate the cylinders with engine oil.

3 Use a new cylinder head gasket and place it in position, noting the words FRONT and TOP on the gasket and positioning it accordingly. Do not use any jointing compound.

53.1 The rear main bearing cap seal

53.3 The oil seal retaining plate

53.4 Refitting the flywheel

54.3 The new gasket in place, prior to fitting the pump

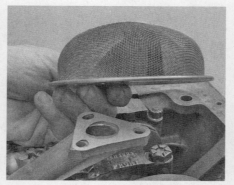
55.2 The oil strainer and gasket (pump removed from the engine)

55.3 Fitting a front main bearing cap seal

55.4 The sump gasket in place

56.2 Placing a valve in the guide

56.7 A valve spring compressed and a new oil sealing ring in place, ready for the collets to be fitted

4   Lower the cylinder head into position, and fit the seven external securing nuts finger tight, ensuring that the vacuum pipe clip is correctly positioned (photo).

5   Refit the pushrods to their original locations, making sure that each one mates properly with its tappet.

6   Refit the rocker shaft as described in Section 59, making sure that the ball ends of the adjusting screws enter the cups in the tops of the pushrods.

7   Fit the remaining cylinder head/rocker pedestal nuts and tighten the cylinder head nuts, half a turn at a time, in the order shown in Fig. 1.5, to the specified torque.

8   Adjust the valve clearances as described in Section 60. This is only a preliminary adjustment – the clearances will have to be reset when the head has been tightened down after the initial run – so it does not matter if the clearance is specified for a hot or warm engine and you are setting with the engine cold.

9   If the engine is in the car, continue refitting by reversing the removal procedure in Section 12.

10   Check the tightness of the cylinder head nuts after the engine is first run and again after 500 miles or so. Slacken a nut ½ a turn and then retighten it to the specified torque before proceeding to the next nut. Always check the valve clearances after doing this.

59 Rockers and rocker shaft – reassembly and refitting

1   Reassemble the shaft in the reverse order to dismantling (see Section 11). Lubricate whilst assembling.

2   Refit to the vehicle in the reverse order to removal (see Section 10).

3   Adjust the valve clearances before running the engine (Section 60). Do not forget to tighten the cylinder head nuts and refill the cooling system if it is only the rocker shaft which has been removed.

58.4 Refitting the cylinder head

60.4 Adjusting the valve clearances

60.7 Adjusting the valve clearances, using a proprietary setting tool

61.1a Refitting the exhaust manifold

61.1b Refitting the inlet manifold

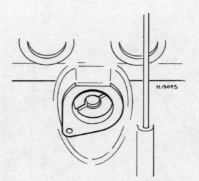

Fig 1.26 Distributor drive – 18G/18GA engines (Sec 63)

60 Valve clearances – adjustment

1   Correct valve clearance is important, both from the point of view of good performance and of engine life.
2   If the engine is in the car, disconnect any attachments to the rocker cover, remove the retaining studs, and remove the cover.
3   Adjust in the following order to save unnecessary turning of the crankshaft.

Valve fully open	Check and adjust Valve No
8	1
6	3
4	5
7	2
1	8
3	6
5	4
2	7

Note that a valve is fully open when the rocker depresses the stem to the maximum, thereby compressing the valve spring.
4   To adjust, slacken the hexagonal locknut whilst holding the ball-ended screw with a screwdriver. Insert the feeler gauge between the rocker arm pad and the valve stem, and adjust the ball screw until the gauge is just held. Tighten the locknut. Recheck the clearance (photo).
5   Continue in the sequence given in paragraph 3, setting the clearances to the figure given in the Specifications. The crankshaft may be turned by using a spanner on the pulley nut, or (if the engine is in the car) by jacking up a rear wheel clear of the ground, engaging top gear and turning the wheel. In either case it will be easier if the spark plugs are removed.
6   Refit the rocker cover and ancillary items.
7   The photograph shows a proprietary tool in use for setting valve clearances. Some owners may find the tool helpful in obtaining the correct settings, and it should be possible to purchase one at any motor accessory shop (photo).

61 Manifolds – refitting

To refit, reverse the removal procedure. Use a new gasket, ensuring first that the mating surfaces are clean (photos).

62 Oil pressure relief valve – refitting

To refit, reverse the removal procedure.

63 Distributor drive – refitting

18G/18GA-engined vehicles

1   Ensure that the crankshaft is turned until No 1 piston is at TDC on the compression stroke. If the cylinder head is in place, observe the valve gear to ensure that, when the groove in the crankshaft pulley is in line with the large pointer on the timing cover, the valves on No 1 cylinder have clearance, and those on No 4 cylinder are rocking. Alternatively, and if the timing cover is removed, ensure that the dots on the chainwheels are adjacent and in line.
2   Screw a 5/16 UNF bolt (a tappet cover bolt will do) into the head of the distributor drive.
3   Hold the drive with the slot just below the horizontal and the large segment uppermost.
4   Enter the gear, allowing it to turn as this happens, when the slot should finish up in the position indicated in Fig. 1.26.
5   Insert the distributor housing, and secure with the bolt and washer.
6   Refit the distributor (see Chapter 4).

18GB and later-engined vehicles

7   Fit the bolt to the spindle (see paragraph 2).
8   Position the pistons half-way up the cylinder bores, and enter the spindle.
9   Turn the crankshaft to the position described in paragraph 1.
10 Withdraw the spindle sufficiently to clear the camshaft gear. Hold it with the slot horizontal and the small offset at the bottom, and re-enter

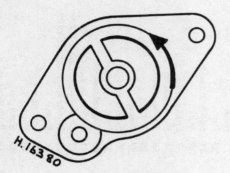

Fig 1.27 Distributor drive, 1978 and later vehicles – slot position upon entering the driveshaft (Sec 63)

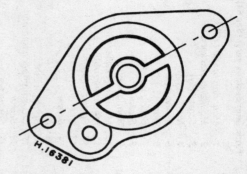

Fig 1.28 Distributor drive, 1978 and later vehicles – slot position when driveshaft is fully entered (Sec 63)

the gear. Note that as engagement takes place the slot will turn to the two o'clock position.
11 Remove the bolt, and refit and secure the distributor housing using the correct bolt and washer.
12 Refit the distributor (see Chapter 4).

1978-on vehicles

13 Proceed as described in paragraphs 1 to 6. However, the positions of the slot before and after entry are shown in Figs. 1.27 and 1.28.

64 Engine mountings – removal and refitting

1 The engine mounting design varies depending upon the year of manufacture, but the basic method of working remains the same.
2 When the engine and transmission unit is out of the vehicle, the mountings are simply unbolted, and renewal made as necessary (see Fig. 1.29).
3 When the unit remains in the car, and referring to the front mountings, take the weight of the engine unit on suitable lifting tackle, remove the fixings, and lift the unit to provide the necessary clearance. Remove the mountings.
4 On certain models, it is necessary to remove the steering rack when changing the LH mounting.
5 Great care should be taken when lifting to ensure that damage or distortion are not caused to adjacent or attached items.
6 Note the positions of any shims fitted.
7 Referring to the rear mountings, and when the engine remains in the vehicle, take the weight of the rear end of the engine and transmission.
8 Disconnect the restraint rod (if fitted) at the gearbox, by removing the nut and bolt.
9 Remove the rear crossmember (see Section 6, paragraphs 33 to 38).
10 Detach the mountings.
11 To refit both front and rear mountings, reverse the removal procedure. Ensure that the shims, where fitted, are correctly relocated. Note the earth strap on the LH mounting bracket (photo).

65 Engine – refitting

1 Obtain the services of an assistant, whenever possible.
2 Refitting is, generally speaking, a reversal of removal, but the points in the following paragraphs should be noted (photos).
3 Ensure that leads and pipes are watched as the unit is positioned, to avoid their being trapped. Additionally, great care should be taken not to allow the fingers and hands to become trapped as the unit is lowered.
4 If the engine and gearbox are to be refitted as a unit, ensure that the starter motor and the upside-down type of oil filter are fitted before refitting the engine, as they are far more difficult to fit with the unit in place.
5 If the engine alone has been removed and is to be mated to the gearbox in the car, make sure before commencing that the clutch driven plate is correctly centred if it has been disturbed (see Chapter 5). It may be necessary to raise the front of the gearbox slightly with a jack under the bellhousing in order to get the input shaft at the correct angle for entering the clutch. Rock the engine whilst pushing rearwards if the splines on the input shaft seem reluctant to enter those on the clutch plate. *At no time allow the weight of the engine to hang on the input shaft.*
6 Note the packing plate on the LH engine mounting only. Connect up the earth strap.
7 Note the correct method of assembly of the stay rod and associated items (see Fig. 1.29) if these have been disturbed.
8 Ensure correct reassembly of the propeller shaft components if appropriate (see Chapter 7).
9 Check that the servo vacuum pipe is connected up.
10 Ensure that the cooling system is filled.
11 Ensure that the engine is filled with the correct grade of oil.
12 Start the engine and check for leaks. Do not be unduly alarmed at the smell and smoke which may come from the outside of a rebuilt unit. This will cease once the unit becomes hot and has burnt off all oil and other deposits which have collected on it whilst being worked on.
13 If new piston rings and/or bearing shells have been fitted, the engine should be treated as if it were new and run-in at reduced revolutions for the first 500 miles or so.
14 Change the oil and the oil filter after the first 500 miles, tighten the cylinder head nuts if necessary and recheck the valve clearances.

64.11 The LH engine mounting in process of being fitted

65.2a General view of engine, (right-hand side), after refitting in the vehicle

65.2b General view of engine, (left-hand side), after refitting in the vehicle

Fig 1.29 Engine mountings – exploded view (Note: later designs vary) (Sec 64)

1　Mounting bracket (RH)
2　Mounting bracket (LH)
3　Screw (RH)
4　Nut
5　Screw (LH)
6　Nut
7　Spring washer
8　Screw
9　Spring washer
10　Mounting rubber (RH)
11　Mounting rubber (LH)
12　Spring washer
13　Nut
14　Screw
15　Nut
16　Spring washer
17　Crossmember assembly
18　Screw
19　Spring washer
20　Bracket
21　Screw
22　Spring washer
23　Stay-rod
24　Buffer
25　Buffer plate
26　Distance tube for stay-rod
27　Spring washer
28　Nut
29　Bush
30　Pin
31　Spring washer
32　Nut
33　Engine mounting
34　Plain washer
35　Spring washer
36　Nut
37　Screw
38　Spring washer
39　Packing plate
40　Control bracket
41　Engine mounting
42　Engine mounting bracket
43　Engine mounting bracket
44　Screw
45　Spring washer
46　Pin
47　Bush pin
48　Plain washer
49　Spring washer
50　Nut

66 Fault diagnosis – engine

Note: *When investigating engine faults, do not be tempted into snap diagnosis. Adopt a logical checking procedure and follow it through – it will take less time in the long run. Poor engine performance in terms of power or economy is not necessarily diagnosed quickly.*

Symptom	Reason(s)
Engine fails to turn when starter motor operated	Flat battery Battery or starter connections corroded or loose Engine and/or battery earth straps loose or missing Starter pinion jammed in mesh with flywheel ring gear Starter solenoid defective Starter motor internal fault (see Chapter 10) Ignition/starter switch defective or disconnected Automatic transmission inhibitor switch defective or disconnected (if applicable)
Starter motor turns engine slowly	Flat battery Battery or starter connections corroded or loose Engine and/or battery earth straps loose Starter motor internal fault (see Chapter 10)
Starter motor turns engine normally but engine will not start	Damp and/or dirty HT leads and distributor cap Dirty or incorrectly gapped contact breaker points No fuel at carburettors (tank empty or pump malfunctioning) Insufficient choke (cold engine) or too much choke (hot engine) Air cleaner(s) clogged Air leaks on induction side Blockage in exhaust system Incorrect ignition timing (after adjustment or rebuild) Incorrect valve timing (after rebuild) Incorrect valve clearances Major mechanical failure (eg broken timing chain) Other ignition system fault (see Chapter 4) Other fuel system fault (see Chapter 3)
Engine lacks power	Ignition timing incorrect (see Chapter 4) Air cleaner(s) clogged Carburation incorrect (see Chapter 3) Overheating (seizure may be imminent!) Distributor worn or auto advance seized Valve clearances incorrect Valve timing incorrect (after rebuild) Brakes binding Poor compression General wear and/or neglect
Engine misfires	Ignition system defect (see Chapter 4) Carburation incorrect (see Chapter 3) Valve clearances incorrect Valve(s) burnt or incorrectly seated Valve spring(s) broken or weak Valve timing incorrect (after rebuild) Fuel contaminated Overheating Poor compression on one or more cylinders
Engine pinks on acceleration	Ignition timing incorrect Incorrect grade of fuel in tank Distributor worn or auto advance seized Carburation incorrect Excessive carbon build-up in combustion chambers Valve timing incorrect (after rebuild) Overheating
Engine backfires or spits back	Carburation incorrect (see Chapter 3) Ignition timing incorrect (see Chapter 4) Emission control defect (see Chapter 3) Valve clearances incorrect Valve(s) burnt or incorrectly seated Valve spring(s) broken or weak Air leak in induction or exhaust systems Valve timing incorrect (after rebuild)

Symptom	Reason(s)
Low oil pressure	Oil level low or in incorrect grade Gauge or sender defective Overheating Oil pump worn or mountings loose Oil pick-up strainer clogged or loose Oil filter blocked or bypass valve stuck open Oil pressure relief valve defective or spring weak Main and/or big-end bearings worn Severe leak on delivery side
Excessive oil consumption	External leakage Crankcase breathing system blocked or defective Pistons, rings and/or bores excessively worn Valves and/or guides worn Valve stem seals defective or omitted after rebuild
Unusual mechanical noises	Unintentional mechanical contact (eg fan blades) Peripheral component fault (eg water pump) Incorrect valve clearances (tapping noise from top of engine) Pinking (see above) Worn timing chain (thrashing and clattering noise from front of engine) Broken piston ring(s) (ticking noise) Worn big-end bearings (knocking noise, perhaps lessening under load) Worn main bearings (rumbling and thumping, perhaps worsening under load)

Chapter 2 Cooling system

Contents

Specifications

System type .... Pressurised, pump and fan assisted, sealed from model No 410002

Coolant type/specification .... Antifreeze to BS 3151, 3152 or 6580

Capacities
Early models .... 9.5 Imp pints (5.4 litres, 11.4 US pints)*
18V engines, GHN5 and GHD5 from model no 410002........ 11.5 Imp pints (6.6 litres, 13.8 US pints)*
18V engines 1976 to 1978 .... 10 Imp pints (5.6 litres, 12 US pints)
All models 1978 onwards.............................. 12 Imp pints (6.8 litres, 14.4 US pints)
Add ½ Imp pint (0.28 litres, 0.6 US pint) for heater if fitted

Thermostat
Hot climate (early models only) .... 74°C (165°F)
Standard:
   Early models .... 74°C (165°F)
   Later models .... 82°C (180°F)
Cold climate:
   Early models .... 82°C (180°F)
   Later models .... 88°C (190°F)

Radiator pressure cap rating
Early models .... 7 lbf/in² (0.492 kgf/cm²)
Later models .... 15 lbf/in² (1.05 kgf/cm²)

Water pump
Type .... Centrifugal
Drive .... Belt from crankshaft
Belt tension:
   Early models .... ½ in (12.8 mm) deflection at the middle of the longest run
   Later models .... ¼ in (6 mm) deflection of belt at an applied load of 7.5 to 8.2 lbf (3.3 to 3.6 kgf)

Belt width:
   Early models .... 3/8 in (9.5 mm)
   Later models .... 15/32 in (11.90 mm)

Cooling fan
Early models .... Belt-driven fan on water pump pulley
Later models .... Electrically operated, thermostatically controlled
Fan thermo switch operating temperature (later models only)........ 90°C (194°F)

Torque wrench setting

	lbf ft	Nm
Water pump-to-crankcase:		
Early models	25	34
Later models	17	23

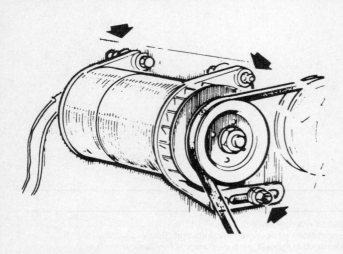

Fig 2.1 Fanbelt adjusting bolts (arrowed) – dynamo fitted (Sec 3)

1   General description

Coolant is circulated by a thermo-syphon, pump-assisted system. The coolant is pressurized, the pressure being limited by a relief valve in the radiator cap.

The condition of the radiator cap is important, and it can be tested by a machine normally kept by most garages.

Cold water circulates from the base of the radiator to the water pump, and on to the passages in the cylinder block and head. Provided the engine is at operating temperature, the water then leaves the cylinder head, and travels via the thermostat to the radiator top tank. As the water moves down inside the radiator it is cooled by the rush of air.

A fan assists with drawing air through the radiator.

Water is only permitted to pass the thermostat when the designed operating temperature has been reached. The thermostat then opens, to permit passage of coolant to the radiator.

If a leak in the cooling system is suspected, a test can be quickly carried out by a garage possessing a pressure tester.

The pressure test should be carried out with the system warm. If the specified pressure will not hold for 10 seconds, check for leaks.

If no leak is visible, an internal leak is likely.

2   Routine maintenance

1   The coolant level should be checked at least weekly. Top up as necessary, using soft water (ie rainwater).
2   Check the fanbelt at the specified intervals, and adjust where necessary (see Section 3).

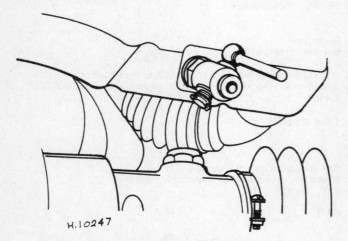

Fig 2.2 Radiator drain tap (Sec 4)

3.3 Adjusting the fanbelt (alternator fitted)

3   On early cars occasionally remove the top plug from the water pump and press in a little grease. Do not pressure lubricate.
4   On later cars, no maintenance is required to the water pump.

3   Fanbelt – adjustment, removal and refitting

Adjustment

1   Check the belt tension and condition frequently. Tension so that the total sideways movement in the longest run of the belt is as indicated in the Specifications.
2   A loose belt will slip, wear rapidly, and cause generator and water pump faults. A tight belt will cause rapid wear of generator and pump bearings.
3   To adjust the belt, slacken the generator securing bolts and move it in or out to obtain the correct tension. It can help to slacken the bolts only slightly so that some force is required to move the generator, thus making the exact setting easier to arrive at (photo).

Removal

4   Renew a worn or stretched belt, and always carry a spare.
5   To remove a belt, loosen the bolts and push the generator in towards the engine.
6   Slip the belt over the pulleys, and remove it.
7   If the belt has broken in service, the procedure is the same except that there is no belt to remove.

Refitting

8   To refit, reverse the removal procedure and adjust the belt.
9   Check a new belt frequently at first, and adjust as necessary to take up initial stretch.

4   Cooling system (early models) – draining, flushing and refilling

The procedures below apply to cars not fitted with an expansion tank.

Draining

1   Remove the radiator cap. If the engine is hot, turn the cap very slightly until the pressure disperses. Do this carefully, using a rag over the cap to protect the hand from escaping steam otherwise severe scalding may be sustained.
2   Antifreeze may be re-used, if not time-expired.
3   On early cars, open the drain taps on the base of the radiator and on the cylinder block. On certain cars, a plug and washer are employed on the engine instead of a tap.
4   On later cars, no provision is made for draining the radiator. This should be done, therefore, by removing the bottom hose at the radiator.

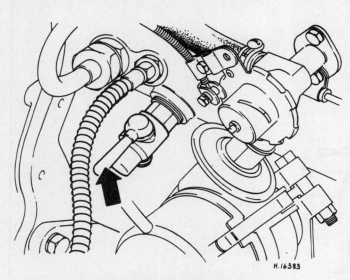

Fig 2.3 Cylinder block drain tap (arrowed) (Sec 4)

Flushing
5   The cooling system will gradually lose efficiency as it becomes choked with rust and other deposits.
6   To clean the system, remove the cap and drain taps and leave a hose running into the radiator cap orifice until the water comes out clear.
7   In bad cases of radiator blockage, reverse flush the radiator by forcing water up through the radiator in the reverse direction. If wished, use a proprietary flushing compound, making sure that the manufacturer's instructions are carefully followed.

Refilling
8   Close all drain taps and check hose connections.
9   Ensure that the heater valve is open, and fill slowly to avoid air locks, using soft water or an antifreeze solution. Do not overfill.
10 Use antifreeze mixture with a glycerine or ethylene base.
11 Refit the filler cap and turn clockwise to lock.
12 Run the engine and check for leaks. Check the coolant level.

5   Cooling system (later models) – draining and refilling

The procedures below apply to models fitted with an expansion tank.

Draining
1   With the car on level ground, remove the expansion tank cap.
2   Remove the filler plug from the coolant outlet pipe.
3   Disconnect the bottom hose at the radiator.
4   Remove the drain plug from the engine block.
5   Flushing procedure is as described in Section 4.

Refilling
6   Refit the drain plug.
7   Refit the bottom hose, and check all others for security and general condition.
8   With the heater temperature control to HOT, top up the expansion tank to half-full. Refit the cap.
9   Fill the system via the filler neck, up to the bottom thread. Refit the plug.
10 Run the engine. When the top hose is warm, switch off.
11 Turn the expansion tank cap to the safety stop, releasing the pressure, and top the tank up to half-full if necessary before refitting the cap.
12 Take out the filler plug. Top up again to the base of the threads, and refit the plug.

6   Antifreeze mixtures

1   Where freezing is likely, drain some of the water to allow a recommended quantity of antifreeze to BS 3151, BS 3152, or BS 6580 to be added. Never use antifreeze with an alcohol base.
2   Maintain the mixture strength by topping up when necessary with the recommended strength of antifreeze solution.
3   The solution may be used for up to two years before draining, flushing and complete replenishment is carried out.
4   The protection afforded by the various mixtures is as follows:

Concentration	Protection down to
25%	-13°C (9°F)
33%	-19°C (-2°F)
50%	-36°C (-33°F)

5   Always check the condition of the cooling system hoses before adding antifreeze, and renew any that are cracked or perished. Antifreeze has a very searching effect and will soon seep through small splits or loose connections.

7   Radiator and surround panel (early models) – removal, inspection, cleaning and refitting

Removal
1   Drain the cooling system (Section 4).
2   Disconnect the top and bottom hoses (photo).
3   Remove the nuts and washers which secure the tie-rods to the body (photo). Free the ends of the rods.
4   Disconnect the oil cooler pipes at the engine (photos).
5   Disconnect the pipes at the oil cooler (photo), leaving the pipes in position in the surround panel.
6   Remove the screws securing the surround panel to the body, and remove the panel with the radiator (photos).
7   To separate the surround and radiator, remove the six bolts and washers, at the same time freeing the drain tube clips. Note the packing pieces.

7.2 Disconnecting the top hose

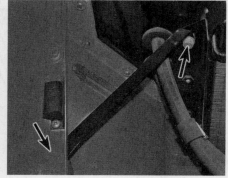
7.3 Disconnecting the tie-rods at the bonnet lock platform

7.4a Remove the oil cooler pipe at the engine block

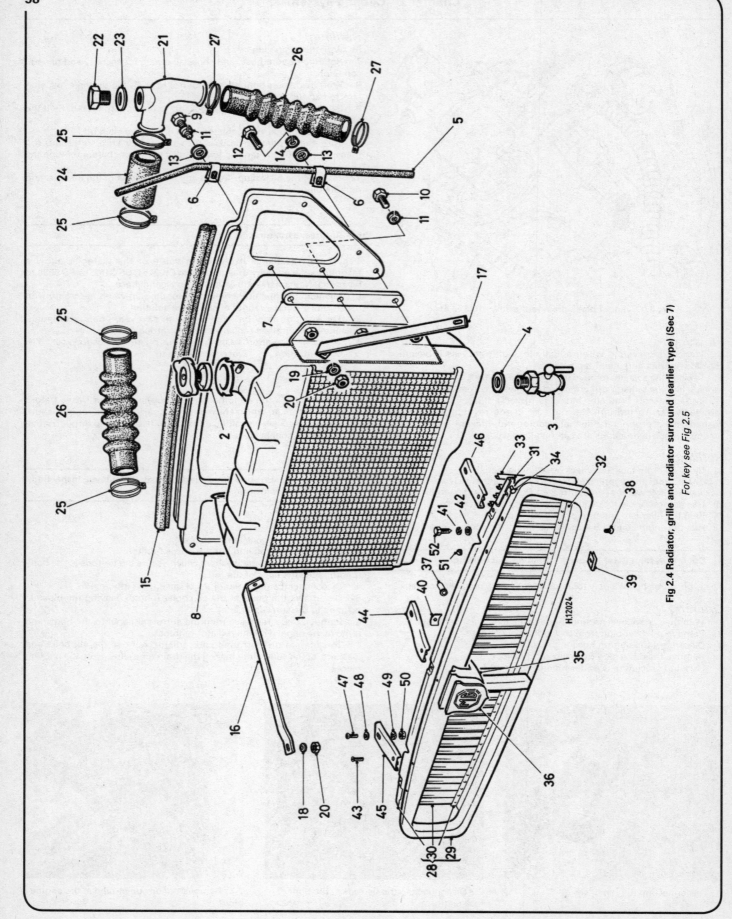

Fig 2.4 Radiator, grille and radiator surround (earlier type) (Sec 7)

For key see Fig 2.5

H.12024

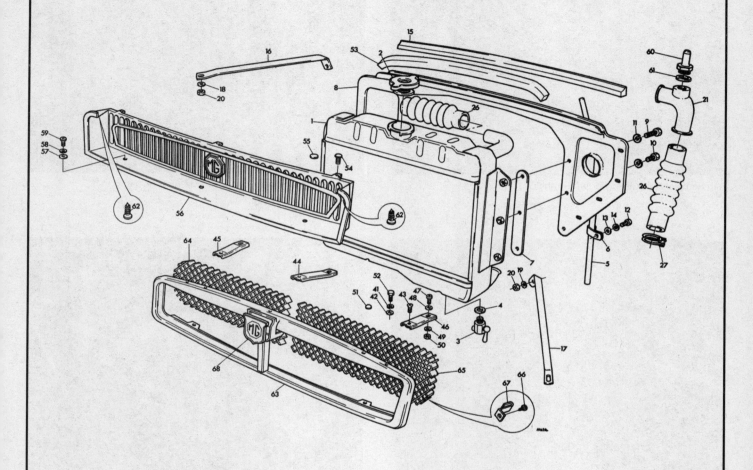

Fig 2.5 Radiator, grille and radiator surround (Sec 8)

1	Radiator	19	Spring washer	36	Badge	**GHN5/GHD5 cars only**	
2	Filler cap	20	Nut	37	Blind badge fixing	53	Radiator air seal
3	Drain tap (Early cars)	21	Pipe	38	Screw	54	Screw
4	Washer for tap (Early cars)	22	Plug	39	Spring nut	55	Sealing plug
5	Drain tube	23	Plug washer	40	Push-on fix	56	Grille assembly
6	Drain tube clip	24	Hose connector	41	Spring washer	57	Washer
7	Packing	25	Hose clip	42	Plain washer	58	Spring washer
8	Radiator diaphragm	26	Hose	43	Screw	59	Screw
9	Long screw	27	Clip	44	Bracket	60	Heater hose connection
10	Short screw	28	Case and grille assembly	45	Bracket (RH)	61	Sealing washer
11	Spring washer	29	Case assembly	46	Bracket (LH)	62	Self-tapping screw
12	Screw	30	Grille assembly	47	Screw	63	Case assembly
13	Plain washer	31	Grille fixing – top	48	Plain washer	64	Grille (RH)
14	Spring washer	32	Grille fixing – bottom	49	Spring washer	65	Grille (LH)
15	Radiator air seal	33	Grille slats	50	Nut	66	Screw
16	Radiator tie (RH)	34	Rivet	51	Buffer	67	Bracket
17	Radiator tie (LH)	35	Bar and badge housing	52	Screw	68	Motif
18	Plain washer						

7.4b Removing the oil cooler pipe at the oil filter

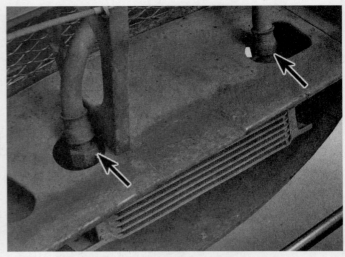

7.5 The unions at the oil cooler, before disconnecting

7.6a Removing the radiator surround panel bolts

7.6b Removing the radiator, complete with the surround and oil cooler pipes

Inspection and cleaning

8   Clean the radiator by reverse flushing (see Section 4) and have any major leaks repaired by a specialist. Minor leaks may be cured using a coolant additive. Clean the exterior by hosing through the matrix.
9   Check the condition of the hoses, and renew if suspect.
10   Check the condition of the drain taps (if fitted) and sealing washers.

Refitting

11   To refit reverse the removal procedure.

---

8   Radiator (later models) – removal and refitting

1   Drain the coolant (Section 5).
2   Disconnect the hose from the expansion tank, and the top hose, at the radiator.
3   Pull the thermostat switch electrical connections apart.
4   Take out the radiator to mounting bracket screws, and those retaining the radiator bracket ties to the bonnet lock platform.
5   Move the ties away, and ease the radiator forwards and out.

6   Cleaning and inspection procedures are as described in Section 7.
7   To refit, reverse the removal procedure.

---

9   Water pump (early models) – removal, examination and refitting

Removal

1   Drain the cooling system (Section 4).
2   Remove the radiator (Section 7).
3   Remove the bolts from the fan and pulley (Fig. 2.6) and remove them (photo).
4   Remove the generator (Chapter 10).
5   Remove the four pump securing bolts. Lift away the pump and gaskets (photo).

Examination

6   If the pump has been leaking or noisy, it is advised that, with exchange pumps available at reasonable prices, it is not worth attempting to rebuild.

Refitting

7   To refit, reverse the removal procedure. Check the fanbelt tension.

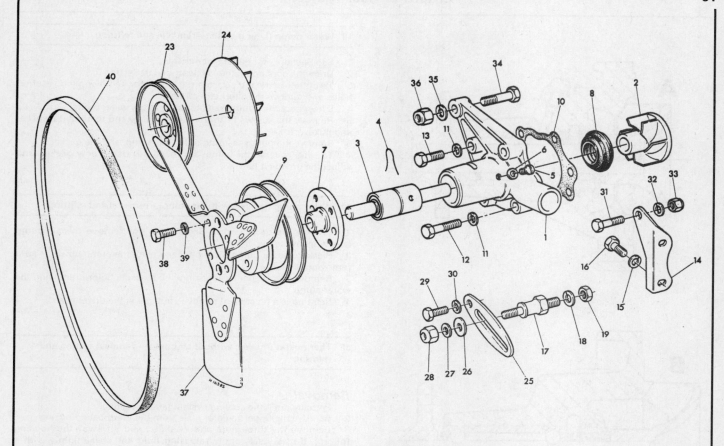

Fig 2.6 Fan and water pump – exploded view (Sec 9)

1	Water pump assembly	11	Spring washer
2	Vane	12	Long screw
3	Bearing assembly	13	Short screw
4	Bearing locating wire	14	Bracket
5	Screw	15	Spring washer
6	Washer	16	Screw
7	Hub	17	Generator adjusting link stud
8	Water pump seal	18	Spring washer
9	Pulley	19	Nut
10	Gasket		

23	Generator pulley	32	Spring washer
24	Generator fan	33	Nut
25	Generator adjusting link	34	Bolt
26	Washer	35	Spring washer
27	Spring washer	36	Nut
28	Nut	37	Water pump fan
29	Screw	38	Screw
30	Spring washer	39	Spring washer
31	Bolt	40	Drivebelt

9.3 Removing the fan and pulley bolts

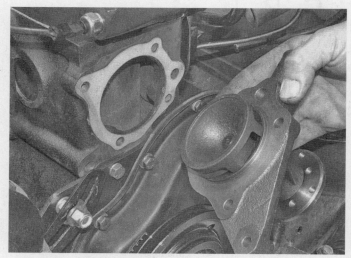

9.5 The water pump and gasket

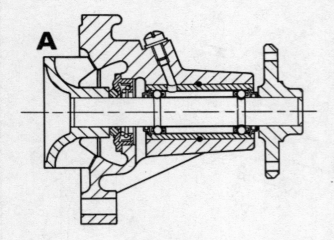

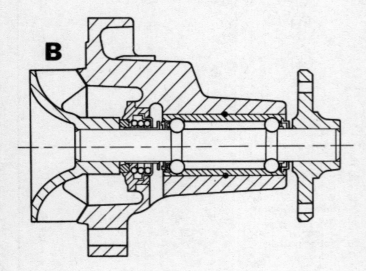

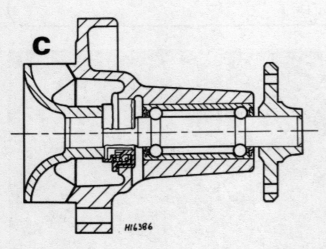

Fig 2.7 The three types of water pump fitted (Sec 9)

A   Early type
B   Second type
C   Late type

10 Water pump (later models) – removal and refitting

1   See Section 9 for general comments.
2   Drain the cooling system as described in Section 5.
3   Take the electrical plug from the alternator, removing the securing bolts, and remove the alternator and belt.
4   Disconnect the bottom radiator hose at the water pump.
5   Remove the screws from the pump pulley, and remove the spacer and pulley.
6   Remove the pump securing bolts, the pump, and the gasket.
7   To refit, reverse the removal procedure. Use a new gasket, and adjust the drivebelt tension.

11 Water pump (models with air pump) – removal and refitting

1   Proceed as described in Section 10, but remove the air pump adjusting link screw.
2   Slacken the air pump pivot bolt, and pivot the pump upwards after removing the belt.
3   Remove the air pump adjusting link brackets before removing the water pump.
4   Refitting is a reversal of removal, but adjust the drivebelts.

12 Thermostat (models without air pump) – removal testing and refitting

Removal
1   Partially drain the cooling system (about 4 pints).
2   Remove the upper radiator hose from the thermostat housing.
3   Remove the three nuts and washers, and lift away the housing (photo). If it is stuck, apply releasing fluid and strike lightly with a wooden mallet.
4   Take out the thermostat.

Testing
5   Immerse the thermostat in cold water, with a thermometer.
6   Heat the water. The thermostat should start to open at the temperature marked upon it. Discard if faulty.
7   Continue to heat until the thermostat is fully open, and then allow it to cool. If it does not both fully open, and then completely close as the water cools, discard it.
8   If the thermostat is stuck open when removed from the housing. discard it.
9   If the housing is badly corroded, fit a new one.

Refitting
10 To refit, reverse the removal procedure, using a new gasket.

12.3 Lifting away the thermostat housing

13 Thermostat (models with air pump) – removal, testing and refitting

1   Remove the filter plug and O seal.
2   Take out the engine block drain plug, partly drain the system, and refit the plug.
3   Remove the screw to release the gulp valve hose from the thermostat housing.
4   Loosen the air pump bolts, and remove the air pump belt. Take out the top air pump mounting bolt.
5   Remove the three nuts and washers, and remove the housing and gasket. Take out the thermostat.

Testing
6   Test as described in Section 12.

Refitting
7   To refit, reverse the removal procedure. Refill the cooling system (Section 5).

14 Cooling fan motor (later models only) – general

Removal
1   Remove the fan guard.
2   Disconnect the fan motor wires.
3   Slacken the fan blade grub screw, and pull the blades off.
4   Loosen the 2 motor bracket clamp screws, and withdraw the motor.

Testing
5   Connect the motor to a 13.5 volt DC supply with a moving-coil ammeter in series. Check the current, which after 60 seconds should not be in excess of 3 amps. Speed should be 3500 to 4000 rpm.
6   High current consumption after dismantling may be caused by a misaligned end cover bearing. Light blows with a soft mallet on the side of the end cover may correct the problem. Alternatively, the armature will be faulty.
7   Low current consumption indicates a dirty commutator or faulty brush gear.

Dismantling
8   Take out the through-bolts and remove the end cover, noting the assembly marks.

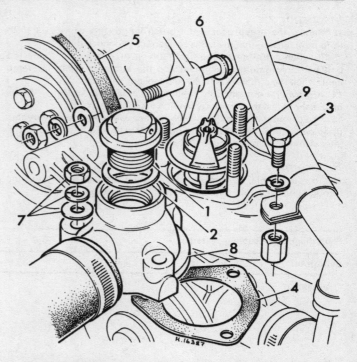

Fig 2.8 Thermostat and housing – vehicles fitted with air pump (Sec 13)

1	Coolant filler plug	5	Air pump belt
2	O-ring seal	6	Air pump top mounting belt
3	Screw retaining gulp valve clip	7	Nut, bolt and washer
4	Gasket	8	Thermostat housing
		9	Thermostat

9   Remove the circlip. the two shims, and the bowed washer, and take the armature from the end cover.
10 Take the thrust washer and circlip from the armature spindle.
11 Take out the three screws, and remove the brush carrier assembly from the end cover.

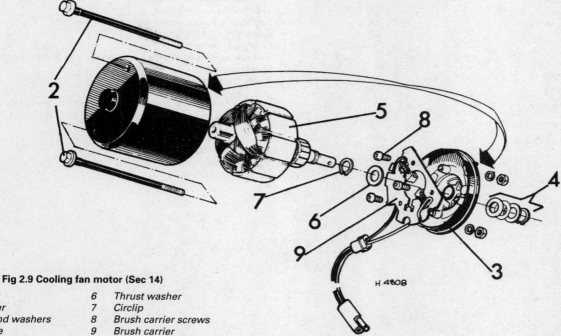

Fig 2.9 Cooling fan motor (Sec 14)

2	Tie bolts	6	Thrust washer
3	End cover	7	Circlip
4	Circlip and washers	8	Brush carrier screws
5	Armature	9	Brush carrier

Inspection

12 Renew the brush gear if the brush length has worn to 3/16 in (4.76 mm). Ensure that the leads are correctly connected.

13 If, when a 15W test lamp and 110 volt AC supply are connected between a commutator segment and the armature shaft, the lamp lights, then the armature is faulty and must be renewed.

14 A growler, normally only available in an auto-electrical works, is necessary to test the armature winding for short-circuiting.

15 The commutator may be cleaned either with petrol, with very fine glass paper, or if necessary may be lightly skimmed in a lathe. Clean after skimming. Do not undercut the segments.

Reassembly

16 To reassemble, reverse the dismantling procedure. Tighten the through-bolts securely, and test the motor (see paragraphs 5-7).

17 When reassembling, lubricate the bearing bushes and armature shaft bearings with Shell Turbo 41 oil or equivalent.

Refitting

18 To refit, reverse the removal procedure. Ensure that the fan end of the motor protrudes 2 in (50.8 mm) from the mounting bracket.

15 Temperature gauge – removal and refitting

1 The gauge unit consists of a thermal transmitter in the cylinder head, connected to the dial indicator on the instrument panel.

2 Checking of the transmitter or indicator is by substitution.

3 Remove the transmitter (capillary type) by removing the gland nut. Unscrew the later type.

4 Remove the indicator gauge by releasing the small bracket behind it. On North American models also remove the speedometer.

Fault diagnosis – cooling system

Symptom	Reason(s)
Overheating	Low coolant level due to leakage or neglect
	Low oil level
	Gauge or sender faulty
	Drivebelt slack or broken
	Thermostat failed in closed position
	Radiator clogged internally
	Radiator or engine waterways clogged internally
	Hose collapsed or blocked internally
	Water pump defective
	Cylinder head gasket blown (combustion gases in coolant)
	Radiator or expansion tank pressure cap defective
	Ignition retarded or auto advance faulty
	Weak mixture
	New or reconditioned engine not yet run-in
	Electric fan malfunction (when fitted)
	Brakes binding
Overcooling	Thermostat failed in open position
	Temperature gauge faulty
	Rich mixture
	Electric fan operating continuously (when fitted)
Coolant loss – external	Perished or damaged hose(s)
	Hose clips loose or broken
	Thermostat housing leaking
	Radiator or heater matrix leaking
	Pressure cap defective
	Core plug leaking
	Cylinder head gasket blown (combustion gasses pressurising system)
	Overheating
	Water pump seal or gasket leaking
Coolant loss – internal	Cylinder head gasket blown (steam in exhaust and/or water in oil
	Cracked head or block
Heater output inadequate	Overcooling (see above)
	Airlock in heater pipes
	Heater matrix clogged internally
	Heater valve defective

Chapter 3
Fuel, exhaust and emission control systems

Contents

Specifications

Note that the following are additional features

Engine Nos

		Key	
18GD – EEC	18V 672 Z – EEC, ELC	CC	Catalytic converter
18GF – EEC	18V 673 Z – EEC, ELC	CCV	Carburettor crankcase ventilation
18GG – EEC	18V 801 AE – CC	EEC	Exhaust emission control
18GH – EEC, CCV	18V 802 AE – CC	ELC	Evaporative loss control
18GJ – EEC, ELC, CCV	18V 883 AE – CC		
18GK – EEC, ELC	18V 884 AE – CC		
18V 584 Z – EEC, ELC	18V 890 AE – CC		
18V 585 Z – EEC, ELC	18V 891 AE – CC		

Carburettors

Type:
   Engine Nos 18G, 18GA, 18GB, 18GD, 18GG, 18GF, 18GH,
   18GJ and 18GK .... Twin SU HS4
   Engine Nos 18V 584 Z, 18V 585 Z, 18V 672 Z, 18V 673 Z, 18V 581 F,
   18V 582 F, 18V 583 F, 18V 581 Y, 18V 582 Y, 18V 583 Y, 18V,
   18V 779 F, 18V 780 F, 18V 846 F and 18V 847 F .... Twin SU HIF4
   Engine Nos 18V 797 AE, 18V 798 AE, 18V 801 AE, 18V 802 AE,
   18V 883 AE, 18V 884 AE, 18V 890 AE, 18V 891 AE,
   18V 892 AE and 18V 893 AE .... Single Zenith 175 CD 5T
Piston damper oil type/specification .... Multigrade engine oil, viscosity SAE 20W/50

Twin SU HS4
Specification:
Engine No 18GF .... AUD 265
Engine No 18GJ .... AUD 326
Engine No 18GK .... AUD 465
Jet size (all models) .... 0.090 in (2.2 mm)
Choke diameter (all models) .... 1½ in (38.1 mm)
Piston spring (all models) .... Red
Needles:

	Standard	Rich	Weak
Engine Nos 18G and 18GA	No 5	No 6	No 21
Engine No 18GB	FX	No 6	No 21
Engine Nos 18GD and 18GG	FX	No 6	GZ
Engine Nos 18GH and 18GJ	AAE	-	-
Engine No 18GK	AAL	-	-

Twin SU HIF4
Specification:
Engine Nos 18V 584 Z and 18V 585 Z .... AUD 493
Engine Nos 18V 672 Z and 18V 673 Z .... AUD 550
Engine No 18V .... AUD 434
Engine Nos 18V 779 F and 18V 780 F .... AUD 616
Engine No 18V 846 F .... FZX 1001
Engine No 18V 847 F .... FZX 1001 or FZX 1229
Needles (standard):
Engine Nos 18V 584 Z and 18V 585 Z .... AAU
Engine Nos 18V 672 Z and 18V 673 Z .... ABD
Engine Nos 18V 581 F, 18V 582 F and 18V 583 F .... AUU
Engine Nos 18V 846 F and 18V 847 F .... ACD

Single Zenith 175 CD 5T
Specification:
Engine Nos 18V 797 AE and 18V 798 AE 3824
Engine Nos 18V 801 AE and 18V 802 AE 3766
Engine Nos 18V 883 AE, 18V 884 AE, 18V 890 AE and 18V 891 AE 3851
Engine Nos 18V 892 AE and 18V 893 AE 3918
Choke needle (all models) .... K
Fast idle setting .... 0.025 in nominal
Needles (standard):
Engine Nos 18V 797 AE, 18V 798 AE, 18V 892 AE and 18V 893 AE 45G
Engine Nos 18V 801 AE and 18V 802 AE 454
Engine Nos 18V 883 AE, 18V 884 AE, 18V 890 AE and 18V 891 AE 45H
Initial needle adjustment .... Needle shoulder flush with underside of air valve

Idling speed
Engine Nos 18G and 18GA .... 500 rpm
Engine Nos 18V 851 F, 18V 582 F and 18V 583 F .... 750 to 800 rpm
Engine No 18V .... 750 rpm
Engine Nos 18V 779 F and 18V 780 F .... 850 rpm
Engine Nos 18V 797 AE, 18V 798 AE, 18V 801 AE, 18V 802 AE,
18V 883 AE, 18V 884 AE, 18V 890 AE, 18V 891 AE, 18V 892 AE
and 18V 893 AE .... 850 rpm
Fast idle speed .... 1000 to 1300 rpm

Exhaust emission
Air pump test speed (if fitted) .... 1000 engine rpm up to 1976, 850 rpm later models
Gas analyser reading at idle speed:
Engine No 18GF .... 4 to 5% CO maximum
Engine Nos 18V 584 Z and 18V 585 Z .... 3.5% CO maximum
Engine Nos 18V 672 Z and 18V 673 Z .... 2.5% CO maximum
Engine No 18V .... 3 to 4.5% CO
Engine Nos 18V 846 F and 18V 847 F .... 3.0% CO
Engine Nos 18V 797 AE and 18V 798 AE .... 5½% ± 1% CO

Fuel pump
Make and type:
Early models .... SU HP electric
Later models .... SU AUF 300 or AUF 305 electric
Minimum delivery:
Early models .... 7 Imp gal (31.8 litres, 8.4 US gal) per hour
Later models .... 15 Imp gal (68.2 litres, 18 US gal) per hour

Torque wrench settings

	lbf ft	Nm
Carburettor stud nuts	15	20
Air pump mounting screws (if fitted)	18	24

1   General Description

The fuel system consists of a fuel tank at the rear of the vehicle, an electric fuel pump, and the necessary fuel lines to the carburettors. Engine emission control systems are specified to suit the requirements of certain territories.

Various carburettors, fuel pumps and other items have been fitted, depending upon the year of manufacture and local territorial regulations. The main differences are given in the Specifications.

2   Routine maintenance

The items requiring periodic attention will be found listed in the Routine Maintenance section of this book. Detailed information on the methods employed in carrying out the tasks will, if necessary, be found elsewhere in this Chapter.

Note that in some countries, local or national laws may forbid carburation or emission control adjustments by unqualified operators. If in doubt consult your dealer.

3   Air cleaners – removal, servicing and refitting

Twin carburettor installation

1   Disconnect the engine rocker cover breather pipe from the front air cleaner. Remove the two bolts securing the air cleaners to the carburettor flanges, and remove the air cleaner assemblies.
2   Part the air cleaner cases, and discard the elements. Thoroughly clean the inside of the cases and intake tubes.
3   Fit new elements. Reassemble the air cleaner cases, and refit them to the vehicle. Renew the breather pipe, if necessary.

Single carburettor installation

4   On later cars. loosen the wing nut on the air cleaner end cover. Pivot the cover, together with the air temperature valve, away from the engine, and remove as a unit.
5   Withdraw the air cleaner element.
6   Clean the casing, and fit a new element, followed by the end cap.
7   Refit the end cover and air temperature control valve assembly, and secure with the wing nut.

4   Fuel pumps, SU types HP and AUF 300 – general description

1   The two pump types differ only in detail, the HP being fitted to early models.
2   A body casing houses the diaphragm, armature and solenoid assembly. At one end is a contact breaker assembly protected by a short cover, and at the other a casting with inlet and outlet ports, filters, valves and pumping chamber.
3   When the ignition is switched on current travels through the solenoid coil, and the armature is drawn in.
4   The armature brings the diaphragm forward against the spring, creating a vacuum in the pump chamber. Fuel therefore fills the pump chamber via the filter and non-return valve.
5   As the armature nears the end of its travel a throwover mechanism operates, separating the points and breaking the circuit.
6   The return spring returns the diaphragm and armature into the pumping chamber, forcing the fuel therein out via the non-return outlet valve.
7   When the armature is nearly fully forward the throwover mechanism again functions, closing the points, re-energising the solenoid, and repeating the cycle.

5   Fuel pumps, SU types HP and AUF 300 – removal and refitting

1   The fuel pump is positioned under the right side of the car; on the heelboard adjacent to the front of the RH leaf spring.

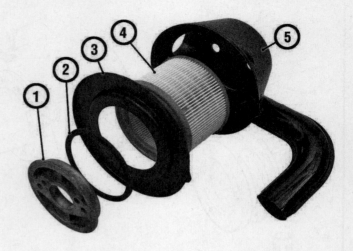

Fig 3.1 Air cleaner – twin carburettor installation (Sec 3)

1	Adaptor	4	Filter
2	Gasket	5	Case
3	Baseplate		

2   Disconnect the battery earth.
3   Disconnect the earth and supply wires from the pump.
4   Remove the fuel inlet and outlet pipes by undoing the nuts or clips. Remove the vent pipe.
5   Remove the two bolts and spring washers, and remove the pump and bracket.
6   To refit, reverse the removal procedure. Ensure that the inlet and outlet pipes are connected correctly, and that a good earth connection is made.

6   Fuel pumps SU types HP and AUF 300 – dismantling

Inlet outlet and filter arrangements

HP pump
1   Clean the exterior. Remove the inlet union, outlet union, outlet valve cage, and the inlet valve disc. Take off the base plug and filter.

AUF 300 pump
2   Remove the screws and clamp plate (59 in Fig. 3.2). and remove the valves, sealing washers and filter. Remove the 2 BA screw, remove the inlet air bottle cover, and unscrew the inlet and outlet connections.

Contact breaker

3   Remove the insulating sleeve (32). terminal nut (31) and the connector and washer (29, 30). Remove the seal (33) and the end cover (28).
4   Remove the screw (23) and ease the capacitor (24) from the clamp. Remove the washer, the long coil wire, and contact blade.

Diaphragm and pump chamber

5   Mark the flange on items (1) and (36). remove the screws, and separate them, taking care not to damage the diaphragm if it sticks to either flange. Remove screw (6) and terminal (8).
6   On the roller type diaphragm, unscrew the diaphragm anti-clockwise until it comes free. Catch the eleven brass rollers (4).
7   On the guide plate type diaphragm, turn back the diaphragm edge, carefully lever the two lobes on the guide plate from the coil housing recess, and unscrew the diaphragm anti-clockwise.

Rocker pedestal

8   Remove nut (19) and screw (15). Cut away lead washer (18) with a knife. Take the spring washer from the terminal tag.

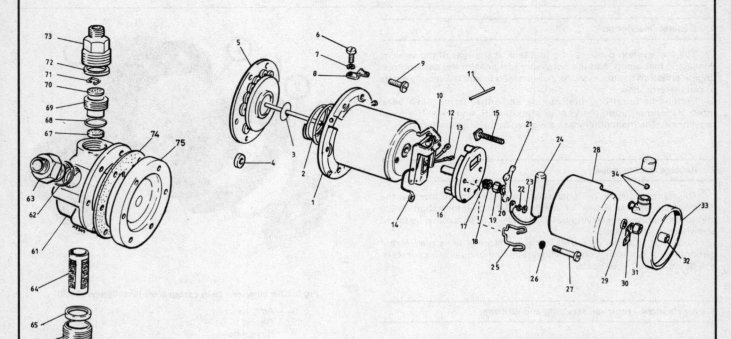

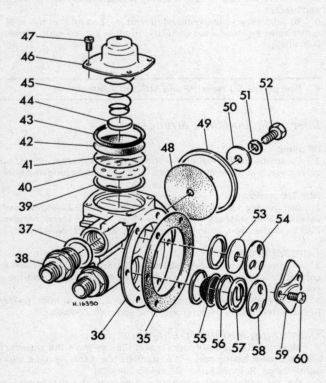

Fig 3.2 Fuel pumps, SU types HP (bottom) and AUF 300 (top) – exploded view (Sec 4)

1	Coil housing	39	Washer
2	Armature spring	40	Diaphragm plate (early models)
3	Impact washer		
4	Armature centralizing roller	41	Plastic diaphragm barrier
5	Diaphragm and spindle assembly	42	Rubber diaphragm (early models)
		43	Rubber O-ring
6	Screw	44	Spring end cap
7	Spring washer	45	Diaphragm spring (early models)
8	Earth connector		
9	Screw	46	Delivery flow smoothing device cover (later models)
10	Rocket mechanism		
11	Rocker pivot pin	47	Screw
12	Terminal	48	Gasket
13	Terminal	49	Inlet air bottle cover
14	Earth tag	50	Washer
15	Stud	51	Spring washer
16	Pedestal	52	Screw
17	Spring washer	53	Outlet valve
18	Lead washer	54	Valve cap
19	Nut	55	Filter
20	Washer	56	Sealing washer
21	Contact blade	57	Inlet valve
22	Washer	59	Clamp plate
23	Screw	60	Screw
24	Condenser	61	Pump body
25	Condenser clip	62	Washer
26	Spring washer	63	Outlet connection
27	Screw	64	Filter
28	End cover	65	Washer
29	Washer	66	Plug
30	Lucar connector	67	Inlet valve
31	Nut	68	Washer
32	Insulating sleeve	69	Outlet valve cage
33	Sealing band	70	Outlet valve
34	Vent valve	71	Spring clip
35	Gasket	72	Washer
36	Pump body	73	Outlet connection
37	Washer	74	Gasket
38	Outlet connection	75	Sandwich plate

9 Take out the two pedestal securing screws (27), remove the earth terminal tag and condenser clip. Take out the terminal stud (15). Remove the pedestal complete with the rocker assembly.

10 Push out pivot pin (11) to remove the rocker assembly.

7 Fuel pumps SU types HP and AUF 300 – reassembly

Rocker pedestal

1 Turn the pedestal upside down. Attach the rocker assembly by inserting the pin through the small hole in the struts and rockers. The pin, a special case-hardened component, must be replaced only by a genuine spare part if lost or damaged.

2 Position the centre toggle so that when the inner rocker spindle is held in tension against the rear of the contact point, the centre toggle spring is above the spindle on which the white rollers run.

3 The rocker mechanism must move freely. Bent parts may be carefully straightened with long-nosed pliers.

4 Fit the terminal stud (15) to the pedestal. Reverse the dismantling procedure (Section 6, paragraphs 8 and 9). Use a new lead washer if necessary.

Diaphragm assembly

5 Place the impact washer on the diaphragm spindle, and against the armature. Fit the diaphragm spring with the wide end into the coil housing. Place the diaphragm spindle through the coil and screw it into the rocker trunnion until the rocker will not operate.

6 On the roller type diaphragm, turn back the edge and insert the eleven brass rollers. On later-type rocker mechanisms possessing adjustable fingers, fit the contact blade and adjust the finger settings as described in paragraph 26. Remove the blade.

7 Hold the pump horizontally. Unscrew the diaphram whilst actuating it, until the rocker will just throw over. Unscrew until the holes are aligned, then unscrew a further quarter-turn.

8 Press the armature centre. Fit the retaining fork at the back of the rocker.

Body items, AUF 300 pump

9 On the guide plate type diaphragm, turn the edge back and position one lobe after the other in the recess between the armature and coil housing. Press the lobes home, firstly in the centre, and following with those at the ends.

10 Note that the recess housing for the inlet valve assembly is deeper than that for the outlet valve, to allow for the filter and sealing washer. Refit the inlet and outlet connections with their sealing rings.

11 Fit the outlet valve components. Firstly the joint washer, followed by the valve (tab side downwards), and the valve cover.

12 Fit the inlet valve components. Firstly the joint washer, followed by the filter (dome side downwards), the valve (tab side upwards), and the valve cover.

13 Refit the clamp plate (59). Refit the air bottle cover with the sealing washer (48, 49), securing with the central screw.

14 On early pumps, fit the sealing ring, the perforated diaphragm plate, round side down (item 40). the plastic disc and the rubber diaphram. Fit seating ring (43) in the recess.

15 Place the large end of the diaphragm spring in the cover (46). Fit the end cap (44) on the small end of the spring, and place the assembly tool through the three items, turning it through 90° to tension the spring.

16 Fit the cap and spring assembly, secure with the four screws, and remove the tool.

17 On later pumps fit the sealing washer, followed by the plastic diaphragm, domed side down, in the air bottle aperture. Fit the O seal, and refit the cap and screws.

Body items – HP pump

18 Place the outlet valve disc (70) in the valve cage and fit the spring clip. Check that the valve rattles freely when the housing is shaken.

19 Fit the inlet valve (67) plain side down in the housing. Fit the thin fibre washer, and drop the outlet valve cage (69) into place. Fit the medium washer (72). Fit the inlet and outlet unions, and the filter, washer and plug.

20 Place the pump body, sandwich plate and coil housing together with the gaskets interposed between them. Ensure correct orientation, line up the holes, and fit the six screws finger tight. Fit the earthing

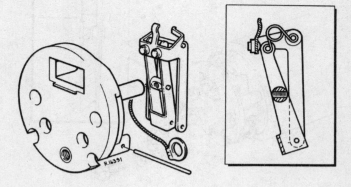

Fig 3.3 The rocker assembly and pedestal (inset – the correct toggle spring position) (Sec 7)

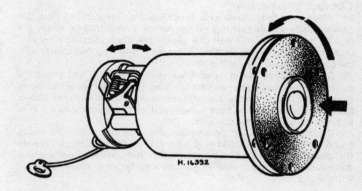

Fig 3.4 Unscrewing the diaphragm until the rocker just throws over (Sec 7)

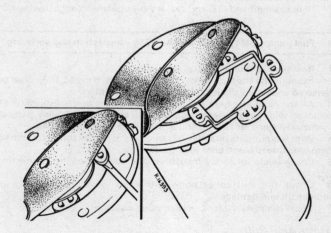

Fig 3.5 Repositioning the armature guide plate (Sec 7)

screw and connector. The two cast lugs on the coil housing should be at the bottom, as should the filter.

21 Carefully remove the roller retaining fork. Tighten the body screws (9) in diagonal sequence.

Contact blade

22 Fit the contact blade, the capacitor and the coil leads to the pedestal. Secure with the washer and screw.

23 Adjust the blade using the slot at the end, so that the points when closed are as shown in Fig. 3.6. They should wipe over the centre-line of each other when they open or close. Tighten the securing screw.

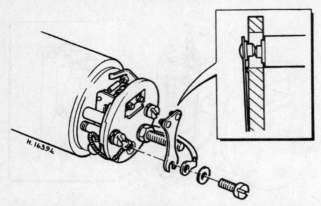

Fig 3.6 The relationship of the rocker contacts and spring blade contacts (Sec 7)

Contact gap setting

24 When the outer rocker is pressed towards the coil housing, the contact blade should just rest on the narrow rib protruding above the face of the pedestal. If there is a gap or the blade rests too heavily, loosen the screw, swing the blade clear, and bend it so that it rests with the correct tension against the rib.

25 On earlier type rocker assemblies, refer to Fig. 3.7, and check the points gap by pressing the contact blade against the pedestal rib, taking care not to press the actual point. Measure the gap between the face of the coil housing and the fibre rollers, and set if necessary to 0.030 in (0.8 mm) by bending the blade tip.

26 On modified rocker assemblies, refer to Fig. 3.8, and check gap A which should be 0.035 in (0.9 mm). Bend the stop finger beneath the pedestal if necessary, to obtain this dimension. Finally check dimension B, and if necessary bend the stop finger to obtain a gap of 0.070 in (1.8 mm).

End cover

27 Fit the seal washer (20) on the terminal stud. Fit the end cover, the washer, terminal and retaining nut (31). Refit the insulating sleeve (32).

28 Refit sealing band (33) and seal it thoroughly with adhesive tape.

---

8   Fuel pumps SU types HP and AUF 300 – inspection and servicing

---

1 Remove the filter and clean in paraffin.

2 Examine the contact points. If they are burnt or pitted, they must be renewed and a new blade and rocker assembly fitted.

3 All traces of any gum-like substance, similar to varnish, must be removed with paint stripper or a suitable solvent. Soak alloy parts in methylated spirit for several hours, and clean them off with rag.

4 With the pump dismantled, clean all parts and examine for cracks, damaged threads, and poor joint faces.

5 Check leads for faulty insulation and security of the connecting tags.

6 Check the end cover non-return vent valve, for freedom of movement and damage.

7 Check the pedestal for cracks or other damage.

Type AUF 300

8 Check the plastic valve assemblies by blowing or sucking, and for obvious damage. Examine the narrow tongue on the valve cage. This should allow the valve to lift about 1/16 in (1.6 mm), and must not be distorted.

9 On early pumps, check all parts of the delivery flow smoothing device, and renew where necessary.

10 On later pumps, check the delivery air bottle diaphragm, the cover, and the gasket. Examine the body valve recesses, and discard the body if they are badly pitted or corroded.

Type HP

11 Take out the outlet valve cage circlip. Examine the inlet and outlet valve discs for wear, and renew if necessary.

12 Check the outlet valve cage and the valve seat in the body for general condition. If necessary, discard the defective part.

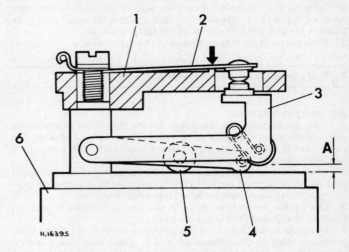

Fig 3.7 Contact setting procedure – early rocker assemblies (Sec 7)

1	Pedestal	5	Trunnion
2	Contact blade	6	Coil housing
3	Outer rocker		A = 0.030 in (0.8 mm)
4	Inner rocker		

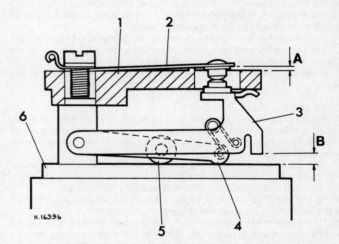

Fig 3.8 Contact setting procedure – later modified rocker assemblies (Sec 7)

1	Pedestal	5	Trunnion
2	Contact blade	6	Coil housing
3	Outer rocker		A = 0.035 in (0.9 mm)
4	Inner rocker		B = 0.070 in (1.8 mm)

---

9   Fuel pumps SU types HP and AUF 300 – fault-finding and rectification

---

Noisy pump

1 Noisy, rapid operation, combined with fuel starvation, indicates a suction side air leak or an empty fuel tank. Check by undoing the fuel pipe at the carburettor and immersing the end in a container of fuel. With the ignition on, a regular stream of air bubbles emerging from the pipe end indicates that air is being taken in on the suction side.

2 To remedy the fault, make sure that:

   (a)   The screws (9) in Fig. 3.2 are secure

   (b)   The inlet union is secure, and the O-ring in good condition

   (c)   All the connections from tank to pump are sound

Fuel feed failure

3   Disconnect the fuel pipe at the carburettor and check as in paragraph 1, when:

(a) *If the flow is satisfactory, examine the float chamber needle valve for obstructions*

(b) *If an initially normal flow diminishes and the pump slows down, remove the tank filler cap. If flow returns to normal, the cap vent is blocked*

(c) *Reduced flow and slow pump operation signifies an inlet side restriction. Check the filter for blockage*

(d) *Reduced flow and rapid operation signifies a suction side air leak, or valve fault*

(e) *If no flow is present check if current is being delivered to the pump terminal*

(f) *With no flow, but current at the terminal satisfactory, short across the contact points. If the pump performs a stroke, service or renew the contacts*

(g) *If the pump operates only with the inlet pipe disconnected, there is obstruction in the pipeline from the tank to pump. Remove the filler cap, and blow down the pipe with an air line*

(h) *No flow can be caused by excessive friction in the rocker mechanism. Apply oil sparingly at the pivot points, and move the mechanism by flexing the diaphragm. Re-test*

(i) *No flow can be caused by stiff ness of the diaphragm. Flex the diaphragm a few times, and retest*

Continuous pump operation, without delivering fuel

4   Likely to be caused by:

(a) *Dirt under a valve, especially the inlet valve*

(b) *A serious suction side air leak. Remedy as described in paragraph 1*

(c) *Empty fuel tank!*

---

10   Fuel pump GHN5 and GHD5 cars from model No 410002 – removal and refitting

---

Removal

1   Disconnect the battery.

2   In the boot, remove the screws securing the fuel pump guard, and remove the guard.

3   Loosen the clip retaining the pump in the support rubber, and remove the electrical lead.

4   Under the vehicle, disconnect the inlet and outlet unions, and the breather tube and lead.

5   Remove the pump.

Refitting

6   To refit, reverse the removal procedure. Angle the inlet and outlet unions at 45° to the pump centre-line.

---

11   Fuel pump, SU type AUF 305 – general description

---

1   The design and performance of this pump is similar to that of the AUF 300 type.

2   Removal and dismantling procedures are covered in the sections referring to the type AUF 300.

---

12   Fuel tank (cars without evaporative loss system) – removal, cleaning and refitting

---

Removal (early tourers)

1   Disconnect the batteries. Raise the rear of the car and support it firmly.

2   Remove the filler cap. Under the vehicle, remove the drain plug and catch the fuel.

3   Disconnect the fuel pipe union.

4   Remove the fuel gauge wires from the right side of the tank.

5   Support the tank. Loosen the two clips on the filler neck hose, and pull out the extension and seal.

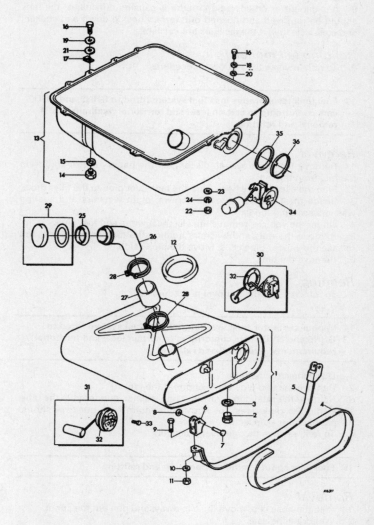

Fig 3.9 Fuel tanks (Sec 12)

1	Tank (earlier type)	19	Washer
2	Drain plug	20	Fibre washer
3	Drain plug washer	21	Fibre washer
4	Rubber packing strip	22	Nut
5	Mounting strap	23	Washer
6	Rear hanger	24	Spring washer
7	Clevis pin	25	Rubber ferrule
8	Washer	26	Filler tube
9	Bolt	27	Connection hose
10	Washer	28	Clip
11	Nut	29	Cap
12	Rubber seal (tank to boot floor)	30	Gauge unit (early)
13	Tank (later type)	31	Gauge unit (early, modified)
14	Drain plug	32	Gasket
15	Washer	33	Screw
16	Bolt – tank to boot	34	Gauge unit (later models)
17	Nut	35	Sealing ring (later models)
18	Washer	36	Locking ring (later models)

6   Undo the strap nuts at the rear of the tank. Move the straps away, and lower the tank.

Removal (later tourer and GT models)

7   Proceed as described in paragraphs 1-7, except that the tank is held to the floor of the boot by setscrews which must be removed before the tank can be lowered. Retainer straps are not fitted.

Cleaning

8   If sediment or other foreign matter is causing difficulties, the tank should be removed and flushed out, turned upside down and shaken, and steam cleaned if the facilities are available.

Refitting (all models)

9   To refit, reverse the removal procedures.

13 Fuel tank (evaporative loss fuel system fitted to GHN5 and GHD5 cars conforming to certain local and territorial requirements) – removal and refitting

Removal

1   Remove the spare wheel, disconnect the battery earth, and drain the fuel from the tank.
2   Free the clips on the hose from the tank inlet pipe to the filler tube.
3   Inside the boot, remove the screws, plain washers and sealing washers securing the tank.
4   Under the vehicle, remove the electrical wires and fuel pipe.
5   Remove the nuts and washers holding the tank to the studs, and release the vapour pipe clips. Move the pipe aside.
6   Remove the tank.

Refitting

7   To refit, reverse the removal procedure.

14 Vapour separator tank (evaporative loss fuel system fitted to GHN5 and GHD5 cars conforming to certain local and territorial requirements) – removal and refitting

1   Disconnect the battery.
2   Remove the two pipe connections at the tank.
3   Remove the retaining screw, nut and washer, and remove the tank. Note that the tank does not normally contain fuel, but care should nevertheless be exercised.
4   To refit, reverse the removal procedure.

15 Fuel filler spout – removal, servicing and refitting

Removal

1   Free the hose clip, move the clip away, and pull out the spout.
2   Withdraw the seal.
3   On North American vehicles, check the restrictor. Ensure that the trap door will open, and that it will close by its own spring pressure.
4   To rectify a faulty restrictor.
    (a) On early cars, fit a new filler spout assembly
    (b) On later cars, fit a new restrictor
5   To renew the restrictor on North American cars:
    (a) Release the three locating tongues, and withdraw the restrictor
    (b) Fit the filler spout sleeve, with the vent hole in line with the mark TOP on the spout
    (c) Secure the sleeve with the three tongues

Refitting

6   To refit, reverse the dismantling procedure. Fit a new seal if necessary, and on North American cars ensure that the spout is fitted with the word TOP uppermost.

16 Fuel tank gauge unit – removal and refitting

Removal (early tourer)

1   Take out the six screws which hold the unit to the tank. Take out the unit, taking care not to damage the float lever.

Removal (later tourer and GT)

2   Remove the locking ring on the tank unit, preferably using service tool 18G 1001. Take out the unit and seal.

Refitting

3   To refit, reverse the removal procedure.

17 Carburettor SU type HS4 (vehicles not fitted with emission control equipment) – general description and maintenance

1   The variable choke SU carburettors are relatively simple instruments and basically the same irrespective of size and type. They differ from most other carburettors in that only one variable jet is fitted to deal with all possible conditions. The two carburettors are linked by rods and levers (photos).
2   Air passing rapidly through the choke draws petrol from the jet, forming a petrol/air mixture. The amount of fuel drawn depends on the position of the tapered needle, which moves up and down the jet orifice according to engine load and throttle opening, effectively altering the size of the jet and metering the fuel to suit the conditions prevailing.
3   The tapered needle is held in a piston which slides up and down the dashpot in response to manifold vacuum, thus determining the position of the needle in the jet and hence the size of the orifice. To prevent piston flutter, and to give a richer mixture when the accelerator is suddenly depressed, an oil damper and light spring are fitted in the dashpot.
4   The central piston rod slides in the piston chamber. All other parts of the piston assembly have clearances to prevent metal-to-metal contact.
5   The fuel level in the carburettor is determined by the level of the float in the float chamber. When the level is correct, a lever resting on top of the float closes the needle valve in the cover of the chamber, cutting off the fuel supply.
6   As fuel is used the float sinks and the needle comes away from its seat allowing more fuel to enter the float chamber and restore the level.

Maintenance

7   Remove the cap from the suction chambers, and top up the hollow piston rod until the oil level is ½ in (12.5 mm) above the top of the rod. Use engine oil (photo).

17.1a A general view of the linkages on the carburettors (removed from engine)

17.1b A general view of the linkages on the carburettors (fitted to engine)

17.7 The cap and damper piston on the carburettor

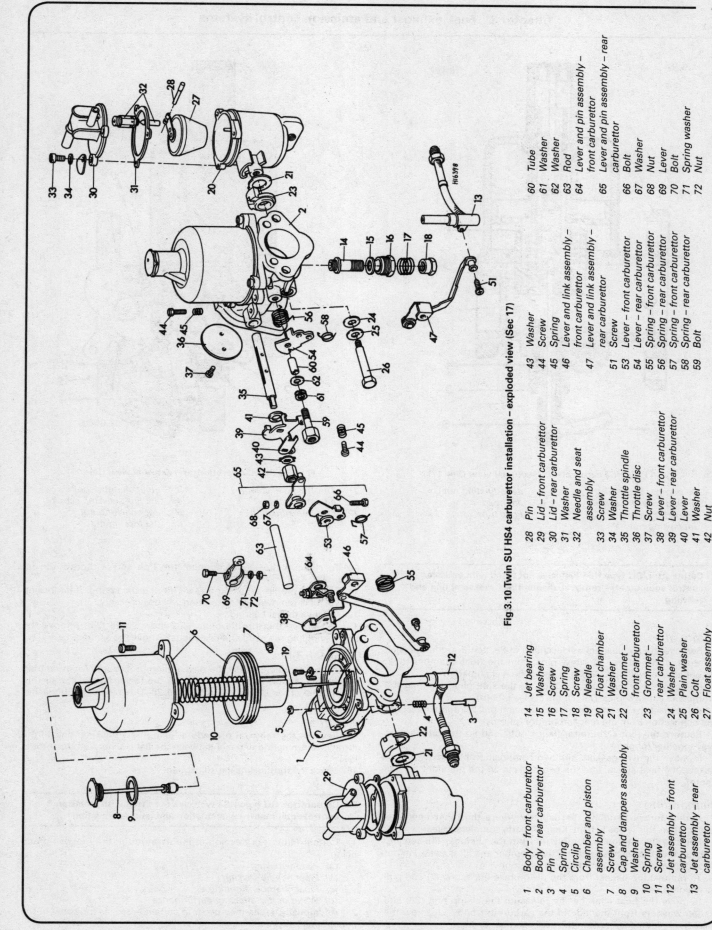

Fig 3.10 Twin SU HS4 carburettor installation – exploded view (Sec 17)

1	Body – front carburettor	28	Pin
2	Body – rear carburettor	29	Lid – front carburettor
3	Pin	30	Lid – rear carburettor
4	Spring	31	Washer
5	Circlip	32	Needle and seat assembly
6	Chamber and piston assembly	33	Screw
7	Screw	34	Washer
8	Cap and dampers assembly	35	Throttle spindle
9	Washer	36	Throttle disc
10	Spring	37	Screw
11	Screw	38	Lever – front carburettor
12	Jet assembly – front carburettor	39	Lever – rear carburettor
13	Jet assembly – rear carburettor	40	Lever
14	Jet bearing	41	Washer
15	Washer	42	Nut
16	Screw	43	Washer
17	Spring	44	Screw
18	Screw	45	Spring
19	Needle	46	Washer
20	Float chamber	47	Lever and link assembly – front carburettor
21	Washer	51	Screw
22	Grommet – front carburettor	53	Lever – front carburettor
23	Grommet – rear carburettor	54	Lever – rear carburettor
24	Washer	55	Screw
25	Plain washer	56	Spring – front carburettor
26	Colt	57	Spring – rear carburettor
27	Float assembly	58	Spring – front carburettor
		59	Bolt
60	Tube		
61	Washer		
62	Washer		
63	Rod		
64	Lever and pin assembly – front carburettor		
65	Lever and pin assembly – rear carburettor		
66	Bolt		
67	Washer		
68	Nut		
69	Lever		
70	Bolt		
71	Spring washer		
72	Nut		

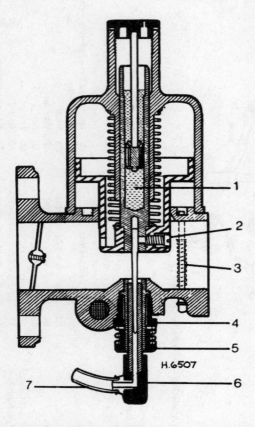

Fig 3.11 SU HS4 carburettor – sectional view (Sec 17)

1	Oil damper reservoir	5	Jet adjusting nut
2	Needle securing screw	6	Jet head
3	Piston lifting pin	7	Feed tube
4	Jet locking nut		

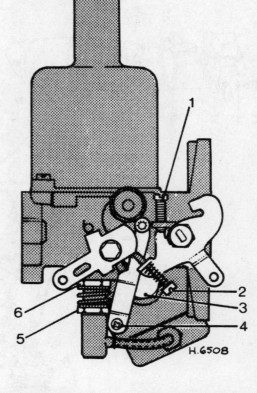

Fig 3.12 SU HS4 carburettor – external view (Sec 17)

1	Throttle (idle speed) adjusting screw	3	Float chamber bolt
2	Fast idle adjusting screw	4	Jet link securing screw
		5	Jet adjusting nut
		6	Jet locking nut

18 Carburettor, SU type HS4 (vehicles not fitted with emission control equipment) – removal, dismantling, reassembling and refitting

Removal

1   Remove the air cleaners as described in Section 3. Undo the clips (if fitted), and pull the overflow pipe from the float chamber tops. Disconnect the fuel pipe hose(s) from the float chamber(s).
2   Remove either the bolts and nuts, or the split pins, securing the throttle and choke cables. Detach the cables (photo).
3   Disconnect the throttle return springs, and pull the rubber vacuum pipe connection from the rear carburettor (photos).
4   Remove the four carburettor flange nuts, and lift the carburettors away together (photos).
5   Remove the two gaskets, the two composition blocks, two more gaskets, the heat shield, and the two gaskets on the manifold flanges (photo).

Dismantling

6   Avoid clumsy handling, particularly where the taper needle is concerned as this is easily bent. Keep all parts completely clean.
7   Remove the damper assembly (8) from the chamber (6), see Fig. 3.10. Remove the screws retaining the chamber and lift it away. Lift out the spring, and the piston and needle assembly.
8   To remove the needle from the piston take out screw (7) and pull the needle away.
9   Remove the float chamber by releasing the clamp bolt (26) and sealing washers from the side of the carburettor body. Unscrew the union holding the feed tube in the float chamber base.

10   To remove the jet, disconnect the link and withdraw the jet assembly.
11   Remove the jet adjusting screw (18) and the spring. If jet locking screw (16) is removed, jet re-centring will be necessary.
12   Remove the jet bearing.
13   To remove the throttle plate (36) and spindle (35), remove the screws holding the plate and take it out Remove the spindle.

Reassembly

14   To reassemble, reverse the dismantling procedure. When refitting the needle, ensure that it is flush with the lower face of the piston. Centre the jet, as described in Section 20. Use new seating washer throughout.

Refitting

15   Reverse the removal procedure, using new gaskets. Locate the throttle return spring end eye between the flat washer and the throttle lever.
16   Check the throttle linkage adjustment

19 Carburettor, SU type HS4 (vehicles not fitted with emission control equipment) – examination and fault rectification

1   Certain faults can develop in the carburettor, the most common being:
   (a) Piston sticking
   (b) Float needle sticking
   (c) Float chamber flooding
   (d) Water or dirt affecting performance
2   Additionally, faults may occur in certain areas, as indicated in the paragraphs which follow.

18.2 Carburettors – removing the throttle cable

18.3a Carburettors – disconnecting the throttle return springs

18.3b Carburettors – pulling off the vacuum pipe

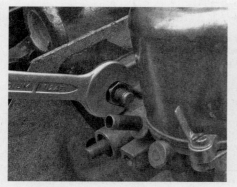

18.4a Carburettors – removing the manifold flange nuts

18.4b Carburettors – lifting the twin instruments from the engine as a pair

18.5 Carburettors – gaskets, distance pieces and heat shield

Needle
3   If a fine ridge can be seen on the jet needle, it implies that the needle has not been centrally located in the jet. The needle should be renewed.

Jet
4   A needle which has become ridged will damage the jet by striking it. The jet can also become worn on the outside diameter. In either case, renew the jet.

Throttle disc and choke tube
5   Examine these items, and renew if worn.

Float needle and seat
6   Examine these items and renew if ridging is evident.

Piston sticking
7   The hardened piston rod, sliding in the centre guide tube in the piston chamber (6), is the only part of the piston assembly that should contact the chamber. However, after high mileages wear in the centre tube may allow the piston to touch the chamber causing piston sticking.
8   To test for piston sticking, rotate the piston in the guide tube whilst sliding it in and out. If any contact takes place between the piston and the chamber wall, polish the relevant area of the wall with metal polish until clearance exists. In extreme cases, use fine emery cloth, but remove only the minimum amount of metal necessary to provide clearance or leakage will occur.
9   Clean the whole assembly thoroughly, and lubricate the piston rod with a spot of oil.
10   Recheck by reassembling and lifting the piston with the lifting pin; the piston when released should fall smartly back onto the seat.

Piston return spring
11   On no account may this be stretched in an attempt to eliminate sticking.

Float needle sticking
12   If the float needle sticks the carburettor will run dry and the engine will stop.
13   Check by removing the inlet pipe at the float chamber, and turning on the ignition. If fuel spurts from the end of the pipe (direct it towards the ground or into a cloth or jar), the fault is probably a sticking float needle.
14   Remove the float chamber and dismantle the needle valve (Section 22). Clean all parts thoroughly.

Float chamber flooding
15   Fuel dripping from the float chamber area is normally caused by dirt between the float chamber needle and seat. This prevents the valve cutting off the fuel supply. Alternatively, the float may be leaking or incorrectly adjusted.
16   Dismantle the float chamber (see Section 22). Clean the needle valve. Check the float setting, and shake it to see if fuel has leaked into it.
17   If, after clearing dirt from the needle valve, flooding quickly recurs, there is no alternative but to make sure that the fuel tank and pipelines are completely free of all foreign material.

---

20   Carburettor, SU type HS4 (vehicles not fitted with emission control equipment) – jet centering

---

1   Remove the feed tube union at the base of the float chamber. disconnect the link to the jet, and withdraw the jet and feed tube assembly.
2   Remove the jet adjusting screw (Fig. 3.10, item 18) and spring (17). Refit screw (18) without the spring, screwing it up to the fullest extent. Refit the jet assembly.
3   Slacken the jet locking screw (16) until the jet bearing (14) can just be rotated with the fingers.
4   Remove the damper assembly, and push the piston assembly

fully down to enter the needle fully into the jet Tighten the jet locking screw (16) whilst ensuring that the jet head remains in the correct angular position.

5   Check by lifting the piston, then releasing it. The piston should hit the jet bridge with a soft metallic click, and the intensity of the click should be the same whether the jet is in its normal position or is fully lowered. A variation in the sound means that the jet is not properly centralised and the process must be repeated.

6   On completion, remove the jet and adjusting screw. Refit the spring, and reassemble the remaining parts.

21 Carburettor SU type HS4 (vehicles not fitted with emission control equipment) – slow running adjustment and synchronisation

1   Before beginning work, the following points should be in good order or adjustment.
(a) General engine condition
(b) Ignition timing
(c) Spark plugs
(d) Contact breaker
(e) Induction system (no air leaks)
(f) Valve clearances
(g) Engine controls
(h) Float chamber petrol level
The engine should be at operating temperature. Remove the air cleaners.

2   Loosen the pinch-bolt on the folded metal clamp on the interconnecting shaft, to allow the carburettors to operate independently.

3   Disconnect the choke cable, slacken the pinch-bolts on levers (64) and (65) in Fig. 3.10. Back off the fast idle screws (44).

4   Remove the chamber and piston assembles, and screw up each jet adjusting nut until the jet is flush with the bridge. Refit the chamber and piston assemblies.

5   Use the lifting pins to check that each piston will fall freely onto the bridge, and if so, turn each jet adjusting nut down exactly two turns. If not, centralise the jet(s) (see Section 20).

6   Start the engine. Synchronise the throttles by turning the throttle adjusting screws whilst listening to the hiss in the intakes alternately, preferably using a rubber tube held to the ear. The throttles will be synchronised when the intensity of the hiss in each intake is similar. There are various balancing instruments on the market which will provide assistance in obtaining accurate synchronisation.

7   When synchronisation is complete, adjust the jet adjusting nuts up and down by equal amounts to give the fastest idle speed consistent with even firing. Keep the jets pressed upwards as this is done.

8   Reset the idle speed (see Specifications) if necessary, by turning the throttle screws equal amounts.

9   Check the mixture setting, by raising each piston in turn about 1/32 in (0.75 mm), using the lifting pins. Compare with the following:
(a) If engine speed increases appreciably, the mixture is too rich
(b) If engine speed immediately decreases, the mixture is too weak
(c) If engine speed increases momentarily very slightly, the mixture is correct

10 Work first on the rear carburettor, then the front, and back to the rear until a satisfactory result is obtained. Check against the following:
(a) If the exhaust gas and tailpipe tend to be blacky the mixture is too rich. Usually accompanied by a regular misfire in the exhaust beat
(b) A colourless exhaust gas, light grey exhaust tailpipe, and irregular misfire, indicate a weak mixture
(c) With the mixture correct, the exhaust note should be regular and even

11 Set the clearance in the throttle operating mechanism. Employing an 0.012 in (0.3 mm) or 0.020 in (0.5 mm) feeler gauge for manual or automatic transmission vehicles respectively, and referring to Fig. 3.13, place the feeler gauge between the indicated items.

12 Press down on each throttle levershaft until the lever pin rests lightly on the lower arm of the fork in the throttle lever. Tighten the lever clamp bolt Carry this operation out on both levers, and remove the feeler gauge.

13 Connect the choke cable. Make sure that the jets return up to the jet adjusting nuts, and that, when the choke control is fully home, the choke levers are fully returned.

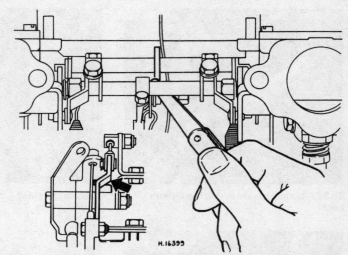

Fig 3.13 Throttle lever adjustment, showing a feeler gauge between the throttle/shaft lever stop and the choke interconnecting spindle. (Inset: feeler position on automatic transmission vehicles) (Sec 21)

14 Adjust the fast idle screws to give 1000 rpm (engine hot), with the choke control pulled out to the point where the linkage is ready to move the jets (a minimum of 1/4 in or 6 mm).

15 Ensure that a small clearance is present between the fast idle cams and screws, when the choke control is fully home.

16 Refit the air cleaners.

22 Float chamber, SU type HS4 carburettor – dismantling examination, adjustment and reassembly

Dismantling
1   Disconnect the inlet pipe.
2   Remove the three screws, and lift off the float chamber cover.
3   If the float only is to be removed, insert a thin piece of bent wire under it, and lift it out.
4   To remove the float chamber, disconnect the feed tube union in the base, and withdraw fixing bolt (26) (Fig. 3.10). Note carefully all grommets and washers.

Examination
5   Check the float for cracks or leaks. Shake it to see if any fuel has leaked into it Renew if defective.
6   Remove hinge pin (28), and examine the tip of the needle, and the

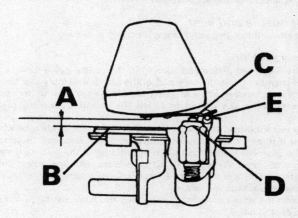

Fig 3.14 Float level setting (Sec 22)

A   1/8 in (3.18 mm) diameter bar
B   Machined lip
C   Lever resetting point
D   Needle valve assembly
E   Hinge pin

needle seating (32). If any ridge is present, screw out the seating, and fit a complete new needle and seat assembly.

Adjustment and reassembly

7   To reassembly, reverse the dismantling procedure. However, adjust the fuel level setting before refitting the float chamber cover.

8   To adjust the fuel level, invert the cover so that the needle valve is closed. With the float needle fully on the seating, the face of the float lever should just rest on a 1/8 in (3.18 mm) diameter bar placed under the lever and across the machined lip, parallel to the float hinge pin. Reset if necessary by bending the float lever at the resetting point (see Fig. 3.14).

---

23   Carburettor, SU type HS4 (emission control equipped vehicles) – basic tuning, dismantling examination, reassembly, and complete tuning

---

1   The carburettors fitted to vehicles equipped with emission control systems are in most respects the same as the basic instrument. However, they are carefully balanced to give the best possible performance with the maximum pollution control.

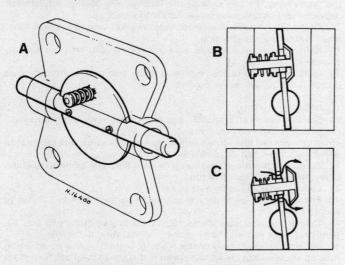

Fig 3.15 SU emission control carburettors – overrun valve in throttle disc (Sec 23)

2   Under no circumstances should parts be interchanged.

3   Certain constructional details differ from those found on the basic instrument. These will be mentioned in the text which follows, at the appropriate point.

Basic tuning

4   All tuning must be carried out with the emission control system connected and operative.

5   Employ a tachometer.

6   Warm the engine at fast idling speed. When the radiator header tank becomes suddenly warm, run the engine for at least a further five minutes. Reset the speed to 2500 rpm and run for one minute.

7   Tune, ensuring that the work is completed within three minutes. If not, clear the engine by running at 2500 rpm for one minute. Continue this procedure until tuning is complete.

8   In no case may the jet adjustment restrictors be removed or repositioned. If satisfactory tuning is not obtainable within the limits provided, the carburetor(s) must be serviced.

9   Top up the piston damper to ½ in (12.7 mm) above the top of the hollow piston rod. (On dust-proofed carburettors with no vent in the cap, ½ in below the top of the piston rod).

10   Remove the air cleaners.

11   Loosen the clamp bolts on the throttle interconnection, and those on the jet control interconnection shaft.

12   Set the throttle screws to give the correct idling speed (see Specification) on the tachometer.

13   Balance the carburettors by adjusting the throttle adjusting screws. Use a balance meter, and finish with the idling speed at the figure given in the Specifications.

14   Assuming the result is satisfactory, proceed as instructed in paragraphs 22 to 24.

15   If the balance is unsatisfactory examine the intake system, such as servos and emission control items, for leaks. If the fault persists, service the carburettor.

16   If balance is acceptable, but idling poor, proceed as instructed in the following paragraphs.

17   Adjust the jet adjusting nut within the limits of the restrictors, on both carburettors, to obtain maximum rpm consistent with smooth running.

18   Adjust the idling speed if necessary, by tuning both throttle adjusting screws by equal amounts. If satisfactory results cannot be obtained, service the carburettors.

19   Set the throttle interconnection clamping levers (Fig. 3.17). Tighten the clamp bolt.

20   Hold both jet levers in their lowest position. Tighten the jet interconnection lever clamp bolts.

21   Check the balance at 1500 rpm.

22   Ensure that there is about 1/16 (1.6 mm) free movement of the choke control wire before it starts to pull on the jet levers.

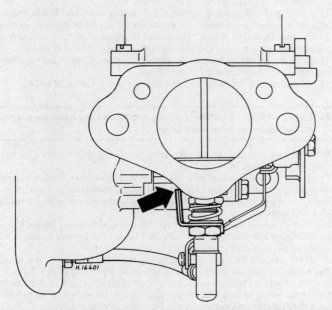

Fig 3.16 SU emission control carburettors – jet adjustment restricted (arrowed) (Sec 23)

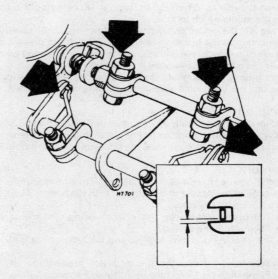

Fig 3.17 SU carburettors – throttle clearance. Arrows indicate pinch-bolts and 0.012 in (0.31 mm) clearance (Sec 23)

home. Screw it back until the arrow on the tool points to the inlet flange. Keep both tool and carburettor in this position during centering.

34   Keep the piston at the bottom of its travel, and the jet hard up against the bearing. Tighten the locknut.

35   During and after tightening, check for binding of the jet in the bearing. If this occurs, release the jet locknut and start again.

36   Remove the loading tool.

37   Take out both the feed tube and the jet. Refit, this time with the spring, the restrictor, and jet adjusting nut at the jet end, and with the gland and washer on the flexible tube. Do not over-tighten the sleeve nut.

38   Some carburettors have the needle held in a spring-loaded mounting in the piston, biased to one side. These needles are supplied with shouldered spring seats. The raised pip form in the needle guide ensures that the needle is correctly centralised.

39   The needle, spring and guide should be assembled in the piston so that the lower edge of the guide is flush with the face of the piston. Where the guide has a line etched on the face, this must be between the two piston transfer holes. Where the guide has a flat on it, position it so that the locking screw tightens down onto it. If the guide is incorrectly positioned the screw will protrude.

40   No jet centering is necessary with the spring-loaded needle. Refit the jet bearing, fit and tighten the locknut, the spring, adjustment restrictor and jet adjusting screw. Screw this right up.

41   Fit the jet. Refit the sleeve nut, washer and gland to the feed tube, and fit without overtightening.

42   Refit the piston assembly, and the spring, and refit the suction chamber and screws.

43   Reassemble the remaining items in reverse order, and tune (see complete tuning procedure below).

Complete tuning

44   Slacken the throttle spindle and jet control interconnections, and remove the mixture control wire.

45   Screw the fast idle screws well away from the cams, and the throttle adjusting screws just clear of their stops.

46   Screw the throttle screws in again until they just begin to operate. Screw them in a further half turn.

47   Leave the jet adjusting nuts as set.

48   Ensure that the conditions described in paragraphs 4 to 7, 9, 10, 12 and 13 apply.

49   During the next operations, described in paragraphs 50 and 53, gently tap each suction chamber neck before taking the readings.

50   Obtain the fastest tachometer reading, by turning the jet adjusting nuts up equally until the engine speed just starts to drop off. Turn them back one flat.

51   Recheck the idle speed (see Specification) and reset if necessary.

52   Recheck the balance.

53   Check the CO reading on an exhaust gas analyser. Reset the jet adjusting nuts if necessary, by equal amounts, to bring the reading within the specified limits. Note that if more than this amount of adjustment is necessary, the test equipment should be checked.

54   Hold the jet adjusting nut. Move the adjustment restrictor tag. Paint the small tag and adjacent flat on the nut.

55   Complete the procedure as described in paragraphs 19 to 24.

---

24   Carburettor, SU type HIF (vehicles not fitted with emission control equipment) – general description

---

1   The basic principle of operation is as described for the HS4 instrument in Section 17.

2   There is no separate, side-mounted float chamber. This is instead integral with the main body, giving the carburettor base a fatter shape. The central position limits fuel level changes during cornering, braking and acceleration.

3   The jet is held by a bi-metallic spring arm which varies the jet height according to temperature. The arm, and hence the jet and mixture, are adjusted by a screw in the side of the body.

4   Rich mixture for cold starting is supplied by a separate jet, which has a progressive control to give progressive enrichment (Fig. 3.20).

5   An emulsion bypass passage allows unevaporated fuel drops to be drawn along at small throttle openings and mixed more completely with the faster travelling air.

6   An overrun valve in the throttle disc, and a spring biased jet needle, are provided.

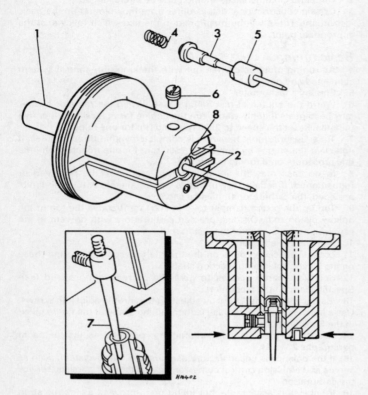

Fig 3.18 SU carburettors – swinging needle arrangement (Sec 23)

1	Piston rod	5	Needle guide
2	Transfer holes	6	Needle locking screw
3	Jet needle	7	Needle biased in jet
4	Needle spring	8	Etch mark

23   Pull the choke control out until the jets are about to move, and with the balance meter in position, set the fast idle screws to give the correct fast idle speed.

24   Refit the air cleaners.

Dismantling

25   Proceed broadly as described in Section 18, paragraphs 6 to 13. Note also the points which follow.

26   The tag on the jet adjustment restrictor (Fig. 3.16) should be unbent. Ensure that the breaking of any seals which are present does not contravene any local regulations, and that test equipment such as an exhaust gas analyser is available if necessary.

27   On instruments with a spring-loaded jet needle, remove the locking screw and pull out the needle assembly with the guide and spring.

Examination

28   Examine all parts, basically as described in Sections 19 and 22. Use no abrasives when attempting to rectify piston sticking, but renew the piston and chamber if thorough cleaning does not rectify the trouble.

Reassembly

29   Refit the needle (fixed needle type) to the piston assembly, with the lower edge of the needle shoulder level with the bottom face of the piston rod. Lock with the screw.

30   Refit the piston assembly, the piston spring and the suction chamber. Secure with the screws.

31   Refit the jet bearing, a new washer, and the locknut. Leave the nut loose.

32   Centralise the jet, using the special piston loading tool, by first loosely refitting the nylon feed tube in the float chamber.

33   Feed the jet into the jet bearing and, with the carburettor resting on the inlet flange, insert the tool into the damper tube and screw it fully

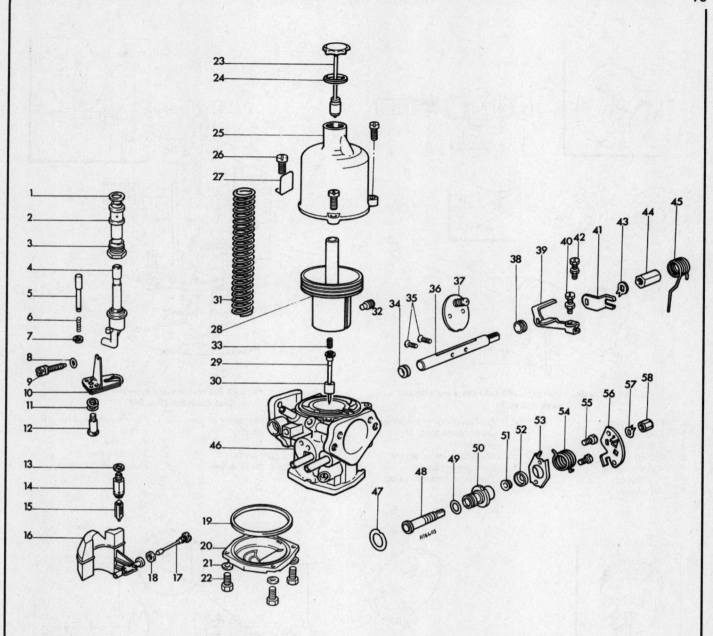

Fig 3.19 SU carburettor type HIF – exploded view (Sec 24)

1	Jet bearing washer	15	Float needle	30	Needle guide	44	Retaining nut
2	Jet bearing	16	Float	31	Piston spring	45	Throttle spring
3	Jet bearing nut	17	Float pivot	32	Needle retaining screw	46	Body
4	Jet assembly	18	Pivot seal	33	Needle spring	47	Cold start seal
5	Lifting pin	19	Float chamber cover seal	34	Throttle spindle seal	48	Cold start spindle
6	Lifting pin spring	20	Float chamber cover	35	Throttle disc screws	49	O-ring
7	Circlip	21	Spring washer	36	Throttle spindle	50	Cold start body
8	Adjusting screw seal	22	Cover screw	37	Throttle disc	51	Spindle seal
9	Jet adjusting screw	23	Piston damper	38	Throttle spindle seal	52	End cover
10	Bi-metallic jet lever	24	Damper washer	39	Throttle actuating lever	53	Retaining plate
11	Jet spring	25	Suction chamber	40	Fast idle screw and nut	54	Cold start spring
12	Jet retaining screw	26	Chamber screw	41	Throttle lever	55	Retaining screw
13	Needle seat washer (if required)	27	Identity tag	42	Throttle adjusting screw and nut	56	Fast idle cam
14	Float needle	28	Piston	43	Tab washer	57	Tab washer
		29	Jet needle			58	Retaining nut

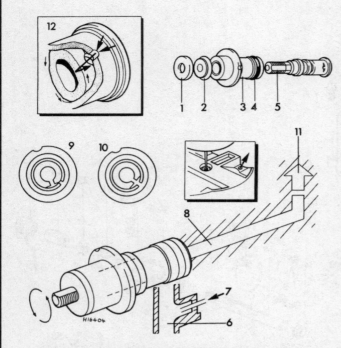

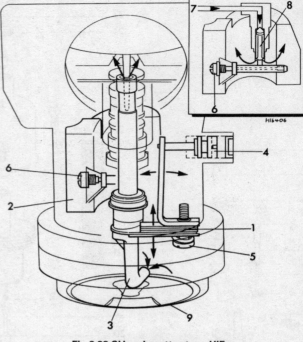

Fig 3.20 SU carburettor type HIF cold start enrichment device (Sec 24)

1	End seal cover	8	Fuel delivery to jet bridge
2	End seal	9	Commencement of
3	Starter valve body		enrichment
4	O-ring	10	Maximum enrichment
5	Valve spindle	11	Enrichment outlet
6	Fuel supply	12	Fuel flow through valve
7	Air bleed		

Fig 3.22 SU carburettor type HIF – float chamber (Sec 24)

1	The bi-metallic assembly	6	Float chamber fulcrum
2	Concentric float		screw
3	Jet head	7	Fuel inlet
4	Jet adjuster screw	8	Needle valve
5	Bi-metallic pivot screw	9	Bottom cover plate

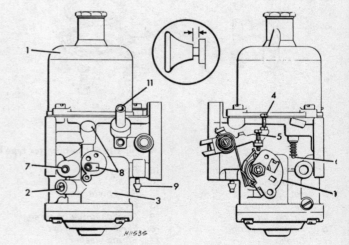

Fig 3.21 SU carburettor type HIF – bypass idle system (Sec 24)

| 1 | Fuel outlet at throttle | 3 | Jet bridge |
| 2 | Cold start enrichment outlet | 4 | Slot in position |

Fig 3.23 SU carburettor type HIF – adjustment and connection details (Sec 24)

1	Piston/suction chamber	8	Vent tube (alternative
2	Jet adjusting screw		positions)
3	Float chamber	9	Auto ignition connection
4	Throttle adjusting screw	10	Cold start enrichment lever
5	Fast idle adjusting screw		(cam lever)
6	Piston lifting pin	11	Crankcase ventilation
7	Fuel inlet		tube

25 Carburettor SU type HIF (vehicles not fitted with emission control equipment) – removal, dismantling, reassembling and refitting

Removal
1 Proceed largely as described in Section 18, paragraphs 1 to 5.

Dismantling
2 Remove the damper cap, and remove the piston damper. Discard the sealing washer.
3 Remove the suction chamber screws and identity tag. Hold the unit upright, and remove the chamber, spring and piston. Ensure that the chambers are marked, so that they are refitted to the correct bodies.
4 If both carburettors are being dismantled, ensure that the components are kept separate for refitting purposes.
5 Remove and discard the needle retaining screw. Withdraw the jet needle, needle guide and needle spring. Separate these components, taking care not to stretch the spring.
6 Remove the circlip and spring from the lifting pin, and remove the pin. Discard the circlip.
7 Remove the float chamber cover screws, washers, and cover. Discard the cover seal.
8 Remove the jet retaining screw and spring. Withdraw the jet assembly and bi-metallic jet lever together. Separate the jet assembly and lever taking care not to damage the plastic moulding at base of the jet assembly.
9 Remove the float pivot, and discard the seal. Remove the float and invert the body, when the float needle will drop out.
10 Remove the jet adjusting screw, remove and discard the seal.
11 Remove the float needle seat, using a spanner.
12 Remove the jet bearing nut and the bearing. Discard the bearing washer.
13 Remove and discard the throttle disc screws. Open the throttle and pull the disc from the slot in the spindle. Remove burrs from the screw holes with a fine file to prevent damage to the PTFE bushes, and withdraw the spindle. Discard the spindle seals.
14 Remove the throttle spring. Bend back the tab washer, remove the nut and washer, the throttle lever, throttle actuating lever, throttle adjusting screw and nut, and fast idle screw and nut.
15 Bend back the tabs of the tab washer. Remove the washer, nut, fast idle cam, cold start spring, end cover and spindle seal. Discard the seal. Remove the screws and retaining plate.
16 Remove the cold start body complete with the cold start spindle. Remove and discard the O-ring and cold start seal.
17 Do not remove the piston key (fitted to the periphery of piston bore at top of the casting) or the throttle spindle bushes unless these parts require renewal. Do not remove any brass orifices, plugs or stub pipes.

Reassembly
18 Clean and dry all parts.
19 Fit a new O-ring to the cold start body. Insert the cold start spindle into the body and fit a new seal over the threaded end of spindle, with the thin, soft flange inwards. Press the seal up to the body.
20 Fit a new cold start seal to the body assembly, and insert it into the carburettor body, with the cut-out on the flange registering with the uppermost carburettor body screw hole.
21 Fit the retaining plate (large flange outward and facing carburettor outlet flange) and the retaining screws. Fit the end cover, cold start spring (with straight tail engaged in the slot in the upper flange of the retaining plate), fast idle cam, tab washer and nut. Tighten the nut and bend over the tab washer.
22 Fit the throttle adjusting screw and nut and fast idle screw and nut to the throttle actuating lever. Do not lock. Fit the throttle actuating lever and throttle lever to the throttle spindle, with the countersunk ends of the screwholes in the spindle facing away from the levers. Fit the tab washer and nut, and bend over the tab.
23 Fit the seal to the throttle spindle (thin, soft flange toward centre), and fit the spindle to the body. Fit the seal to the exposed end of the spindle and press up into the recess. Fit the actuating lever, the throttle lever, the tab washer and retaining nut. Lock up the tab.
24 Fit the throttle spring, resting the straight tail against the underside of the throttle lever. Pre-load the spring by rotating it one turn clockwise and engaging the hook in the slot in the lever. Engage the straight tail with the outer slot in the lower flange of the retaining plate.

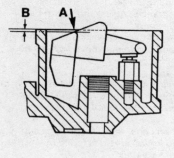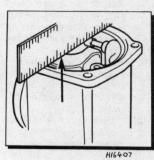

HI6407

Fig 3.24 SU carburettor type HIF – float setting (Sec 24)
A Measuring point on the float
B 0.04 in ± 0.02 in (1.0 mm ± 0.5 mm)

25 Open the throttle against the spring load, and slide the throttle disc into the slot in the spindle. The disc must be fitted with the head of the overrun valve towards the engine flange, ie above the spindle when the valve is closed. Close the throttle to centre the plate in the bore. Check that the cut-out at the bottom of the disc registers. Fit new throttle disc screws. Adjust the disc until accurately centred, and tighten the screws. Spread the ends just sufficiently to prevent unscrewing.
26 Fit a new washer to the jet bearing. Fit the bearing to the carburettor body with the jet bearing nut. Tighten the nut.
27 Fit the float needle seat using a spanner. Do not overtighten.
28 Fit a new seal to the jet adjusting screw, and screw into the body until the end is flush with the inside wall of the float chamber.
29 Fit the float needle into the needle seat. Fit a new pivot seal to the float, position the float, and secure it with the pivot.
30 Invert the carburettor and check that the point indicated on the float (Fig. 3.24) is 0.04 in (±0.02 in)/1.0 mm (±0.5 mm) below the face of the float chamber. Bend the brass tab if necessary to adjust
31 Assemble the jet assembly and lever. Insert the assembly into the jet bearing and secure the bi-metallic lever to the body with the spring and screw.
32 Fit the float chamber cover with a new seal. Secure with the screws and new spring washers, tightening evenly in a diagonal sequence.
33 Fit the needle spring to the needle, and assemble it to the needle guide. The pip on the needle guide must be in contact with the flange on the jet needle, and the scribed line on the lower face of the guide must be parallel with, and between the milled channels at the bottom of the piston. Fit the assembly to the piston with a new needle locking screw.
34 Fit the piston to the carburettor body. Fit the piston spring, suction chamber, identity tag and screws. Fit a new damper washer to the cap, and screw in the damper.

Refitting
35 To refit, reverse the removal sequence. Fit new gaskets wherever these are used, and adjust the carburettor settings.

26 Carburettor, SU type HIF (vehicles not fitted with emission control equipment) – inspection and fault rectification

1 Inspect the float needle seat and needle for damage or wear. Renew if necessary.
2 Renew any seals showing signs of deterioration. Renew the float chamber cover seal.
3 Check the body casting for damage.
4 Examine the piston and suction chamber for signs of abrasion.
5 Check the throttle spindle and bearings, and renew as necessary.
6 Clean the suction chamber and piston rod guide with fuel or methylated spirit.
7 Check for security of all the brass connections, and the piston key.

8   If the carburettor is malfunctioning, but all the foregoing points are in order, proceed to the following timing check:

(a) *Temporarily plug the piston transfer holes, and fit it to the suction chamber without the spring.*

(b) *Secure a large washer to one of the suction chamber fixing holes using a small screw and nut so that it overlaps the bore of the chamber.*

(c) *Refit the damper and washer.*

(d) *Ensure that the piston is fully down, and invert the assembly to allow the chamber to fall until the piston strikes the washer*

(e) *Check the time taken for the chamber to fall the full piston travel*

(f) *If the time is outside 4 to 6 seconds, check for damage and cleanliness, and retest. If no improvement is found renew the suction chamber and piston assembly.*

27 Carburettor, SU type HIF (vehicles not fitted with emission control equipment) – slow running adjustment and synchronisation

1   Tuning procedure is largely as described in Section 21, but with reference being made to Fig. 3.19. Certain differences in procedure do, however, exist

2   When setting the mixture, the side screw is used, operating the jet via the bi-metallic spring. However, before removing any seat on the side screw, ensure that no regulation is being broken.

3   After dismantling, screw the jet up as far as it will go, and then turn the screw clockwise. Note when the jet starts to move down, and thereafter screw down two further turns.

4   To weaken the mixture turn the screw out (anti-clockwise). As the screw is coupled through the spring there may be some lag in the movement of the jet Tap the carburettor body to encourage it to find its new position. Move the screw in and out by small amounts, until the optimum position is determined.

5   Reset the engine idling if necessary, moving each throttle adjusting screw by the same amount.

6   Very accurate setting can be achieved using an exhaust gas analyser, and this may be essential to meet local regulations.

28 Carburettor, SU type HIF (emission control equipped vehicles) – tuning, dismantling, inspection and reassembly

Tuning

1   Proceed as in Section 21, paragraph 1.

2   Check for smooth throttle action, and back off the adjusting screws until just clear of the levers. Turn them clockwise again by two full turns.

3   Use the lifting pin to raise each piston. If it does not fall freely, service the carburettors.

4   Lift the piston, and turn the jet adjusting screw anti-clockwise until the jet is flush with the bridge (or as high as possible if it will not reach the bridge). Both jets must be in the same positions.

5   Ensure that the needle guides are flush with the bottom of the piston groove.

6   Turn the jet adjusting screws clockwise by two turns. Refit the suction chamber.

7   Continue as in Section 23 paragraphs 4 to 7.

8   Slacken the throttle spindle and jet control spindle interconnections.

9   Employ a balance meter, and balance the carburettors by altering the throttle adjustment screws to obtain correct idle speed and balance.

10   Proceed as described in Section 23, paragraphs 49 to 53.

11   Proceed as described in Section 23, paragraphs 19 to 24.

Dismantling

12   Proceed as described in Section 25.

Inspection

13   Proceed as described in Section 26.

Reassembly

14   Proceed as described in Section 25.

29 Carburettor, Zenith type 175 CD 5T – maintenance

Damper oil level – checking and topping up

1   Unscrew the cap, raise it, and lower again until resistance is felt. This should be when a 1/4 in (6 mm) gap remains at A in Fig. 3.26.

2   To top up, remove the three bolts securing the air cleaner to the carburettor. Release the air temperature control valve from the hose, and lift the assembly away.

3   Take out the damper cap. Raise the piston, release the damper retaining cap. and remove the damper assembly.

4   Keep the piston raised. Top up the piston rod with engine oil until 1/4 in (6 mm) below the top of the rod. Refit the damper, retaining cap, and damper cap. Refit the air cleaner.

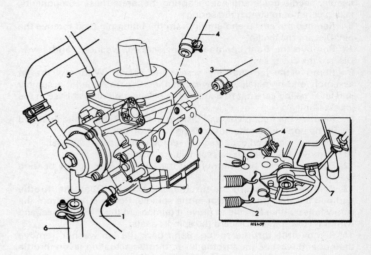

Fig 3.25 Zenith carburettor type 175 CD 5T – installation details (Sec 29)

1 Fuel feed hose	5 EGR valve pipe
2 Throttle return spring	6 Water hose
3 Absorption canister pipe	7 Throttle quadrant
4 Crankcase breather pipe	

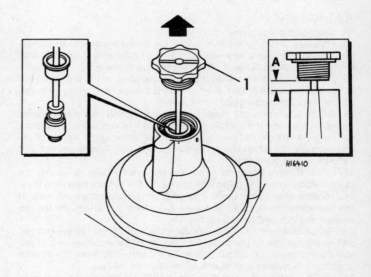

Fig 3.26 Zenith carburettor details (Sec 29)

1   Damper cap   A ¼ in (6 mm) resistance point

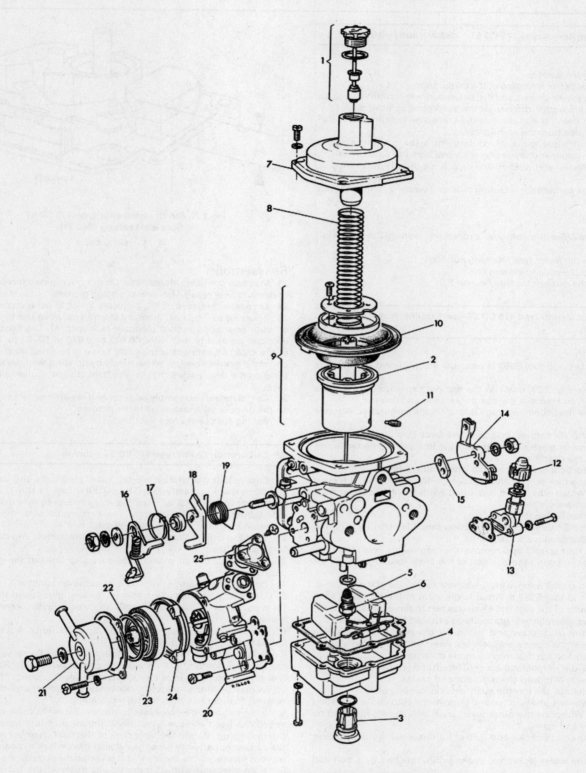

Fig 3.27 Zenith carburettor type 175 CD 5T – exploded view (Sec 29)

1 Damper assembly	8 Spring	15 Locating plate	21 Water jacket
2 Air valve piston	9 Air valve unit	16 Automatic choke operating	22 Sealing rim
3 Float chamber plug	10 Diaphragm	lever unit	23 Heat mass
4 Float chamber	11 Air valve grub screw	17 Outer spring	24 Insulator
5 Float	12 Idle air regulator cover	18 Inner operating lever	25 Vacuum kick piston
6 Needle valve	13 Idle air regulator	19 Inner spring	cover
7 Top cover	14 Throttle quadrant	20 Automatic choke	

30 Carburettor, Zenith type 175 CD 5T – removal and refitting

Removal

1   Disconnect the battery.
2   Remove the petrol feed pipe at the carburettor.
3   Disconnect the air cleaner, and the air temperature control valve unit.
4   From the carburettor, disconnect the absorption canister pipe.
5   Undo the hose clip and remove the crankcase breather pipe. Pull the EGR valve pipe from the carburettor.
6   Drain about three pints of coolant from the cooling system. Disconnect the upper and lower coolant pipes from the auto choke.
7   Unscrew the nut and washer, and detach the throttle quadrant (Fig. 3.27 item 14).
8   Remove the carburettor retaining nuts and washers, and withdraw the instrument.

Refitting

9   To refit, reverse the removal procedure, noting the following points.
   (a) Locate the lower rear retaining nut first
   (b) Top up the cooling system
   (c) Tune the carburettor (see Section 32)

31 Carburettor, Zenith type 175 CD 5T– dismantling, inspection and reassembly

Dismantling

1   Note that Leyland tool S353 is essential if complete dismantling is undertaken.
2   Referring to Fig. 3.27, unscrew the damper cap, carefully raise the air valve piston and remove the damper retainer and damper.
3   Pull out the float chamber plug (3) to drain the carburettor. Remove the O-ring.
4   Remove the six screws, and then the float chamber and gasket. Note that the metal plate which supports the floats is positioned facing the outside of the chamber.
5   Remove the float chamber needle valve and washer.
6   Unscrew the four screws and remove the top cover from the main body, noting which way round it is fitted (with the offset cover neck casting facing the air intake).
7   Withdraw the spring (8).
8   Remove the air valve assembly, noting how the outer location tag and air valve diaphragm are positioned.
9   Undo the four screws and remove the diaphragm, retaining ring. and nylon spacer, noting the position of the inner locating tag and air valve diaphragm.
10 Loosen but *do not remove* the grubscrew in the side of the air valve.
11 With Leyland tool S353 inserted in the stem of the air valve, twist the centre spindle of the tool anti-clockwise two to three turns, when the needle housing assembly will gradually be exposed from the air valve.
12 Remove the grubscrew and withdraw the needle and housing assembly. **Note:** *the needle adjuster is a fixed unit within the stem of the air valve and no attempt may be made to remove it.*
13 Unclip the idle air regulator cover (if fitted) and remove the regulator retaining screws. Withdraw the regulator and gasket.
14 Remove the nut, the throttle quadrant and locating plate.
15 Unscrew the nut and washer, and remove the auto choke operating lever spacer. Withdraw the outer lever, bush and spring, followed by the inner lever and spring.
16 Remove the auto choke and gasket by unscrewing the retaining screws.
17 Remove the water jacket and sealing ring. retained by a bolt and washer.
18 Remove the heat mass and insulator by unscrewing the three screws and washers.
19 Remove the vacuum kick piston cover and gasket

Inspection

20 Clean and dry all parts.
21 Examine the parts for damage, general wear, and hairline cracks. Check in particular the air valve diaphragm and float chamber needle. Renew any defective parts.
22 A defective auto choke should be renewed as a unit. Overhauling is not recommended.

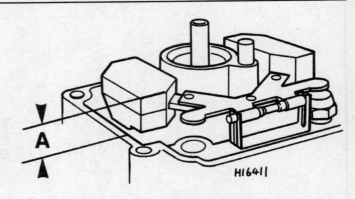

Fig 3.28 Zenith carburettor type 175 CD 5T – float level setting (Sec 31)

A   Checking point

Reassembly

23 Maintain complete cleanliness. Do not overtighten threaded parts, or damage may result. Use new seals and gaskets.
24 To reassemble, reverse the sequence given in paragraphs 5 to 19.
25 Referring to Fig. 3.28, measure the gap between the highest point on each float and the float chamber face (gap A). The floats must be adjusted parallel to and within 0.625 to 0.672 in (15.87 to 17.07 mm) of the face. Adjustment is made by using a selected washer located under the needle valve, or alternatively by bending the float tabs. When bending the tabs, ensure that they remain at right angles to the needle valve.
26 Complete the reassembly as described in paragraphs 1 to 4. topping up the damper with engine oil in the process.
27 Set the auto choke (see Section 33).

32 Carburettor, Zenith type 175 CD 5T – tuning

1   Ensure that the ignition timing, spark plug gaps and valve rocker clearances are correctly set. The oil filler cap in the rocker cover must have a good seal as must the rocker cover to cylinder head, the side tappet covers and dipstick. The carburettor inlet manifold and carburettor spindle seals must be efficient.
2   Start the engine, warm up to normal temperature, and drive the car for five minutes.
3   Disconnect the air manifold-to-air pump hose at the pump, and plug it.
4   Pull the float chamber vent pipe from the carburettor.
5   Using an accurate tachometer, increase engine speed to 2500 rpm for a period of 30 seconds. Repeat at three minute intervals during tuning.
6   Check the idle speed against the Specifications. Adjust the idle speed screw, Fig. 3.29, if necessary.
7   Adjust the idle mixture by turning the fine idle screw to obtain the fastest smooth idle. If an exhaust gas analyser is available, check that the CO percentage at idle speed is to specifications. The fine idle screw may be further adjusted, clockwise to enrich or anti-clockwise to weaken, in order to obtain the correct reading.
8   If an exhaust gas analyser is not available, but the correct idle speed has been achieved, reconnect the air manifold hose to the air pump (unplug it), refit the vent pipe to the float chamber and then at the earliest opportunity have the exhaust gas emission reading checked by your local agent to ensure that it is within the regulations.
9   If on checking with an exhaust gas analyser the CO percentage reading is unobtainable by adjustment of the idle screws, proceed as follows.
10 Turn the fine idle screw to the limit in a clockwise direction and then unscrew 2 1/2 turns. The screw is now centred in the adjustment range.
11 Remove the suction chamber and air valve unit from the carburettor. Check that the initial needle adjustment conforms to the Specifications.
12 To adjust the needle, obtain special tool S353 from an MGB agent. Withdraw the damper and insert the tool so that the outer tool (A in Fig. 3.30) is engaged with the air valve. Inner tool B locates in the hexagon recess in the needle adjuster plug.

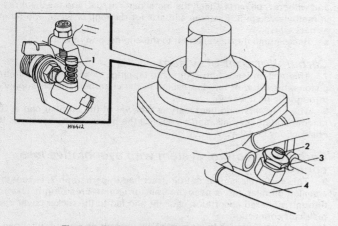

Fig 3.29 Zenith carburettor type 175 CD 5T – external detail (Sec 32)

1 *Idle speed screw*
2 *Fine idle screw*
3 *Coarse idle nut*
4 *Float chamber vent tube*

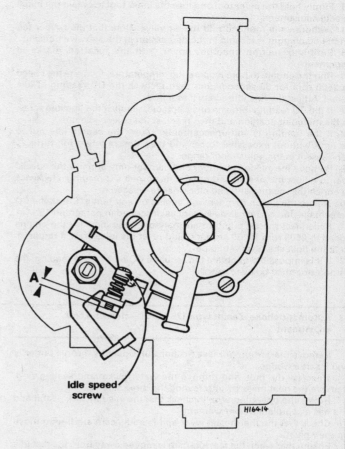

Fig 3.31 Zenith carburettor type 175 CD 5T – choke/throttle lever gap (Sec 33)
A = 3/32 in (2.40 mm)

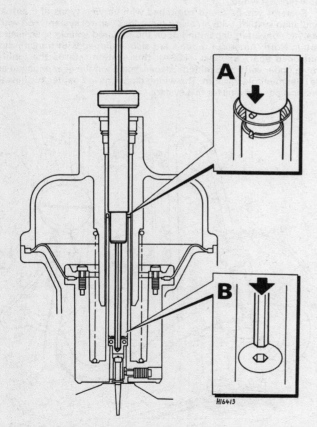

Fig 3.30 Zenith carburettor type 175 CD 5T – needle adjustment (Sec 32)

A Outer tool engagement pin, and air valve slot
B Inner tool, and needle adjustment point

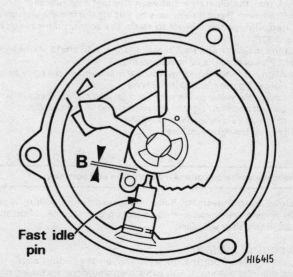

Fig 3.32 Autostart, Zenith carburettor type 175 CD 5T – fast idle pin-to-cam adjustment (Sec 33)
B = 0.025 in (0.63 mm)

13 Firmly hold the outer tool and turn the inner tool to obtain the initial needle adjustment.

14 Withdraw the tool and refit the air valve. Note that the rubber tag on the diaphragm is located in the depression in the air valve housing.

15 Refit the suction chamber cover with the location marks in alignment.

16 Run the engine to obtain operating temperature. Increase the speed to 2500 rpm for 30 seconds and then recheck the CO reading at idle speed. Adjust the fine idle screw if required.

17 If the CO reading remains unacceptable, readjust the fine idle screw to the midpoint position and then readjust the coarse idle nut.

18 If the reading is still unacceptable, screw the coarse idle nut to its limit without excessive force, and then unscrew two full turns to centralise it in the adjustment range.

19 Remove the suction chamber and damper unit. and use the special tool to adjust the needle and obtain the correct CO reading, clockwise to enrich the mixture and anti-clockwise to weaken it.

20 Top up the piston damper with engine oil and refit it. Check the CO percentage and correct as necessary as described in paragraph 19.

21 Reconnect the air pump to air manifold hose increase the engine speed to 2500 rpm for 30 seconds, and reset the idle screw if required. Refit the float chamber vent pipe.

22 If it is impossible to obtain the required CO percentage reading, the carburettor must be overhauled.

33 Automatic choke, Zenith type 175 CD 5T – checking and adjustment

1 Remove the carburettor (see Section 30). Open the throttle butterfly and insert a wedge.

2 Unscrew the bolt, and remove the water jacket and scaling ring. Remove the heat mass by unscrewing the three screws.

3 Rotate the operating arm, to check that the vacuum kick piston and rod has a complete free movement.

4 Check that the thermostat lever and fast idle cam are free to move on their pivot.

5 Ensure that when the fast idle cam is moved away from the fast idle lever, it returns under spring tension to the lever. Check also that when the fast idle lever is rotated, the cam remains in contact with it.

6 Withdraw the wedge from the throttle butterfly.

7 Check the gap between the choke and throttle lever. Adjust if necessary (see Fig. 3.31) using the idle speed screw.

8 Check that the clearance between the fast idle pin and cam is 0.025 in (0.63 mm). Reset if necessary by turning the throttle stop screw as required. Tighten the locknut to retain the screw, and recheck the gap (Fig. 3.32).

9 Refit the insulator and heat mass. and the auto choke water jacket assembly. Please note the following points:

　(a) *Align the index marks on the heat mass and choke body before tightening the clamp plate screws*

　(b) *Locate the water jacket with the inlet and outlet pipes in the correct position. Tighten the central bolt to the specified torque. Use a new seal and washer*

10 Refit the carburettor, and tune.

34 Crankcase emission control – description and servicing

1 Various control systems have been used for removing fumes from the engine crankcase, and for directing them to the combustion chambers where they are burnt.

Valve control system

2 Fumes are fed from the oil separator on the timing cover to a valve on the inlet manifold. The valve diaphragm varies the opening presented to the inlet manifold, depending upon the pressure or depression which acts upon it.

3 To test the system, run the engine at idling speed and remove the oil filler cap. If the engine speed rises noticeably, the control valve is functioning correctly.

4 To service the system, renew the oil filler cap at the recommended intervals.

5 Renew the valve assembly, or alternatively remove the spring clip and withdraw all parts. Clean the metal parts in fuel, and the diaphragm in methylated spirit. Examine all parts for damage or wear, and renew as necessary.

6 Reassemble the valve, refit it to the engine, and re-test.

Carburettor control system

7 This system leads fumes direct to tappings close to the carburettor pistons, by virtue of the depression in the chamber. The air supply is through the oil filler cap.

8 The only servicing necessary is renewal of the oil filler cap at the recommended intervals, and a check of the hoses and connections for obstructions and leaks.

Carburettor control system with evaporative loss control

9 This system is similar to that described in paragraph 7, except that a sealed oil filler cap is used, and air for engine breathing is taken in through a filtered absorption canister and fed to the rocker cover via a restrictor connection.

10 Servicing is limited to renewal of the absorption canister filter pad at the recommended intervals, and checking of the hoses for obstructions and leaks.

35 Exhaust emission control (EEC) – general description

1 Exhaust emission control systems, where fitted, will vary in detail depending upon the age of the vehicle, and upon the requirements of the territories for which the vehicle is intended. Figs. 3.33 and 3.34 show typical layouts.

2 Systems will be found combined with varying types of crankcase ventilation system, with an evaporative loss control system, and with a catalytic converter, depending upon the required vehicle specification. Certain North American models are also equipped with transmission-controlled spark advance (TCSA): this system retards the ignition timing under certain conditions, depending upon the gear engaged and the inlet manifold vacuum. The wiring diagrams in Chapter 10 show the electrical connections for this system.

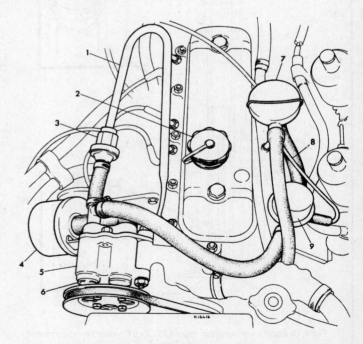

Fig 3.33 A typical earlier emission control system (Sec 35)

1	*Air manifold*	6	*Relief valve*
2	*Filtered oil filler cap*	7	*Crankcase emission valve*
3	*Check valve*	8	*Vacuum sensing tube*
4	*Air pump air cleaner*	9	*Gulp valve*
5	*Air pump*		

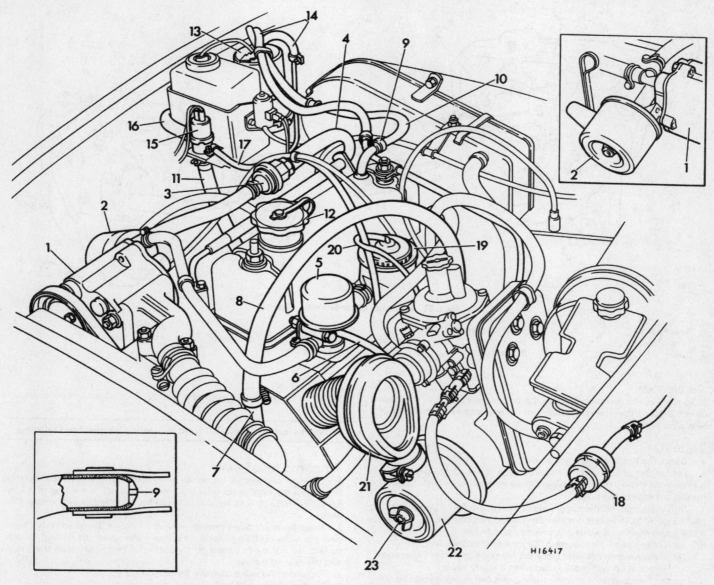

Fig 3.34 A later emission control system (Sec 35)

1 Air pump
2 Air pump air cleaner
3 Check valve
4 Air manifold
5 Gulp valve
6 Sensing pipe
7 Oil separator/flame trap

8 Breather pipe
9 Restricted connection
10 Purge line
11 Air vent pipe
12 Oil filler cap (sealed)
13 Absorption canister
14 Vapour lines

15 Running-on control valve
16 Running-on control hose
17 Running-on control pipe
18 Fuel line filter
19 Exhaust gas recirculation
     valve (EGR)

20 EGR valve hose
21 Air temperature control
     valve
22 Air cleaner case
23 Wing nut retaining air cleaner
     cover

3   The EEC blows air into the exhaust ports to bum off any hydrocarbons (unacceptable emissions in certain territories) which would otherwise be given off to atmosphere.
4   The air pump draws air through an air cleaner and delivers it to an air manifold along the cylinder head.
5   Drillings pass through the cylinder head to each exhaust port. A check valve in the delivery pipe to the manifold prevents blow back of high pressure exhaust to the pump, and in the event of failure of the pump stops exhaust gases passing that way.
6   When slowing down with the engine on overrun the air pump supplies air to the inlet manifold through a gulp valve.
7   The pump is a rotary vane type driven by a belt from the water pump pulley. The belt is tensioned by moving the pump away from the engine block.

8   The pump air cleaner has a renewable filter element, and a relief valve to allow excessive air pressure to be blown off to the atmosphere.

36 Air pump, exhaust emission control

Drivebelt tension

1   The belt should be tensioned to allow a total deflection of ½ in (13 mm), using hand pressure, at the centre of the belt run.
2   To adjust, loosen the main mounting bolt, and the bolts on the adjusting link. Use hand pressure to move the pump, until the correct tension is obtained. Tighten the bolts to the specified torque.

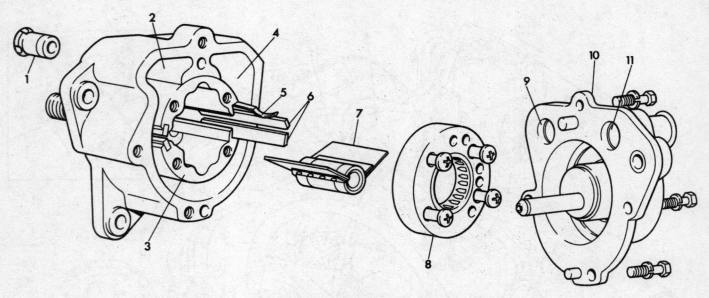

Fig 3.35 Air pump, exploded view (Sec 36)

1	Relief valve	4	Outer chamber	7	Vanes	10	Port-end cover
2	Inlet chamber	5	Springs	8	Rotor bearing – end plate	11	Inlet port
3	Rotor	6	Carbons	9	Outlet port		

Air cleaner

3   To remove the element, remove the nut and washer, and the casing cover. Discard the element, clean the casing, and reassemble with a new element.

Testing

4   Check the tension of the drivebelt.
5   Disconnect and plug the air supply hose at the gulp valve.
6   Remove the air manifold supply hose at the check valve. Connect a pressure gauge to the hose.
7   Run the engine at the specified engine rpm, when a gauge reading of 2.75 lbf/in² (0.19 kgf/cm²) minimum should be obtained.
8   If a low reading is achieved, proceed as follows:
   (a) *Clean the air cleaner, and fit a new element. Re-test*
   (b) *If the reading remains incorrect blank off the relief valve and retest. A correct reading indicates a faulty valve*
   (c) *An unacceptable reading means that the pump should be serviced*

Removal

9   Disconnect the air hoses from the pump. Remove the two nuts and washers, and remove the air pump air cleaner.
10   Loosen the pump bolts, and remove the drivebelt.
11   Remove the top adjusting link bolt and the mounting bolt. Remove the pump.

Dismantling and servicing

12   Remove the four port-end cover bolts and take off the cover.
13   Remove the four screws securing the rotor bearing endplate and remove it. Lift out the vanes and take the carbon strips and springs from the rotor.
14   Clean all parts, using lint-free cloth.
15   Repack the bearings with Andok 260, or equivalent.
16   Renew worn or damaged vanes.
17   Fit new carbons. The slots which carry the carbon and springs are the deeper ones. The carbons are fitted with the chamfered edge to the inside.

Reassembly

18   To reassemble, reverse the dismantling procedure. Smear a thread locking compound on the underside of the heads of the screws retaining the rotor bearing endplate.

Refitting

19   To refit, reverse the removal procedure. Adjust the belt tension.

---

37   Valves, exhaust emission control – testing, removal and refitting

Air pump relief valve

1   Connect a pressure gauge as described in Section 36, paragraph 6, and run the engine up until the valve blows off. A reading of 4.5 to 6.5 lbf/in² (0.32 to 0.45 kgf/cm²) should be obtained. If not, renew the valve.
2   If the blow-off point proves difficult to detect, place adhesive tape over the blow-off hole to form an orifice from which the flow of air can be felt. Do not try to detect air by putting a finger between the valve and the driving pulley.
3   To renew the valve, remove the air pump.
4   Remove four bolts and washers, and remove the drive pulley.
5   Using a ½ in (12.7 mm) diameter soft drift in the pump discharge connection, drift out the relief valve.
6   Enter the new valve complete with copper seating washer into the pump body, and employ the tool shown in Fig. 3.36 to drift the valve firmly home. Do not compress the washer.
7   Refit the pulley, and the pump.

Check valve

8   Disconnect the air supply pipe. Hold the air manifold connection to prevent twisting, and unscrew the check valve.
9   Blow through the valve by mouth, in each direction. Air should only pass through from the air supply hose side. Do not use compressed air.
10   If air passes in the wrong direction, renew the valve.
11   Refit carefully, to avoid twisting the inlet manifold.

Gulp valve

12   The gulp valve prevents sudden enrichment of the mixture following the closing of the throttle after running on full power.
13   Disconnect the air supply hose to the valve at the air pump, and connect a vacuum gauge with T connection to the hose.
14   Start the engine, and allow it to idle.
15   Place a finger on the T-piece open connection, and check that a zero gauge reading is shown for at least 15 seconds. Do not increase the engine speed above idling. Renew the valve if any vacuum is registered.

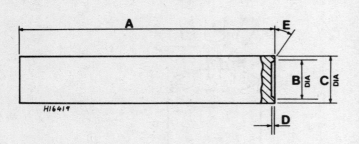

Fig 3.36 Refitting tool – air pump relief valve (Sec 37)

A = 5 in (127 mm)   D = 0.05 in (1.27 mm)
B = 0.986 in (25 mm)   E = 30°
C = 1.062 in (27 mm)

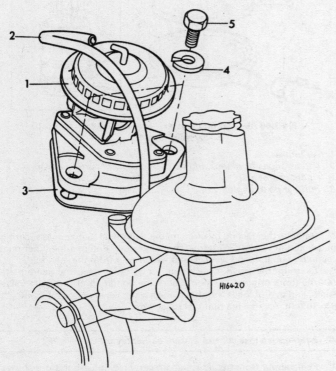

Fig 3.37 Exhaust gas recirculation (EGR) valve (Sec 37)

1 Valve   4 Spring washer
2 Vacuum hose   5 Bolt
3 Gasket

16 Open the throttle, allow the engine to speed up, and shut it sharply. As the engine speed falls the gauge should register a vacuum. Remove the finger from the end of the pipe to release the vacuum, and then repeat the test a number of times. If the gauge fails to register a vacuum, renew the valve.
17 To remove the valve, disconnect the hoses, take out the mounting screw(s) and remove the valve.
18 To refit the valve, reverse the removal procedure.

Inlet manifold depression limit valve
19 A small valve, fitted in the throttle disc, limits the manifold depression under overrun conditions.
20 To check, disconnect the gulp valve pipe from the inlet manifold, and connect a vacuum gauge to the manifold union.
21 Warm the engine at fast idle speed until normal operating temperature is reached.
22 Speed the engine up to 3000 rpm and release the throttle quickly,

when the vacuum gauge reading should immediately rise to a pressure of between 20.5 to 22 inches of Mercury (Hg).
23 If the vacuum reading is outside the given limits the limit valve is faulty, and a new disc with valve must be fitted. Re-tune the carburettors after fitting the new valve.

Exhaust gas recirculation valve (EGR)
24 The EGR valve is mounted on the engine inlet manifold, and controls the flow of exhaust gases to the manifold.
25 To service the valve, warm up the engine, and switch off.
26 Remove the vacuum hose.
27 Remove the gulp valve vacuum pipe and, using an extra length of pipe, connect it to the EGR valve.
28 Observe that, when the engine is started and the speed increased, the spindle rises, so opening the valve. Also that, when the vacuum pipe is removed, the spindle drops, closing the valve.
29 Stop the engine.
30 Reconnect the gulp valve vacuum pipe.
31 Remove the EGR valve retaining bolts, and then the valve.
32 Check that the valve is closed, and renew if defective.
33 Clean all surfaces and remove all deposits, ensuring that they do not fall into the manifold. Do not touch the valve disc, the seat, and the protruding valve spindle.
34 Refit the valve with a new gasket, and reconnect the vacuum hose.
35 Check for correct operation as described in paragraphs 24 to 30.

38 Air manifold and injectors, emission control system – testing and servicing

1 To test the airflow, disconnect the air manifold at the cylinder head connections, slacken the air supply hose at the check valve, and rotate the manifold until the pipes point upwards. Retighten the hose clip.
2 Run the engine at idle speed. Check:
   (a) That air comes equally from all the pipes
   (b) That exhaust gases blow from each of the injectors in the cylinder head vacated by the air pipes
3 Take care not to displace any cylinder head injectors which may be free.
4 If an injector is blocked, turn the engine to shut the relevant exhaust valve. Using a hand drill only, pass a 1/8 in (3.17 mm) twist drill into the injector bore, taking care not to touch the exhaust valve stem at the other end. Blow out the carbon.

39 Hot air duct, emission control system – removal and refitting

1 To remove the duct, loosen the air cleaner wing nut and pivot the cleaner and air temperature control assembly away.
2 Detach the hose from the duct.
3 Remove the nut and washer, and bolt and washer, retaining the outer duct. Remove the duct.
4 Remove the nut and washer retaining the inner duct. Remove the duct.
5 To refit, reverse the removal procedure.

40 Catalytic converter, exhaust emission control – removal and refitting

1 Certain models are fitted with this equipment, located between the exhaust manifold and the downpipe.
2 Raise and securely support the front of the vehicle.
3 Release the pipe from the converter, remove the pipe support bolt, and remove the pipe gasket.
4 Free the springs attached to the air casing, and remove the three bolts and casing.
5 Disconnect the hose from the air temperature control valve.
6 Detach the air cleaner case, and the heat shield screws and nut.
7 Release the water rail stud from the heat shield, and remove the shield by bringing it to the rear and turning anti-clockwise.
8 Remove the converter nuts, and the converter.
9 Fit a new converter by reversing the removal procedure.

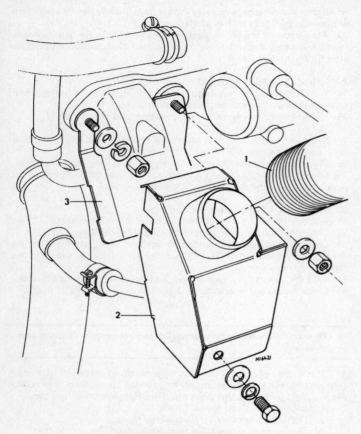

Fig 3.38 Hot air duct (Sec 39)

1   Hot air duct   3   Inner duct
2   Outer duct

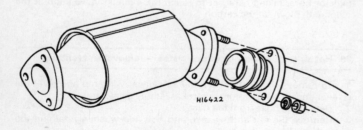

Fig 3.39 The catalytic converter (Sec 40)

10   Renew all gaskets when reassembling,
11   Service the EGR valve, and reset the warning indicator if fitted by zeroing the counter with the key.

41   Air temperature control valve, emission control system

1   Certain single carburettor models, equipped with exhaust emission control systems, are also fitted with this valve. It is of bi-metallic type, connected to the carburettor air cleaner intake, and controls the airflow temperature.
2   The intake air is dueled near the exhaust manifold. As the engine warms up, the valve opens to allow cooler air to blend with the hot air, thus maintaining a constant temperature supply.
3   To remove the valve and ducting, unscrew the air cleaner end cover wing nut. Remove the cover and valve by pivoting the assembly away from the engine.

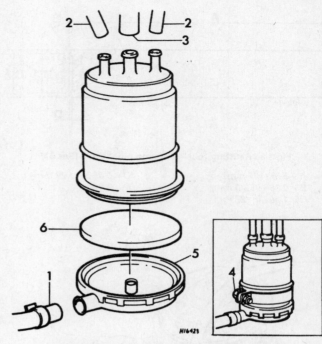

Fig 3.40 Absorption canister – evaporative loss control system (Sec 42)

1   Air intake   4   Clamp
2   Vapour pipes from tank and   5   Screwed bottom cover
     float chambers   6   Renewable filter pad
3   Purge pipe to engine

4   Remove the ducting by undoing the outer duct to manifold securing nut, bolt and washer. Withdraw the outer duct. Remove the inner duct retaining nut, bolt and washer, and withdraw it from the manifold.
5   Examine the valve. Check that, when depressed, the valve plate returns to its original position. Check the condition of the foam valve seats, and that of the hot air hose. Renew the valve or hose if faulty.
6   To refit, reverse the removal procedure.

42   Evaporative loss control system earlier layout

1   Fuel vapour from the tank, and on certain twin-carburettor vehicles from the float chambers, is stored in an absorption canister when the engine is not running. When the engine is running, all vapours are drawn directly to the crankcase emission control system.
2   An air-lock chamber in the fuel tank prevents it being completely filled with fuel. thus ensuring that fuel displaced by expansion due to high ambient temperatures can be accommodated.

Absorption canister

3   The canister contains charcoal granules contained between filter pads. Renew the pads on early canisters, and the complete canister on later versions.
4   To service the canister, disconnect the vent tube from the bottom, and the vapour and purge pipes from the top.
5   Take out the securing clip screw, and remove the canister.
6   To change the pad, unscrew the bottom cap, remove the pad, clean the cap, and reassemble with a new pad. Refit the connections.

Fuel line filter

7   A filter is fitted on some models, and should be renewed at the specified intervals.
8   To renew, ensure that the ignition is off, remove the filter and renew it.
9   Switch on the ignition, check for leaks, start the engine, and check, again.

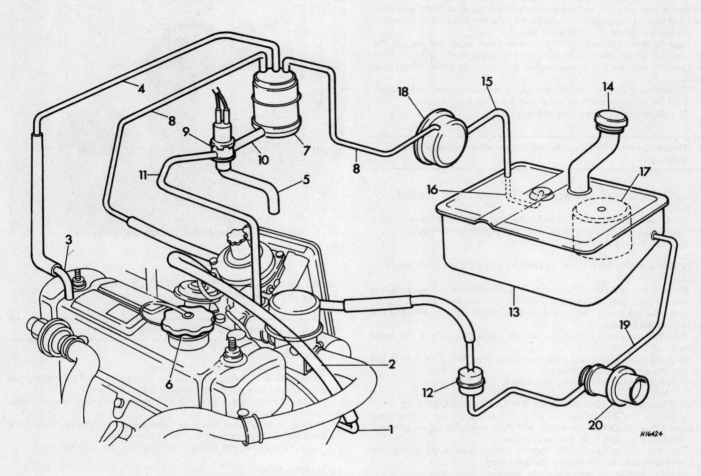

Fig 3.41 Evaporative loss control system – typical later layout (Sec 43)

1 Oil separator/flame trap	6 Sealed oil filler cap	11 Running-on control pipe	16 Vapour tube
2 Breather pipe	7 Charcoal absorption canister	12 Fuel line filter	17 Capacity limiting tank
3 Restrictor connection	8 Vapour lines	13 Fuel tank	18 Separation tank
4 Purge line	9 Running-on control valve	14 Sealed fuel filler cap	19 Fuel pipe
5 Air vent pipe	10 Running-on control hose	15 Vapour line	20 Fuel pump

Mixture temperature compensator

10   On certain vehicles this valve may be fitted between the air cleaner and carburettor depression chamber. The temperature-sensitive device allows a small quantity of air into the carburettor, bypassing the jet, when fuel is for any reason entering the carburettor at high temperatures.

Leak testing

11   If a running-on control valve is fitted, block its vent pipe with the engine idling, when the engine should stop. If it continues to run, an air leak exists.

12   To pressure-test the system, ensure that there is a minimum of one gallon of fuel present in the tank, and switch on the ignition until the fuel system is primed.

13   Switch the ignition off, remove the fuel tank ventilation pipe from the absorption canister connection, and connect the pipe to a 0 to 10 lbf/in² (0 to 0.7 kgf/cm²) pressure gauge, a Schrader valve, and a low-pressure air supply (a tyre pump will do).

14   Pressure to 1 lbf/in² (0.07 kgf/cm²) only, and check that no more than 0.5 lbf/in² (0.03 kgf/cm²) is lost over a period of 10 seconds.

15   In the event of leaks, check the fuel filler cap and seal, the tank. and all connections whilst still pressurised.

16   If a satisfactory reading is obtained and held, remove the tank cap and check that the gauge falls to zero. Remove the gauge, and remake the connections.

43 Evaporative loss control system, later type

1   Certain differences to the system will be found, depending upon the year of manufacture and upon the market for which the vehicle is intended.

Absorption canister, twin fitting

2   Where a twin fitting is found, renewal of the canisters is basically carried out as for the single fitting (Section 42, paragraphs 3 to 6).

Fuel line filter

3   Squeeze the clips on the feed and delivery hoses, and remove the hoses.

4   Remove the clamp screw, and remove and discard the filter.

5   Fit the new filter with the end marked IN downward. Secure the clamp, and refit the hoses.

44 Running-on control valve evaporative loss control system

1   Low octane fuel and the lean mixtures required to meet anti-pollution standards make the engine liable to run-on after switching off the ignition. This puts great stress on the engine. It will try to run backwards, and there may be blow back through the carburettor.

2   The anti-run-on valve cuts off fuel to the carburettor jet when the ignition is switched off, and the engine will quickly stop. The valve is on the right rear of the engine compartment near the absorption canister.
3   To test the valve, first check the fuse.
4   With ignition off, remove the control valve electrical lead at the oil pressure switch, and touch the lead to a good earth. The valve will be heard to operate if it is serviceable and if the electrical circuit is in order.
5   To remove the valve, remove the pipes, hoses and electrical leads.
6   Turn the valve through 45°, and remove it from the bracket.
7   To refit, reverse the removal procedure.

---

45   Throttle pedal, throttle cable and choke cable – removal and refitting

---

Throttle pedal, GHN5 and GHD5 cars from model No 41002

1   To remove, take out the split pin at the end of the pedal, and remove the cable. Take out the pedal pivot bolt, and withdraw the pedal.
2   To refit, reverse the removal procedure.

Throttle cable, GHN5 and GHD5 cars from model No 41002

3   Remove the cable from the throttle interconnection rod by removing the securing clip and taking out the clevis pin and washers.
4   Unscrew the lower nut on the throttle cable adjuster. Release the cable from the bracket.
5   Take the screw out to free the throttle cable clamp from the pedal bracket.
6   Take the split pin from the throttle pedal, free the cable, and pull it out into the engine compartment.
7   To refit, reverse the removal procedure.

Throttle cable, later models for USA and Canada

8   Unscrew the lower nut holding the cable to the carburettor abutment bracket. Detach the cable, and disconnect the return springs.
9   Remove the cable from the carburettor.
10 Take out the split pin in the throttle pedal, release the cable, and pull the cable out into the engine compartment
11 To refit, reverse the removal procedure.

Choke cable, later models for UK

12 Disconnect the cable return spring at the carburettor trunnion. Free the screw in the trunnion, releasing the cable.
13 Unscrew the nut on the carburettor control, behind the fascia. Pull the cable carefully out through the fascia and bulkhead.
14 To refit, reverse the removal procedure. Ensure that 1/16 in (1.5 mm) free movement exists at the cable.

46.2 The exhaust flange sealing rings

Choke cable, GHN4/5 and GHD4/5 cars

15 Refer to Chapter 10, Section 46.

---

46   Exhaust system – removal and refitting

Earlier types

1   A one-piece welded assembly is fitted.
2   To remove the exhaust, remove the nuts at the manifold and allow the pipe to drop away. Note the sealing rings (photo).
3   Loosen the rear mounting pipe bolt, remove the front support bolt, and withdraw the assembly.
4   To refit, reverse the removal procedure. Leave all fixings loose until the front fixings have been tightened at the manifold.
5   Tighten the remaining fixings, working from front to rear.

Later models

6   Disconnect the system from the manifold, catalytic converter, or exhaust front pipe, depending upon the system fitted.
7   In turn, remove the bolts from the front stay, the front mounting, and the rear mounting.
8   Withdraw the system. Note the sealing rings.
9   To refit, reverse the removal procedure. Ensure that the front fixings are secured tightly, before working backwards to tighten those remaining.

47   Fault diagnosis – fuel, exhaust and emission control systems

Unsatisfactory engine performance and excessive fuel consumption are not necessarily the fault of the fuel system or carburettor. In fact they more commonly occur as a result of ignition and timing faults. Before acting on the following it is necessary to check the ignition system. Even though a fault may lie in the fuel system it will be difficult to trace unless the ignition is correct. The faults below, therefore, assume that this has been attended to first (where appropriate).

Symptom	Reason(s)
Difficult starting when cold	Defective fuel delivery (empty tank, blocked filter or pump malfunction) Needle valve(s) stuck in closed position Fuel level in float chamber incorrect Choke control maladjusted or automatic choke malfunction Air leaks in induction system Carburettor(s) defective or worn
Difficult starting when hot	Excessive choke (control maladjusted or automatic choke malfunction) Defective fuel delivery Air cleaner(s) clogged Needle valve(s) stuck in closed or open position Fuel level in float chamber incorrect Vapour lock in fuel line Carburettor(s) maladjusted or worn
Excessive fuel consumption	Unfavourable operating conditions (short journeys, heavy traffic) Leakage from unions, hoses or tank Mixture too rich (maladjusted or choke malfunction) Needle valve(s) leaking Float(s) punctured or wrong height setting Air cleaner(s) clogged Carburettor(s) worn Emission control system defects
Engine starts but cuts out	Anti-run-on valve defective or connections faulty Fuel tank vent blocked Piston(s) sticking (SU carbs)
Backfiring or spitting back	Air leaks in induction and/or exhaust systems Mixture too weak Emission control defect Engine defect (see Chapter 1)

Faults in specific components are dealt with in the Sections concerned

Chapter 4 Ignition System

Contents

Specifications

Note that the following are additional features

Engine Nos		Key	
18GD – EEC	18V 672 Z – EEC, ELC	CC	Catalytic converter
18GF – EEC	18V 673 Z – EEC, ELC	CCV	Carburettor crankcase ventilation
18GG – EEC	18V 801 AE – CC	EEC	Exhaust emission control
18GH – EEC, CCV	18V 802 AE – CC	ELC	Evaporative loss control
18GJ – EEC, ELC, CCV	18V 883 AE – CC		
18GK – EEC, ELC	18V 884 AE – CC		
18V 584 Z – EEC, ELC	18V 890 AE – CC		
18V 585 Z – EEC, ELC	18V 891 AE – CC		

General

System type	12 volt, coil ignition, contact breaker or electronic triggering (later models)
Firing order..	1-3-4-2
Location of No 1 cylinder	Adjacent to the radiator

Distributor

Make .... Lucas

Type:

Engine Nos 18G, 18GA, 18GB, 18GD, 18GG, 18GF, 18GH, 18GJ, 18GK, 18V 584 Z, 18V 585 Z, 18V 672 Z, 18V 673 Z, 18V 581 F, 18V 582 F, 18V 583 F, 18V 581 Y, 18V 582 Y, 18V 583 Y, 18V, 18V 779 F and 18V 780 F	25D4
Engine Nos 18V 846 F, 18V 847 F, 18V 797 AE, 18V 798 AE, 18V 892 AE and 18V 893 AE	45D4
Engine Nos 18V 801 AE, 18V 802 AE, 18V 883 AE, 18V 884 AE, 18V 890 AE and 18V 891 AE	45DE4 (electronic triggering)

Serial No:

	High compression	Low compression
Engine Nos 18G, 18GA, 18GB, 18GD, and 18GG	40897	40916
Engine Nos 18GF, 18GH, and 18GJ	40897 or 41155	-
Engine No 18GK	41339	-
Engine Nos 18V 584 Z and 18V 585 Z	41370	-
Engine Nos 18V 672 Z and 18V 673 Z	41491	-
Engine Nos 18V 581 F, 18V 582 F, 18V 583 F, 18V 581 Y, 18V 582 Y and 18V 583 Y	41288	41290
Engine No 18V	41032	-
Engine Nos 18V 779 F and 18V 780 F	41234 or 41391	-
Engine Nos 18V 846 F and 18V 847 F	41610	-
Engine Nos 18V 797 AE and 18V 798 AE	41599	-
Engine Nos 18V 892 AE and 18V 893 AE	41692	-
Engine Nos 18V 801 AE and 18V 802 AE	41600	-
Engine Nos 18V 883 AE and 18V 884 AE	41693	-
Engine Nos 18V 890 AE and 18V 891 AE	41695	-

Static timing:

	High compression	Low compression
Engine Nos 18G, 18GA, 18GB, 18GD, 18GG, 18GF, 18GH, 18GJ, 18GK, 18V 584 Z, 18V 585 Z, 18V 672 Z and 18V 673 Z.....................	10° BTDC	8° BTDC
Engine Nos 18V 581 F, 18V 582 F, 18V 583 F, 18V 581 Y, 18V 582 Y and 18V 583 Y	10° BTDC	10° BTDC
Engine No 18V	5° BTDC	-
Engine Nos 18V 779 F and 18V 780 F..................................	6° BTDC	-
Engine Nos 18V 846 F, 18V 847 F, 18V 797 AE, 18V 798 AE, 18V 801 AE, 18V 802 AE, 18V 883 AE, 18V 884 AE, 18V 890 AE, 18V 891 AE, 18V 892 AE and 18V 893 AE	7° BTDC	-

Dynamic timing:

Engine Nos 18G, 18GA, 18GB, 18GD, 18GG, 18GF, 18GH, 18GJ, 18GK, 18V 584 Z, 18V 585 Z, 18V 672 Z and 18V 673 Z	14° BTDC at 600 rpm 12° BTDC at 600 rpm
Engine Nos 18V 581 F, 18V 582 F, 18V 583 F, 18V 581 Y, 18V 582 Y and 18V 583 Y	13° BTDC at 600 rpm 13° BTDC at 600 rpm
Engine No 18V	15° BTDC at 1000 rpm -
Engine Nos 18V 779 F and 18V 780 F	11° BTDC at 1000 rpm -
Engine Nos 18V 846 F, 18V 847 F	10° BTDC at 1000 rpm -
Engine Nos 18V 797 AE, 18V 798 AE and 18V 892 AE and 18V 893 AE	13° BTDC at 1300 rpm -
Engine Nos 18V 801 AE, 18V 802 AE, 18V 883 AE, 18V 884 AE, 18V 890 AE and 18V 891 AE	10° BTDC at 1500 rpm -

Dwell angle:

25D4 distributor	60° ± 3°
45D4 and 45DE4 distributors	51° ± 5°
Rotation of rotor	Anti-clockwise
Condenser capacity	0.18 to 0.24 mf
Contact breaker gap (25D4 and 45D4) distributor	0.014 to 0.016 in (0.35 to 0.40 mm)
Pick up air gap (45DE4 distributor)	0.010 to 0.017 in (0.25 to 0.43 mm)
Timing mark	Pointer on timing case and notch on crankshaft pulley

Spark plugs

Type (all models)	Champion N9YCC or N9YC

	N9YCC	**N9YC**
Electrode gap:		
Lucas 25D4 distributor	0.032 in (0.081 mm)	0.024 to 0.026 in (0.61 to 0.66 mm)
Lucas 45D4 and 45DE4 distributors	0.035 in (0.89 mm)	0.035 in (0.89 mm)

Coil

Make	Lucas
Type:	
Early models	HA12 (12 volt)
Later models	16C6 (6 volt with ballast resistor)
Primary resistance:	
HA12	3.1 to 3.5 ohms (cold)
16C6	1.43 to 1.58 ohms

Torque wrench setting

	lbf ft	**Nm**
Spark plugs	18	24

1   General description

An electrical spark is required to ignite the fuel/air mixture in the combustion chamber at exactly the right moment in relation to engine speed and load. The ignition system feeds low tension voltage from the battery to the coil where it is converted to high tension voltage. This is powerful enough to jump the sparking plug gap, providing that the system is in good order.

The low tension (or primary) circuit consists of the battery, battery lead to the control box, control box lead to the ignition switch, ignition switch lead to the coil primary, and the coil primary lead to the contact breaker points and condenser.

The high tension circuit consists of the secondary coil windings, the ignition lead from the centre of the coil to the centre of the distributor cap, the rotor arm, and the sparking plug leads and plugs.

The coil changes low tension voltage into high tension voltage by the opening and closing of the contact breaker points in the low tension circuit. High tension voltage is fed via the carbon brush in the distributor cap to the rotor arm. Each time the rotor arm comes in line with one of the four metal segments in the cap, the opening and closing of the contact breaker points causes the high tension voltage to build up, jump the gap from the rotor arm to the appropriate metal segment, and travel via the plug lead to the sparking plug, where it finally jumps the spark plug gap before going to earth.

Some later models are fitted with electronic ignition, which does away with conventional contact breaker points. The low tension current is interrupted electronically in response to signals received from a pickup adjacent to the distributor rotor.

The ignition is advanced and retarded automatically, to ensure the spark occurs at the right moment for the prevailing load/engine speed combination. Control of the spark is by mechanical and (on most models) vacuum systems.

Mechanical spark control is by two weights, which move out from the distributor shaft as the engine speed rises due to centrifugal force, rotating the cam relative to the distributor shaft and advancing the spark. The weights are restrained by two springs, the rating of which determine the movement of the weights and hence the amount of spark advance.

Vacuum spark control is by a diaphragm, one side of which is connected via a tube to the carburettor, and the other side to the contact breaker plate. Depression in the inlet manifold causes the diaphragm to move, so moving the contact breaker plate, and advancing or retarding the spark. Fine control is achieved by a spring in the vacuum assembly.

Where an exhaust emission control system is fitted, an exhaust emission check should be carried out after work has been done upon the distributor, or if the ignition timing has been varied.

2   Sparking plugs and leads – maintenance

Sparking plugs

1 The correct functioning of the spark plugs is vital for the correct running and efficiency of the engine. It is essential that the plugs fitted are appropriate for the engine, and the suitable type is specified at the beginning of this chapter. If this type is used and the engine is in good condition, the spark plugs should not need attention between scheduled replacement intervals.

2 Spark plug cleaning is rarely necessary and should not be attempted unless specialised equipment is available as damage can easily be caused to the firing ends.

3 Set the plug gap to the specified dimension. Never bend the centre electrode. When refitting the plugs, use new washers if available. Refit the leads in the order 1, 3, 4, 2, No 1 cylinder being the one nearest the radiator.

Plug leads

4　Examine the leads, and renew any with cracked, perished or damaged insulation. Check the ends of the cables for corrosion and proper connections. Filling the holes in the distributor cap with silicone grease before fitting the cables will help to exclude water.

5　On later vehicles with radio-frequency-suppressed HT cables, the older type of end fittings are unsuitable and the type shown in Fig. 4.1 must be used.

3　Contact breaker points, Lucas distributor type 25D4 – cleaning, adjusting, removal and refitting

---

Cleaning

1　Pull away the two clips securing the distributor cap to the body, and lift away the cap. Clean the cap inside and out with a dry cloth. If cracks

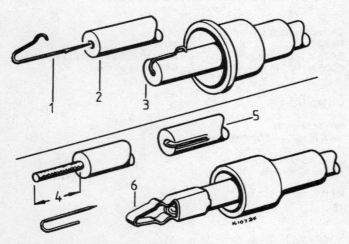

Fig 4.1 End fitting arrangements for later type suppressed HT cables (Sec 2)

Coil lead
　1　Fish-hook connector
　2　Cable end cut square
　3　Lead cover fitted, and hook pressed in
Plug lead
　4　Strip insulation back for ½ in (12.7 mm)
　5　Fold the inner cord back, and push the staple home
　6　Fit the connector body, ensuring a good contact with the cord and staple

or burning exist, or if the four segments are burnt badly, renew the cap. Check that the carbon brush moves freely.

2　Examine the contact points. If pitted or dirty, remove them for resurfacing, or preferably renewal.

Adjustment

3　Check the points gap by turning the engine over until the contact breaker arm is on the peak of one of the four cam lobes (photo). If it varies from the specified value, slacken the contact plate securing screw and adjust the gap. Turn clockwise to decrease and anti-clockwise to increase. Tighten the securing screw and check the gap.

4　Refit the rotor arm and distributor cap. If the points gap has been altered, check the ignition timing.

Removal

5　Unscrew the terminal nut and remove it with the steel washer. Remove the flanged nylon bush, the condenser lead and the low tension lead from the terminal pin. Lift off the contact breaker arm and the large fibre washer, where fitted. Remove the contact breaker plate by removing the one holding down screw, complete with spring and flat washer.

6　To reface the points, rub their faces on a fine carborundum stone, or on fine emery paper. The faces must be flat and parallel to each other. Completely remove the built-up deposits, but not necessarily all pitting. Clean the faces of new points with methylated spirit.

Refitting

7　To refit, position the adjustable contact breaker plate (photo), and

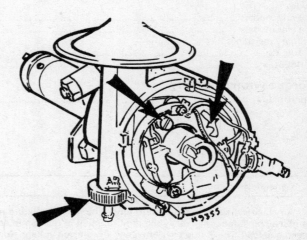

Fig 4.2 Lucas 25D4 distributor – arrowed are the contact securing screw, the adjusting notches, and the fine adjustment screw (Sec 3)

3.3a Contact breaker arm (arrowed) on the peak of a cam lobe

3.3b Alter the gap by slackening the screw and moving the plate

3.7a Position the adjustable plate on the pivot pin

3.7b Fit the securing screw and washers

3.7c Fit the sprung contact breaker arm on the pivot post

fit the securing screw with spring and plain washers (photo). Place the fibre washer on the pivot pin, where fitted, and fit the contact breaker spring arm (photo).

8 Place the nylon bush over the terminal bolt, followed by the eye of the moving contact spring and the capacitor and low tension lead terminals (photos).

9 Fit the flanged nylon bush over the terminal bolt and secure with the washer, star washer, and nut.

10 Reset the gap, and refit the rotor arm and distributor cap.

4 Contact breaker points, Lucas distributor type 45D4 – cleaning, adjusting, removal and refitting

Cleaning

1 Proceed as described in Section 3, paragraph 1 and 2.

Adjusting

2 Proceed as described in Section 3, paragraphs 3 and 4.

3 If the contact breaker points are to be set by the setting of the dwell angle, use the equipment recommended by the manufacturers. The dwell angle is reduced by increasing the contact breaker gap, and vice versa. Finally, recheck the ignition timing.

Removal

4 Remove the distributor cap and rotor arm. Remove the securing screw and washers, and lift away the contact set. Release the terminal plate by pressing the end of the spring.

Refitting

5 Clean the contact faces with methylated spirit, lubricate the pivot post, and connect the terminal plate to the end of the contact breaker spring.

6 Refit the contact set, lightly secure it with the screw and washers, check the spring in the insulator register, and set the contact gap.

5 Capacitor (condenser) – description

1 The capacitor has a dual function. Firstly to reduce arcing at the contacts, resulting in heavy and rapid burning, and secondly to cause a more rapid collapse of the magnetic field with a consequently greater induced voltage in the coil secondary winding.

2 If the capacitor fails in the short-circuit mode, the contact breaker points will be prevented from interrupting the LT circuit and total ignition failure will result.

3 If the capacitor fails in the open-circuit mode, there will be excessive arcing and burning at the points and a poor spark at the plug. The engine will run badly or not at all.

4 Special equipment is necessary to make any conclusive tests of a capacitor, and in view of the low cost of the item it is suggested that a suspect capacitor be tested by substitution.

6 Distributor, Lucas type 25D4 – servicing, removal, dismantling, inspection, reassembly and refitting

Servicing

1 Lubricate the distributor cam with petroleum jelly at the specified intervals.

2 Lubricate the bearings by removing the rotor, and dropping two drops of oil on the exposed screw head.

3 Lubricate the automatic advance mechanism by allowing a few drops of oil through the hole in the contact breaker baseplate.

3.8a Fit the nylon bush (arrowed) to the terminal bolt

3.8b Refit the capacitor and low tension leads

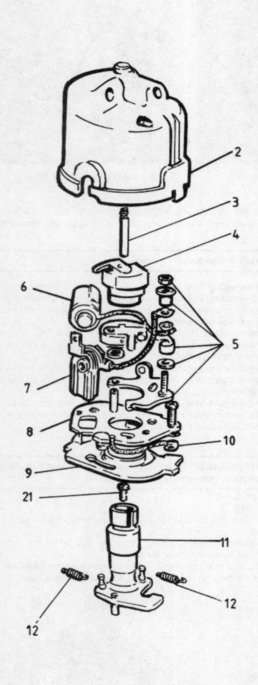
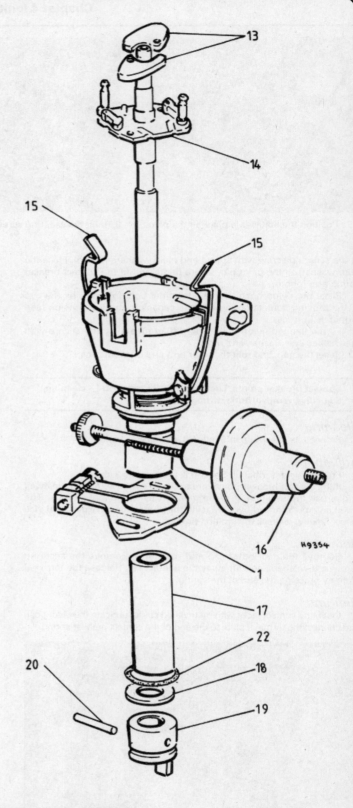

Fig 4.3 Lucas 35D4 distributor – exploded view (Sec 6)

1	Clamping plate	7	Terminal and lead (low tension)	11	Cam	17	Bush
2	Moulded cap			12	Automatic advance springs	18	Thrust washer
3	Brush and spring	8	Moving contact breaker plate	13	Weight assembly	19	Driving dog
4	Rotor arm			14	Shaft and action plate	20	Parallel pin
5	Contacts (set)	9	Contact breaker baseplate	15	Cap retaining clips	21	Cam screw
6	Capacitor	10	Earth lead	16	Vacuum unit	22	O-ring oil seal

4   Apply a small spot of oil to the moving contact pivot post, removing any excess.

5   Do not use excesses of lubricant, which can cause burning and misfiring.

Removal

6   Pull the leads from the sparking plugs. Remove the low tension connection on the side of the distributor, remove the HT lead from the coil, and disconnect the vacuum tube to the distributor vacuum housing.

7   Remove the distributor body clamp plate bolts, and remove the distributor. If it is removed without the clamp being loosened from the body, the timing will not be lost.

Dismantling

8   Remove the contact points as described in Section 3. Remove the capacitor.

9   Disconnect the vacuum unit spring from its mounting pin on the moving contact breaker plate. Remove the two screws and lockwashers, together with the earth lead, and lift out the contact breaker baseplate.

10   Note the position of the rotor drive slot relative to the offset drive dog, for reassembly purposes.

11   Remove the cam securing screw, the springs, the cam assembly, and the weights. Test the endfloat of the driveshaft, and the shaft clearance in the body bushes, before further dismantling.

12   If necessary, remove the distributor driveshaft by driving the pin out of the driving dog, using a thin punch. Remove the shaft.

13   To remove the vacuum unit, spring off the small circlip securing the adjustment nut and remove the nut. Remove the spring and clip.

14   To dismantle the baseplates, rotate the moving plate, disengage the stud, and disengage the plate from the C-spring.

Inspection and repair

15   Check the contact points (see Section 3). Check the distributor cap (see Section 3, paragraph 1). Renew the rotor arm if it is burnt, or loose on the spindle.

16   Test the fit of the breaker plate on the bearing plate, and the breaker arm pivot for looseness or wear. Renew as necessary. Examine the balance weights and pivot pins for wear, and renew the weights or cam assembly.

17   Examine the shaft and the fit of the cam assembly on it. Renew either or both if excessive wear is evident.

18   Check the shaft and bush, and renew if excessive wear exists. Remove the bush by pressing it out from inside the body, insert the new bush as far as possible by hand, and finish by pressing it in using a mandrel in a vice or under a press, until flush with the end of the body. Drill through the existing body hole, and through the bush, and remove all swarf. Ensure that the shaft when lubricated is not excessively tight in the bushes. Note that overboring is not permissible. Ensure that the bush is soaked in engine oil for 24 hours before being fitted.

19   Compare the length of the balance weight springs with new parts. Renew them if stretched.

Reassembly

20   To reassemble, reverse the dismantling procedure, lubricating the mechanism generally with engine oil where relevant. Do not over-oil.

21   Ensure that the action of the weights between the retarded and advanced extremes is quite free. Set the micrometer adjusting nut to the centre of its travel. Check the contact breaker gap.

Refitting

22   To refit, reverse the removal procedure. If the engine has been turned, or the clamp bolt loosened, retime the ignition.

---

7   Distributor, Lucas type 45D4 – servicing, removal, dismantling, inspection, reassembly and refitting

Servicing

1   See Section 6, paragraphs 1 to 5. However, when removing the rotor, add oil to the felt pad which is exposed.

Removal

2   Proceed as described in Section 6; paragraphs 6 and 7.

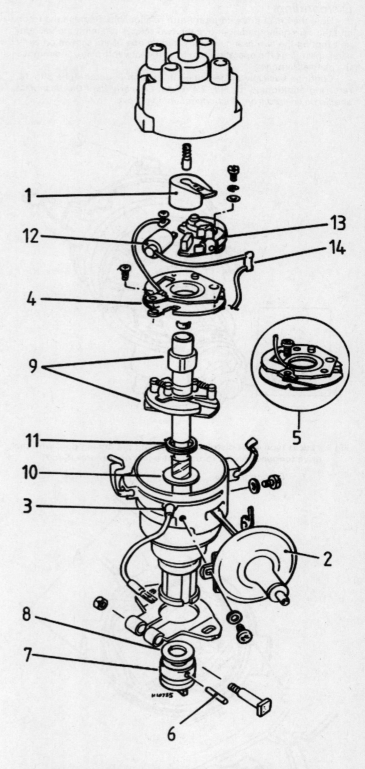

Fig 4.4 Lucas type 45D4 distributor – exploded view (Sec 7)

1	Rotor arm	9	Cam spindle and automatic advance weights assembly
2	Vacuum unit	10	Steel washer
3	Low tension lead	11	Spacer
4	Baseplate	12	Capacitor
5	Baseplate (early cars)	13	Contact set
6	Retaining pin – drive dog	14	Low tension lead
7	Drive dog		connector
8	Thrust washer		

Dismantling

3   Note the offset drive dog/rotor arm relationship. Remove the rotor, and the cam oiling pad. Remove the two screws retaining the vacuum unit (noting the two prongs which straddle one of the screws on early cars), disengage the operating arm from the movable plate, and remove the plate assembly.

4   Continue basically as described in Section 6, paragraphs 8 to 14, referring additionally to Fig. 4.4. **Note:** *On early cars the baseplate should be levered from the body retaining groove.*

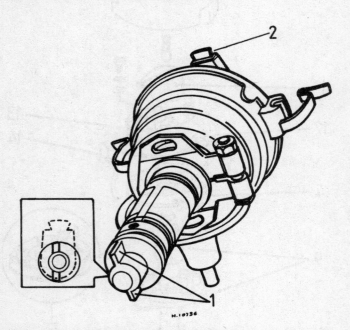

H.10736

Fig 4.5 Lucas type 45D4 distributor – refitting the driving dog, with the drive tongues parallel to the centre-line of the rotor (Sec 7)

1	*Driving tongues*	2	*Rotor arm*

Fig 4.6 Lucas type 45D4 distributor (early cars) – refitting the baseplate (Sec 7)

1	*Baseplate*	4	*Prongs*
2	*Slot in baseplate*	A	*Checking diameter*
3	*Screw hole*		

Inspection

5   If the spindle, or moving parts of the automatic advance mechanism (other than the springs), are worn, renew the complete spindle assembly. If the spindle bearing is worn, the complete distributor must be renewed.

6   Check the cap. rotor and pick-up brush for damage, burning or tracking.

7   Check the spring between the baseplates, and the plates for excessive wear or seizure. Renew complete if necessary.

Reassembly

8   To reassemble, reverse the dismantling procedure. Lubricate the spindle cam and moving contact pivot post with general purpose grease, and the weight pivots and spindle bearing with Rocol MP (Molypad). Oil the oiling pad, using engine oil.

9   If a new spindle is fitted, drill through the hole in the drive dog using a 3/16 in (4.76 mm) drill. During drilling, push the spindle from the cam end. thus pressing the drive dog against the body flange. Remove the pin, tap the dog to partially flatten the pips on the thrust washer and reassemble the pin. Adopt a similar procedure if the thrust washer is renewed.

10   On early cars only, when fitting the baseplate, ensure that the plate is pressed against the register in the distributor body with the chamfered edge engaging the undercut. Check the dimension A indicated in Fig. 4.6, at right-angles to the baseplate slot. Tighten the securing screw. Recheck dimension A, which should increase at least by 0.006 in (0.152 mm). If this does not occur, renew the baseplate.

Refitting

11   Refer to Section 6, paragraph 22.

---

8   **Distributor, Lucas type 45 DE4 – removal, dismantling, inspection, reassembly and refitting**

Removal

1   Disconnect the battery. Remove the distributor as described in Section 6, paragraphs 6 and 7. Note that the wires are fitted with a multi-plug connector.

Dismantling

2   Remove the rotor arm, and the anti-flash shield, by lifting them off. Disconnect the pick-up unit from the moving plate by removing the two screws, spring and plain washers.

3   Remove the three screws from the amplifier module, and detach the retard link from the moving plate pin. Withdraw the module together with the pick-up, grommet, and leads. If the vacuum retard unit is to be removed from the module, drive out the pin and withdraw the unit.

4   Remove the timing rotor and rubber O-ring by withdrawing the retaining circlip and washer. Remove the baseplate by unscrewing the two retaining screws.

5   Drive out the pin, and remove the drive dog and thrust washer. Withdraw the drive spindle and shims.

Inspection

6   Refer to the relevant parts of Section 6. paragraphs 15 to 19. If the return springs are suspect, renew them. Always renew the O-ring and also the retaining pins if they were easy to withdraw.

Reassembly

7   Reverse the dismantling procedure. Lubricate the spindle, moving plate pin and return springs with Rocol Molypad or similar grease. Ensure when refitting the timing rotor that the large location lug is in the related slot.

8   Before tightening the amplifier module retaining screws check that it is seated correctly. Check the correct positioning of the wiring grommet.

9   Adjust the pick-up air gap (see Section 9).

Refitting

10   Refit as described in Section 6, paragraph 22. If the crankshaft is turned whilst the distributor is removed or the timing is otherwise lost, turn the crankshaft to bring No 1 piston to TDC on the firing stroke and fit the distributor so that the rotor arm points to No 1 segment in the distributor cap. This should enable the engine to be run for a dynamic timing check to be carried out (see Section 11).

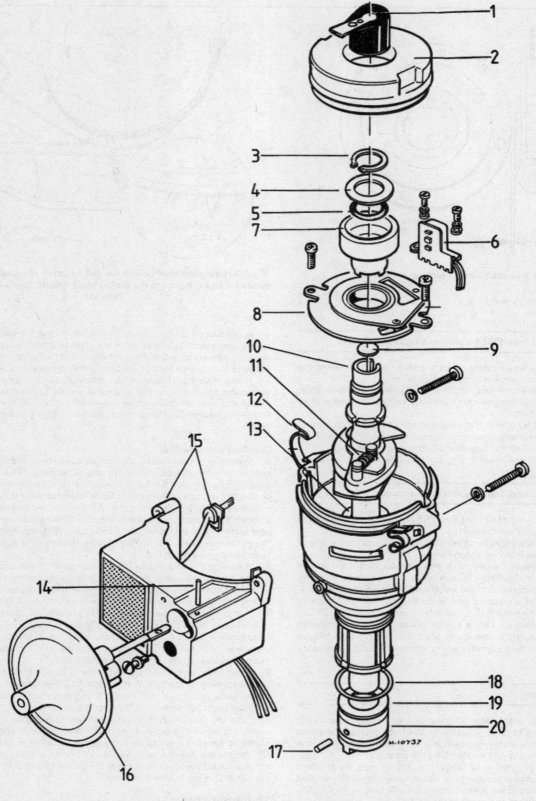

Fig 4.7 Lucas type 45DE4 distributor – exploded view (Sec 8)

1	Rotor	6	Pick up	11	Return spring	16	Vacuum unit
2	Anti-flash shield	7	Timing rotor	12	Spring clip	17	Driving dog pin
3	Circlip	8	Baseplate	13	Shim	18	O-ring
4	Washer	9	Felt pad	14	Pin	19	Thrust washer
5	O-ring	10	Spindle	15	Amplifier module	20	Driving dog

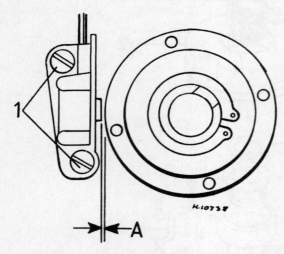

Fig 4.8 Lucas type distributor – pick-up air gap (Sec 9)

1 *Adjustment screws*
A = 0.010 to 0.017 in (0.25 to 0.43 mm)

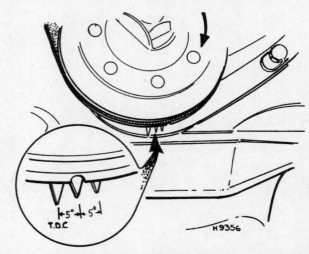

Fig 4.9 The timing marks, with the pulley notch approaching TDC for pistons 1 and 4. Inset are the timing scale details. (Early arrangement) (Sec 11)

9 Distributor, Lucas type 46DE4 – pick-up air gap adjustment

1 Disconnect the battery – *never insert the feeler gauge between the pick-up air gap with the ignition circuit switched on!*
2 Remove the distributor cap, liftoff the rotor arm and anti-flash shield, and using feeler gauges check that the air gap clearance is as given in the Specification.
3 Adjust if required by undoing the two securing screws and pivoting the pick-up to obtain the correct setting. Tighten the screws and re-check to ensure that the gap has not been disturbed whilst tightening.
4 Refit the anti-flash shield, rotor arm and distributor cap.

10 Ignition coil – removal, refitting and maintenance

1 To remove the coil, remove the LT and HT connections, remove the coil securing bolts, and then the coil.
2 Maintenance consists simply of keeping the area around the top of the coil clean, and free from oil and moisture.
3 Testing calls for special equipment, and an auto-electrician should be consulted. If a multi-meter is available, the primary winding resistance can be compared with the value given in the Specification.
4 The surest test of a suspect coil is by substitution of a new or proven unit. Note however that some later models of the MGB use a 6 volt coil in conjunction with a ballast resistor, the resistor being bypassed when the starter motor is operated. The two types of coil are not interchangeable unless corresponding alterations to the wiring are also made.

11 Timing the ignition

1 It is necessary to check, and perhaps adjust, the ignition timing whenever the contact breaker points gap has been altered, or when the distributor-to-clamp plate alignment has been disturbed. Check, the contact breaker points gap before checking the timing.
2 If contact breaker ignition is fitted, the timing may be checked statically (with the engine stopped) or dynamically (with the engine running). If electronic ignition is fitted, only dynamic timing is possible. Dynamic timing is quicker and more accurate.

Static timing

Initial setting
3 If timing has been lost completely (eg during engine rebuild). commence by turning the crankshaft in the normal direction of rotation until No 1 piston is rising on the compression stroke. This can be ascertained by removing No 1 spark plug and feeling the compression

being developed in the cylinder, or by removing the rocker cover and noting when both valves on No 4 are open and both valves on No 1 are closed. Continue to rotate the crankshaft until the notch in the crankshaft pulley is in line with the correct timing pointer (see Specifications).
4 If the distributor has been removed, refit it now, turning the distributor shaft so that the rotor arm points to No 1 segment in the distributor cap. Set the vernier adjuster (if fitted) to the middle of its travel and slacken the clamp plate pinch-bolt Now proceed as described below.

Checking and adjusting
5 With the timing marks aligned as described in paragraph 3. the contact breaker points should be just separating. (The marks will be aligned when either No 1 or No 4 cylinder is commencing the firing stroke, but as long as the distributor is fitted correctly it does not matter which cylinder is firing.) To check when the points are separating, connect a 12V test lamp between the coil LT connection to the distributor and earth (any bare metal part of the car). With the ignition on, when the points are open, the lamp will light. Remove the distributor cap so that the engine cannot fire.
6 Rotate the crankshaft in the normal direction of rotation until the timing marks are again approaching correct alignment and observe when the test lamp lights. (It will come on and go out again during rotation for the firing stroke of No 2 or No 3 cylinder – ignore this).
7 If the lamp lights before the marks are aligned, the ignition timing is advanced. With the marks correctly aligned, slacken the distributor clamp plate pinch-bolt and slowly turn the distributor body anti-clockwise until the test lamp goes out, then turn it clockwise until the lamp comes on again. Tighten the pinch-bolt.
8 If the lamp does not light until after the timing marks are aligned, ignition timing is retarded. With the marks correctly aligned, slacken the clamp plate pinch-bolt and slowly turn the distributor body clockwise until the lamp just comes on. Tighten the pinch-bolt.
9 Turn the crankshaft through a complete revolution until the timing marks are again aligned and check that the test lamp lights at the right moment. Small errors can be corrected by rotating the vernier adjuster (if fitted) in the direction arrowed A to advance or R to retard.
10 Switch off the ignition, remove the test lamp and refit the distributor cap. Static timing is now complete.

Dynamic timing
11 Connect a stroboscopic timing light to No 1 spark plug lead in accordance with the manufacturer's instructions. Mark the notch on the crankshaft pulley and the correct dynamic timing mark (see Specifications) with quick-drying white paint – typist's correcting fluid is ideal. Disconnect the distributor vacuum pipe (if fitted) and plug it.
12 Start the engine and adjust the tickover to that specified. Shine the timing light onto the timing marks, when they will appear stationary and, if the timing is correct, in alignment.

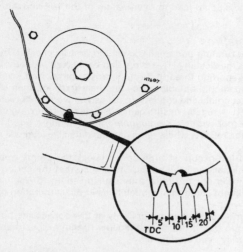

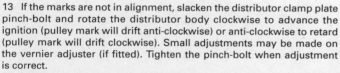

Fig 4.10 Timing marks, later arrangement (Sec 11)

Fig 4.11 Timing marks, later arrangement (TDC position shown)
(Sec 11)

13   If the marks are not in alignment, slacken the distributor clamp plate pinch-bolt and rotate the distributor body clockwise to advance the ignition (pulley mark will drift anti-clockwise) or anti-clockwise to retard (pulley mark will drift clockwise). Small adjustments may be made on the vernier adjuster (if fitted). Tighten the pinch-bolt when adjustment is correct.

14   Increase the engine speed and check that the pulley mark drifts anti-clockwise as the centrifugal advance mechanism comes into operation. Reconnect the distributor vacuum pipe (if fitted) and look for a small further advance from the vacuum advance unit

15   If the pulley mark appears blurred or jerks about, this may be due to a worn distributor or to general wear in the timing gear. If the automatic advance mechanisms are jerky or inoperative they should be investigated.

16   Stop the engine, disconnect the timing light and remake the original connections.

17   Small readjustments under running conditions can be beneficial. Start the engine, allow to warm up to normal temperature, accelerate in top gear from 30 to 50 mph and listen for heavy pinking. If this occurs, retard the ignition slightly until just the faintest trace of pinking can be heard under these conditions.

18   The fullest advantage of any change of fuel will only be attained by readjustment of the ignition settings. Vary the setting on the vernier adjuster (where fitted) by one or two divisions until the best all-round result is achieved.

12 Fault diagnosis – ignition system

1   With the exception of timing maladjustment or advance-retard defects, both of which will be evident as lack of performance and possibly pinking (pre-ignition) or overheating, ignition faults can be divided into two types: total failure (engine fails to start, or cuts out completely, perhaps intermittently) and partial failure (misfiring, regular or otherwise, on one or more cylinder).

2   Electronic ignition, where fitted, is normally very reliable. Fault diagnosis should be confined to checking the pick-up air gap, the continuity of leads and the security of connections, and the dryness and condition of insulation on the HT side. In particular, it is not advisable to remove HT leads when the engine is running, as the voltage present is considerably higher than that in a conventional ignition system, and there is a risk both of personal injury and of damage to the coil insulation. The checks below apply only to contact breaker ignition systems.

3   The commonest cause of difficulty in starting, especially in winter, is a slow engine cranking speed combined with a poor spark at the plugs. Before commencing the checks below, ensure that the battery is fully charged, that the HT leads and distributor cap are clean and dry, that the points and plugs are in good condition and correctly gapped,

and that all LT connections (including the battery terminals) are clean and tight.

Engine will not start

4   Remove the plug cap and hold the metal end of the lead about ¼ in (6 mm) away from the block. *Hold the lead with insulating material – eg a rubber glove, a dry cloth, or insulated pliers – to avoid electric shocks.* Have an assistant crank the engine on the starter motor a fat blue spark should be seen and heard to jump from the end of the lead to the block. If it does. this suggests that HT current is reaching the plugs, and that either the plugs themselves are defective, the timing is grossly maladjusted, or the fault is not in the ignition system. If the spark is weak or absent although the cranking speed is good, proceed with the checks below. If the cranking speed is low check the battery and starter motor.

5   Remove the HT lead which enters the centre of the distributor cap, hold the end near the block and repeat the check described above. A good spark now, if there was none at the plug lead, indicates that HT current is not being transmitted to the plug lead. Check the carbon brush and the plug lead terminals inside the distributor cap, the inside of the cap itself for dampness, cracks or tracking marks (black lines formed where insulation defects allow the passage of current), and the rotor arm for cracks or tracking. If tracking is evident on the distributor cap or rotor arm, the component must be renewed, although in an emergency it may be possible to interrupt the track by scraping or filing. If there is no spark at the HT lead from the coil, carry on to the next check.

6   The HT system has now been checked, with the exception of the HT lead from the coil to the distributor and the HT terminal on the coil itself. If these seem to be in order, start checking the LT system. With the distributor cap and rotor arm removed, turn the engine if necessary until the points are closed, then switch on the ignition and separate the points with an insulated screwdriver. A strong blue spark suggests condenser failure in the open circuit mode: fit a new one and the engine should run. No spark at all when the points are separated could be due to condenser failure in the short circuit mode: temporarily disconnect it and check again. If there is still no spark, either the point faces are contaminated – clean them with methylated spirit – or the fault is elsewhere in the LT system. For further checking a 12 volt test lamp or a voltmeter will be required.

7   Connect the test lamp or voltmeter between the coil contact breaker (CB) terminal and earth. Turn on the ignition and separate the points with a piece of cardboard. A reading suggests that the fault is either a broken lead between the coil and distributor or an internal fault in the coil. No reading indicates a fault further up the line, or a short circuit to earth in the distributor. Disconnect the distributor-to-coil LT lead, leaving the test lamp connected to the coil: a reading now where there was none before indicates a short circuit to earth somewhere between the lead and the fixed contact. Check the insulating washers on the moving contact pivot, the lead from the distributors LT terminal

to the moving contact and the contact itself. No reading still means that further checking is required.

8   Connect the test lamp or voltmeter to the other coil LT terminal, separate the points and turn on the ignition. A reading here with none at the CB terminal confirms an internal fault in the coil, which will have to be renewed. (A reading at *both* terminals suggests an internal short circuit, but if everything else is in order this would probably blow a fuse.) No reading indicates a break in supply from the battery to the coil via the ignition switch. The fuse which protects the ignition circuit also protects a number of other items (see Chapter 10), and presumably it will be noticed if these are not working either. As a 'get-you-home' measure it may be possible to connect a wire directly from the coil to the battery live terminal, but check the wiring from the coil to the ignition switch and from the switch to the battery first.

Engine fires but will not run

9   If the coil ballast resistor (if fitted) is defective, the ignition system will function normally whilst the starter motor is operating, but will cut out as soon as the ignition key returns to its normal position. This condition is confirmed if voltage is present at the supply (ignition switch) side of the resistor but not at the coil side. It is inadvisable to bypass the resistor, as this could lead to overheating of the coil and subsequent damage.

Engine misfires

10   Uneven running and misfiring should first be checked by seeing that all leads, particularly HT, are dry and connected properly. See that they are not shorting to earth through broken or cracked insulation. If they are, you should be able to see and hear it. If not, then check the plugs, contact points and condenser just as you would in a case of total failure to start. A regular misfire can be isolated by removing each plug lead in turn *(not with electronic ignition)*; removing a good lead will accentuate the misfire, whilst removing the defective lead will make no difference.

11   If misfiring occurs at high speed check the points gap, which may be too small, and the plugs. Check also that the spring tension on the points is not too light thus causing them to bounce. If the trouble is still not cured then the fault lies in the carburation or engine itself.

12   If misfiring or stalling occurs only at low speeds the points gap is possibly too big. If not, then the slow running adjustment on the carburettor may need attention.

Chapter 5   Clutch

Contents

Specifications

General

Make	Borg and Beck
Type	Dry single plate, diaphragm spring, hydraulic actuation
Clutch fluid type/specification	Hydraulic fluid to SAE J1703

Driven plate

Diameter	8 in (203 mm)
Friction material..	Wound yarn
No of damper springs	6
Damper spring colour	Black/light green

Release bearing

Type	Graphite MY3D

Torque wrench setting

	lbf ft	Nm
Clutch-to-flywheel bolts	25 to 30	34 to 41

1   General description

The clutch consists of a cover assembly bolted to the flywheel, between which is held the driven plate. The clutch release mechanism is hydraulically operated by means of the foot pedal attached to the clutch master cylinder. Pressure is transmitted to the slave cylinder, and then on to the release bearing.

2   Maintenance

1   Check the fluid level in the master cylinder at the specified intervals, and top up as necessary with the correct fluid. Any noticeable fall in the fluid level indicates a leak, which should be investigated. Do not allow dirt or oil to contaminate the hydraulic system, and do not overfill.
2   No adjustment is required to the clutch.

3   Bleeding the hydraulic system

1   It is necessary to bleed the clutch hydraulic system whenever air has been allowed to enter it, either as a result of some part of the system having been disconnected, or if the fluid level in the reservoir has been allowed to fall so far that air has been introduced into the master cylinder.
2   Employ a clean jam jar, a 9 in length of rubber or plastic tubing which fits tightly over the bleed screw on the slave cylinder, and a quantity of the recommended hydraulic fluid. Obtain an assistant. Top up the master cylinder, if necessary, and put a little clean hydraulic fluid in the jar.
3   Remove the dust cap, open the bleed screw one turn, place the tube on the screw, and immerse the other end in the jar.

4   Have your assistant pump the clutch pedal up and down slowly until air bubbles cease to emerge from the end of the tube. Keep the reservoir well topped up. When the air bubbles cease, tighten the bleed screw at the end of downstroke.
5   Remove the bleeding apparatus, top up the reservoir and refit the cap. Discard the fluid bled from the system as it is unsuitable for re-use.

4   Clutch – removal, dismantling, inspection reassembly and refitting

Removal

1   Remove either the engine, or the engine and gearbox, as described in Chapter 1, the simplest way being to remove the engine alone. Separate the engine and gearbox if they have been removed together.
2   Mark the cover and flywheel for reassembly, and remove the clutch assembly by unscrewing the six bolts holding the cover to the flywheel. Unscrew the bolts diagonally half a turn at a time to prevent distortion of the cover flange.
3   Lift the clutch assembly from the locating dowels, when the driven plate will fall out (photo).

Dismantling

4   Normally, clutch renewal involves only the fitting of a new driven plate and release bearing. It is false economy not to renew the release bearing, which may otherwise have to be changed at a later date when wear on the clutch linings is still very small. It is also advised that, if the clutch cover unit is to be renewed, an exchange unit should be fitted, rather than carrying out a repair. This will ensure that the unit is properly balanced. It is not possible to dismantle the cover on cars manufactured from 1978 on.
5   If the cover is to be rebuilt, remove the circlip holding the release plate in position (early models only), and remove the plate. Remove the

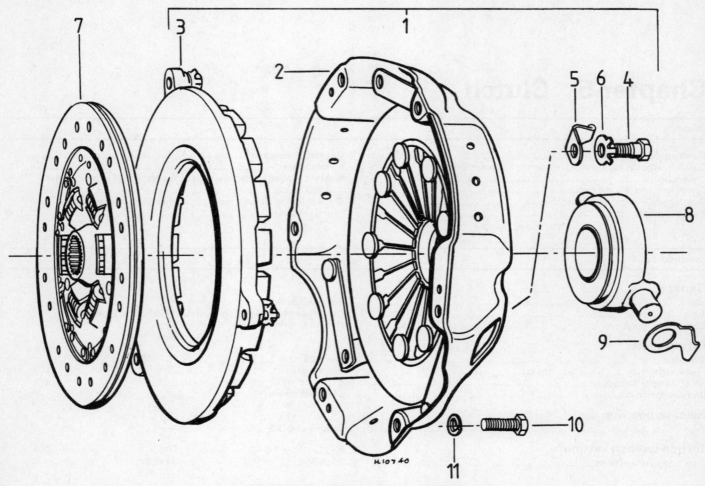

Fig 5.1 The clutch – exploded view (early models) (Sec 4)

1	Cover assembly	4	Strap bolt
2	Cover with straps, diaphragm	5	Pressure plate clip
	spring and release plate	6	Tab washer
3	Pressure plate		

7	Driven plate assembly	10	Cover assembly retaining
8	Release bearing assembly		screw
9	Bearing retainer clip	11	Spring washer

4.3 Removing the clutch cover and friction plate

three strap bolts a turn at a time, through the holes in the cover. Lift out the pressure plate. Turn the release bearing spring retainers through 90° and pull out the bearing.

Inspection

6   Examine the driven plate assembly for worn friction linings, loose rivets, distortion, cracks, loose or broken springs, and worn splines. It is advised that the friction linings alone should not be changed, but a complete new driven plate should be fitted.

7   Check the machined faces of the flywheel and pressure plate. If either are grooved, cracked or split, renew or recondition as necessary.

Reassembling

8   To reassemble, reverse the dismantling procedure, noting the reassembly marks.

Refitting

9   No oil or grease is permissible on the pressure plate, the flywheel, or friction linings. Use clean hands, and wipe the plate and flywheel faces with a clean rag before assembly.

10   Place the driven plate against the flywheel, with the shorter end of the driven plate hub facing the flywheel. Note the words FLYWHEEL SIDE which normally appear on the driven plate as an additional aid to

4.11 The clutch cover locating dowel

4.12 Lining up the driven plate, using an old input shaft

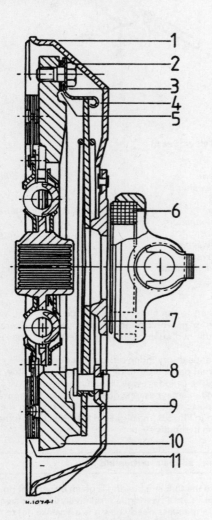

Fig 5.2 The clutch – sectional view (Sec 4)

1 Cover	7 Release plate
2 Strap bolt	8 Strap – release
3 Tab washer	plate/cover
4 Clip	9 Diaphragm spring
5 Strap – diaphragm cover	10 Pressure plate
6 Release bearing	11 Driven plate

correct fitting. If the plate is fitted the wrong way round, the clutch will not work.

11 Refit the cover assembly on the dowels (photo). Fit the six bolts and spring washers and tighten finger tight so that the driven plate is gripped but can still be moved.

12 Centralise the driven plate, preferably using an old gearbox input shaft if this is available (photo). If not, insert a round bar through the hole in the centre of the clutch and move the driven plate about until coincident with the hole in the cover assembly.

13 Tighten the cover bolts to the specified torque in a diagonal sequence. Check the release bearing (see Section 7).

14 Mate the engine and gearbox, if both are out of the vehicle. Refit the unit to the car (see Chapter 1).

---

5 Master cylinder, clutch – removal, dismantling, reassembly and refitting

---

Early cars

Removal

1 Remove the four screws and washers, and the cover, from the master cylinders.

2 Drain the fluid from the reservoir. Attach a rubber tube to the slave cylinder bleed screw, undo the screw one turn, and have an assistant pump out the fluid using the clutch pedal. Hold the pedal against the floor at the completion of each stroke and tighten the bleed screw before allowing the pedal to return. Repeat, until the master cylinder is empty.

3 Undo the hydraulic pipe union at the master cylinder. Free the clutch pedal from the pushrod by removing the split pin and the clevis pin.

4 Remove the two securing bolts, nuts and washers, and remove the cylinder.

Dismantling

5 Pull off the boot (11) (Fig. 5.3), press the pushrod (13) into the cylinder (8) and remove the circlip (12). Pull the pushrod, piston, and associated components from the bore.

6 Clean all parts in methylated spirit. Inspect the seals for swelling and other faults, and the piston and cylinder for wear and score marks. Probe the bypass ports gently with a thin wire. It is sound practice to always renew the rubber seals. Renew the cylinder complete if piston or bore wear is evident.

Reassembly

7 Wet all parts with hydraulic fluid when refitting them. Fit all rubber parts using fingers only.

8 Fit the secondary cup (14) over the piston (15). Ensure that the cup is fully home in the groove, and that the lip faces into the cylinder bore. Fit the retainer (18) in the small end of the spring (19).

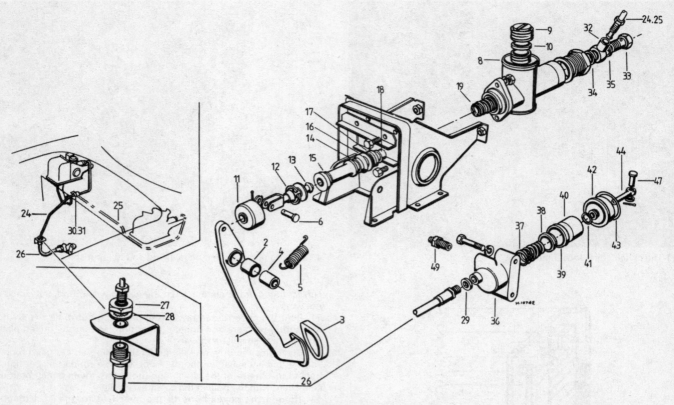

Fig 5.3 The clutch control gear – exploded view (Sec 5)

1	Clutch pedal	12	Circlip	27	Locknut	37	Spring
2	Bush	13	Pushrod	28	Lockwasher	38	Piston cup filler
3	Pedal rubber pad	14	Secondary cup	29	Copper washer	39	Piston cup
4	Distance tube	15	Piston	30	Pipe clip	40	Piston
5	Spring	16	Piston washer	31	Pipe clip	41	Boot clip – small
6	Clevis pin	17	Main cup	32	Banjo connection	42	Boot
8	Master cylinder and	18	Spring retainer	33	Banjo bolt	43	Boot clip – large
	reservoir	19	Spring	34	Sealing washer	44	Pushrod
9	Cap	24	Metal pipe (RHD)	35	Sealing washer	47	Clevis pin
10	Seal	25	Metal pipe (LHD)	36	Slave cylinder body	49	Bleed screw
11	Boot	26	Hose				

9   Fit the spring in the cylinder, large-end first, followed by the main cup (17) (lip edge first), the piston washer (16), the piston and secondary cup (14, 15) and the pushrod (13).
10   Fit circlip (12), and the rubber boot.

Refitting

11   To refit, reverse the removal sequence. Note that the longer cylinder securing bolt is refitted in the top hole which also carries a stiffener plate. Refill and bleed the hydraulic system (Section 3).

Later cars

12   The procedure is largely as for early vehicles, but access is obtained to the lower master cylinder bolt via the bulkhead access plug.

USA/Canada vehicles

13   Proceed as in paragraph 12, but note that the facia left-hand lower panel must be removed.

6   Slave cylinder, clutch – removal, dismantling, reassembly and refitting

1   The cylinder is on the right-hand side of the bellhousing, and is held in place by two bolts and spring washers. To remove, disconnect the hydraulic pipe at the cylinder, catch the hydraulic fluid that will spill, undo the two bolts, and pull the cylinder away from the pushrod which is left attached to the clutch release fork. Note that, when removing the cylinder for gearbox removal purposes only. there is no need to disconnect the hydraulic pipe. Simply tie the cylinder back out of the way.

2   To dismantle the cylinder, remove the boot (42 in Fig. 5.3) and shake out the internal parts. If tight, tap on the bench or blow out with an air line (holding the cylinder away from the person).

3   Clean and examine as described in Section 5 paragraph 6.

4   Wet all parts with hydraulic fluid when refitting them. Refit in the order shown in Fig. 5.3, making sure that the cup is fitted lip first. Refill and bleed the hydraulic system.

7   Clutch fork and release bearing

1   Access to the fork and bearing is given by separating the engine and gearbox. The release bearing is a relatively inexpensive but important component, and unless nearly new it is a mistake not to renew it during an overhaul of the clutch (photos).

2   To remove the bearing from the operating fork, turn the spring clips through 90° and remove them. Lift out the bearing.

3   Check the clutch withdrawal lever for excessive play, and have the bushes renewed, if necessary, by a specialist engineer. To remove the lever, remove the locknut, washer and bolt (photo), and disengage the dust cover.

4   To refit, reverse the removal procedure.

7.1a A worn release bearing

7.1b A release bearing in unworn condition

7.3 The clutch fork securing bolt and nut

8   Clutch pedal – removal and refitting

Early cars

1   Follow the instructions given for removal of the brake pedal (see Chapter 9).

Later cars

2   Remove the pedal box cover, and take out the clevis pin joining the pedal to the pushrod. Take the three bolts securing the pedal box out, from the engine compartment side.

3   On North American cars, free the throttle springs, slacken and pivot the air cleaner assembly away from the engine. Remove the three bolts securing the air cleaner casing, and manoeuvre the air cleaner towards the radiator. Remove the facia left-hand lower panel.

4   Inside the vehicle, remove the five bolts remaining in the pedal box, free the spring, and manoeuvre the box towards the engine without straining any fluid pipes.

5   Withdraw the pedal pivot bolt, the pedal, the bush and the spacer.

6   Refitting is a reversal of the removal procedure.

Fault diagnosis – clutch

1   There are four main faults which the clutch and release mechanism are prone to. They may occur by themselves or in conjunction with any of the other faults. They are clutch squeal, slip, spin, and judder.

Clutch squeal

2   If on taking up the drive or when changing gear, the clutch squeals, this is a sure indication of a badly worn clutch release bearing.

3   As well as regular wear due to normal use, wear of the clutch release bearing is much accentuated if the clutch is ridden, or held down for long periods in gear, with the engine running. To minimise wear of this component the car should always be taken out of gear at traffic lights and for similar hold-ups.

Clutch slip

4   Clutch slip is a self-evident condition which occurs when the clutch friction plate is badly worn, the release arm free travel is insufficient, oil or grease have got onto the flywheel or pressure plate faces, or the pressure plate itself is faulty.

5   The reason for clutch slip is that, due to one of the faults listed above, there is either insufficient pressure from the pressure plate, or insufficient friction from the friction plate to ensure solid drive.

6   If small amounts of oil get onto the clutch, they will be burnt off under the heat of clutch engagement, in the process gradually darkening the linings. Excessive oil on the clutch will burn off leaving a carbon deposit which can cause quite bad slip, or fierceness, spin and judder.

7   If clutch slip is suspected, and confirmation of this condition is required, there are several tests which can be made.

8   With the engine in second or third gear and pulling lightly up a moderate incline, sudden depression of the accelerator pedal may cause the engine to increase its speed without any increase in road speed. Easing off on the accelerator will then give a definite drop in engine speed without the car slowing.

9   In extreme cases of clutch slip the engine will race under normal acceleration conditions.

10   If slip is due to oil or grease on the linings a temporary cure can sometimes be effected by squirting a volatile organic solvent into the clutch. The permanent cure is, of course, to renew the clutch driven plate and trace and rectify the oil leak.

Clutch spin

11   Clutch spin is a condition which occurs when there is a leak in the clutch hydraulic actuating mechanism where this system of actuation is used, the release arm free travel is excessive, there is an obstruction in the clutch either on the primary gear splines, or in the operating lever itself, or the oil may have partially burnt off the clutch linings and have left a resinous deposit which is causing the clutch disc to stick to the pressure plate or flywheel.

12   The reason for clutch spin is that due to any, or a combination of, the faults just listed, the clutch pressure plate is not completely freeing from the centre plate even with the clutch pedal fully depressed.

13   If clutch spin is suspected, the condition can be confirmed by extreme difficulty in engaging first gear from rest, difficulty in changing gear, and very sudden take-up of the clutch drive at the fully depressed end of the clutch pedal travel as the clutch is released.

14   Check the operating lever free travel. If this is correct examine the clutch master and slave cylinders and the connecting hydraulic pipe for leaks. Fluid in one of the rubber boots fitted over the end of either the master or slave cylinders, where fitted, is a sure sign of a leaking piston seal.

15   If these points are checked and found to be in order then the fault lies internally in the clutch, and it will be necessary to remove the clutch for examination.

Clutch judder

16   Clutch judder is a self-evident condition which occurs when the gearbox or engine mountings are loose or too flexible, when there is oil on the faces of the clutch friction plate, or when the clutch pressure plate has been incorrectly adjusted.

17   The reason for clutch judder is that due to one of the faults just listed, the clutch pressure plate is not freeing smoothly from the friction disc, and is snatching.

18   Clutch judder normally occurs when the clutch pedal is released in first or reverse gears, and the whole car shudders as it moves backwards or forwards.

Chapter 6
Gearbox, overdrive and automatic transmission

Contents

Specifications

Manual gearbox – early models (18G, 18GA and 18GB)
Type .... Four forward speeds and one reverse with synchromesh on 2nd, 3rd
and 4th gears

Overdrive where fitted.. Type D

Gear ratios
1st	3.64 to 1
2nd	2.21 to 1
3rd	1.37 to 1
4th	1.00 to 1
Reverse	4.76 to 1
Overdrive..	0.802 to 1

Component dimensional limits and tolerances
Laygear endfloat...	0.002 to 0.003 in (0.051 to 0.076 mm)
Mainshaft 2nd and 3rd gear endfloats...........................	0.004 to 0.006 in (0.102 to 0.152 mm)
Overdrive spring free lengths:	
Pump spring..	2.00 in (50.8 mm)
Clutch spring..	1.51 in (38.4 mm)

Lubricant
Type/specification...	Multigrade engine oil, viscosity SAE 20W/50
Capacity:	
Gearbox...	4.5 pints (2.56 litres, 5.6 US pints)
Gearbox with overdrive	5.5 pints (3.36 litres, 6.0 US pints)

Manual gearbox – later models
Type .... Four forward speeds, all with sychromesh and one reverse

Overdrive (where fitted).. Laycock type LH

Gear ratios
1st	3.44 to 1 (post 1978 3.333 to 1)
2nd	2.167 to 1
3rd	1.382 to 1
4th	1.000 to 1
Reverse	3.095 to 1
Overdrive..	0.82 to 1

Component dimensional limits and tolerances

1st and 3rd speed gear endfloat	0.005 to 0.008 in (0.13 to 0.20 mm)
2nd gear endfloat	0.005 to 0.008 in (0.13 to 0.20 mm)
Laygear endfloat	0.002 to 0.003 in (0.05 to 0.08 mm)

Lubricant

Type/specification	Multigrade engine oil, viscosity SAE 20W/50
Capacity:	
Gearbox	5.25 pints (3.0 litres, 6.0 US pints)
Gearbox and overdrive	6.0 pints (3.4 litres, 7.0 US pints)

Automatic transmission

Type

Borg-Warner type 35

Torque converter ratio

2.2 : 1 to 1 : 1

Gear ratios

1st	2.39 to 1
2nd	1.45 to 1
3rd	1.00 to 1
Reverse	2.09 to 1

Lubricant

Type/specification	ATF to BLMC type F
Capacity	10.5 pints (6.0 litres, 2.7 US pints) approx.

Torque wrench settings

	lbf ft	Nm
Manual gearbox		
Mounting to gearbox case	15 to 20	20 to 27
Driveflange nut, gearbox without overdrive	150	203
Driveflange nut, overdrive:		
Type D	100 to 130	136 to 176
Type LH	55 to 60	75 to 81
Automatic transmission		
Front brake band adjusting screw locknut	15 to 20	20 to 27
Rear brake band adjusting screw locknut	25 to 30	34 to 41
Filler tube connector sleeve to transmission case	20 to 30	27 to 41
Filler tube to connector sleeve nut	17 to 18	23 to 24
Drive flange nut	55 to 60	75 to 81
Centre support bolts	10 to 18	14 to 24

1   General description

All models are fitted with a gearbox containing four forward and one reverse gears. Earlier models do not have synchromesh fitted to first gear. Overdrive units and an automatic gearbox are also available.

Certain modifications have been made to gearbox components during production, and any Leyland parts department will provide the latest parts, where applicable, as a matter of routine, by referring to the latest issue of the Parts List.

Tow starting is not possible where automatic transmissions are fitted. To tow the vehicle, refer to *Towing*.

2   Routine maintenance – all gearboxes

Manual gearboxes

1   A combined filler plug/dipstick is located beneath a rubber cover in the gearbox tunnel on earlier models, with access from under the carpet. On later models, a combined filler/level plug is fitted to the side of the gearbox, with access from under the vehicle.

2   Check the oil level at the recommended intervals, and top up as required with the correct lubricant.

3   Drain the gearbox at the recommended intervals by removing the drain plug. Refill with the correct lubricant, after refitting the drain plug.

Overdrive models

4   The overdrive is lubricated by the gearbox oil, and the instructions in paragraphs 1 to 3 apply. However, when draining, the plug in the overdrive marked DRAIN must be removed as well as that beneath the gearbox. *Do not* use anti-friction additives in the gearbox oil on overdrive models.

5   Clean the filter at the recommended intervals by removing the bolts and washers from the coverplate (14), Fig. 6.13, on the left-hand side of the overdrive, and removing the plate and gasket (14, 15). Pull out the filter gauze (11) with the filter seals and magnetic rings (12, 13). Clean the filter and rings in petrol.

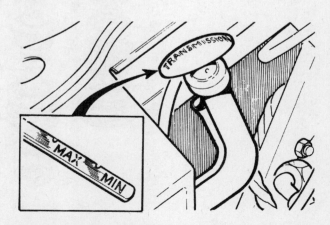

Fig 6.1 Automatic transmission – combined dipstick/filler tube (Sec 2)

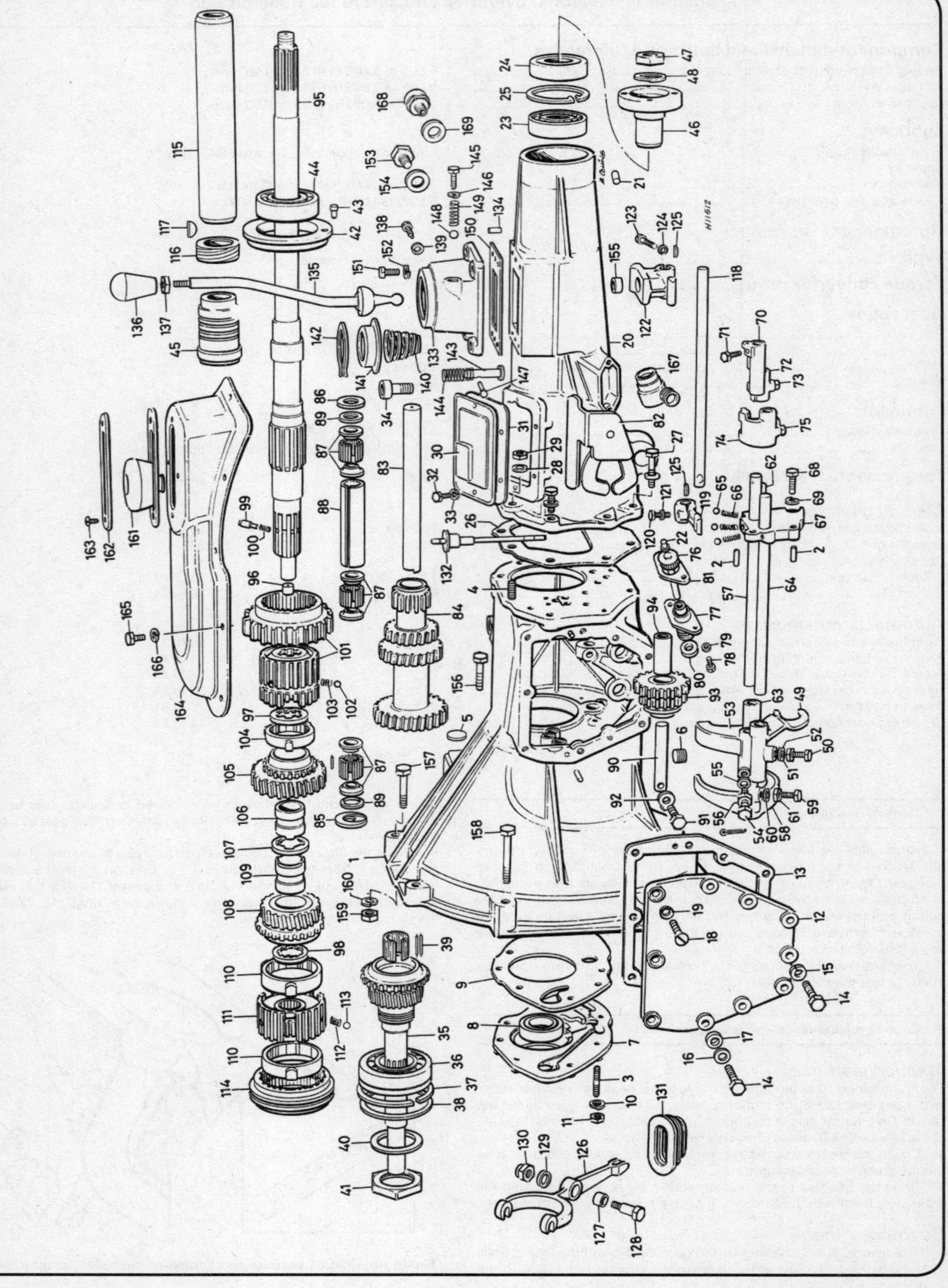
H11612

Fig 6.2 Manual gearbox, early type, non overdrive – exploded view (Sec 4)

#	Part	#	Part
1	Casing assembly	34	Breather assembly
2	Dowel	35	Shaft
3	Stud	36	Bearing
4	Stud	37	Ring
5	Plug	38	Shim
6	Plug	39	Needle
7	Cover assembly	40	Washer
8	Oil seal	41	Nut
9	Gasket	42	Rear bearing
10	Washer	43	Peg
11	Nut	44	Bearing
12	Cover	45	Distance piece assembly
13	Gasket	46	Flange
14	Bolt	47	Nut
15	Spring washer	48	Washer
16	Plain washer	49	Fork
17	Fibre washer	50	Screw
18	Screw	51	Washer
19	Washer	52	Nut
20	Plug	53	Fork
21	Plug	54	Screw
22	Thrust button	55	Washer
23	Rear bearing	56	Nut
24	Oil seal	57	Rod
25	Circlip	58	Fork
26	Gasket	59	Screw
27	Screw	60	Washer
28	Spring washer	61	Nut
29	Nut	62	Rod
30	Cover	63	Distance piece
31	Gasket	64	Rod
32	Screw	65	Ball
33	Spring washer	66	Spring

#	Part	#	Part
67	Block	101	First speed gear and synchroniser assembly
68	Screw	102	Ball
70	1st and 2nd gear selector	103	Spring
71	Screw	104	Baulk ring
72	3rd and 4th gear selector	105	Gear
73	Screw	106	Bush
74	Reverse gear selector	107	Ring
75	Screw	108	Gear
76	Pinion	109	Bush
77	Bush	110	Baulk ring
78	Screw	111	Synchroniser
79	Washer	112	Spring
80	Oil seal	113	Ball
81	Gasket	114	Coupling
82	Interlock plate	115	Distance piece
83	Layshaft	116	Gear
84	Gear unit	117	Key
85	Thrustwasher	118	Shaft
86	Thrustwasher	119	Lever
87	Needle bearing	120	Screw
88	Distance tube	121	Washer
89	Ring	122	Lever
90	Reverse shaft	123	Screw
91	Screw	124	Spring washer
92	Washer	125	Key
93	Gear assembly	126	Lever
94	Bush	127	Bush
95	Shaft	128	Bolt
96	Oil restrictor	129	Washer
97	Thrustwasher	130	Nut
98	Thrustwasher	131	Cover
99	Peg	132	Dipstick
100	Spring		

133	Tower
134	Dowel
135	Lever
136	Knob
138	Pin
139	Spring washer
140	Spring
141	Cover
142	Circlip
143	Plunger
144	Spring
145	Screw
146	Washer
147	Pin
148	Ball
149	Spring
150	Gasket
151	Screw
152	Washer
153	Plug
154	Gasket
155	Bush
156	Bolt
157	Bolt
158	Bolt
159	Nut
160	Washer
161	Grommet
162	Retainer
164	Cover
167	Box
168	Reverse light switch (later cars)
169	Washer for switch (later cars)

6   Refit the filter seal, noting that the metal surface faces inwards. Ensure that the coverplate does not leak when the gearbox is refilled.

Automatic transmission

7   The oil level is checked with the engine running. The level should be to the full mark when warm, but 5/16 in (8 mm) below if cold. The difference between the max and min marks is 1 pint (1.2 US pints/0.57 litres).

8   To check the level, apply the handbrake and place the selector to P, ensuring that the vehicle is on level ground. Start the engine and idle for two minutes.

9   Leave the engine idling. Take out the dipstick and wipe it with paper (not rag), refit it, withdraw again immediately, and check the reading.

10 Add the required amount of fluid through the dipstick/filler tube, using only a recommended type. Keep everything clean, and do not overfill.

11 If the unit has been drained, it will have an indeterminate amount of fluid of up to 5 pints (6 US pints, 2.8 litres) remaining in the torque converter. Thus the refill quantity is variable.

---

3   Manual gearbox – removal and refitting

1   The easiest method is to remove the gearbox in unit with the engine through the engine compartment (see Chapter 1). Alternatively, if heavy lifting tackle is not available, the engine and gearbox can be separated at the gearbox bellhousing and first the engine, and then the gearbox, lifted out (see Chapter 1).

2   To refit, reverse the removal procedures described in Chapter 1.

---

4   Manual gearbox – dismantling

Early type

1   If overdrive is fitted, refer to Section 11 before proceeding further.

2   Referring to Fig. 6.2, pull out the dipstick. Remove the two bolts, the spring washers and the speedometer pinion bush (77). Remove the gasket and speedometer pinion.

3   Undo the nut and spring washer retaining the mainshaft flange (46) on non-overdrive models. Use a long strong screwdriver through one of the flange bolt holes to prevent it moving (or Leyland tool 18G 2). Remove the flange.

4   Remove the bolts holding the remote control extension (overdrive models) or remote control tower (133) (non-o/d models) in place, and remove the extension or tower.

5   On non-overdrive gearboxes undo the bolts and washers which hold the extension side cover (30). Remove the cover and gasket.

6   Lift out the interlock plate (82) and bracket. Undo the bolt and spring washer from the front selector lever (119). Undo the nuts, bolts, and spring washers which hold the extension (20) to the gearbox, and pull it off. Note that the lever (119) will fall free as the extension is pulled back.

7   Remove the screws and bolts, and the side cover and gasket (12, 13). Note the fibre and plain washers (17, 16) which must be placed under the correct bolt head to prevent a severe oil leak developing.

8   To remove the selectors (70, 72, 74), cut through the locking wire, undo the retaining bolts (71, 73, 75) and pull the selectors away.

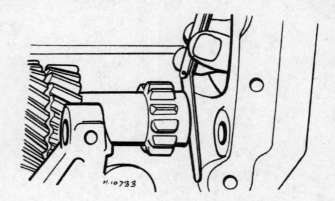

Fig 6.3 Measuring the laygear endfloat (Sec 4)

9   Remove screws (68) and take the block (67) from the gearbox face, recovering the three balls and springs which will be released. Note the two locating dowels. Release the change speed forks (49, 53, 58) by removing the locating screws and sliding out rods (57, 62, 64). Remove the reverse, fourth and third speed, second and first speed rods, in that order. Note that, if the rods are tight, it may be better to remove the front cover and use a soft drift to tap them out. Note also the distance tube over the third and fourth gear selector rod on some models.

10 Remove the bolt (91).

11 Remove the nuts and washers retaining front cover (7), and remove the cover, gasket and shims. Remove the reverse gear and shaft.

12 Measure the endfloat of the laygear, Fig. 6.3, with a feeler gauge. If this exceeds 0.003 in (0.08 mm), new thrustwashers must be fitted on reassembly.

13 With a suitable soft rod. drift out the layshaft (83). Lower the laygear and thrustwashers to the bottom of the gearbox casing as the drift is withdrawn.

14 Remove from the gearbox case the mainshaft (95), the large ball bearing (44) and the bearing housing (42), as a complete assembly. If the housing is tight, try gently tapping the bearing housing at alternate, diagonally opposite, points from inside. When the housing is far enough out, place levers under the lip to accelerate removal. Take great care not to damage the bearing housing, the gearbox case, or the laygear.

15 Locate a rod in the hole in the inner end of the first motion shaft (35). Tap out the shaft into the bellhousing. Lift out the laygear.

Later type (all synchromesh)

16 Use the instructions for the early type for general guidance, in conjunction with these instructions. If overdrive is fitted, refer to Section 17 before proceeding further.

17 Drain the gearbox and remove the propeller shaft flange (photo) on non-overdrive models. On all models remove the bolts from the remote control housing, and remove the housing (photo). On overdrive models remove the overdrive. Select top gear and remove the interlock arm assembly (photo).

18 Remove the nuts retaining the rear extension on non-overdrive models and remove the extension. Retain the shims.

4.17a A method of holding the propeller shaft flange

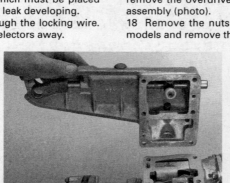

4.17b Remove the remote control housing

4.17c Remove the interlock arm assembly

Fig 6.4 Manual gearbox remote control arrangement, overdrive fitted – exploded view (Sec 4)

1	Rear selector screw
3	Woodruff key
10	Dipstick
11	Remote control tower
12	Dowel
13	Welch plug
14	Gearchange lever
15	Gearlever knob
17	Locating pin
19	Spring
20	Cover
21	Circlip
22	Reverse selector plunger
23	Spring
24	Reverse selector plunger peg
25	Ball
26	Spring
27	Spring retainer plug
28	Washer
29	Gasket
33	Plunger
34	Plunger spring
35	Cap
36	Washer
37	Selector lever shaft
38	Screw
39	Bracket
44	Isolation switch, overdrive
45	Gasket
47	Plunger spring
48	Locating pin
51	Mainshaft clip
52	Reverse selector plunger (alternative design)
53	Detent plunger
54	Plug
55	Reverse light switch
56	Fibre washer

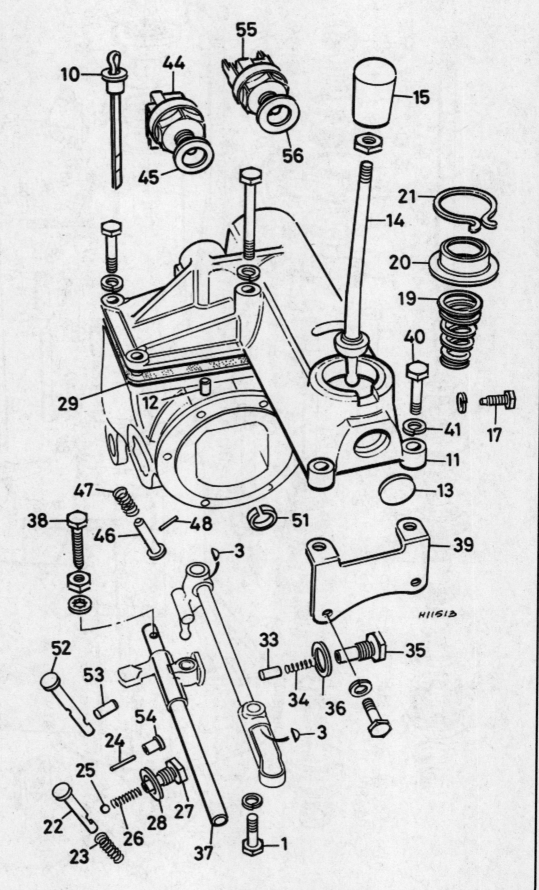

H11513

M.1074S

Fig 6.5 Manual gearbox, later type, all synchromesh, non-overdrive – exploded view (Sec 4)

1	Side cover	27	Front thrustwasher
2	Gasket	28	Rear thrustwasher
3	Dust cover	29	Third motion shaft front nut and
4	Pivot bolt		lockwasher
5	Bush	30	Baulk ring
6	Clutch withdrawal lever	31	3rd/4th synchroniser coupling
7	Front cover	32	3rd/4th sychroniser hub
8	Gasket	33	Synchroniser ball and spring
9	Oil seal	34	Sleeve
10	Gearbox case	35	Third speed gear
11	First motion shaft	36	Bush
12	Spigot bearing	37	Thrustwasher
13	Bearing	38	Second speed gear
14	Circlip	39	Bush
15	Shim	40	Thrustwasher
16	Nut and lockwasher	41	1st/2nd speed synchroniser
17	Locking screw and lockwasher		coupling
18	Reverse shaft	42	1st/2nd speed synchroniser hub
19	Bush	43	Third motion shaft
20	Reverse idler gear	44	Reverse light switch
21	Breather	45	1st speed gear
22	Layshaft	46	Bush
23	Laygear	47	Reverse gear
24	Bearing for laygear	48	Bearing housing
25	Distance tube	49	Roller housing
26	Circlip for laygear	50	Circlip

51	Shim	76	3rd/4th speed selector
52	Distance piece	77	Reverse selector fork
53	Speedometer drivegear	78	Reverse selector rod
54	Distance tube	79	Reverse selector
55	Shim	80	Drain plug
56	Bearing	81	Detent plug and washer
57	Circlip	82	Detent spring and plunger
58	Oil seal	83	Rear extension
59	Drive flange	84	Gasket
60	Nut and lockwasher	85	Gearchange lever
61	Selector lever	86	Seating cone
62	Bush	87	Gear lever knob and nut
63	Selector lever shaft	88	Gear lever retainer
64	Locking screw and lockwasher	89	Retaining cap
65	Spring	90	Damper plunger and spring
66	Locating pin	91	Remote control housing
67	Reverse plunger	92	Gasket
68	Detent plug and washer	93	Dowel
69	Detent spring and plunger	94	Locating pin
70	Interlock arm	95	Bush
71	1st/2nd speed selector fork	96	Retaining clip
72	1st/2nd speed selector rod	97	Damper plunger and spring
73	1st/2nd speed selector	98	Remote control shaft
74	3rd/4th speed selector fork	99	Selector key
75	3rd/4th speed selector rod	100	Key

19 Remove the front cover by removing the clutch release bearing and rubber boot from the lever. Remove the cover retaining nuts and the cover, retaining the shims revealed (photo).

20 Remove the side cover bolts and cover, and the three detent plugs, springs and plungers (photos).

4.19 Withdraw the front cover

4.20a Remove the side cover

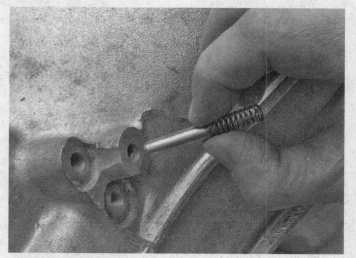

4.20b Removing a detent spring and plunger

4.21a   Remove the selector fork bolts

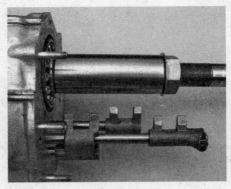
4.21b   Remove the selector rods

4.21c   Remove the selector forks

4.22   Take out the reverse gear

4.23   Withdraw the first motion shaft

4.24a   Remove the needle rollers

4.24b   Withdraw the third motion shaft assembly

4.25   Remove the laygear

5.8   Driving on the first motion shaft bearing

21   Remove the selector fork bolts, the selector rods, and the forks (photos).

22   Remove the reverse shaft by knocking up the tab, removing the retainer bolt, and withdrawing the shaft. Take out the gear (photo).

23   Remove the layshaft (see paragraphs 12 and 13). Drift the first motion shaft assembly forward and out, using a soft metal drift on the outer track of the bearing (photo).

24   Remove the needle rollers and third/fourth synchro unit from the nose of the third motion shaft (photo). Use a piece of hard wood on the nose to tap the assembly out. Keep the shaft square or jamming will occur, and ensure that the laygear is kept clear (photo).

25   Remove the laygear and thrustwashers (photo).

5   Manual gearbox, early version – examination and renovation

Examination of parts

1   Examine the baulk rings for damage. Check the mating coned surfaces, which should have clearly-defined machined lines on them.

If the faces are smooth or uneven, renew the rings. When the cones on baulk ring and gear are placed together, there should be no rock. Check by trying a new ring.

2   Examine the gears for wear and chipped teeth, and the shafts for wear and damage to splines.

3   Renew the laygear thrustwashers if endfloat was outside the limits (Section 4, paragraph 12). Thrustwashers are available as follows: 0.154 to 0.156 in (3.91 to 3.96 mm), 0.157 to 0.159 in (3.99 to 4.04 mm), 0.160 to 0.161 in (4.06 to 4.09 mm), 0.163 to 0.164 in (4.14 to 4.17 mm).

4   All bearings should be examined for pitting, condition of the cages, overall looseness, and fit on their journals or in their housings.

5   Examine the bushes fitted to the third motion shaft, reverse gear, and clutch withdrawal fork.

6   Examine all small parts for obvious defects. Renew oil seals as necessary.

First motion shaft

7   Hold the shaft in a soft-jawed vice. Free the lockwasher and the nut *(left-hand thread)*. Support the bearing, place a suitably sized piece of

5.14 Third motion shaft assembly

5.16a Fitting the second gear baulk ring

5.16b The second gear bush, correctly fitted

5.17a Fitting the second speed gear

5.17b Fitting the interlocking ring

5.18 Fitting the third speed gear bush. Cut-out (arrowed) must be over hole in mainshaft

tube over the shaft against the shoulder, and carefully drive the shaft through the bearing.

8   To reassemble, reverse the procedure. Drive the bearing on using a piece of tube (photo).

Third motion shaft

9   Referring to Fig. 6.2, slide the third and fourth gear synchroniser (111) complete with baulk rings (110) and the coupling sleeve (114) as one assembly from the mainshaft (if not removed before). Do not pull the coupling sleeve from the hub (111) or the springs and balls may jump out and become lost.

10   With a thin probe, depress the peg (Fig. 6.6) through the hole provided in third gear, rotate the washer (98) so that a spline holds the peg down, and slide off the washer.

11   Remove the peg and spring, followed by third gear (108), the third gear bush (109), the interlock ring (107), second gear (105), the second gear bush (106), the synchroniser ring (104), and the thrustwasher (97).

12   Slide off the first and second gear synchroniser and first gear (101). Ensure that first gear remains in place, or the balls and springs (102, 103) may be lost. Remove the speedometer drivegear, the Woodruff key, and distance piece (45, 116, 117).

13   To fit new bushes to the third motion shaft, heat them to between 180° and 200°C (356° and 392°F). Ensure that the locating tongues are in line with the splines on the shaft and that the oil holes are in line.

14   To reassemble, generously lubricate all parts as they are fitted. Press the rear bearing into the housing, and the combined bearing and housing onto the tail end of the shaft. Fit the first gear and the second gear synchromesh assembly together with the rear thrustwasher from the opposite end of the shaft (photo).

15   Fit the distance piece (45), speedometer drivegear and key.

16   Fit the second gear baulk ring synchroniser (photo) and the rear thrustwasher. Heat the second gear bush (106) as described in paragraph 13, and fit with the oil holes in alignment and with the lugs facing the splined end of the shaft (photo). Lubricate the bush.

17   Slide on second gear (105), and fit ring (107) with the lugs correctly engaged (photos).

18   Fit the third gear bush (109), lug end first, with the oil hole in line

with the hole in the shaft. Heat before fitting (paragraph 13). Engage the lugs in the interlocking ring, noting that the bush cut-out should be adjacent to the mainshaft hole (photo).

19   Fit the pin and spring (99, 100), and then third gear (108). Rotate the gear until the hole in the cone is over the pin. and depress the pin with

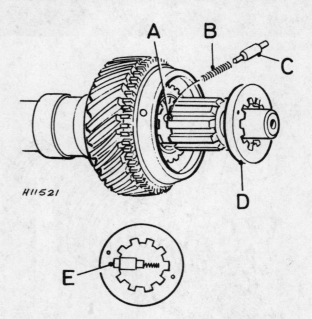

H11521

Fig. 6.6 Mainshaft gear retention (Sec 5)

A Hole, for spring and peg	D Locking wash
B Spring	E Peg location in locking
C Peg	washer

5.19a Fit the spring and pin

5.19b Fit the third speed gear

5.19c Depressing the pin and spring

5.19d Rotating the thrustwasher

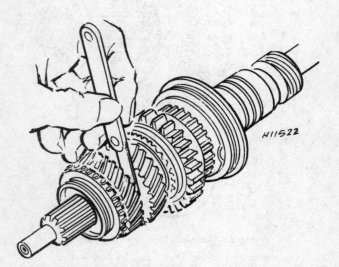

Fig 6.7 Measuring the third gear endfloat (Sec 5)

a thin stiff piece of wire. Fit the thrustwasher over the splines and push it over the depressed pin. Rotate the washer to allow the pin to rise and lock the washer (photos).

20 Check the endfloat between second and third gear with a feeler gauge. Adjust if necessary by choosing from the following available thrustwashers: 0.1565 to 0.1575 in (3.98 to 4.00 mm), 0.1585 to 0.1595 in (4.03 to 4.05 mm) and 0.1605 to 0.1615 in (4.08 to 4.10 mm).

21 Fit the third and fourth gear rear baulk ring, the third and fourth gear synchroniser and coupling sleeve, and the front baulk ring (photo).

Laygear

22 To examine the needle bearings, pull out the spring rings (89). With a finger, pull out the rollers (87) and distance tube (88). Renew if worn. On early cars the rollers are loose, and on later models caged.

23 To reassemble the early type, fit the stepped end of the layshaft in a vice, grease the shaft, and fit the bottom rollers, distance tube and top two sets of rollers to the shaft. Slip the spring ring into its groove in the front end of the laygear and slide the laygear over the shaft, taking care not to dislodge the rollers. Remove the gear and shaft from the vice and fit the remaining spring ring.

24 To reassemble the later type, oil all parts and slip the distance tube and two bearings in at the small end of the gear, followed by the remaining two bearings at the larger end.

5.21 Fitting third and forth gear synchroniser parts

5.32 Tapping home a new oil seal

Rear extension

25 If necessary remove the bolt securing the lever (122), and remove the lever, key and shaft (118).

26 Renew the oil seal after removing it with Leyland service tools 18G 389 and 18G 389C, if available. Alternatively, carefully prise the seal out. Remove the bearing by taking out the circlip and tapping the bearing out with a long drift, bearing against the outer race.

27 Fit a new bearing and seal by carefully drifting them into place. (Employ Leyland tools 18G 134 and 18G 134N to fit the seal, if available). Remember to fit the circlip after the bearing.

28 Refit the lever (122) in reverse order.

Control tower

29 Remove the circlip (142) and pins (138). Take out the lever.

30 Remove the screw, spring and ball (145, 148, 149). Remove the plunger and spring (143, 144), by removing the locating pin (147).

31 To reassemble, reverse the dismantling procedure.

Front cover

32 If necessary, carefully drift out the old oil seal and tap in a new one using a suitable sized socket or the old seal as a drift (photo).

---

6 Manual gearbox, later version – examination and renovation

---

1 Refer to Section 5, paragraphs 1 to 6.

First motion shaft

2 Refer to Section 5, paragraph 7 and 8.

Third motion shaft

3 Refer to Section 5, paragraph 9. Tap back the tabs which lock the front gear nut, (Fig. 6.5, item 29), hold the shaft in a soft-jawed vice, and remove the nut, using Leyland tool 18G 1024, or by tapping carefully with a punch (photo).

4 Remove the sleeve, third speed gear and thrustwasher, and second speed gear and thrustwasher. Withdraw the first and second speed synchroniser assembly (photos).

5 Remove the speedometer drivegear and key, and the distance piece.

6 Press the shaft out of first gear, reverse gear and the bearing. Alternatively, support the first gear, and tap the shaft through with a soft hammer (photo). Press the bearing from the housing (50).

7 To refit, reverse the dismantling procedure. Take care to line up the lugs on the sleeve (34) with the interlocking thrustwashers. Recheck first, second and third gear endfloats.

Laygear

8 Take the needle roller assemblies from each end of the laygear (photo). Examine them, together with the layshaft, for wear and damage. Inspect the gear teeth. If there is no apparent wear or damage refit the bearings in the laygear.

Rear extension

9 If necessary, carefully prise out the oil seal. Remove the circlip, and press it out. Alternatively carefully tap it out with a long drift. To refit, reverse the dismantling sequence.

Front cover

10 Refer to Section 5, paragraph 32.

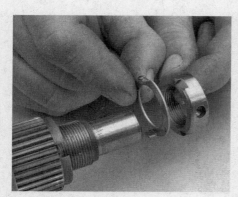

6.3 Third motion shaft front nut

6.4a Remove the sleeve, third speed gear and thrustwasher

6.4b Remove the first/second speed synchroniser assembly

6.6 Removing the third motion shaft

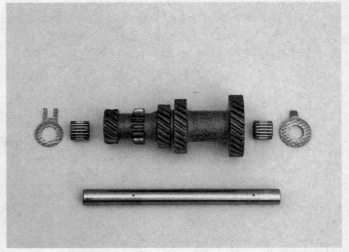

6.8 The layshaft components

7   Manual gearbox, early version – reassembly

1   Place the laygear and thrustwashers in the bottom of the casing (photo).
2   Fit the built-up mainshaft from the rear of the gearbox (photo). Employ the gearbox extension gasket to align the dowel which mates with the extension. Tap the bearing down flush.
3   Grease the orifice in the inner end of the first motion shaft and fit the needle rollers into position. Fit the first motion shaft to the bellhousing end of the gearbox and tap it home, ensuring that no needle rollers are dislodged (photos).
4   Employ a rod to pick up the laygear and thrustwashers. Push the rod through with the layshaft, keeping the shaft and rod pressed together until the layshaft is fully inserted, and has pushed the rod out at the other end. Make sure the cutaway end of the shaft faces forwards (photo).
5   Generously lubricate the gears and bearings throughout assembly.
6   Fit the reverse gear and shaft, noting that the cut-out (arrowed) in the shaft must line up under the threaded hole in the case (photo). Refit the locating bolt (arrowed) and tab washer, and lock the tab (photo).
7   Position shims (38 in Fig. 6.2) against the first motion shaft, tape the splines with plastic tape to avoid damaging the oil seal, and temporarily fit the front cover to check that the step on the end of the layshaft lines up with the cut-out in the cover (photo). Check that the cover is free to move on the studs very slightly in all directions, so allowing the oil seal to centralise over the first motion shaft. If the cover binds at any point, the holes should be relieved just enough to permit the cover to float. Remove the cover.

8   Fit the cover and gasket, pushing them firmly home. Secure the spring washers and nuts finger tight, and tighten them half a turn at a time in a diagonal sequence. Remove the plastic tape.
9   Place the selector forks in position in the order first/second, reverse, and third/fourth (photo).
10   Bolt the selector rod block (67) to the rear face, invert a spring and ball, and hold down the ball slide in the selector rod, picking up the selector fork in the process. Do this with each rod, but ensure that the distance tube is fitted to the third/fourth rod (photos).
11   Align the holes in the forks and shafts, fit the fork locating bolts and locknuts, and tighten the bolts firmly. Secure the locknuts (photos).
12   Assemble the selectors (70, 72, 74) to the exposed ends of the selector rods, secure them with the locating bolts, and lock the bolt heads to the selectors with wire. When correctly assembled the cut-outs in the selectors should line up as shown (photo).
13   Refit the distance tube (115) to the mainshaft.
14   Fit the Woodruff key (125) and front selector lever (119) to the shaft (118). Do not tighten the pinch-bolt.
15   Clean the gearbox rear face, coat with jointing compound, and fit the gasket Coat the extension with jointing compound, place in position, and fit and tighten the spring washers and nuts.
16   Fit the interlock plate with the arms in the cut-out of the selectors, and the side plate in its recess.
17   Tighten the pinch-bolt (120). Refit the cover (30) with its gasket (31).
18   Refit the side cover (12) and gasket (13). Note the fibre washer (17) which must be in position on the bolt shown in Fig. 6.2.
19   Refit the flange (46) on non-overdrive models, the drain plug, dipstick, and speedometer drive pinion (76).
20   Refit the control tower (133). Refill the gearbox with oil.

7.1 Position the laygear

7.2 Refit the third motion shaft

7.3a Fit the needle rollers

7.3b Fit the first motion shaft

7.3c The third motion shaft in place

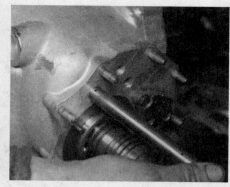
7.4 Fit the layshaft

7.6a The reverse gear shaft cut-out (arrowed)

7.6b The reverse shaft locating bolt and tab washer

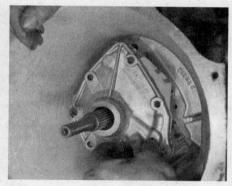
7.7 Offering up the front cover

7.9 The selector forks in place

7.10a Holding down a ball and spring in the selector rod block

7.10b Sliding home a selector rod

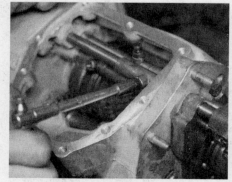
7.11a Tighten the fork locating bolts

7.11b Tighten the locking nuts

7.12 The selectors, correctly positioned

8.1a Position the laygear thrustwashers . . .

8.1b . . . with grease or a magnet

8   Manual gearbox, later version – reassembly

1   Reassembly is largely as for the earlier type gearbox, described in Section 7. Position the laygear thrustwashers (photos).
2   Note the following points:
   (a) *Select fourth gear before fitting the interlock arm (70 in Fig.6.5)*
   (b) *See Section 9 or 10 if the rear extension, mainshaft components, front cover or first motion shaft components have been changed.*
   (c) *Before refitting the flange (59), put the flange bolts through from the back*
   (d) *Pull items 45 to 49 into place, using a piece of tube and a puller (photo)*
   (e) *Note that the baulk rings of the two synchroniser assemblies must not be interchanged. First and second speed rings only have either a fillet at the base of the lugs, or a drift mark for identification purposes.*

9   Shim calculations – new rear cover or third motion shaft components fitted to later type manual gearbox

1   When a new rear cover or third motion shaft components have been fitted, it is essential to recalculate and fit the shims required between the gearbox rear bearing and extension housing (see Fig. 6.8). Proceed as follows:
   (a) *Measure the depth from the gearbox rear face to the rear face of the rear bearing, and call this A*
   (b) *Measure the depth from the bearing register protrusion on the rear extension, to the face which mates with the gearbox. Call this B*
   (c) *Measure the gasket thickness, and call this C (the compressed thickness of the joint can be assumed to be 0.012 in 10.30 mm))*
   (d) *Call the shim thickness required D*
2   To calculate the shim thickness D required, substitute the dimensions measured in 1(a), 1(b) and 1(c) in the following formula:
   D = (A+C-B) +0.000 in (0.00 mm) or -0.001 in (0.03 mm)
Shims are available in two sizes, 0.002 in (0.05 mm) and 0.004 in (0.10 mm).
3   Calculate the shims required between the distance tube and the third motion shaft rear bearing, after fitting the extension in accordance with paragraph 1 and 2.
   (a) *Measure from the distance tube to the extension rear face. Call this E*
   (b) *Measure from the bearing reqisterto the extension rear face. Call this F*
   (c) *Call the shim thickness required G*
4   To calculate shim thickness G, substitute the dimensions measured in 3(a), 3(b) and 3(c) in the following formula:
   G = (E-F) +0.001 in (0.08 mm) or -0.000 in (0.00 mm)
Shims are available in the following sizes: 0.002 in (0.05 mm), 0.005 in (0.13 mm) and 0.010 in (0.25 mm).
5   Retain the bearing with the thickest circlip that will fit the groove, selected from the following available range:
   0.096 to 0.098 in (2.43 to 2.49 mm)
   0.098 to 0.100 in (2.49 to 2.54 mm)
   0.100 to 0.102 in (2.54 to 2.59 mm)

8.2 Positioning the third motion shaft bearing with a puller and packing piece

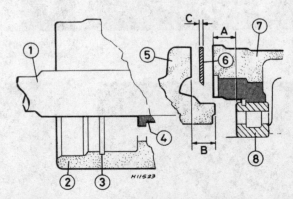

**Fig 6.8 Shim calculations, relating to the gearbox rear extension
For A, B, and C, see text (Sec 9)**

1	Shaft	6	Gasket
2	Rear extension	7	Main casing
3	Circlip groove	8	3rd motion shaft front
4	Distance tube		bearing
5	Rear extension		

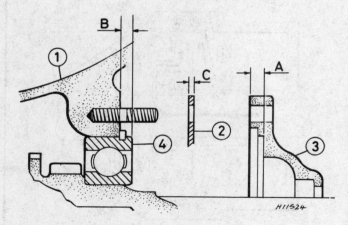

Fig 6.9 Shim calculations, relating to the gearbox front cover. For A, B and C, see text (Sec 10)

1	Gearbox main casing	3	Front cover
2	Cover gasket	4	1st motion shaft bearing

10 Shim calculations – new front cover or first motion shaft components fitted to later type manual gearbox

1 When a new cover or first motion shaft components have been fitted, it is essential to recalculate and fit the shims required between the front bearing and cover. Proceed as follows:
    (a) Measure the depth from the cover mating surface to the surface against which the bearing registers. Call this A
    (b) Call the gasket thickness C (C = .012 in, 0.31 mm)
    (c) Measure the protrusion of the bearing from the case. Call this B
    (d) Call the shim thickness required D
2 Substitute the values A, B and C in the formula below:
$$D = (A+C-B) +0.000 \text{ in } (0.00 \text{ mm}) \text{ or } -0.001 \text{ in } (0.03 \text{ mm})$$
Shims are available in two sizes, 0.002 in (0.05 mm) and 0.004 in (0.10 mm).

11 Overdrive, type D – removal and refitting

1 To remove the overdrive unit, the complete engine, overdrive and gearbox must be removed from the vehicle as described in Chapter 1.
2 Remove the bolts, washers and screws which hold the remote control in position.
3 Remove the eight nuts from the ¼ in (6.35 mm) diameter studs, noting the extra length of one stud, and separate the overdrive casing from the gearbox extension. Carefully pull the overdrive off the end of the mainshaft (photo).
4 To refit the overdrive, place the unit in an upright position and line up the splines of the clutch and planet carrier by eye, turning them anti-clockwise only, with the aid of a long thin screwdriver. The gearbox mainshaft should now enter the overdrive easily.
5 If trouble is experienced do not use force, but separate and re-align the components. Place the gearbox in top gear while refitting, and gently rotate the input shaft to and fro to help in feeding the mainshaft into the splines. At the same time make certain that the lowest portion of the cam on the mainshaft will rest against the pump, and that as the gearbox extension and overdrive come together the end of the mainshaft enters into the needle roller bearing in the tailshaft.
6 Fit the remaining items in reverse of the removal procedure.

12 Overdrive, type D – dismantling, examination and reassembly

Dismantling

1 Referring to Fig. 6.13. remove the operating valve plug (20), spring (22), plunger (23), and ball (24).
2 Bend back the tabs on the four lockwashers (63) and undo the nuts from the bolts (55). Remove the two bridge pieces (62), and the two operating pistons (1) from their cylinders in the main casing assembly (2).
3 Cut the locking wire on the non-return relief valve plug (49); undo the plug and remove the spring (48) and ball (46). The valve body (45) can then be unscrewed from the pump body (43). Undo the grub screw (47) and pull the pump body (43) from the casing (2).
4 Undo the eight nuts and spring washers securing the rear casing (8) a turn at a time. As this is done the pressure of the springs (56) will be released. Take off the main casing (1) and brake ring (7), pull the four clutch springs (56) from their guide bolts (55), and remove the clutch (51) together with the sun wheel assembly (65). If the brake ring (7) sticks to the casing (1), separate them by tapping gently on the flange with a soft hammer.
5 Release the circlip (59) on the splined end of the sun wheel, and push out the wheel (65) from the centre of the clutch assembly.
6 Remove the circlip (58) with circlip pliers, and pull the bearing housing (52) complete with thrust bearing (53) from the clutch assembly (51).
7 Lift the planet carrier (66) from the annulus (75). To remove the uni-directional roller clutch (not recommended unless the rollers are thought to be chipped or worn), take off the circlip and brass retaining washer in front of the clutch. As the inner member (68) is removed the roller bearings (70) will fall out.
8 On no account should the outer bearing ring be removed as it is expanded into the annulus. To renew the roller bearing (76) carefully lever it out or use an extractor if available.
9 Remove the combined output shaft and annulus (75) from the rear casing (8) by removing the locking screw (86) to free the speedometer pinion and bush (88, 89). Remove nut (103) from the rear of the output shaft, and pull off the coupling flange (101). Use a drift to tap out the output shaft and annulus from the rear of the casing. Note that the larger inner bearing will come away with the output shaft. The smaller outer bearing will remain in position, and must be extracted from the rear of the casing.

Examination

10 Clean and inspect all parts, for any obvious wear or flaws. Check that the oil pump plunger and pin are not worn, and that the plunger spring still conforms to the Specifications and is not distorted. Examine the O-rings from the operating pistons and renew them if they are worn or becoming hard. Check that the cylinder bores are free from score marks and wear.
11 Check all bearings for roughness, all splines for burrs and wear,

11.3 Withdrawing the overdrive assembly (Type D)

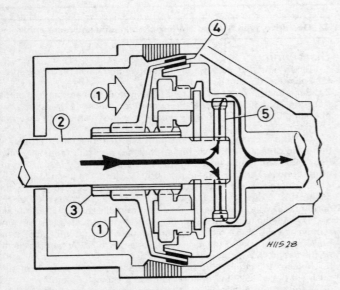

Fig 6.10 Overdrive power train – overdrive not in use (Sec 11)

1 Spring pressure
2 3rd motion shaft
3 Sun wheel
4 Cone clutch
5 Uni-directional clutch

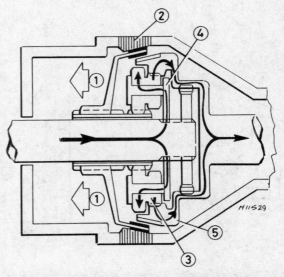

Fig 6.11 Overdrive power train – overdrive in use (Sec 11)

1 Hydraulic pressure
2 Brake ring
3 Planet wheel
4 Planet carrier
5 Annulus

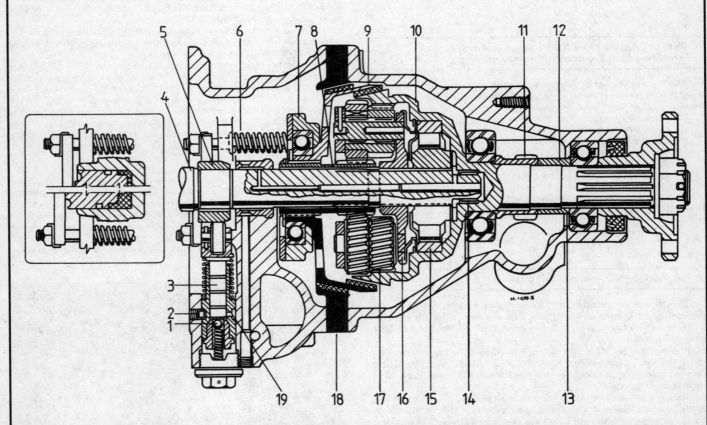

Fig. 6.12 Overdrive unit type D – sectional view. Upper half shows overdrive disengaged, lower half shows overdrive engaged. (The separate detail is of the operating cylinder) (Sec 11)

1 Non-return valve
2 Grub screw – pump body
3 Pump plunger
4 Mainshaft
5 Cam
6 Clutch spring
7 Thrust bearing
8 Sun wheel
9 Cone clutch assembly
10 Annulus
11 Speedometer driving gear
12 Spacer
13 Shim
14 Needle roller bearing
15 Uni-directional clutch
16 Planet carrier
17 Planet wheel
18 Brake ring
19 Oil inlet

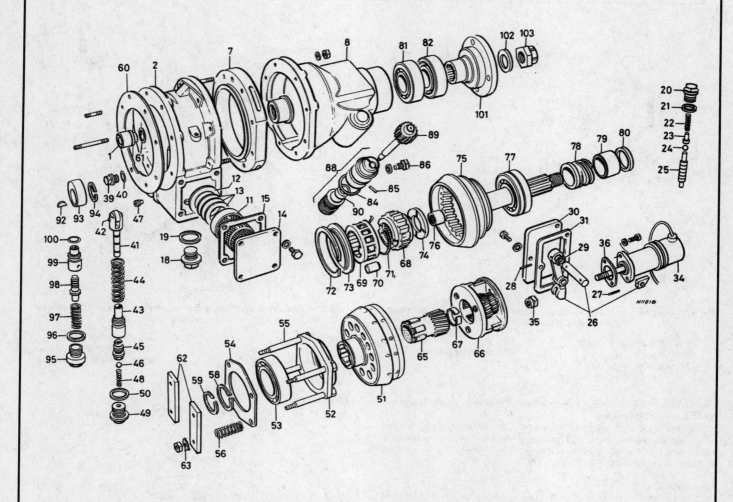

Fig 6.13 Overdrive unit, type D – exploded view (Sec 12)

1	Operating piston	42	Pin	73	Oil thrower
2	Main casing assembly	43	Pump body	74	Thrust bearing
7	Brake ring	44	Pump plunger spring	75	Annulus assembly
8	Intermediate casing	45	Non-return valve body	76	Bearing
11	Filter	46	Steel ball	77	Inner bearing
12	Sealing plate	47	Screw	78	Speedometer driving gear
13	Magnetic rings	48	Spring	79	Bush
14	Side cover plate	49	Plug	80	Thrustwasher
15	Gasket	50	Washer	81	Bearing
18	Drain plug	51	Clutch assembly	82	Oil seal
19	Washer	52	Bearing housing	83	Steady bush – 3rd motion shaft
20	Plug	53	Thrust bearing	84	O-ring
21	Washer	54	Plate	85	Pin
22	Spring	55	Bolt	86	Locking screw
23	Plunger	56	Spring	88	Speedometer drive bearing assembly
24	Steel ball	58	Circlip	89	Speedometer driven gear
25	Operating valve	59	Circlip	90	Oil seal – speedometer bearing
26	Operating valve lever assembly	60	Gasket	92	Key
27	Mills pin	61	O-ring	93	Cam
28	Mills pin	62	Bridge piece	94	Circlip
29	O-ring	63	Lockwasher	95	Plug
30	Cover – solenoid	65	Sun wheel assembly	96	Washer
31	Gasket	66	Planet carrier	97	Spring
34	Solenoid	67	Locating ring – 3rd motion shaft	98	Plunger
35	Self-locking nut	68	Inner member – uni-directional clutch	99	Body
36	Gasket	69	Cage – uni-directional clutch	100	O-ring
39	Plug	70	Roller – uni-directional clutch	101	Flange
40	Washer	71	Spring for clutch	102	Washer
41	Pump plunger	72	Circlip	103	Nut

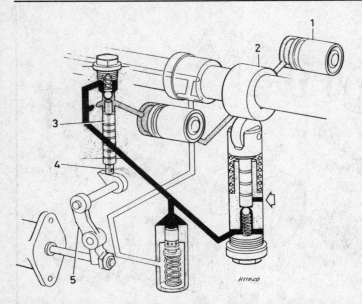

Fig 6.14 Overdrive hydraulic system components, with overdrive not in use (Sec 12)

1　Operating cylinders	4　Jet
2　Cam	5　Operating linkage
3　Operating valve	

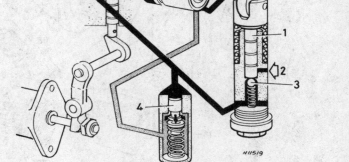

Fig 6.15 Overdrive hydraulic systsem components, with overdrive in use (Sec 12)

1　Oil pump	4　Oil relief valve
2　Oil inlet	5　Axial mainshaft drilling
3　Non-return valve	6　Mainshaft steady bush

and the clutch rollers for any visual defects. Check the bush (83) and the thrustwasher (74) for wear.

12　Renew the clutch linings if they are burnt or worn. Examine the gear teeth for cracks, chips, and general wear, and the sealing balls for ridges which will prevent them seating properly. Check the free length of the springs against the Specifications.

Reassembly

13　Obtain new gaskets and seals as necessary. Refit the annulus and output shaft (75) in the rear casing (10). Do not omit to fit the speedometer drivegear (78), bush (79), and thrustwasher (80). When fitting a new bearing note that four different thicknesses of shim are available, namely, 0.090 in (2.28 mm), 0.095 in (2.41 mm), 0.100 in (2.54 mm), 0.105 in (2.67 mm). Output shaft endfloat is 0.005 to 0.010 in (0.13 to 0.25 mm).

14　Refit the coupling flange (101), the flange washer (102), and the castellated nut (103). Tighten it to the specified torque, and lock with a split pin.

15　Refit the speedometer drivegear (89) and the drive bearing assembly (88), securing the latter with the washer (87) and lockscrew (86).

16　Refit the thrust bearing (74). Reassemble the uni-directional clutch, holding the rollers (70) in place in the cage (69) with grease prior to fitting the inner member (68). Ensure that the spring (71) is fitted in such a way that it pushes the rollers up the ramp on the inner member (68). Fit the oil thrower (73) and circlip (72).

17　Turn the planet gearwheels to permit the line etched on each wheel to line up with one of the three corresponding lines on the periphery of the planet carrier (see Fig. 6.16). Insert the sun wheel (65) into the carrier to keep the planet gearwheels in the correct positions, and fit the complete sun wheel and carrier assembly to the annulus. The sun wheel may then be withdrawn. Note that the sunwheel can now be inserted or removed as required, but if the planet carrier is removed from the annulus. the carrier gear wheels will have to be reset.

18　Slide the splined end of the sun wheel (65) into the centre of the clutch assembly and secure it with the snap ring (59). If the thrust bearing was removed for renewal, press the new bearing (53) in its housing (52); insert the four bolts (55) into the housing threaded ends facing forwards, and fit the bearing and housing assembly (53, 55) over the centre of the clutch assembly (51). Lock the bearing and housing with the circlip (58) which fits in a groove on the clutch.

19　Carefully fit the clutch and sun wheel assembly to the planet carrier

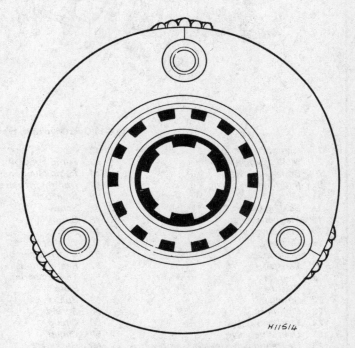

Fig 6.16 Overdrive type D – lining up the etched lines on the planet wheel with those on the planet carrier, before fitting the carrier to the sun wheel (Sec 12)

in the annulus. Refit the retainer plate (54) and clutch springs (56) over the bolts (55).

20　Coat the mating faces of the main casing (2) and the brake ring (7) with jointing compound. Note: that the smaller diameter of the brake ring abuts the main casing, and fit the ring and casing together.

21　Coat the mating surfaces of the brake ring (7) and rear casing (8) with jointing compound. Offer up the rear casing to the brake ring and front casing. Slide the four bolts (55) through their holes in the main casing and refit and tighten down a turn at a time the nuts and washers which hold the casings together.

22 Fit the 0-rings (61) to the two operating pistons (1). Lubricate the pistons generously with oil, and slide them into their cylinders in the housing, with the spigoted ends facing the front of the overdrive assembly. Slip the two bridge pieces (62) over the ends of the four bolts (55) and refit the washers and nuts. Turn up the lockwasher tabs.

23 Refit the oil pump body, small end first, into the centre hole at the bottom of the casing making sure the oil inlet faces the rear. Gently tap it into position until the groove lines up with the grub screw hole. Fit and tighten the grub screw.

24 Refit the components of the relief valve, operating valve, and nonreturn valve and do up the three plugs. Lock together the heads of the relief valve and non-return valve with wire.

13 Operating lever, type D overdrive – adjustment

1   If the overdrive does not engage or release, and if the solenoid is in order, the operating lever will probably require adjustment.

2   Remove the three bolts and washers, and the cover plate (30 in Fig. 6.13).

3   Switch the ignition on, put the car in top gear, and flick the actuating switch to the overdrive position. If a 3/16 in (4.76 mm) diameter rod will now pass through hole A in the operating arm (see Fig. 6.17), adjustment is correct.

4   If adjustment is necessary, hold the solenoid plunger by the two flats machined on its shank and, pressing the plunger tightly into the solenoid, screw the self-locking nut B in or out until the test rod can be pushed fully home into the casing.

5   Operate the switch several times, and check the adjustment. Measure the current consumed by the solenoid which, with the operating arm correctly set, should be 2 amps. If a reading of about 17 amps is obtained, the solenoid plunger is not moving sufficiently to switch to the holding coil from the operating coil. If very fine adjustment will not remedy this condition, fit a new solenoid and plunger.

14 Relief, non-return and operating valves, type D overdrive – removal, inspection and refitting

Relief and non-return valves

1   Access to the valves in the bottom of the overdrive is gained after removing the engine steady rod and bracket from the rear crossmember. Drain the oil from the gearbox and overdrive.

2   Cut through the locking wire, unscrew the plugs and remove and clean the components. The valve cap and non-return valve body are unscrewed from the pump, and the relief valve body is removed with circlip pliers.

3   Examine the seatings for pits or chips, and the balls for wear, and ridges. If the non-return valve ball is undamaged and the seating is suspect, tap the ball firmly into its seat with a soft metal drift.

4   To refit, reverse the removal procedure. Remember the copper washer on the relief valve between the cap and main casing. Hold the non-return valve ball to its spring with petroleum jelly whilst fitting.

Operating valve

5   Remove the remote control assembly from inside the car. Undo the plug and check that the ball is lifted 1/32 in when the solenoid is actuated. Failure to move points to a fault in the solenoid or operating arm.

6   Remove the ball with a magnet, and the valve with a piece of 1/8 in wire. Check the ball and seat and clean out the small hole in the side of the valve tube. Check the oil pump by jacking the rear of the car off the ground, engage top gear and overdrive, and with the engine running watch for oil being pumped into the valve chamber.

7   To refit, reverse the removal procedure.

15 Oil seal and driveshaft bearings, type D overdrive – removal and refitting

Oil seal

1   The seal may be renewed with the unit still in the vehicle. Remove the propeller shaft and flange, and remove the seal using an extractor or by careful prising. Tap in a new seal squarely (photo).

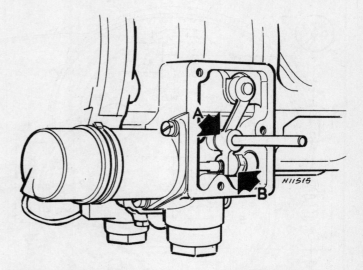

Fig 6.17 Solenoid operating lever – checking and adjustment. For A and B, see text (Sec 13)

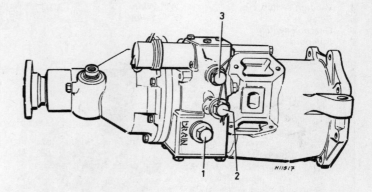

Fig 6.18 Overdrive type D – underside (Sec 14)

1	Drain plug	3	Relief valve plug
2	Non-return valve plug		

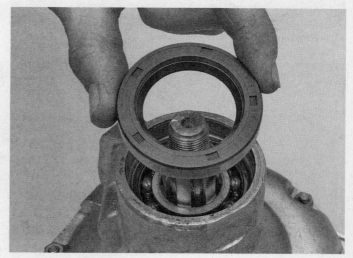

15.1 A new rear oil seal

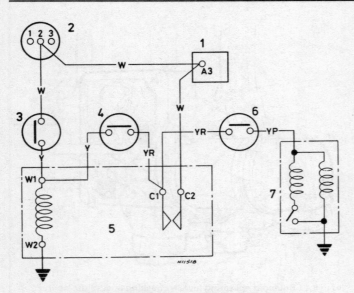

Fig 6.19 Electrical circuit – overdrive type D (Sec 16)

1	Fuse block	Cable colours	
2	Ignition switch	P	Purple
3	Driver's switch	R	Red
4	Vacuum switch	W	White
5	Relay	Y	Yellow
6	Gearbox switch		
7	Solenoid		

Bearings

2   Remove the combined annulus and output shaft (Section 12), and remove the front driveshaft bearing, preferably using a press. Fit a new bearing using a press, or by carefully tapping it on using a piece of tube over the shaft and up against the bearing inner track.

3   Press or tap the rear bearing from the housing. Press the new bearing into position, or use a suitable piece of tube against the outer track, and tap it into place.

16   Relay operation, type D overdrive

1   Primary operation of the overdrive unit is by a manually-operated switch on the facia, which operates a solenoid.

2   When overdrive is engaged the contacts of the actuating switch are closed and current is fed through the ignition switch and A3 fuse to the relay operating coil. The contacts of the relay close, connecting the A3 terminal to the gear switch, and as long as the car is in third or fourth gears the pushrod in the solenoid will move the operating arm in the overdrive, bringing indirect third or top into operation.

3   When the actuating switch is moved to the NORMAL position with the accelerator held down to open the vacuum switch, the circuit is broken and direct drive is re-engaged. Direct drive is also obtained if second gear is selected as this opens the gear switch contact. If the accelerator is not depressed when the switch is moved from OVERDRIVE to NORMAL the vacuum switch overrides the electrical switch until the speeds in the overdrive are the same to give a snatch-free change into direct drive.

17   Overdrive, Laycock type LH – removal and refitting

1   Remove the engine and gearbox complete from the vehicle (see Chapter 1). Drain the gearbox and overdrive oil.

2   Remove the bolts, and the remote control housing (photo). Unscrew the eight nuts securing the overdrive unit to the gearbox adaptor, and withdraw the overdrive unit (photo).

3   Slide the pump driving cam from the gearbox shaft, and withdraw the cam locking ball from the pocket in the shaft. Remove the pump cam circlip using tool number 18G1004 or circlip pliers. The selector interlocking arm and plate assembly can now be withdrawn. Remove the adaptor securing nuts, followed by the adaptor (photos).

4   To refit, reverse the removal procedure.

18   Overdrive, Laycock type LH – dismantling, examination and reassembly

Dismantling

1   Remove the solenoid cover and plunger, the relief valve assembly, the sump and filter and the pump items (see Section 19).

2   Remove the speedometer drive clip, gear and seal.

3   Remove the nuts and withdraw the rear casing from the main casing. Remove the planet gear assembly.

4   From the main casing, remove the bridge pieces, the pistons, clutch

17.2a Removing the remote control housing

17.2b Withdraw the overdrive unit (Type LH)

17.3a Removing the pump drive cam

17.3b Remove the gearbox adaptor

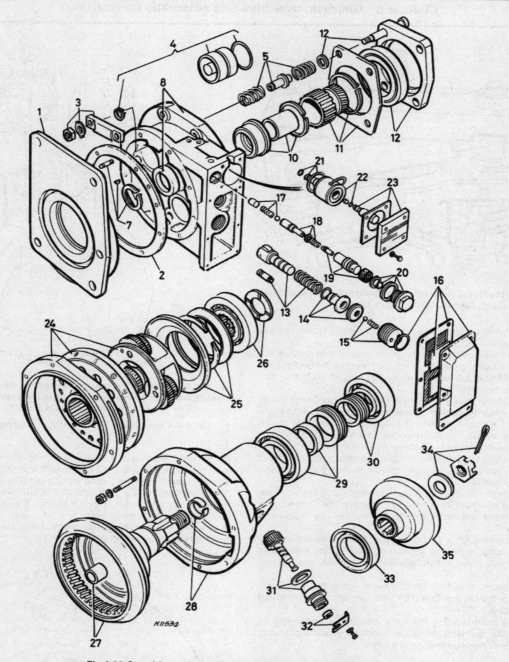

Fig 6.20 Overdrive unit, Laycock type LH – exploded view (Sec 18)

1 Adaptor plate
2 Gasket
3 Bridge piece, tab washer and locknut
4 Operating piston, O-ring and circlip
5 Thrust rod and springs
6 Thrust housing pin and washer
7 Circlip, stud and key
8 Pump cam and main casing
9 Ball, plug and grommet
10 Thrust bush, sun wheel bush and circlip
11 Sun wheel, circlip and retainer plate
12 Thrust ball race and thrust ring
13 Pump suction tube, pump plunger and spring
14 O-ring, pump body and non-return valve seat
15 Valve ball, spring and pump plug
16 O-ring, sump filter and gasket, magnets and sump
17 Low pressure valve plug, spring and ball
18 Low pressure valve body, washer and relieff valve spring

19 Valve plunger, valve body and filter
20 O-ring, O-ring washer and plug
21 O-ring, solenoid valve body and O-ring
22 Solenoid coil, valve ball and O-ring
23 Solenoid plunger, gasket and solenoid cover
24 Brake ring, clutch siding member and planet carrier
25 Oil catcher, circlip and oil thrower
26 Uni-directional clutch, thrustwasher
27 Bush and annulus
28 Spring ring and rear casing
29 Annulus front bearing, spacer and speedometer drivegear
30 Selective spacer and rear bearing
31 Speedometer driven gear, sealing washer and bearing
32 Oil seal and retaining clip
33 Oil seal
34 Washer, nut and split pin
35 Drive flange

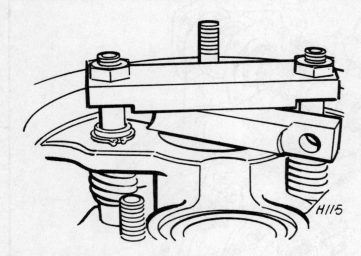

Fig 6.21 Removing the thrust rods, using the bridge pieces – overdrive unit, Laycock type LH (Sec 18)

sliding member, brake-ring and sun wheel. Remove the clutch springs and selective washers.

5   Prise the sun wheel retaining ring from the groove, and remove the wheel. Withdraw the bearing retainer plate, and remove the circlip. Drift the clutch sliding member carefully from the bearing, which in turn can be pressed from the housing.

6   To remove the thrust rods and springs, fit four studs into the thrust ring and insert the studs through the thrust rods from the rear. Lay one bridge piece across a piston chamber on its side, fit the other to the normal assembly position but inverted over the adjacent thrust ring studs and secure with two nuts. Tighten the nuts until the springs compress sufficiently, and remove the circlips retaining the thrust rods and springs. Unscrew the two nuts evenly. Repeat the process to remove the other thrust rods.

7   Remove the flange nut. Prevent it from turning using Leyland tool number 18G34A, if available or locate two studs in the flange holes and place a suitable bar between them. An assistant will be required to support the casing.

8   Withdraw the annulus from the front of the case. If the front bearing remains in the housing, remove it if necessary by drifting it carefully against the inner track. Press or carefully drift out the rear bearing and seal.

9   Remove the spacer, speedometer drivegear and selective spacer, noting the selective spacer position. The selective spacer is identified by a peripheral groove.

10   To remove the front bearing from the annulus, a puller will be required. Remove the split ring, oil thrower and uni-directional clutch, and collect the rollers. Remove the thrustwasher.

Examination

11   Proceed as in Section 12, paragraphs 10, 11 and 12. In particular check the pistons and bores for scoring, and inspect the shaft splines for signs of wear or damage. New selective washers must also be obtained (a set of four) if the existing ones are worn.

Reassembly

12   Press the front bearing into place, ensuring that the outer track butts against the casing shoulder. Press the annulus into position and fit the spacer, speedometer gear and selective washer. If any of these items have been renewed, a dial gauge will be required to check the endfloat, first from the selective washer rear face and second from the shoulder of the rear bearing housing. The correct reading should be 0.010 in (0.254 mm), +0.000 -0.005 in (0.128 mm) larger than the second. If incorrect readings are obtained, check that the bearing is correctly located. If adjustment is required, selective washers are available in seven sizes from 0.360 in (9.1 mm) to 0.390 in (9.9 mm).

13   Fit the rear bearing. Lubricate and fit the flange oil seal. Fit the flange, fit and tighten the nut to the specified torque, and secure with a new split pin (early type).

14   Refit the thrust ring and uni-directional clutch unit. Assemble the oil thrower and split ring and ensure that the clutch turns anti-clockwise.

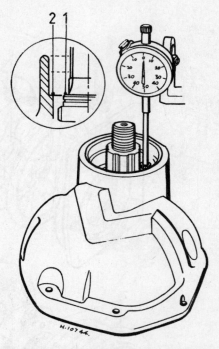

Fig 6.22 Using a dial gauge to ascertain the selective washer requirement between the bearings in the casings – overdrive unit Laycock type LH (Sec 18)

1   Selective washer rear face   2   Bearing housing shoulder

15   Before inserting the sun wheel into the planet carrier, locate each planet wheel with its punch mark and keyway outwards and in alignment with the wheel shaft locking pin (Fig. 6.23). Insert the planet carrier in the annulus and remove the sun wheel. Align the splines in the carrier and uni-directional clutch. If available use special tool 18G185 for accurate alignment.

16   To refit the clutch release thrust rods, reverse the dismantling procedure given in paragraph 6.

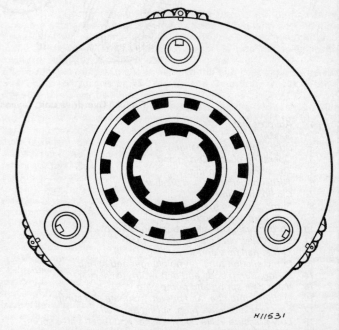

Fig 6.23 The correct position of the planet wheels, when fitting the sun wheel and assembly the annulus (Sec 18)

19.1a Remove the solenoid cover

19.1b Withdraw the solenoid assembly

19.1c The solenoid components

19.8 Remove the sump cover and filter

17 Refit the pistons. Refit the clutch sliding member and related components, in the reverse order of dismantling. Ensure that the selective washers fitted, whether old or new, are a complete set.
18 Refit the sun wheel, brake ring and clutch sliding member, reversing the procedures given in paragraphs 4 and 5. Smear the joint faces of the brake ring with jointing compound. Lock the nuts with new tab washers on early models.
19 Smear the joint faces of the two casings with jointing compound. When assembling, ensure that the sun wheel and planet gears are correctly meshed.
20 Reverse the dismantling procedure for the remaining items.

19 Solenoid and operating components, type LH overdrive – removal, dismantling, reassembly and refitting

Solenoid

1 To remove, drain the gearbox, remove the four screws which retain the solenoid cover, and remove the cover and gasket. Prise out the solenoid with a screwdriver do not pull on the supply lead (photos).
2 Press the coil and base cap from the housing, and remove the operating valve plunger and ball by shaking from the rod.
3 Clean and examine the ball and rod for scoring or pitting. Renew if necessary. Using a suitable drift the ball may be tapped onto the seat to reseat it. Renew the 0-ring seals.

4 To reassemble, reverse the dismantling procedure. Refit to the overdrive unit, pressing the lead grommet into the slot, and using a new gasket under the cover.

Relief and low pressure valve

5 To remove, drain the gearbox, and unscrew and remove the relief valve plug and sealing washer. Take out the assembly.
6 To dismantle, remove the filter, spacer tube, valve unit and relief valve spring. Examine the plunger and seat. If pitted or worn renew it. Renew the 0-rings and any other parts which are worn or suspect, particularly the relief valve spring.
7 To reassemble and refit, reverse the dismantling and removal procedures. Ensure that the spacer tube slotted end is farthest from the filter, and that the slots are lined up with the oil outlet hole and the locating stud.

Filters

8 Drain the gearbox, clean the sump area and remove the sump screws, followed by the cover and filter (photo).
9 Clean the two internal magnets, and wash the filter and cover in fuel.
10 Take out the relief valve body, and the filter. Clean the filter in fuel, and refit it, followed by the body assembly, sealing washer and plug.
11 Refit the filter and sump cover, and refill the gearbox with oil.

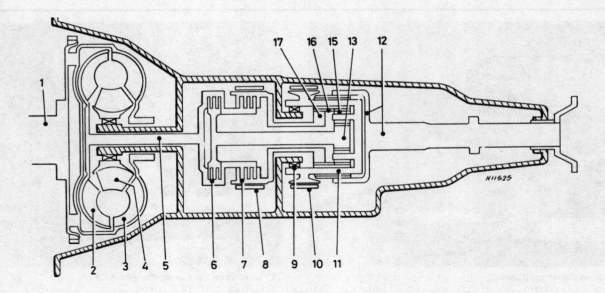

Fig 6.24 Automatic transmission – diagram of the main mechanical components (Sec 21)

1 Engine crankshaft	5 Input shaft	9 Uni-directional clutch	13 Forward sun gear and shaft
2 Turbine	6 Front clutch	10 Rear brake band	15 Short planet pinion
3 Impeller	7 Rear clutch	11 Plant pinion carrier	16 Long planet pinion
4 Stator	8 Front brake band	12 Ring gear and output shaft	17 Reverse sun gear

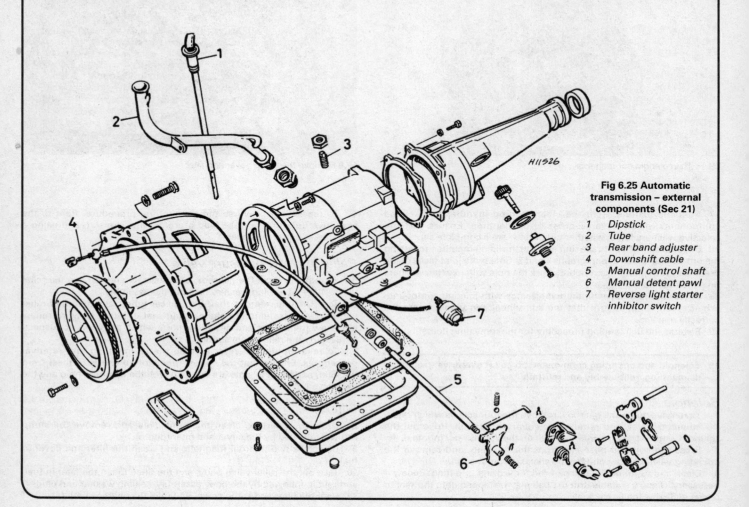

Fig 6.25 Automatic transmission – external components (Sec 21)

1 Dipstick
2 Tube
3 Rear band adjuster
4 Downshift cable
5 Manual control shaft
6 Manual detent pawl
7 Reverse light starter inhibitor switch

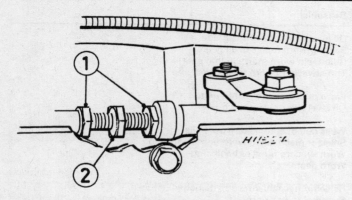

Fig 6.26 Selector rod adjuster, automatic transmission (on left-hand side of the unit) (Sec 21)

1   Locknuts   2   Adjuster

Pump and non-return valve

12   Proceed as in paragraph 8. Preferably using tool 18G1118, remove the pump retaining plug followed by the spring and ball, the pump body, plunger spring and plunger.
13   Carefully part the non-return valve seat from the body, check the ball and seat condition, and renew if necessary. Tap the ball lightly on to the seat Renew 0-rings if suspect.
14   To reassemble, refit the seat to the pump body. Fit the plunger to the casing with the flat side to the rear of the overdrive, retaining it in place with Leyland tool 18G1117. Refit the remaining parts in reverse order.

---

20   Selector switch and isolation switch, Laycock type LH overdrive – removal and refitting

Selector switch

1   To remove, take out the centre console where fitted (see Chapter 12), lift the gaiter up and pull the electrical leads apart. Lever off the cap on the gear lever, disconnect the leads, remove the retaining screws and switch.
2   To refit, reverse the removal procedure.

Isolation switch

3   Support the rear of the engine/gearbox unit, and take out the nut and bolt holding the engine restrainer to the gearbox bracket. Remove the screws holding the rear mounting to the extension, and the bolts holding the bottom tie-bracket to the crossmember. Remove the screws holding the rear crossmember to the body. and take it away. Lower the engine/gearbox assembly. Remove the console (see Chapter 12), disconnect the switch leads, and with a long punch through the gear lever aperture, remove the switch.
4   To refit, fit the switch and the backing washers. Place a test lamp across the switch terminals, switch on the overdrive, and see that the lamp lights when 4th gear is selected, but no other. Adjust by means of the packing washers, which should be added or subtracted as required. Refit the remaining items in reverse order.

---

21   Automatic transmission – testing and adjustment

1   Extensive dismantling of the automatic transmission requires specialised knowledge and skills which are felt to be outside the scope of this manual. Owners who feel competent enough to undertake this work are advised to obtain a copy of the manual published by the transmission manufacturer. Additionally, it should be mentioned that if it is necessary to dismantle the unit to renew one failed component, then others may also be close to failure, and the purchase of a reconditioned unit may be the most economic course of action.

Reverse light/starter inhibitor switch

2   Disconnect the leads from the switch, connect a test lamp and battery across the reverse terminals, and another lamp and battery across the starter terminals. Select D, L1 or L2. Unscrew the switch till the reverse contacts make. Now screw it in counting the amount turned until the starter circuit is made. Halfway between these points is the correct setting.

Selector adjustment

3   A malfunction requiring selector adjustment can be confirmed by noting when changes such as Neutral to Drive or to Reverse occur in relation to the detents in the selector.
4   Place the selector lever to N. Remove the nut and the manual lever from the selector shaft on the gearbox. With a spanner on the flats on the end of the shaft turn it to P, which is as far as it will go anti-clockwise. Then bring it clockwise two clicks. Undo the two locknuts and turn the adjuster so that the lever will fit straight back on the shaft.

Stall test

5   Stall speed is that obtainable at full throttle, with the vehicle stationary. To test, select a deserted open space, ensure that the vehicle is warmed up, and apply the handbrake. Select P and check the fluid level.
6   Apply the footbrake hard, select L1 or R and push down the accelerator pedal to the kickdown position *for a maximum period of 10 seconds*. Note the maximum engine speed reached, and relate to the following table:
   (a) *Stall test below 1250 rpm: Stator slip or engine condition poor*
   (b) *Stall test 1800 to 2100 rpm: Normal*
   (c) *Stall test over 2700 rpm: Transmission slip*

Slip test

7   If there is slip (usually accompanied by squawking) note when it occurs. Note also whether there is flare-up (engine speed increasing between gear shifts, especially when changing up). Slip will usually be a band or clutch not applied either from lack of oil pressure, a wrongly set valve, or most unlikely, worn friction members. Flare-up is when a gear is out of adjustment, and one is let go before the other is engaged.

Brake band adjustment

8   The rear band can be adjusted by the screw on the right side outside the casing. Tighten it to 10 lbf ft (13.6 Nm), back it off one turn, then tighten the locknut to the specified torque.
9   To reach the front band the oil must be drained and the gearbox sump removed. Pull back the adjuster and place a gauge block 0.250 in (6.35 mm) thick between the adjusting screw and the servo piston pin. Undo the locknut and tighten the adjuster screw to a torque of *only* 10 lbf in (1.13 Nm), and tighten the locknut to the specified torque.

Downshift cable assembly

10   To check the cable adjustment first ensure that, with the carburetors set at normal idle, the crimped stop on the inner cable just contacts the abutment on the outer downshift cable. Apply the handbrake.
11   Remove the line pressure take-off plug from the rear face of the fat part of the gearcase, off centre to the left. just above the rear face of the gearbox sump. Fit a pressure gauge reading up to 150 lbf/in² (10.50 kgf/cm²). Start the engine and warm up. With the engine idling in N the pressure should be between 55 and 65 lbf/in² (3.60 to 4.20 kgf/cm²).
12   Engage D, and hold the brakes hard on with the left foot. Increase engine speed to 1000 rpm. The pressure should now be 90 to 100 lbf/in² (6.10 to 7.00 kgf/cm²). If it is too high alter the cable adjuster to shorten the outer cable: if too low lengthen it.

---

22   Fault diagnosis – manual gearbox, overdrive and automatic transmission

Manual gearbox and overdrive

It is sometimes difficult to decide whether it is worthwhile removing and dismantling the gearbox for a fault which may be nothing more than a minor irritant. Gearboxes which howl, or where the synchromesh can be 'beaten' by a quick gear change, may continue to perform for a long time in this state. A worn gearbox usually needs a complete rebuild to eliminate noise because the various gears, if re-aligned on new bearings, will continue to howl when different wearing surfaces are presented to each other.

The decision to overhaul, therefore, must be considered with regard to time and money available, relative to the degree of noise or malfunction that the driver can tolerate.

Symptom	Reason(s)
Gearbox noisy	Oil level low or incorrect grade Bearing worn (noise in all gears) Gear teeth worn (noise in that gear) Thrustwashers worn or incorrect size
Sychromesh ineffective	Worn or defective synchro unit(s) Oil level low or incorrect grade
Jumping out of gear	Weak detent springs or worn balls Selector mechanism worn or maladjusted Worn synchro hubs or baulk rings Worn gears
Difficulty in engaging gear	Selector mechanism worn, damaged or loose Synchro unit(s) worn Mainshaft endfloat excessive Clutch fault (see Chapter 5)
Overdrive will not engage	Oil level low or filter clogged Electrical system defect (wire disconnected, switch/relay/solenoid malfunction or madadjustment Hydraulic system defect
Overdrive will not disengage (*do not reverse vehicle*)	Electrical system defect (short-circuit or faulty switch) Solenoid sticking or maladjusted Vacuum switch sticking (Type D only) Cone clutch sticking to brake ring Clutch springs weak or broken Hydraulic system defect

Automatic transmission

If the automatic transmission fluid is in good condition and at the correct level, and the checks and adjustments described in Section 21 have been carried out, there is little more that the home mechanic can do. Diagnostic work should be left to a specialist and the transmission should not be removed from the car until diagnosis has been carried out. Typical shift speeds are listed below for the guidance of owners who wish to ascertain whether or not a fault exists.

Driving conditions		Upshifts mph (kph)		Downshifts mph (kph)		
		1 to 2	2 to 3	3 to 2	3 to 1	2 to 1
D selected:	Min throttle	8 to 12 (13 to 19)	13 to 17 (21 to 27)			
	Full throttle	22 to 29 (35 to 46)	41 to 48 (65 to 78)			
	Kickdown	30 to 37 (48 to 60)	57 to 62 (91 to 100)	50 to 57 (80 to 91)	20 to 26 (32 to 41)	20 to 26 (32 to 41)
L2 selected:	Full throttle					2 to 5 (3 to 8)
	Kickdown					20 to 26 (32 to 41)
L1 selected:	Min throttle					10 to 15 (16 to 24)

Chapter 7 Propeller Shaft

Contents

Specifications

Type .... Tubular, telescopic, with needle roller universal joints

Overall length
Fully extended:
    Standard .... 30 3/4 in (78.1 cm)
    Overdrive .... 31 7/8 in (81.0 cm)
Fully compressed:
    Standard .... 29 1/16 in (74.0 cm)
    Overdrive .... 30 3/16 in (76.5 cm)

Length of shaft assembly
Standard .... 25 11/32 in (64.3 cm)
Overdrive .... 26 15/32 in (67.0 cm)

Lubricant
Type .... Multi-purpose lithium based grease

Torque wrench setting

	lbf ft	Nm
Flange nuts	30 to 35	41 to 47

1 General description

The drive is transmitted from the gearbox to the rear axle by a Hardy Spicer tubular propeller shaft, fitted with a universal joint at each end to accommodate vertical movement of the rear axle. A sliding spline at the front of the shaft absorbs fore-and-aft movement of the axle. Two types of universal joint are fitted, the sealed and the non-sealed.

It should be noted that shafts of differing overall lengths are used on standard and overdrive vehicles.

2 Routine maintenance

1   On shafts with non-sealed joints, a grease nipple is provided on each joint and a third at the sliding yoke. On the sealed type, the only nipple is on the sliding yoke.

2   To lubricate, wipe the nipples clean and give three or four strokes of the grease gun.

3 Propeller shaft – removal and refitting

1   Place the vehicle over a pit or on a ramp, or jack the rear of the vehicle, making sure that it is very firmly supported. Apply the handbrake and place the car in gear.
2   The propeller shaft is balanced to fine limits and it is important that it is refitted in the position it was in prior to removal. Scratch a mark on the four flanges to ensure accurate reassembly.
3   Remove the self-locking nuts, bolts and washers which hold the flanges together. Lower the propeller shaft to the ground.
4   To refit, reverse the removal procedure. Line up the mating marks, ensuring that the flanges are clean, before tightening the bolts to the specified torque. Use new self-locking nuts if possible.

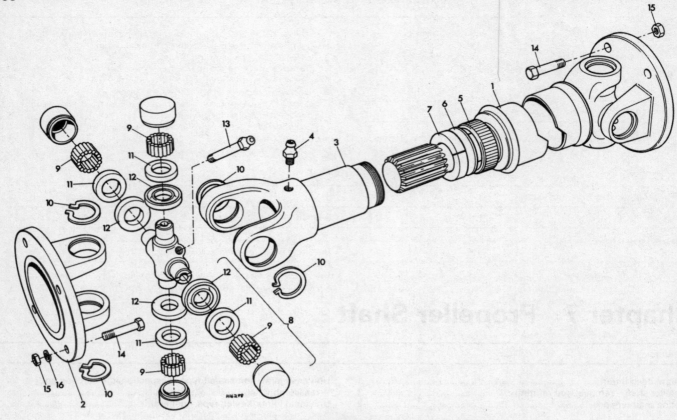

Fig 7.1 Propeller shaft, non-sealed type – exploded view (Sec 4)

1	Shaft assembly	5	Dust cap	9	Needle bearing assembly	13	Lubricator
2	Flange yoke	6	Steel washer	10	Circlip	14	Flange bolt
3	Sleeve assembly	7	Cork washer	11	Gasket	15	Nut
4	Lubricator	8	Journal assembly	12	Gasket retainer	16	Washer

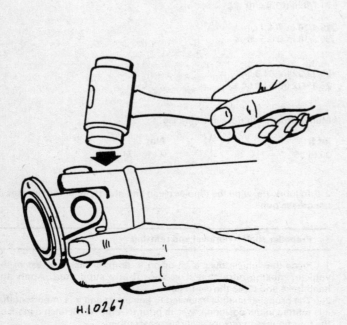

Fig 7.2 Tapping the yoke to free a bearing (circlip removed) (Sec 4)

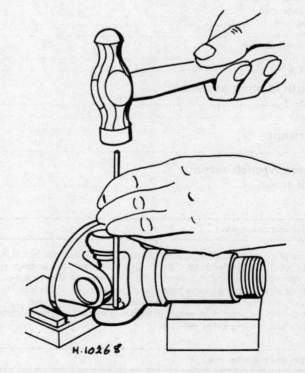

Fig 7.3 To remove a tight bearing, tap it out from the inside using a thin drift (Sec 4)

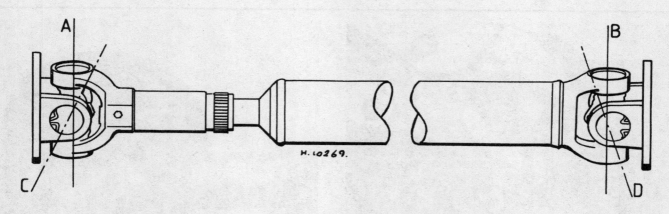

Fig 7.4 The assembled propeller shaft, showing yokes A and B and flanges C and D in alignment (Sec 4)

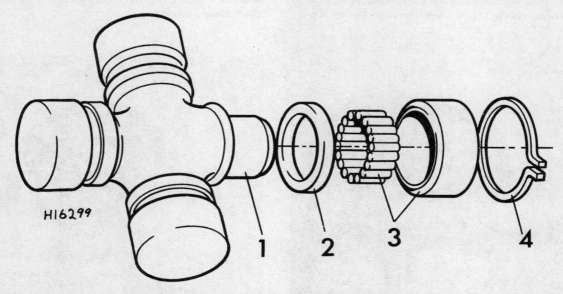

Fig 7.5 Universal joint, sealed type – component parts (Sec 5)

1	*Journal spider*	2	*Rubber seal*	3	*Needle rollers and bearing cup*	4	*Circlip*

4   Universal joint, non-sealed type – inspection, dismantling and reassembly

Inspection

1 Wear at the joints is characterised by transmission vibration, clonks on taking up the drive, and in extreme cases of lack of lubrication, metallic sounds as the bearings break up.

2 Check the needle roller bearings with the propeller shaft in position. Test the rear universal joint by trying to turn the shaft with one hand. whilst holding the rear axle flange with the other. Repeat the test whilst holding the shaft and the front gearbox flange. Any movement discernible in the joints is indicative of wear, and a complete repair kit should be purchased.

3 Examine the propeller shaft splines. Unscrew the dust cap from the sleeve and slide the sleeve from the shaft. Take off the steel washer and the cork washer, and inspect the splines. Wear means that the sleeve assembly must be renewed.

4 Examine the condition of the yokes. Look for fractures and cracks, and for ovality of the bearing bores and fixing bolt holes. Discard the yoke if worn.

Dismantling

5 Clean the whole joint area, and remove the circlips. If they are difficult to remove, tap the bearing face to ease the pressure against the clip. Hold the propeller shaft in one hand and remove the bearing cups by tapping the yoke at each bearing with a copper or hide-faced hammer. As the bearings emerge, draw them out with the fingers.

6 If a bearing cup refuses to move, place a thin bar against the inside of the bearing and tap it gently until the cup starts to emerge. With the bearings removed, extract the spiders from the yokes. Inspect all parts for wear.

Reassembly

7 Thoroughly clean all parts, and apply a coat of shellac to the shoulders on the spiders, to assist with sealing.

8 Refit the gasket retainer, using a hollow drift. Fit new gaskets. Assemble the needle rollers in the bearing races with the assistance of some thin grease.

9 Insert the spiders in the yoke flanges with the lubricating nipples (where fitted) facing the propeller shaft, and not the yoke flanges. Refit the bearing cups, tapping them home with a soft drift. Refit the circlips. and lubricate the joint assembly via the grease nipple.

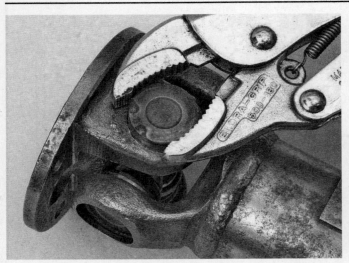

5.2 A self-grip wrench can be of help when removing a bearing cup

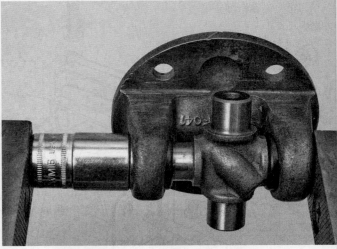

5.4a Refitting a bearing cup

5.4b A bearing cup can be pressed into place by using a vice and a suitable sized socket

5.4c Fitting a bearing cup

10 Fit the dust cap, steel washer, and a new cork gasket over the splined part of the propeller shaft.

11 Grease the splines and sleeve. Line up the arrow on the sleeve with that on the splined shaft, and push the sleeve over the splines. Fit the washers to the sleeve and screw up the dust cap. If correctly assembled the forked yokes on the shafts will have their axes parallel. This is essential if vibration is to be eliminated.

5 Universal joints, sealed type – general

1   The sealed universal joints employ a rubber seal instead of a gasket and retainer, and have no lubricating nipples. No maintenance is possible.

2   Dismantling and reassembly are essentially as described in Section 4. If the bearing cups are reluctant to be withdrawn, a self-grip wrench may be of help (photo).

3   When reassembling, ensure that everything is perfectly clean. Fill the grease holes in the spiders with grease, ensuring that bubbles are eliminated. Fill each bearing assembly with grease to a depth of approximately 1/8 in (3 mm).

4   Fit new rubber seals when reassembling. Refit the spiders to the yokes, press in the bearing cups and fit new circlips (photos).

5.4d A bearing cup being pressed into the propeller shaft yoke

Chapter 8 Rear axle

Contents

Specifications

Axle type
Early models (18G and 18GA) .... Three-quarter floating
Later models .... Semi-floating

Ratio .... 3.909 : 1 (43/11)

Lubricant
Type/specification .... Hypoid gear oil, viscosity SAE 90EP
Capacity:
   Three-quarter floating .... 2.5 Imp pints (1.28 litres, 2.75 US pints)
   Semi-floating .... 1.5 Imp pints (0.85 litre, 1.8 US pints)

Torque wrench settings

	lbf ft	Nm
Axleshaft nut (semi-floating axle)*	150	203
Pinion bearing nut (three-quarter floating axle†)	135 to 140	183 to 190

* Further tighten to align split pin hole
† Refer to text for semi-floating valve

---

1 General description

Two types of axle have been employed, either of three-quarter floating or of semi-floating design. The differential assembly on the three-quarter floating design is easily removed, but that on the semi-floating design requires special equipment to enable it to be removed.

Complete dismantling of either differential unit calls for specialised knowledge and equipment, and the average owner is advised to consult the local main dealer if such work is necessary.

2 Routine maintenance

1   At the recommended intervals, remove the combined filler/level plug on the rear face of the axle. Top up to the level of the plug with the recommended lubricant. Refit the plug only when any excess oil has run out, or oil may find its way onto the brake linings.
2   At the recommended intervals, drain the oil when hot after a run. Refit the drain plug and refill with new oil.
3   From time to time, remove the breather from the top of the axle casing (where fitted) and clean it in petrol. A clogged breather can cause oil leaks.

3 Rear axle, three-quarter floating and semi-floating – removal and refitting

1   Loosen the rear wheel nuts, or in the case of cars with knock-on hub caps, undo the caps a turn. Raise the rear of the vehicle and support it firmly on the body. Remove the roadwheels. Support the axle with a trolley jack.

2   Remove the bolts from the propeller shaft rear flange after marking the drive flanges for refitting purposes.
3   Pull out the split pin and clevis pin holding each brake cable (or rod) to a handbrake lever on the backplates. Remove the handbrake cable clip from the axle casing.
4   Remove the nut and washer securing the brake balance lever to the pivot on the axle casing. Remove the nuts and washers holding the check straps in position on the anchor pins. Free the straps.
5   Free the brake pipe by undoing the union nut on the battery box bracket. Remove the nut and washer holding the shock absorber links to each bottom bracket, and pull out the link. Unbolt the anti-roll bar where fitted. Unscrew the U-bolt nuts.
6   Remove the exhaust pipe and silencer by releasing it at the bolts at the manifold clamp, and at the two brackets under the car.
7   Lower the jack and remove the assembly from under the car.
8   To refit, reverse the removal procedure. Tighten the U-bolt nuts with the full weight of the car on the rear springs.

4 Axleshaft (three-quarter floating axle) – removal and refitting

1   Raise the vehicle, and place on stands under the axle casing. Note that if the axleshaft is removed with the car level, oil will run out and contaminate the brake linings. To avoid this, and if only one shaft is being removed, jack up that side of the car. To remove both, drain the oil from the differential before proceeding.
2   Remove the wheel and release the handbrake. Free the brake adjusters right off.

Disc wheels
3   Unscrew the two countersunk screws, and pull off the brake drum. If necessary tap the drum off with a wooden or hide hammer.

4   Unscrew the single flange locating screw, and pull the shaft by its flange from the axle casing. Note the paper gasket and bearing spacer.

Wire wheels

5   Remove the drum by undoing the four nuts, and tapping it off with a wooden or hide hammer.
6   Unscrew the extension flange screw, and pull off the flange. Withdraw the axleshaft, noting the O-ring seal.

Refitting

7   To refit, reverse the removal procedure. Renew the paper gasket or O-seal as appropriate.

5   Rear hub (three-quarter floating axle) – removal and refitting

1   Remove the axleshaft as described in Section 4, and remove the bearing spacer.

2   Knock back the tab of the locking washer and unscrew the hub retaining nut. Note that the left-hand nut has a left-hand thread. Remove the lockwasher.
3   With a hub puller, draw off the hub complete with the bearing and seal.
4   To refit, reverse the removal procedure, noting the following points:

   (a) Drift a new oil seal into place, lip facing outwards away from the differential, before fitting the bearing
   (b) Before refitting the bearing lubricate with a recommended grease
   (c) Renew the paper washer between the hub and half shaft flange
   (d) The outer face of the bearing spacer (where fitted) should protrode 0.001 to 0.004 in (0.025 to 0.102 mm) from the outer face of the hub after the bearing has been pressed into place, to ensure that the bearing is clamped by the axleshaft driving flange and the abutment shoulder in the hub
   (e) Knock back the tab on the locking washer.

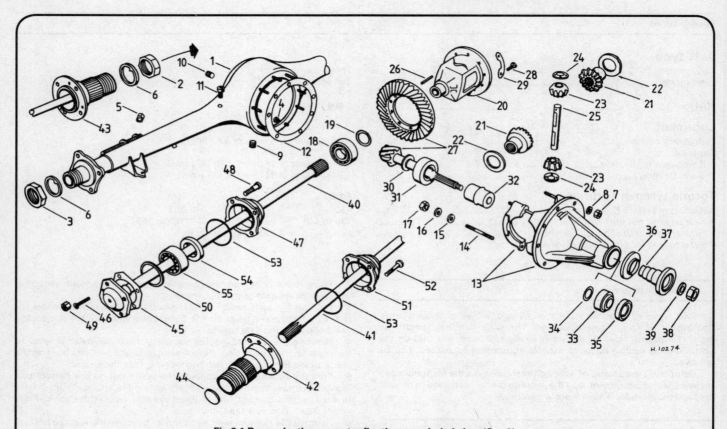

Fig 8.1 Rear axle, three-quarter floating – exploded view (Sec 3)

1 Case	18 Differential bearing	30 Thrust washer – 0.112 to 0.126 in (2.85 to 3.20 mm)	43 Hub extension, LH (wire wheels)
2 Bearing nut (LH thread)	19 Packing washer – 0.002 to 0.010 in (0.051 to 0.0254 mm)	31 Rear pinion bearing	44 Welch plug (wire wheels)
3 Bearing nut (RH thread)	20 Differential cage	32 Bearing spacer	45 Joint
4 Gear carrier stud	21 Differential wheel	33 Front pinion bearing	46 Screw, shaft to hub
5 Rebound spindle nut	22 Thrust washer	34 Shim (0.004 to 0.030 in (0.102 to 0.762 mm)	47 Hub assembly (disc wheels)
6 Locking washer	23 Differential pinion	35 Oil seal	48 Wheel stud (disc wheels)
7 Nut	24 Thrust washer	36 Dust cover	49 Wheel nut (disc wheels)
8 Spring washer	25 Pinion shaft	37 Flange	50 Bearing spacer (disc wheels)
9 Drain plug	26 Pinion peg	38 Nut	51 Hub assembly (wire wheels)
10 Filler plug	27 Crown wheel and pinion	39 Spring washer	52 Wheel stud (wire wheels)
11 Breather assembly	28 Bolt – crownwheel to differential cage	40 Axleshaft (disc wheels)	53 Oil seal
12 Gasket	29 Lockwasher	41 Axleshaft (wire wheels)	54 Oil seal
13 Differential carrier		42 Hub extension, RH (wire wheels)	55 Bearing
14 Stud			
15 Plain washer			
16 Spring washer			
17 Nut			

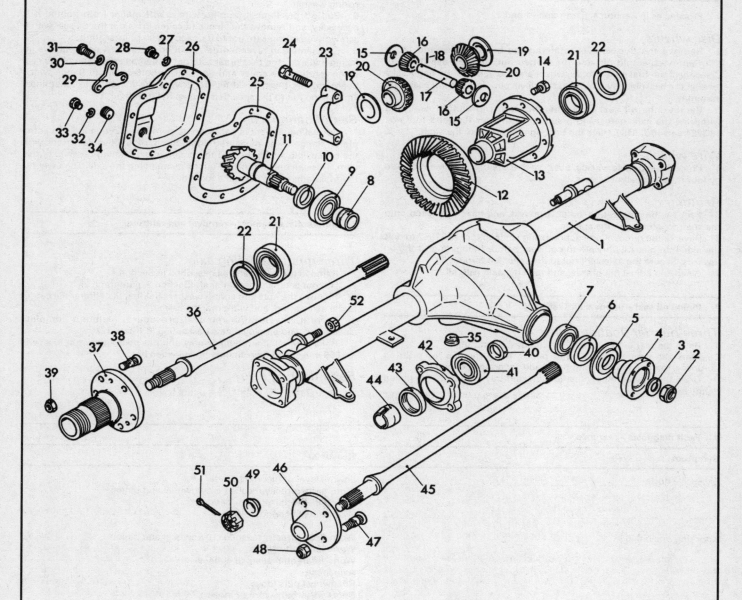

Fig 8.2 Rear axle, semi-floating – exploded view (Sec 3)

1	Case	15	Thrust washer
2	Nut	16	Differential pinions
3	Plain washer	17	Pinion pin
4	Flange	18	Roll pin
5	Dust cover	19	Thrust washer
6	Oil seal	20	Differential wheels
7	Outer pinion bearing	21	Differential bearing
8	Bearing spacer	22	Distance collars
9	Inner pinion bearing	23	Bearing cap
10	Pinion thrust washer	24	Bolt
11	Pinion	25	Gasket
12	Crownwheel	26	Axle case cover
13	Differential cage	27	Spring washer
14	Bolt	28	Setscrews

29	Compensating lever bracket	41	Bearing
30	Spring washer	42	Bearing cap
31	Set screw	43	Oil seal
32	Spring washer	44	Collar
33	Set screw	45	Axleshaft (disc wheels)
34	Filler and level plug	46	Driving flange (disc wheels)
35	Drain plug	47	Wheel stud (disc wheels)
36	Axleshaft (wire wheels)	48	Wheel nut (disc wheels)
37	Driving flange (wire wheels)	49	Axleshaft collar
38	Stud (wire wheels)	50	Nut
39	Nut (wire wheels)	51	Split pin
40	Spacer		

6   Axleshaft and hub (semi-floating axle) – removal and refitting

1   Proceed as in Section 4, paragraphs 1 and 2.

Disc wheels

2   Remove the two screws retaining the brake drum, and tap it off. Remove the split pin and the slotted nut, and remove the hub. Disconnect the brake pipe to the wheel and the cable to the handbrake lever at the backplate by removing the clevis pin. Remove the backplate assembly.

3   Remove the oil seal collar, bearing hub cap and oil seal, and withdraw the axleshaft using a suitable extractor (Leyland tool nos 18G284 and 18G284D). Have the bearing pressed from the shaft.

Wire wheels

4   Proceed as for disc wheels, but note that the brake drum is secured by four nuts, instead of screws.

Refitting

5   Pack the bearing with a suitable grease, and have it pressed onto the shaft together with the spacer.

6   Reverse the removal procedure, using Leyland tool 18G1067 to drift the axle into place. Lubricate the oil seal before fitting, and fit the lip inwards. Secure the axleshaft nut to the specified torque.

7   Bleed and adjust the brakes, and refill the axle with oil.

7   Pinion oil seal – removal and refitting

Three-quarter floating axle

1   Raise the rear of the vehicle, or employ a pit or ramp.

2   Mark the propeller shaft and pinion drive flanges for refitting purposes, remove the nuts and bolts, and separate the flanges.

3   Drain the axle oil. Apply the handbrake firmly to prevent the pinion flange moving.

4   Unscrew the nut in the centre of the pinion drive flange. Use a long extension arm and the appropriate socket spanner. Remove the nut and spring washer.

5   Pull off the flange, tapping with a soft mallet from behind it if necessary, and remove the steel end cover. Prise out the oil seal with a screwdriver, taking care not to damage the lip of its seating.

6   Reassemble in reverse order. Push home the new seal with the lip facing inwards, and take great care not to damage the edge of the seal when refitting the cover and flange. Oil the face of the flange which bears against the oil seal before driving the flange onto its splines. Tighten the nut to the specified torque. Refill with oil.

Semi-floating axle

7   Special equipment is necessary to permit the torque loading at the pinion flange to be measured. In addition, difficulties can occur with the collapsible spacer behind the pinion, necessitating renewal of this item. This can only be carried out by dismantling the axle. The owner is therefore advised to consult a main dealer.

8   Differential assembly – removal and refitting

Three-quarter floating axle

1   Remove the axleshafts as described in Section 4.

2   Disconnect the propeller shaft (Section 7, paragraph 2).

3   Remove the nuts and spring washers holding the differential carrier to the axle casing, and withdraw the carrier.

4   To refit, reverse the removal procedure. Maintain complete cleanliness, and employ a new gasket (Fig. 8.1 item 12).

5   Refill with oil. If a rebuilt or new unit has been fitted, run in slowly for 500 miles, and then change the oil when hot.

Semi-floating axle

6   See Section 1, paragraph 1.

9   Fault diagnosis – rear axle

Symptom	Reason(s)
Excessive noise	Low oil level or incorrect grade Worn or incorrectly meshed crownwheel and pinion Worn differential gears or bearings Worn wheel bearings
Knocking or clunking	Worn or incorrectly meshed crownwheel and pinion Worn halfshaft splines Worn differential gears or splines Axle loose Roadwheel nuts loose Shock absorbers worn or loose Propeller shaft loose or defective
Vibration	Flange bolts or wheel nuts loose Bearings worn Wheels in need of balancing Propeller shaft defective
Oil leaks	Overfilling Breather clogged Seal(s) defective Cover gasket leaking

Chapter 9   Braking system

Contents

Specifications

| System type.. | Discs front, drums rear, hydraulically actuated. Servo-assisted on later models. Handbrake mechanical to rear wheels |
| Brake fluid type/specification............................ | Hydraulic fluid to SAE J1703 |

Hydraulic system

System type:
Early models ....
Single circuit
Later models ....
Dual circuit with pressure differential warning switch

Front brakes

Disc diameter ....
10.75 in (273 mm)
Disc thickness:
    New ....
    0.34 to 0.35 in (8.64 to 8.89 mm)
    Minimum after refinishing..
    0.30 to 0.31 in (7.62 to 7.87 mm)
Maximum disc runout..
0.006 in (0.15 mm)
Pad minimum thickness...
1/16 in (1.6 mm)

Rear brakes

Drum internal diameter..
10 in (254 mm)
Lining minimum thickness:
    Bonded linings...
    1/32 in (0.79 mm)
    Rivetted linings ....
    Flush with rivets

Torque wrench settings

	lbf ft	Nm
Caliper securing bolt	40 to 45	54 to 61
Front servo bolts...	8 to 13	11 to 18
Rear servo bolts	13 to 27	18 to 37
Stone guard screws..	17 to 19	23 to 26
Master cylinder port adaptors (later models)..........................	33	45
Pressure differential switch end plug (later models)...................	17	23

1   General description

A Lockheed hydraulic braking system is fitted. Application of the footbrake creates pressure in the master cylinder (a tandem type is fitted to certain models), and fluid under pressure transmits the braking effort to the mechanisms at the wheels (photo).

The front brake unit, one per wheel, consists of a rigidly mounted caliper carrying two friction pad assemblies, between which revolves a disc attached to the wheel. Upon footbrake application, the disc is gripped by the pads.

The rear brake unit, one per wheel, consists of a drum and an internally expanding pair of friction shoes. Application of the shoes can be either by the footbrake or the handbrake.

1.1 Location of brake (non-tandem type) and clutch master cylinders

2 Maintenance – braking system

1   No adjustment is necessary to the front brakes. Examine the pads at the recommended intervals and renew if necessary. Pads must always be renewed in complete axle sets – ie all four pads – even if only one is worn to the limit. Examine the condition of the rear brake shoes at the Specified intervals, and adjust when the brake pedal travel appears to be increasing.

2   Periodically check the fluid level in the master cylinder, and maintain it at 1/4 in (6.35 mm) below the bottom of the filler neck. Check that the breather hole in the cap is clear. Note that any significant drop in fluid level indicates a leak which must be investigated immediately.

3   Examine all flexible hoses and metal pipes at the recommended intervals for perishing or corrosion. Change the brake fluid completely at the specified intervals. Examine all fluid seals, and piston and cylinder bores, as recommended.

4   Do not re-use old brake fluid, and maintain complete cleanliness. Use only a recommended fluid, and keep it in sealed containers to prevent moisture absorption. Do not spill fluid on paintwork.

5   Lubricate the nipple on the handbrake cable with grease, and all linkages with engine oil.

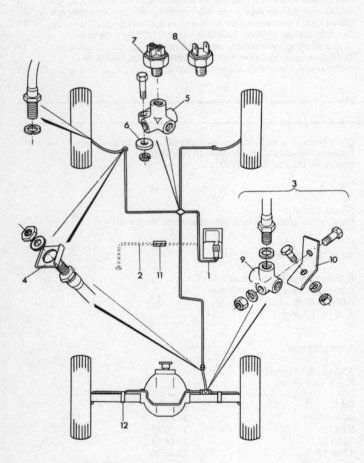

Fig 9.1 Hydraulic brake system – basic layout (Sec 1)

1	Pipe – master cylinder to 4-way connector	7	Stoplamp switch
2	Alternative to 1	8	Stoplamp switch (alternative design)
3	3-way connection assembly	9	3-way connection
4	Locking plate	10	Bracket
5	4-way connection	11	Heat shield
6	Spacer	12	Clip

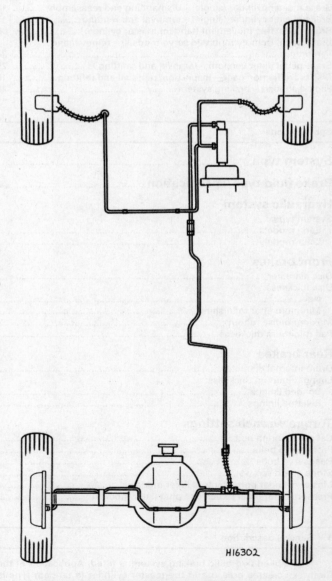

H16302

Fig 9.2 Hydraulic brake layout, later type (RH drive) with tandem master cylinder and servo (Sec 1)

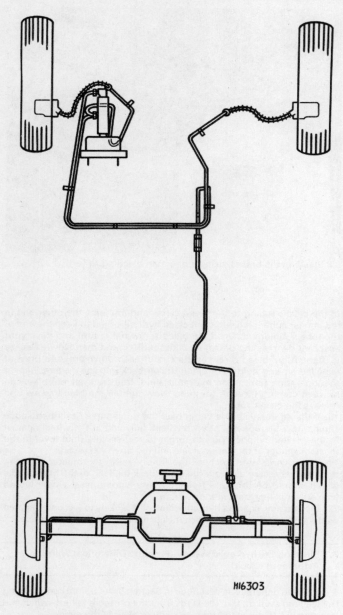

Fig 9.3 Hydraulic brake layout, later type (LH drive) with tandem master cylinder and servo (Sec 1)

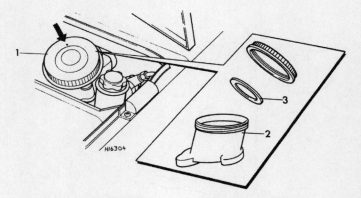

Fig 9.4 Hydraulic fluid reservoir (later type) (Sec 2)

1   Cap – tandem master cylinder
2   Fluid level mark
3   Centre disc – cap

3.3 Rear brake adjustment. Note use of correct tool

3   Adjustment – front and rear brakes

1   Adjustment is not required to the front brakes.
2   Adjust the rear brakes when pedal travel increases noticeably. Chock the front wheels, ensure the handbrake is off, and jack up each side of the car in turn.
3   Turn the square-headed adjuster, one on each rear backplate (photo), in a clockwise direction until both shoes are firmly against the brake drum, locking the wheel. Turn the adjuster back one notch and check for drag. Do not confuse the drag of the differential gears with a locking brake.
4   Adjustment of the brake shoes automatically adjusts the handbrake.
5   If the adjuster is very stiff or impossible to turn, apply a little releasing fluid to it. Check that it has not simply reached the end of its travel (in which case the brake shoes are almost certainly due for renewal). It is well worth purchasing the correct brake adjusting spanner the heads of the adjusters are easily damaged.

4   Handbrake – description and adjustment

1   Adjustment of the rear brake shoes automatically adjusts the handbrake also, and only if cable stretch has occurred will separate adjustment be necessary.
2   To adjust the cable, place chocks at the front wheels, raise the rear of the vehicle, release the handbrake, and check the brake shoe adjustment. Adjust the cable by turning the brass adjusting nut on the lower end of the handbrake lever under the car floor, until the brake shoes are solidly locked on when the lever is pulled up by 4 or 5 notches. Release the lever and check that the brakes are free.

5   Brake pedal free movement (tandem master cylinder)

There must be 1/8 in (3 mm) free movement at the brake pedal pad. This is adjusted by undoing a locknut and turning the stoplight switch. Note that with these brakes the switch is mechanically operated.

6   Bleeding the hydraulic system (vehicles without PDWA)

1   If any of the hydraulic components in the braking system have been removed or disconnected, or if the fluid level in the master cylinder

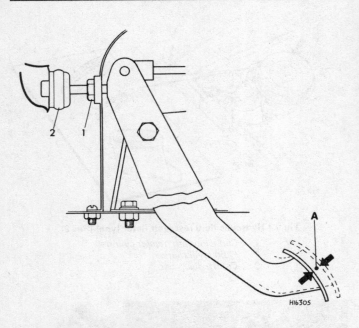

Fig 9.5 Brake pedal free movement, vehicles with tandem master cylinder (Sec 5)

1   *Locknut*
2   *Switch*
A = 1/8 in (3.2 mm) free play

6.8 Bleeding the brakes, using a one-man bleeding kit

has been allowed to fall appreciably, it is inevitable that air will have been introduced into the system. The removal of all this air from the hydraulic system is essential if the brakes are to function correctly, and the process of removing it is known as bleeding.

2   There are a number of one-man, do-it-yourself, brake bleeding kits currently available from motor accessory shops. It is recommended that one of these kits should be used wherever possible as they greatly simplify the bleeding operation and also reduce the risk of expelled air and fluid being drawn back into the system.

3   If one of these kits is not available then it will be necessary to gather together a clean jar and a suitable length of clear plastic tubing which is a tight fit over the bleed screw, and also to engage the help of an assistant.

4   Before commencing the bleeding operation, check that all rigid pipes and flexible hoses are in good condition and that all hydraulic unions are tight. Take great care not to allow hydraulic fluid to come into contact with the vehicle paintwork, otherwise the finish will be seriously damaged. Wash off any spilled fluid immediately with cold water.

5   If hydraulic fluid has been lost from the master cylinder, due to a leak in the system, ensure that the cause is traced and rectified before proceeding further or a serious malfunction of the braking system may occur.

6   To bleed the system, clean the area around the bleed screw at the wheel cylinder to be bled. If the hydraulic system has only been partially disconnected and suitable precautions were taken to prevent further loss of fluid, it should only be necessary to bleed that part of the system. However, if the entire system is to be bled, start at the wheel furthest away from the master cylinder.

7   Remove the master cylinder filler cap and top up the reservoir. Periodically check the fluid level during the bleeding operation and top up as necessary.

8   If a one-man brake bleeding kit is being used, connect the outlet tube to the bleed screw and then open the screw half a turn. If possible position the unit so that it can be viewed from the car, then depress the brake pedal to the floor and slowly release it. The one-way valve in the kit will prevent dispelled air from returning to the system at the end of each stroke. Repeat this operation until clean hydraulic fluid, free from air bubbles, can be seen coming through the tube. Now tighten the bleed screw and remove the outlet tube (photo).

9   If a one-man brake bleeding kit is not available, connect one end

of the plastic tubing to the bleed screw and immerse the other end in the jam jar containing sufficient clean hydraulic fluid to keep the end of the tube submerged. Open the bleed screw half a turn and have your assistant depress the brake pedal to the floor and then slowly release it. Tighten the bleed screw at the end of each downstroke to prevent expelled air and fluid from being drawn back into the system. Repeat this operation until clean hydraulic fluid, free from air bubbles, can be seen coming through the tube. Now tighten the bleed screw and remove the plastic tube.

10   If the entire system is being bled the procedures described above should now be repeated at each wheel, finishing at the wheel nearest to the master cylinder. Do not forget to recheck the fluid level in the master cylinder at regular intervals and top up as necessary.

11   When completed, recheck the fluid level in the master cylinder, top up if necessary and refit the cap. Check the 'feel' of the brake pedal which should be firm and free from any 'sponginess' which would indicate air still present in the system.

12   Discard any expelled hydraulic fluid as it is likely to be contaminated with moisture, air and dirt which makes it unsuitable for further use.

---

7   Bleeding the hydraulic system (Pressure Differential Warning Actuator in circuit)

---

1   Proceed generally as described in Section 6, but before commencing to bleed the system, take the leads from the pressure failure switch and unscrew it 3 1/2 turns to bring the plunger clear of the piston.

2   Bleed the front caliper nearest to the master cylinder first, followed by the other front caliper and then the rear brakes.

3   After checking for a firm pedal, tighten the pressure failure switch and reconnect the wiring. Switch on the ignition, and check that the warning light glows when the handbrake is operated. Free the handbrake. Apply the footbrake, when the warning light should remain off. If it glows, repeat the bleeding procedure.

4   Check all round for leaks.

---

8   Flexible hoses – inspection, removal and refitting

---

1   Visually inspect the flexible hoses, and renew them if in any way suspect.

2   To remove a hose, place a piece of plastic sheet under the fluid reservoir cap to minimise fluid loss, and refit the cap. Unscrew the union nut where the metal pipe joins the hose. Hold the hexagon on the hose with a spanner, and unscrew the attachment nut and washer. Pull the hose end from the chassis bracket. Disconnect the hose from the calipers (front) or from the three-way connector on the rear axle casing.

3   To refit, reverse the removal procedure. Remove the plastic from the fluid reservoir cap, top up the reservoir, and bleed the brakes.

9 Metal brake pipes – general

1   These should be periodically checked for corrosion, particularly in exposed places.

2   Replacement pipes are beginning to become more readily available, made up ready to fit. The average owner is not advised to attempt to make his own pipes up, because of the different types of ends which can be involved, and because of the special tools necessary. A specialist in this field should be consulted, and the owner should supply him with the old pipes as patterns, even if they break into several pieces when they are removed, as frequently happens.

3   Replacement pipes made of copper or copper-based alloys are available from some firms. If these pipes are used, remember that copper can suffer from fatigue fractures if subject to vibration. Follow the pipe manufacturer's instructions and fit extra pipe support clips if these are called for. The main advantage of copper pipes is that they are immune from rust.

10 Disc brake friction pads – inspection, removal and refitting

1   Apply the handbrake, loosen the front wheel nuts, jack up the front of the car, and remove the roadwheels. Ensure that the friction material left on the pads is more than the minimum specified thickness (photo).

2   To remove the pads, press down on the pad retaining spring and extract the split pins. Pull out the pads.

3   Clean the caliper recesses and the exposed piston faces. Remove the cap from the master cylinder. Place a large rag beneath the cylinder to absorb any overflow, and press the caliper pistons right in.

4   Check that the relieved face of each piston is facing the centre of the hub (Fig. 9.6). Fit the new pads, ensuring that they move freely in their recesses. Remove high spots from the edge of the pad backing plate if necessary, by filing.

5   Check the condition of the pad retaining clips. Refit the clips and split pins.

6   Refit the wheels, lower the car to the ground, and press the brake pedal several times to adjust the brakes. Top up the master cylinder.

11 Brake disc and caliper – removal and refitting

1   To remove the caliper without disconnecting the hydraulic line, apply the handbrake, loosen the wheel nuts, raise the vehicle and remove the wheel.

2   Lever back the ears of the lockwasher, remove the two securing bolts, and remove the caliper. Place the caliper on a support, or tie it up, to avoid the weight being taken by the hydraulic hose.

3   To remove a caliper from the vehicle, disconnect the flexible hose from the metal pipe and detach it from the caliper (Section 8). Catch the fluid, and plug the brake pipe to keep out foreign matter. Lever back the ears of the lockwasher, remove the securing bolts, and remove the caliper.

4   To remove a disc, remove the caliper as described in paragraphs 1 and 2. Remove the hub as described in Chapter 11, remove the four bolts and washers, and remove the disc. Make a mark to show the relationship of the hub and disc.

5   To refit, reverse the removal procedures. Bleed the hydraulic system where relevant. The run-out of the disc should not exceed the maximum specified when checked by a dial gauge. If necessary obtain specialist grinding services, or renew the disc. Tighten the caliper bolts to the specified torque.

12 Brake caliper – dismantling and reassembly

1   Remove the caliper (Section 11, paragraphs 1 and 2). Clamp the piston in one half of the caliper and gently apply the footbrake, thereby forcing the undamped piston out until it can be removed by hand.

2   Gently prise the dust seal retainer out by inserting a blade between the retainer and seal. Remove the inner hydraulic fluid seal from the groove in the cylinder with a blunt-nosed toot. Take care not to damage the cylinder or the groove. Use only methylated spirit or brake fluid for cleaning.

3   Coat a new seal with disc brake lubricant and fit it to the inner groove in the cylinder. Slacken the caliper bleed screw.

10.1 The assembled front brake caliper

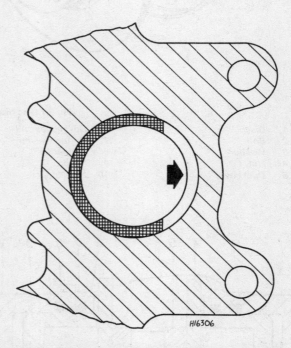

Fig 9.6 Brake caliper piston correctly fitted, with the piston cutaway towards the hub (Sec 10)

4   Coat the piston with disc brake lubricant and press it into the cylinder with the undercut towards the hub as shown in Fig. 9.6 until 1/4 in (6.35 mm) protrudes from the cylinder. Ensure the piston does not tilt in its bore.

5   Coat a new dust seal with disc brake lubricant, fit it to the metal retainer, place the assembly on the protruding piston, and press the piston and seal home with a suitable clamp. Tighten the bleed screw.

6   Carry out the same procedure in respect of the other cylinder.

7   If scoring or scuff marks are evident on the piston(s) and/or bore(s), renewal is necessary. Do not attempt to polish out wear marks.

8   Refit all parts as described in Section 11 and bleed the hydraulic system on completion.

9   If preferred, and in the interests of cleanliness of the hydraulic system, the caliper can be removed from the car for dismantling. In that case the pistons can be ejected using low-pressure compressed air (eg from a foot pump).

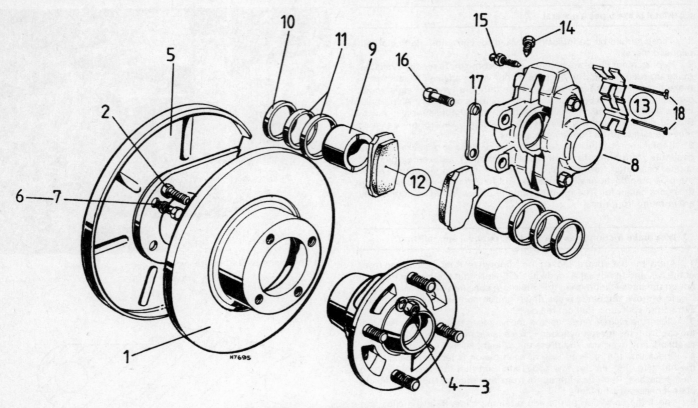

Fig 9.7 Disc brake – exploded view (Sec 12)

1	Disc	6	Dust cover bolt	11	Dust seal and retainer
2	Bolt	7	Spring washer	12	Brake pads
3	Washer	8	Caliper (RH)	13	Clips
4	Nut	9	Piston	14	Plug
5	Dust cover	10	Seal, inner		

15	Bleed screw
16	Caliper bolt
17	Tab washer
18	Split pins

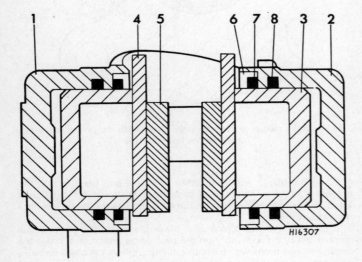

Fig 9.8 Disc brake caliper – sectional view (Sec 12)

1	Caliper – mounting half	5	Friction pad
2	Caliper – rim half	6	Dust seal retainer
3	Hydraulic piston	7	Dust seal
4	Pad backing plate	8	Fluid seal

13 Rear brake shoes and adjusters – removing and refitting

1   The easiest method of renewing the rear brake linings is to purchase exchange shoes, which are factory fitted with new linings. However, when adequate facilities are available linings may be fitted to the old shoes providing a complete axle set is used. Fitting linings to one wheel only is not permissible.

2   To remove the brake shoes, remove the hub cap, loosen the rear wheel nuts, jack up and support the car, and remove the wheel. Chock a wheel, and release the handbrake.

3   Fully back off the brake adjustment, take out the two setscrews (or four nuts – wire wheels) and remove the drum (photo). If the drum is tight, tap the rim with a soft hammer. Examine the shoes, and renew them if the linings are near or below the minimum specified thickness. Make scratch marks on the shoes, to assist with correct refitting of the return springs.

4   Press and turn each steady washer, and remove it with the spring (photo). Retain the steady pins. Pull one shoe against the springs, disengage it at each end. and take away both shoes. (Note the 3 springs on later vehicles).

5   Remove the 2 nuts and washers behind the backplate, and remove the adjuster. Remove the tappets and screw out the adjuster.

6   Wipe and brush away all brake dust. *Brake dust contains asbestos and must not be inhaled.* Preferably wear a mask to prevent inhalation of the dust, and do not blow it about with compressed air. Brake dust can cause squeal and judder and it is important to clean the assemblies thoroughly. Check that the pistons are free in their cylinders, that the rubber covers are undamaged and that there are no leaks. Secure the pistons with wire or string.

7   Smear a little high melting-point grease on all sliding surfaces. The shoes should be free to slide on the ends of the cylinder and on the pivot posts. Do not allow lubricant to contact the brake drums or linings.

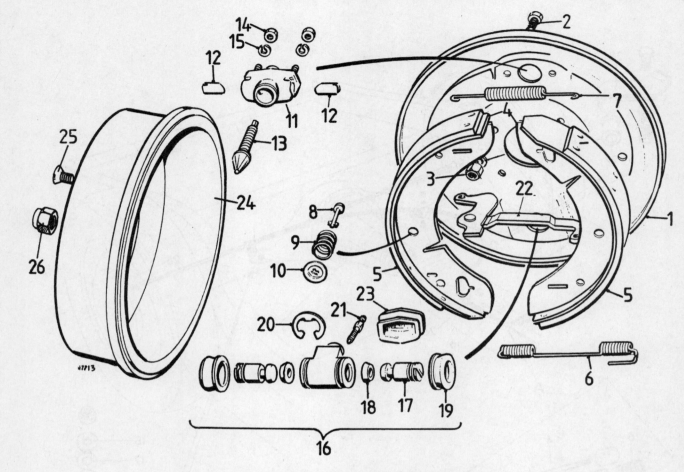

Fig 9.9 Rear brake – exploded view (Sec 13)

1	Backplate	7	Pull-off spring, adjuster end	14	Adjuster retaining nut	21	Bleed screw
2	Backplate bolt	8	Steady pin	15	Spring washer	22	Handbrake lever
3	Nut	9	Steady spring	16	Wheel cylinder assembly	23	Handbrake lever boot
4	Spring washer	10	Steady washer	17	Piston	24	Brake drum
5	Shoe assembly	11	Adjuster assembly	18	Seal	25	Brake drum screw
6	Pull-off spring, cylinder end	12	Tappet	19	Boot	26	Brake drum nut (wire wheels only)
		13	Wedge	20	Wheel cylinder retaining clip		

13.3 The assembled rear brake (drum removed)

13.4 Removing the steady spring and washer

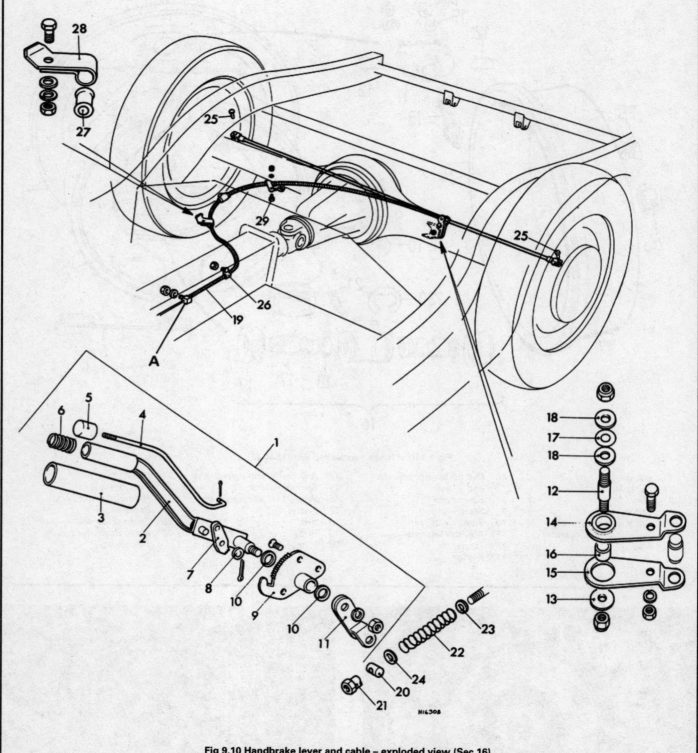

Fig 9.10 Handbrake lever and cable – exploded view (Sec 16)

1	Handbrake assembly	9	Ratchet plate	16	Lever bush	24	Plain washer
2	Handle	10	Washer	17	Anti-rattle washer	25	Clevis pin
3	Handle grip	11	Operating lever	18	Plain washer	26	Clip
4	Pawl rod	12	Compensator fulcrum	19	Cable	27	Cable ferrule
5	Knob	13	Plain washer	20	Trunnion	28	Clip
6	Spring	14	Inner compensating	21	Adjustment nut	29	Clip
7	Pawl		lever	22	Cable spring	A	Cable front abutment
8	Plain washer	15	Outer compensating lever	23	Plain washer		

8   To refit, reverse the removal procedure. Ensure that the adjusters are slackened right off, and that the return springs are correctly refitted. Adjust the brakes after reassembly.

14   Rear brake cylinders and seals – removal, inspection, overhaul and refitting

1   Remove a brake drum and shoes, as described in Section 13. Leave the other brake drum in position.
2   Apply gentle pressure to the footbrake, causing the pistons to be ejected from the wheel cylinder. Catch the hydraulic fluid which will be lost.
3   Examine the cylinder bore and pistons for scoring and corrosion, and renew the complete unit if any is found. Clean the cylinder and pistons in brake fluid.
4   The old seals will probably be worn and swollen. Fit the new seals to the pistons using fingers only, and ensuring that the sealing edge (ie the largest diameter) is towards the centre of the cylinder. Dip the pistons in clean brake fluid, refit to the cylinder, and refit the piston boots.
5   Refit all parts, top up the brake fluid reservoir, and bleed the hydraulic system.
6   If the wheel cylinder is in poor condition, disconnect the brake pipe, remove the cylinder retaining clip (and washer where fitted), and take out the cylinder.
7   To fit a new cylinder, reverse the removal procedure and bleed the hydraulic system. Remember to adjust the brakes on completion.

15   Rear brake backplates – removal and refitting

Three-quarter floating axle
1   Remove the brake drum (see Section 13). Remove the halfshaft and hub, as described in Chapter 8, Section 5.
2   Detach the handbrake cable from the l ever on the backplate, and the brake pipe from the wheel cylinder.
3   Remove the 4 bolts, nuts and washers securing the backplate to the axle flange, and remove the plate complete with brake shoes etc.
4   To refit, reverse the removal procedure. Bleed the hydraulic system, and adjust the brakes.

Semi-floating axle
5   The removal and refitting procedure is described in Chapter 8, Section 6.

16   Handbrake cable and lever – removal and refitting

Earlier layout
1   Refer to Fig. 9.10. Remove the adjusting nut, and pull out the cable. Retain the spring and washers.
2   Remove the lever by removing the nut and washer and pulling it out.
3   Take out the RH seat (see Chapter 12). Remove the 3 bolts and take out the ratchet plate. Raise the carpet and remove the nut and washer to release the cable front abutment.
4   Remove the nuts and release the cable clips.
5   Remove bolt, loosen nut, and free the cable abutment from the compensating lever.
6   Remove the split pins and clevis pins, releasing the brake rods from the levers. Remove the cable assembly.
7   To refit, reverse the removal procedure. Check the handbrake operation, and adjust as necessary (Section 4).

Later layout
8   Remove the handbrake lever as described above, but unscrew the locknut to remove the warning light switch. When refitting, adjust the switch by placing the handbrake lever in the off position. Switch on the ignition, and adjust the switch to the point where the warning light just goes out.
9   Screw the switch in further, by one complete turn. Tighten the locknut, remove the wires, untwist them and refit. Check the warning

16.10 The cable to the handbrake lever (later layout)

light operation, and switch off the ignition. Check the handbrake adjustment.
10   The cable, although of a different design to earlier models, is removed in basically the same way. At the rear division of the cables, remove the screw securing the support strap to the cable on the bracket Cables are employed from the rear division of the cables to the brake backplates (photo).

17   Brake master cylinder (single) – removal and refitting

1   Remove the four screws and washers, and remove the protecting cover from the ends of the brake and clutch master cylinders.
2   Drain the fluid from the master cylinder. Attach a tube to a brake bleed screw. Undo the screw one turn, and pump the fluid into a suitable container using the brake pedal. Hold the pedal against the floor at the end of each stroke and tighten the bleed screw. Return the pedal to its normal position, loosen the bleed screw, and repeat the process until the reservoir is empty.
3   Free the brake pedal lever from the end of the pushrod by pulling out the split pin, the washer, and the clevis pin.
4   Clean the union where the pipe joins the master cylinder, and disconnect the union. Remove the bolts and washers, and remove the cylinder.
5   To refit, reverse the removal procedure. Note that the longer of the securing bolts is refitted in the top hole. Top up the cylinder, and bleed the brakes.

18   Brake master cylinder (single) – dismantling and reassembly

1   Referring to Fig. 9.11, pull off the boot, press in the pushrod, and remove the circlip. Pull out the pushrod and internal components. Clean all parts using methylated spirit.
2   Make certain that the compensating hole in the cylinder bore is clear by probing with a piece of wire. Check all parts for damage or deterioration, renewing where necessary. If the bore of the cylinder is scored, renew the complete unit It is advised that all rubber parts be renewed regardless of their apparent condition.
3   Lubricate all parts as they are refitted in the cylinder, using clean brake fluid. Fit the secondary cup in the groove in the piston, with the lip facing the piston head.
4   Fit the retainer in the small end of the spring, and the valve assembly in the large end. Fit the assembled spring in the bore, valve assembly first. Push the main cup, lip end first, into the bore and press it against the spring retainer. Fit the piston washer with the concave face against the main cup.
5   Fit the piston assembly in the cylinder bore, plain end first, ensuring that the lip of the secondary cup is not turned back. Refit the pushrod, secure it with the circlip and refit the rubber boot.

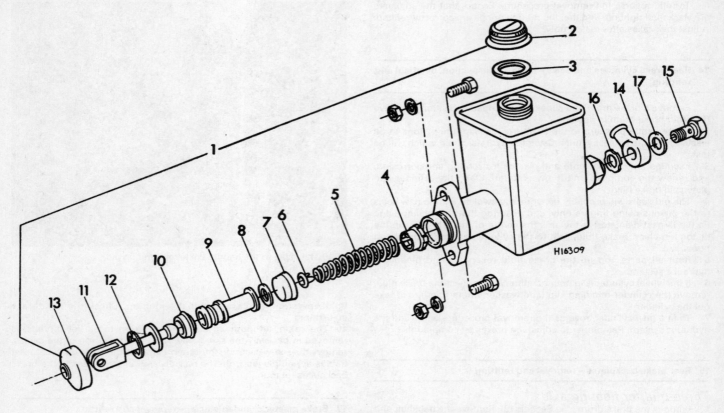

Fig 9.11 Single brake master cylinder and supply tank assembly – exploded view (Sec 17)

1	Cylinder and tank	6	Spring retainer	10	Secondary cap
2	Cap	7	Main cup	11	Pushrod
3	Cap seal	8	Piston washer	12	Circlip
4	Valve assembly	9	Piston	13	Boot
5	Piston return spring				

14	Banjo connector
15	Banjo bolt
16	Gasket
17	Gasket

19 Tandem master cylinder (without integral PDWA) – removal, dismantling, reassembly and refitting

Removal

1   Remove the four screws from the master cylinder cover. Remove the cover.
2   Drain the reservoir. Attach tubes to one front and to one rear brake bleed screw. Slacken both screws one turn. Depress the brake pedal, hold it down and tighten the bleed screws. Repeat until the reservoir is empty. Drain the clutch master cylinder in the same way from the slave cylinder bleed screw.
3   Disconnect the pipes from the brake master cylinder and plug their ends. Similarly, disconnect the pipe from the clutch master cylinder and plug the pipe connections.
4   Remove the split pins and clevis pins from the pushrods, disconnect the pedal levers, and free the clutch and brake pedal return springs.
5   Remove the LH lower facia panel (see Chapter 12).
6   Unscrew the two bolts securing the pedal box to the toeplate. Remove the nut retaining the pedal pivot bolt, withdraw the bolt, remove the centre spacer and temporarily refit the bolt.
7   Remove the six bolts securing the pedal box to the bulkhead, and withdraw the box complete with the cylinder and pedals. Remove the bolts securing the brake master cylinder, and remove the cylinder.

Dismantling

8   Plug the pipe connections, fit the reservoir cap, and clean the exterior of the assembly. Detach the rubber boot and withdraw the pushrod.
9   Hold the cylinder body in a soft-jawed vice, bore uppermost. Compress the return spring and remove the Spirolox ring from the

groove in the primary piston. Take care not to distort the coils of the ring or score the cylinder bore.
10   Remove the piston retaining circlip. Move the piston up and down in the bore to free the nylon guide bearing and seal cup. Remove both items.
11   Remove the plain washer, and the inner circlip. Withdraw the primary and secondary piston assembly, with the stop washer.
12   Compress the spring between the pistons, and tap out the link pin. Note the positions of the rubber cups by their moulded indentations and remove the cups and washers from the pistons.
13   Unscrew the four bolts securing the reservoir, remove it, and take off the two sealing rings.
14   Unscrew the front brake pipe connection adaptor and discard the copper gasket. Withdraw the springs and trap valves from the connection ports.
15   Clean all the parts in brake fluid, and dry them. Examine the metal parts for wear and damage, and the rubber items for deterioration. Renew where necessary. It is advised that the rubber items, which are cheap, should be renewed regardless of their apparent condition.

Reassembly

16   Lubricate all parts in clean brake fluid and assemble whilst still wet.
17   Place the piston washer on the head of the secondary piston, convex surface first. Using fingers, ease the secondary main cup, lip last, over the end of the piston, and seat it in the groove adjacent to the washer. Do the same for the washer and main cup of the primary piston. Continue to reassemble in reverse of the dismantling sequence.

Refitting

18   To refit, reverse the removal sequence. Top up the brake and clutch master cylinders, and bleed both systems. Check the brake pedal free movement (Section 5) and reset the pressure warning switch (Section 23).

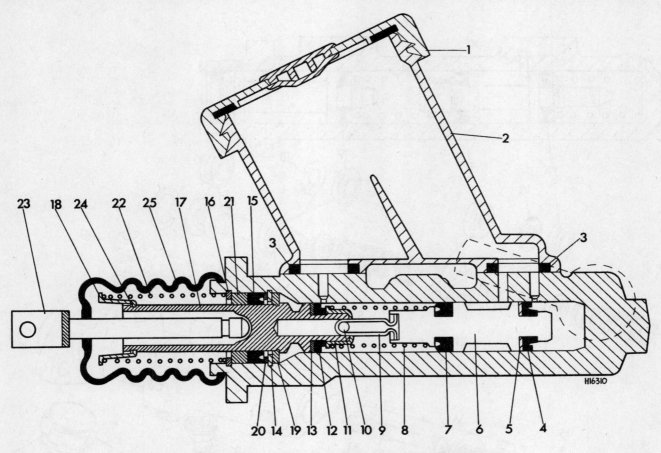

Fig 9.12 Tandem brake master cylinder – sectional view (Sec 19)

1	Filler cap	8	Separating spring
2	Reservoir	9	Piston link
3	Reservoir seals	10	Link pin
4	Second main cup	11	Pin retainer
5	Piston washer	12	Main cup
6	Secondary piston	13	Piston washer
7	Separating cup		

14	Circlip	20	Washer
15	Seal cup	21	Guide bearing
16	Circlip	22	Return spring
17	Primary piston	23	Pushrod
18	Spring retainer	24	Spirolox ring
19	Stop washer	25	Rubber boot

20 Tandem master cylinder, later type with integral Pressure Differential Warning Actuator (PDWA) – removal, dismantling, reassembly and refitting

Removal
1 Drain the hydraulic fluid (Section 19, paragraph 2), and disconnect the fluid pipes.
2 Remove the leads from the pressure failure switch, and unscrew the nuts retaining the master cylinder to the servo unit. Remove the cylinder.

Dismantling
3 Remove the pressure failure switch. Support the master cylinder in a soft-jawed vice and unscrew the reservoir retaining screws. Lift the reservoir from the cylinder.
4 Withdraw the seal and adaptor from the primary feed port. Extract the seal from the secondary feed port.
5 Remove the circlip from the cylinder, and extract the primary piston, return spring and cup.
6 With a soft metal rod depress the secondary piston, withdraw the stop pin from the secondary feed port, and remove the piston, return spring and cup by air pressure.
7 Remove the end plug and washer, leaving the distance piece in position on the end plug spigot. Extract the pressure differential piston by air pressure through the primary outlet port.

8 Clean and examine all parts, as described in Section 19, paragraph 15.

Reassembly
9 Lubricate all parts with brake fluid, and fit all seals using the fingers only.
10 Fit the 0-rings to the pressure differential piston.
11 Fit the shim washers to the secondary and primary pistons. Take the two identical seals, and fit them to the primary and secondary pistons with the lip directed away from the shim washer.
12 Of the two remaining seals, fit the thin one to the secondary piston with the lip directed towards the primary spring seat. Fit the second seal to the primary piston, lip facing the first seal.
13 Fit the shorter of the return springs and cup to the secondary piston. Insert the assembly, being careful not to turn back the seal lips. Holding the secondary piston down against the spring pressure with a soft metal rod, insert the stop pin when the piston head has passed the port.
14 Place the cup and spring on the primary piston. Insert the assembly, taking care not to turn back the seal lips. Refit the circlip.
15 Refit the pressure differential piston, the distance piece, new sealing washer and end plug. Tighten to the specified torque.
16 Fit the 0-ring and seal to the primary feed port adaptor and place in the recess. Fit the secondary feed port seal.
17 With the reservoir thoroughly clean, locate it properly on the cylinder and secure with the screws. Fit the pressure failure switch.

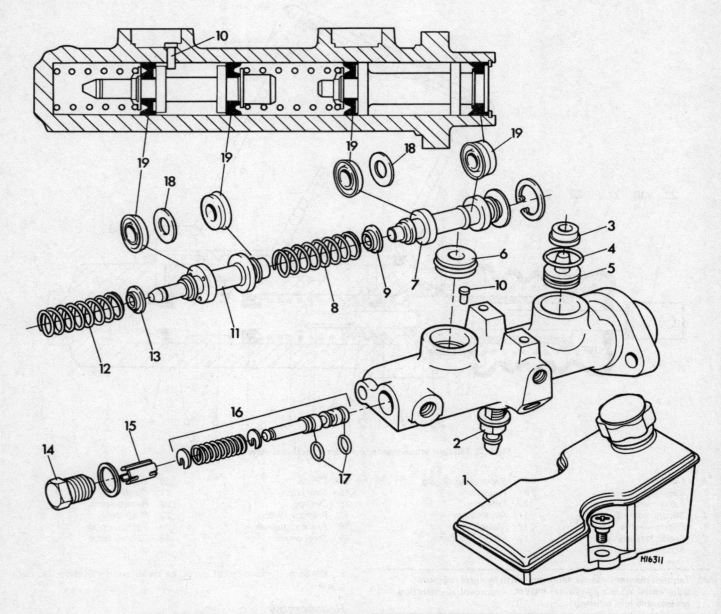

Fig 9.13 Tandem master cylinder with Pressure Differential Warning Actuator (Sec 20)

1	Fluid reservoir	6	Secondary feed port seal	11	Secondary piston	16	Pressure differential unit
2	Pressure failure switch	7	Primary piston	12	Return spring	17	O-ring
3	Primary feed port seal	8	Return spring	13	Cup	18	Shim washer
4	Primary feed port O-ring	9	Cup	14	End plug	19	Seals
5	Primary feed port adaptor	10	Stop pin	15	Distance piece		

Refitting

18 Refit the master cylinder to the servo, but do not tighten the securing nuts until the brake pipe unions have been started in their respective threads. Tighten the master cylinder nuts, followed by the brake pipe unions. Connect the leads to the pressure failure switch, and bleed the brakes.

21 Servo unit, Lockheed Type 6 – removal and refitting

1   Dismantling and servicing of servo units calls for the use of special tools, and it is recommended that specialist advice should be obtained.

Removal and refitting

2   Disconnect the battery, and remove the two screws retaining the base of the servo bracket (one screw on right-hand drive models). Unbolt the vacuum hose clip from the cylinder bracket.
3   Disconnect the feed from the master cylinder at the servo, and plug the pipe.
4   On RH drive models, remove the three nuts and spring washers securing the servo unit to the rear bracket. On LH drive models, remove the bulkhead grommet from inside the car before removing the three nuts and spring washers. Lift away the servo unit, and withdraw the vacuum hose from the servo.
5   To refit, reverse the removal procedure. Bleed the brakes, and reset the pressure warning switch if necessary.

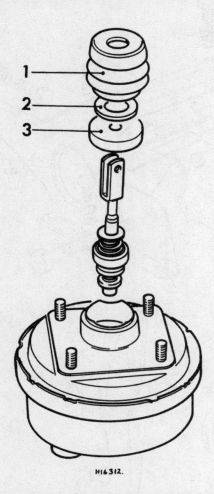

Fig 9.14 Air filter components on the Bendix servo unit (Sec 22)

1 Dust cover	2 End cap	3 Filter

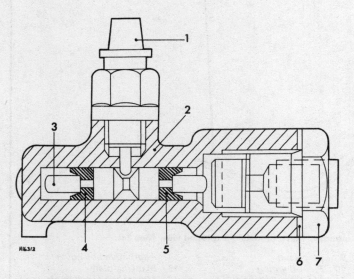

Fig 9.15 Brake failure warning switch – sectional view (Sec 23)

1 Nylon switch	5 Piston seal
2 Switch body	6 Copper washer
3 Shuttle valve piston	7 End plug
4 Piston seal	

22 Servo unit, Bendix type – removal, refitting and air filter renewal

1   Remove the air cleaner assembly, and the pedal box cover and seal.
2   Release the clips which secure the brake fluid pipes. Remove the two nuts and spring washer, detach the master cylinder from the servo, and suitably support it.
3   Loosen the vacuum hose-to-servo securing clip. Disconnect the return springs from the clutch and brake pedals. Take out the split pins, and then the clevis pins, from the brake and clutch pedal pushrods.
4   Remove the four nuts and washers retaining the servo unit to the pedal box. Remove the unit and disconnect the vacuum hose.
5   To refit, reverse the removal procedure. Check the pedal free travel (see Section 5), start the engine, and check servo and brake operation.

Air filter renewal
6   Remove the pedal cover, and pull the dust cover from the servo unit. Remove the end cap by tapping carefully with a screwdriver. (Excessive force may damage the servo body). Extract the filter.
7   Cut the new filter in one place and press it into position. Refit the remaining items in reverse order.

23 Brake failure warning switch (remote type) – description and overhaul

1   This switch gives warning should pressure fall in one of the brake lines. It has a shuttle valve which normally, with brake fluid pressure equal on either side, sits centrally in the cylinder. Loss of pressure on one side causes the valve to move over to the other, closing the switch contacts. Satisfactory functioning of the switch can be established when bleeding the brakes.
2   To overhaul the switch, remove it from the vehicle after draining both brake lines (Section 19). Place a rag round the valve to catch dripping fluid. Remove the air cleaner(s) for better accessibility.
3   Unplug the wires, undo the unions, and remove the bolt holding the valve.
4   Remove the end plug. Unscrew the plastic switch. Remove the shuttle valve, noting assembly details.
5   Clean all parts using methylated spirit or brake fluid. Examine the bore condition and, if it is faulty, renew the complete assembly. Test the switch by reconnecting its wires and operating the plunger with the ignition on.
6   To reassemble, reverse the dismantling procedure. Use a new copper washer for the plug, and new seals on the piston. Dip the parts in brake fluid before fitting.
7   Refill the system. Bleed the brakes as described in Section 6, noting that the warning light should operate when doing so if the ignition is on. Check for leaks.

Centralising the brake pressure switch
8   During bleeding, the loss of pressure in one brake system will force the shuttle valve of the warning switch over to one side. Thus after the last wheel has been bled it will be off centre, and the warning light still on. (Note some cars are wired through the ignition switch, so this must be on to check).
9   Refit the bleed pipe to a bleed screw on the circuit other than that last bled. An assistant should then apply the brakes firmly and watch the warning light.
10 Slacken the bleed screw a little, when the assistant may feel pedal movement as the shuttle moves. As soon as the warning light extinguishes, shut the bleed screw. If this is shut too late the valve will move past centre, and the light will come on again. The procedure must then be repeated, but more quickly, on a bleed screw on the other pipe circuit.

24 Brake pedal (remote mounted servo models) – removal and refitting

1   Referring to Fig. 9.16, remove the screws and washers, and the protective cover.
2   Pull out the split pin from clevis pin and lift off the brake pedal return spring. Undo the nut and spring washer from the fulcrum pin

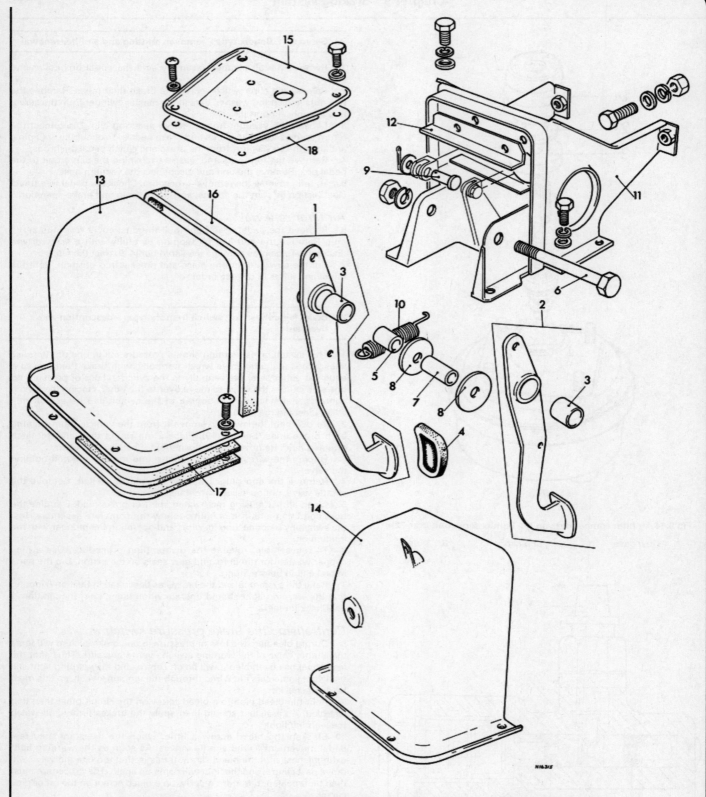

Fig 9.16 Brake pedal and associated items (remote mounted servo models) – exploded view (Sec 24)

1	Brake pedal assembly (RHD)	4 Rubber pedal pad	9 Clevis pin	14 Alternative box cover
2	Brake pedal assembly (LHD)	5 Distance tube	10 Pull-off spring	15 Blanking plate
3	Bush	6 Bolt	11 Master cylinder box	16 Master cylinder box cover
		7 Pedal spacer	12 Stiffener	17 Bottom cover
		8 Plain washer	13 Box cover	18 Blanking plate

bolt Pull out the pin, plain washer and spacer, and pull the brake pedal down and out.

3   To refit, reverse the removal procedure. The head of the fulcrum pin bolt should fit against the clutch pedal end of the assembly.

25 Brake pedal (later version) – removal and refitting

1   Remove 8 screws and take the lid from the pedal box. Retain the

seal. Take out the split pins and clevis pins securing the pushrods to the brake and clutch pedals. Detach the return springs.

2   Release the clips securing the hydraulic fluid pipes and the fuel pipe.

3   Remove the 4 nuts and washers securing the servo to the pedal box, the 2 lower nuts being inside the car.

4   Undo the locknut and remove the pedal fulcrum bolt, move the servo forward and support it, and free the pedal from the pushrod. Take the pedal assembly out from below.

5   To refit, reverse the removal procedure. Check the brake pedal free movement (Section 5).

26 Fault diagnosis – braking system

Symptom	Reason(s)
Excessive pedal travel	Low fluid level (leakage or neglect) Pads and/or shoes excessively worn Rear brakes need adjusting Disc run-out excessive (may be due to defective wheel bearings) Flexible hose(s) leaking or bulging under pressure
Brake pedal spongy or soggy	Air in system Hydraulic system seal(s) defective Flexible hose(s) leaking or bulging Master cylinder cap vent blocked
Brake pedal springy	New pads and/or shoes not yet bedded in, or incorrect grade Master cylinder mountings loose Discs and/or drums badly worn or cracked
Excessive effort required to brake vehicle	New pads/shoes not yet bedded in, or incorrect grade Servo (where fitted) defective or disconnected Pads/shoes contaminated or excessively worn Discs/drums in poor condition
Brakes pull to one side	Lining(s) contaminated on one side or unevenly worn Rear brakes unevenly adjusted Pads/shoes renewed on one side only, or different grades fitted on opposite sides Wheel cylinder or caliper piston seized Disc, caliper or backplate loose Tyre pressures uneven Steering or suspension fault
Brakes binding	Rear brakes overadjusted Handbrake overadjusted or cable seized Caliper piston(s) or wheel cylinder(s) seized Master cylinder faulty or vent hole blocked

Chapter 10 Electrical system

Contents

Specifications

System type

Early models (Engine Nos 18G, 18GA and 18GB)........................ 12V, positive earth
All other models .... 12V, negative earth

Batteries

Quantity:
    Early models .... Two 6V
    Later models .... One 12V

Type:

	Early cars	Later cars
Engine Nos 18G, 18GA and 18GB	Lucas SG9E or STGZ9E	Lucas BT9E or BTZ9E
Engine Nos 18GD, 18GG and 18V	Lucas BT9E or BTZ9E	Lucas CA9E or CP11

Capacity .... 51 to 66 Ah depending on model and territory

Dynamo and control box (positive earth vehicles)

Dynamo:
Type	Lucas C40/1 12V
Maximum output	22 amps
Number of brushes	2
Minimum permissible brush length	0.282 in (7.14 mm)
New brush length	0.718 in (18.233 mm)

Control box:
Type	Lucas RB340
Cut-in voltage	12.7 to 13.3 volts
Drop-off voltage	9.5 to 11.0 volts
Voltage setting at 3000 rpm:	
At 10°C (50°F)	14.9 to 15.5 volts
At 20°C (68°F)	14.7 to 15.3 volts
At 30°C (86°F)	14.5 to 15.1 volts
At 40°C (104°F)	14.3 to 14.9 volts
Reverse current	3.0 to 5.0 amps
Current regulator	22 ± 1 amps

Alternator and control box (negative earth vehicles)

	Engine 18GD	Engine 18GG	Engine 18V
Type	Lucas 16AC	Lucas 16ACR	Lucas 18ACR
Output	34 amps	34 amps	43 amps at 6000rpm
Brush length new	½ in (12.6 mm)		
Brush spring tension	7 to 10 ozf (198 to 283 gf) with brush face flush with brush box		

Control box (16AC alternators):
Type	4TR electronic
Voltage setting	14.3 to 14.7 volts at 5000 rpm

Starter motor

Type:
Engine Nos 18G, 18GA and 18GB	Lucas M418G inertia type
Engine Nos 18GD and 18GG	Lucas M418G pre-engaged
Engine No 18V	Lucas 2M100 pre-engaged
Number of brushes	4
Starter gear ratio	13.3 to 1
Relay (M418G pre-engaged starter motor)	Lucas 6RA-33243
Minimum brush length:	
M418G	5/16 in (8 mm)
2M100	3/8 in (9.5 mm)

Windscreen wiper motor

Type:
Engine Nos 18G, 18GA and 18GB	Lucas DR3A single speed
Engine Nos 18GD, 18GG and 18V	Lucas 14W two-speed
Armature endfloat:	
DR3A	0.008 to 0.012 in (0.2 to 0.3 mm)
14W	0.004 to 0.008 in (0.1 to 0.2 mm)
Normal running current	2.7 to 3.4 amps
Drive to wheel boxes	Rack and cable

Horns

Type	Lucas 9H12
Maximum current consumption	3½ amps

Bulbs

The numerous combinations of vehicle models and territorial regulations make it difficult to give specific recommendations. Owners are advised, in the event of difficulty, to consult either the relevant driver's handbook or their main dealer.

Torque wrench settings

	lbf ft	Nm
Alternator shaft nut	25 to 30	34 to 41
Alternator mounting bolt	20	27
Alternator pulley nut	25	34
Starter motor mounting bolts	30	41

---

1 General description

The electrical system is of the 12 volt earth return type. The earth polarity on early cars is positive, and on later cars negative.

The main items employed are either a dynamo or an alternator for charging, an electro-mechanical starter motor, and two 6-volt batteries wired in series to provide a 12 volt source. (Later vehicles have a single 12 volt battery).

Care should be taken when fitting service replacements to ensure that they are compatible with the electrical system polarity. If this is not done, irreversible damage can be sustained by certain units.

2   Batteries – removal and refitting

1   To remove, lift the rear carpet, release the quick release screws in the access panel or panels (photo) and disconnect the electrical leads, earth lead first. Undo the securing bolts, remove the clamp plates, and lift the battery or batteries away.

2   To refit, reverse the removal procedure. Smear petroleum jelly (not grease) on the terminals. Fit the earth lead last.

3   Battery – maintenance and inspection

1   Check the electrolyte level weekly, by lifting off the cover or by removing the individual cell plugs. Distilled water should be added if necessary, until the tops of the plates are just covered. Batteries fitted to certain later vehicles have a filling device which automatically ensured the correct level when topping up. If no electrolyte is visible when the cover is removed on the later type, add distilled water to the filling trough, until the tubes and trough are filled. Refit the cover. Note that on the later type the cover must be kept fitted except when topping up or taking hydrometer readings, and that the electrolyte will flood if the cover is removed during or within 30 minutes of the battery being charged.

2   Keep the batteries clean and dry. A damp surface can cause leakage and consequent loss of power.

3   Periodically, remove the battery and check the trays, clamps and terminals for corrosion. Wash any off with diluted ammonia, paint affected metal areas, and smear the terminals with petroleum jelly. Repair any cracks with a proprietary sealer, and check the electrolyte as described in Section 4.

4   If topping up becomes excessive, and the cases have been inspected for leakage but none found, the batteries are being overcharged and the voltage regulator will have to be checked and reset (this may not apply with an old battery).

5   If a battery has become discharged, it should be recharged from an external source. If towards the end of a charging period one or more cells do not appear to be gassing as freely as the remainder, it is probable that the cell or cells in question are breaking down, and that the battery life is limited.

4   Battery – charging and replenishment of electrolyte

1   The dangers of explosion with a battery, particularly where it is well-charged and gassing, must be emphasised. It cannot be too strongly stressed that a battery should be kept away from all naked lights and sources of sparks. A single spark can be enough to cause the battery to explode and be thrown in many pieces over a considerable distance. The danger to the person is therefore obvious.

2   In winter when heavy demand is placed upon the battery, such as when starting from cold and when much electrical equipment is in use, occasionally have the battery charged from an external source at the rate of 3.5 to 4 amps. Charge until no rise in specific gravity is noted over a four hour period. Alternatively, a trickle charger charging at the rate of 1.5 amps can be used overnight. Rapid boost charges which are claimed to restore the power of the battery in 1 to 2 hours are not advised. These can cause serious damage to the battery plates. Note also when charging that the temperature of the electrolyte should never exceed 100°F.

3   Electrolyte replenishment should not be necessary unless spillage has occurred. Top up the cell with a solution of mixed electrolyte obtainable from a motor store or garage. When the cell is topped right up and the Specific Gravity is still low. withdraw some of the electrolyte with a pipette and renew it with new solution. Recharge the battery and check the Specific Gravity with a hydrometer. Compare the readings with those given in paragraph 4. When making up electrolyte at home, great care must be taken *that WATER IS NEVER ADDED TO SULPHURIC ACID,* or an explosion will occur. Always pour the acid slowly on to water, using a glass vessel and stirring continuously with a glass rod. The correct proportions of the mixture are 1 part of sulphuric acid (SG 1.840) added to 3.2 parts of distilled water by volume (climate up to 27°C or 80°F), or to 4.3 parts of distilled water (climate over 27°C or 80°F).

2.1 The battery access panel

4   Hydrometer readings should be as follows:
For climates below 27°C (80°F)
    Cell fully charged 1.270 to 1.290
    Cell half charged 1.190 to 1.210
    Cell discharged 1.110 to 1.130
For climates above 27°C (80°F)
    Cell fully charged 1.210 to 1.230
    Cell half charged 1.130 to 1.150
    Cell discharged 1.050 to 1.070

5   These figures are for an electrolyte temperature of 16°C (60°F). For every 3°C (5°F) above 16°C (60°F) add 0.002. For every 3°C (5°F) below 16°C (60°F) subtract 0.002.

5   Dynamo – maintenance and testing

1   Check the fanbelt tension frequently and adjust if necessary as described in Chapter 2.

2   Periodically apply three drops of engine oil in the oil hole in the commutator end bracket. The front bearing requires no attention.

3   Check that the leads from the control box to the dynamo are firmly attached. The control box D terminal to the dynamo D terminal and similarly the F terminals.

4   Ensure that there is no electrical equipment switched on, pull the leads off the dynamo terminals D and F and join the terminals together with a short length of wire. Attach the negative lead of a 0-20 volt voltmeter to this wire, and earth the other lead on the dynamo yoke. Idle the engine at 750 rpm. The voltmeter should read about 15 volts. Do not increase the engine speed above a fast idle.

5   If no reading is obtained, check the brushes. If a reading of approximately 1 volt is observed, the field winding may be suspect. A reading of between 4 to 6 volts indicates that the armature winding is probably faulty.

6   If the voltmeter shows a good reading then with the temporary link still in position connect both leads from the control box to D and F on the dynamo (D to D and F to F). Release the lead from the D terminal at the control box, clip one lead from the voltmeter to the end of the cable, and the other lead to a good earth. Idle the engine at 750 rpm, when an identical voltage to that recorded at the dynamo should be obtained. If no voltage is recorded, there is a break in the wire. If the reading is as recorded at the dynamo, check the F lead in similar fashion. If both readings are the same as at the dynamo, test the control box.

6   Dynamo – removal and refitting

1   Slacken the two retaining bolts and the nut on the sliding link, move the dynamo towards the engine, and remove the fanbelt. Disconnect

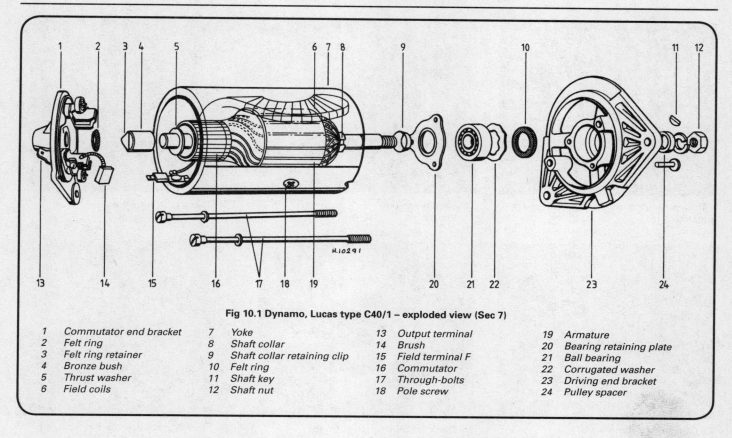

Fig 10.1 Dynamo, Lucas type C40/1 – exploded view (Sec 7)

1	Commutator end bracket	7	Yoke	
2	Felt ring	8	Shaft collar	
3	Felt ring retainer	9	Shaft collar retaining clip	
4	Bronze bush	10	Felt ring	
5	Thrust washer	11	Shaft key	
6	Field coils	12	Shaft nut	
13	Output terminal	19	Armature
14	Brush	20	Bearing retaining plate
15	Field terminal F	21	Ball bearing
16	Commutator	22	Corrugated washer
17	Through-bolts	23	Driving end bracket
18	Pole screw	24	Pulley spacer

the two leads from the dynamo terminals. Remove the nut from the sliding link bolt, and the two upper bolts. Lift the dynamo away.

2   To refit, reverse the removal procedure. Do not finally tighten the retaining bolts and nut until the fanbelt has been tensioned correctly.

7   Dynamo – dismantling, inspection, repair and reassembly

1   Mount the dynamo in a vice and remove the two through bolts from the commutator end. Mark the commutator end bracket and the dynamo casing for reassembly purposes, and remove the bracket (photo).

2   Lift the springs and draw the brushes out of the holders (photo). Measure the brushes and if worn down to the specified minimum, or less, take out the screws holding the brush leads to the end bracket. Remove the brushes (photo).

3   Mark the drive end bracket and the casing and pull out the bracket complete with armature (photo). Check the endplate bearing by firmly holding the plate and noting if there is visible side movement of the

armature shaft. If play is present hold the armature (or mount it carefully in a vice, using soft jaws), and remove the nut, the pulley wheel and fan. Remove the key and the locating ring (photo). Place the bracket across the open jaws of a vice, armature downwards, and gently tap the shaft from the bearing with a drift (photo).

4   Inspect the armature and check for open or short-circuited windings. An indication of an open-circuited armature is when the commutator segments are burnt. If the armature has short-circuited, the segments will be very badly burnt, and the overheated windings badly discoloured. If open or short-circuits are suspected then test by substituting the suspect armature for a new one.

5   Check the resistance of the field coils. Connect an ohmmeter between the field terminal and the yoke. The reading should be about 6 ohms. If the reading is infinity this indicates an open-circuit in the field winding, whilst a reading below 5 ohms indicates that one of the field coils is faulty. Field coil renewal is considered to be beyond the scope of most owners, and if these are defective either purchase a rebuilt dynamo, or take the yoke to a specialist.

6   Check the commutator condition. If it is dirty and blackened clean

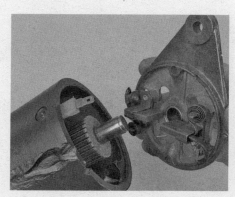

7.1 Removing the commutator end bracket

7.2a Removing the brushes from the holders

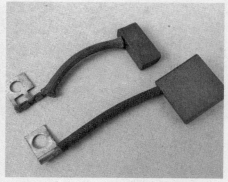

7.2b A new and a worn bush, compared

7.3a Removing the drive end bracket and armature

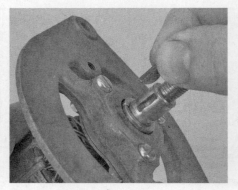

7.3b Remove the key

7.3c Drift out the armature

7.6 Cleaning the commutator

7.8 Check the bush (arrowed) in the commutator end bracket

7.9a Tapping in the new drive end bearing

7.9b Fitting the new bolts

7.9c Using threadlock on the new nuts

7.10a Drifting on the end bracket

7.10b The drive end bracket reassembled

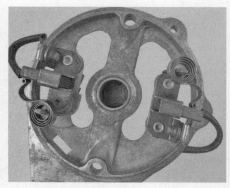

7.12a Raising the brushes in their holders

7.12b Hooking the spring ends on to the brush heads

it with a petrol damped rag. A commutator in good condition will be smooth and quite free from pits or burnt areas, with the insulated segments clearly defined. If after the commutator has been cleaned pits and burnt spots are still present, wrap a strip of glass paper round and rub it, taking care to move the commutator 1/4 of a turn every ten rubs till it is clean (photo). In cases of heavy wear, the armature may be mounted in a lathe and a fine cut taken from the commutator, using high speed. Polish with glass paper.

7 If the commutator has worn so that the insulators between the segments are level with the top of the segments, undercut the insulators to a depth of 1/32 in (0.8 mm). The best tool for this purpose is half a hacksaw blade ground to the thickness of the insulator.

8 Check the bush (photo) in the commutator end bracket by noting if the armature spindle rocks in it. If worn, remove the bearing using a suitable extractor, or by screwing a 5/8 in tap into the bush for several turns. Pull the tap and bush out. Allow the new bush to stand in engine oil for at least 24 hours before fitting. In an emergency, immerse in hot oil (100°C) for 2 hours. Press the bearing in until flush with the inner side of the endplate. If available, use a smooth-shouldered mandrel of the same diameter as the armature shaft.

9 To renew the ball-bearing at the drive end, drill out the rivets holding the retainer plate. Press the bearing from the bracket, and remove the corrugated and felt washers. Clean all parts, and pack the new bearing with high melting-point grease. Place the felt and corrugated washers in the bearing housing and fit the bearing, gently tapping it in with a suitable drift (photo). Refit the retainer plate and secure it with new nuts and bolts (photos).

10 Refit the drive end bracket to the armature shaft. Tap the bracket down gently, using a socket of a suitable size against the inner ring of the bearing (photo). Refit the spacer, the key, the fan and pulley. Fit the spring washer and nut and tighten (photo).

11 If the brushes are to be used again, place them in the holders from which they were removed. Check that the brushes move freely in their holders, and if sticking occurs clean with a petrol-moistened rag. If still stiff, polish the sides of the brush with a fine file. Tighten the screws and washers retaining the brush leads.

12 Refit the armature to the casing. Raise the brushes in their holders (photo), retaining them by the pressure of the springs on their flanks. Fit the end plate and secure it with the through bolts. Hook the ends of the two springs onto the brush heads forcing them into contact with the armature (photo).

8 Control box, Lucas type RB340 – general description

1 The control box comprises two separate vibrating armature-type single contact regulators, and a cut-out relay. One regulator is sensitive to changes of current, and the other to changes in voltage.

2 The regulators control dynamo output depending upon the state of charge of the battery and upon the demands of the electrical equipment, and ensure that the battery is not overcharged. The cut-out is an automatic switch, which connects the dynamo to the battery when the dynamo is turning fast enough to produce a charge. Similarly, it disconnects the battery from the dynamo when the engine is idling or stationary, thus preventing the battery from discharging back through the dynamo.

9 Control box, Lucas type RB340 – maintenance

1 Every 10 000 miles check the contacts. If necessary, clean as described, first disconnecting the battery.

2 Clean the cut-out contacts by placing a piece of fine glass paper between them and drawing it through several times whilst holding the contacts together. Do not use emery or carborundum paper.

3 Clean the regulator contacts as described in paragraph 2, but employ emery or carborundum paper. On completion clean all contacts with methylated spirit, and reconnect the battery.

10 Control box, Lucas RB340 – adjustments

The unit normally requires little attention, and if malfunctioning is suspected certain initial tests should be made. Check the fanbelt tension, and check the battery for a faulty cell, or for corroded terminals. Ensure that the generator leads have not become crossed. Check for broken or

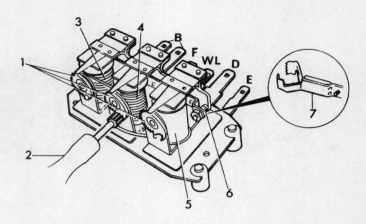

Fig 10.2 Control box, Lucas type RB340, with cover removed (Sec 10)

1	Adjusting cams	5	Voltage regulator
2	Lucas setting tool	6	Voltage regulator contacts
3	Cut-out relay	7	Clip
4	Current regulator		

loose leads at the dynamo and control box. If after these checks it is still necessary to test the unit, this should only be carried out by a capable electrician.

11 Alternator – general description and precautions

1 The alternator generates alternating current which is rectified to direct current for use in the vehicle electrical system. The main advantages of the alternator are lightness, robust construction, and a high output at low engine revolutions. Various types have been fitted to the MGB range.

2 The system is of negative earth polarity. The alternator is provided with diodes which rectify the alternating current produced, and also prevent reverse current flow. No cut-out or current regulator is needed.

3 Certain precautions should be observed to avoid damage to the charging system:

(a) Do not run the engine if the battery or charging circuit cables are removed

(b) Correct battery polarity must be maintained

(c) When arc welding, disconnect all cables from the alternator and control box

(d) Keep all connections tight and clean

12 Alternator, Lucas type 16AC – general description

The alternator is of rotating field design incorporating a three-phase output winding on a laminated stator. The rotor runs in bearings which are sealed for life. An integral rectifier pack is fitted but the voltage regulator is of the remote type.

13 Alternator, Lucas type 16AC – testing in the vehicle

Check the fan belt for correct tension (see Chapter 2), and ensure that all electrical connections are tight. Further testing requires both specialised knowledge and equipment, and should be referred to an auto electrician.

14 Alternator, Lucas type 16AC – checking when removed from vehicle

1 Remove the alternator, as described in Section 15. Remove the screws and cover. Unsolder the connections from the rectifier pack, noting the positions. When soldering, hold the diode pins with long-nosed pliers to conduct heat from the diodes. Do not bend the

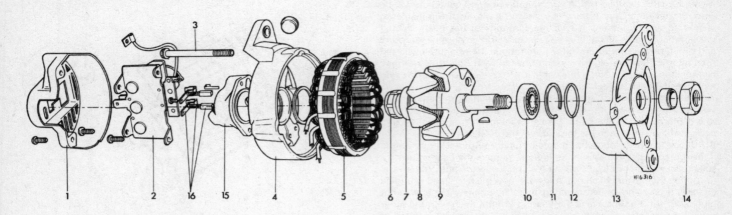

Fig 10.3 Alternator, Lucas type 16AC – exploded view (Sec 12)

1	Cover	5	Stator	9	Field windings
2	Rectifier pack	6	Slip rings	10	Drive end bearing
3	Through-bolt	7	Slip ring end bearing	11	Circlip
4	Slip ring end bracket	8	Rotor	12	Oil sealing ring

13	Drive end bracket
14	Shaft nut
15	Brush box moulding
16	Brush assembly

pins. Remove the screws securing the brush box moulding, remove the nuts retaining the rectifier pack, and withdraw both items.

2   Measure the brush length protruding beyond the brushbox. Renew the brushes if this dimension is less than 0.2 in (5 mm). Ensure that the brushes are free in their holders, and clean them with fuel or polish the sides with a fine file if necessary. Clean the slip rings using fuel, and remove burn marks using very fine glass paper. Do not machine the rings, or use emery cloth.

3   Testing is considered to be beyond the scope of the average owner, because of the test equipment and detailed knowledge required.

15   Alternator, Lucas type 16AC – removal and refitting

1   Where an exhaust emission control air pump is fitted, disconnect the air pump discharge hose, loosen the air pump mounting bolt, remove the adjusting link bolt, remove the belt and raise the pump.

2   On all models, remove the alternator terminal block, take out the adjuster link bolt, slacken the mounting bolts, lower the alternator and take off the belt. Take out the bolts, and remove the alternator.

3   Refit the alternator in reverse of the removal sequence.

16   Control unit, Lucas type 4TR – removal and refitting

1   To remove the unit, disconnect the battery, pull the terminal block from the control unit and remove the securing screws.

2   Testing of the unit should be referred to an auto electrician.

3   To refit, reverse the removal procedure.

17   Alternator, Lucas type 16ACR – general description

This alternator is basically the same as the type 16AC. the only major difference being that a voltage regulator is built into the unit.

18   Alternator, Lucas type 16ACR – testing in the vehicle

Check the fanbelt for correct tension (see Chapter 2) and ensure that the electrical connections are tight. Further testing should be referred to an auto electrician.

19   Alternator, Lucas type 16ACR, regulator packs types 8TR and 11TR – removal and refitting

1   Remove the alternator as described for the 16AC in Section 15. and remove the moulded end cover.

2   The 8TR type has two short screws at each end, and two legs locating in the brush box moulding. Disconnect the coloured leads from the brush box, and also the black earth lead, after removing the lower mounting screw. Remove the remaining screw securing the regulator pack.

3   The 11TR type has a single long mounting screw and spacer, screwed into the brush box moulding top lug, and two locating legs. Disconnect the coloured leads from the brush box, and also the black earth lead after removing the brush box retaining screw. Remove the remaining screw, and collect the spacer.

4   To refit either type, reverse the removal procedure.

20   Alternator, Lucas type 18ACR – description, removal and refitting

1   This alternator has a higher output than other types specified for the MGB range, and has detail differences in construction.

2   Removal is as described in Section 15.

3   To refit, reverse the removal procedure.

21   Alternator, Lucas type 18ACR – dismantling and reassembly

1   Remove the alternator from the vehicle. Remove the two screws and take off the end cover, detach the rectifier plate leads, and remove the four screws which retain the brush assemblies and leads, noting the leaf spring fitted at the side of the brush box. Remove the screw to release the surge protection device lead from the brush holder, and the bolts retaining the brush holder and regulator assembly from the slip ring end bracket Further dismantling should be undertaken by an auto electrician.

2   To reassemble, reverse the dismantling procedure.

22   Alternator, Lucas type 18ACR – inspection and servicing

1   Dismantle as described in Section 21. Clean the slip ring surfaces with fuel, and if necessary remove any burn marks with fine glass paper. Check the brush lengths against the Specification, and renew where necessary.

2   Further servicing and testing should be entrusted to an auto electrician.

23   Starter motor, Lucas type M418G inertia engaged – general description

1   The starter motor is mounted on the right-hand lower side of the engine, and is held by two bolts. The motor is of the four field coil, four

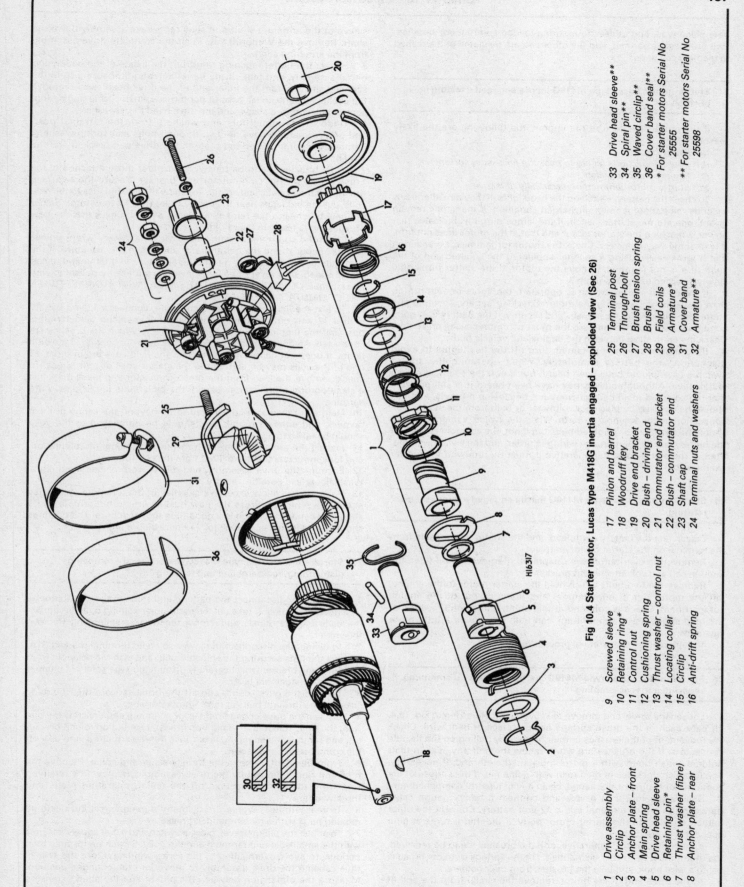

Fig 10.4 Starter motor, Lucas type M418G inertia engaged – exploded view (Sec 26)

1	Drive assembly	9	Screwed sleeve	17	Pinion and barrel	25	Terminal post	33	Drive head sleeve**
2	Circlip	10	Retaining ring*	18	Woodruff key	26	Through-bolt	34	Spiral pin**
3	Anchor plate – front	11	Control nut	19	Drive end bracket	27	Brush tension spring	35	Waved circlip**
4	Main spring	12	Cushioning spring	20	Bush – driving end	28	Brush	36	Cover band seal**
5	Drive head sleeve	13	Thrust washer – control nut	21	Commutator end bracket	29	Field coils	* For starter motors Serial No
6	Retaining pin*	14	Locating collar	22	Bush – commutator end	30	Armature*	25555
7	Thrust washer (fibre)	15	Circlip	23	Shaft cap	31	Cover band	** For starter motors Serial No
8	Anchor plate – rear	16	Anti-drift spring	24	Terminal nuts and washers	32	Armature**	25598

pole piece type, and utilises four spring-loaded commutator brushes. Two brushes are earthed, and the other two are insulated and attached to the field coil ends.

24 Starter motor, Lucas type M418G inertia engaged – testing in position

1   If the motor fails to turn the engine, the following are the likely reasons:
   (a) Faulty battery
   (b) Poor connections failing to pass the necessary current
   (c) Faulty solenoid switch
   (d) Starter motor jammed or electrically defective

2   To check the battery, switch on the headlights. If they dim after a few seconds the battery is in an uncharged condition. If the lamps remain bright, operate the starter switch. If the lamps dim, this indicates that power is reaching the starter motor and that, if the motor does not turn, it is in some way defective. Check the motor for jamming by ensuring that it turns easily, using a spanner applied to the squared end of the shaft. If it is not jammed, remove the motor. If the starter turns only slowly, proceed as in paragraph 3.

3   If, when the starter switch is operated, the lights remain bright, then power is not reaching the motor. Check all battery, solenoid and starter connections for cleanliness and security. If the battery is in good condition, poor connections are the most common causes of trouble. Check the earth strap between the engine and vehicle body.

4   If no improvement is obtained, turn off the headlights to avoid discharging the battery completely. When operating the starter switch a click should have been heard, but if not, the solenoid switch is defective. Although a click may have been heard it is still possible that the solenoid main contacts may not be closing properly, and this should be checked by placing a voltmeter or bulb from the starter side connection on the solenoid to earth. When the switch is operated there should be a reading or a lighted bulb, but if not, the solenoid is faulty. If the battery is fully charged, the wiring in order, and the switch working, then, if the starter is still inoperative it must be removed for further examination.

25 Starter motor, Lucas type M418G inertia engaged – removal and refitting

1   Disconnect the battery earth lead, and the starter motor cable from the terminal on the starter motor endplate.

2   Remove the distributor (see Chapter 4). Remove the oil filter, the ignition coil and coil attachment bracket.

3   Remove the two bolts which hold the starter motor to the engine. Lift the motor out of engagement and upwards out of the engine compartment. Space is confined at this point, and careful levering of the engine against the mountings can help to provide a little more clearance.

4   To refit, reverse the removal procedure.

26 Starter motor, Lucas type M418G inertia engaged – dismantling, servicing and reassembling

1   Loosen the screw and remove the cover band. Referring to Fig. 10.4, lift back each of the brush springs using a piece of bent wire. Check the movement of the brushes in their holders by pulling on the flexible connectors. If the brushes are worn, renew them. If any stick in their holders, wash them with a petrol-moistened cloth and, if necessary, lightly polish the sides of the brush with a fine file. If the surface of the commutator is dirty or blackened, clean it with a petrol dampened rag.

2   Secure the motor in a vice and connect a heavy gauge cable between the motor terminal and a 12-volt battery. Connect the other battery terminal to the starter motor body. If the motor turns at high speed it is in good order.

3   If the motor is still inoperative, or if the brushes are to be renewed, the motor must be further dismantled. Lift the springs from the brushes using a wire hook, and take the brushes from their holders.

4   At the drive end of the motor, remove the circlip from the end of the drive head sleeve. Remove the front spring anchor plate, the main spring and the rear anchor plate. Pull out the pin holding the drive head

sleeve to the armature shaft and slide the sleeve assembly down the shaft. Remove the Woodruff key. Push the complete drive assembly from the armature shaft.

5   Extract the barrel retaining ring from the inside of the pinion and barrel assembly, and pull off the barrel and anti-drift spring from the screwed sleeve. From the inner end of the drive head sleeve remove the circlip, locating collar, control nut thrustwasher, cushioning spring, control nut, screwed sleeve and the drive head thrustwasher.

6   Undo the terminal nuts and washers from the terminal post, and unscrew and remove the two through bolts and spring washers. Remove the commutator end bracket, the drive end bracket, and the armature.

7   If the brushes are to be renewed, unsolder those attached to the brush boxes on the commutator end bracket. Secure the two new brushes to the eyelets, and solder. To renew the two brushes to the field coils, cut the old leads near the coils, but leaving 1/4 in (6 mm). Solder the new brushes to the remaining pieces of lead. Check that the new brushes move freely in their holders.

8   Clean the commutator with petrol, or if necessary wrap a piece of glass paper round the commutator and rotate the armature. If the commutator is badly worn, mount the armature in a lathe and, using a high speed, take a very fine cut. Finish the surface by polishing with glass paper. DO NOT UNDERCUT THE MICA INSULATORS BETWEEN THE COMMUTATOR SEGMENTS.

9   To test the field coils for an open circuit, connect a 12 volt battery with a 12 volt bulb in one of the leads between the field terminal post and the tapping point of the field coils to which the brushes are connected. An open circuit is proved by the bulb not lighting. If the bulb lights, it does not necessarily mean that the field coils are in order, as one of the coils may be earthing to the starter yoke or pole shoes. To check, remove the lead from the brush connector and place it against a clean portion of the starter yoke. If the bulb lights the field coils are earthing.

10   Field coil renewal is considered to be beyond the scope of most owners, and either a rebuilt unit should be purchased or the yoke should be taken to a specialist.

11   Inspect the armature, looking for signs of burning, discolouration, and for conductors that have lifted from the commutator.

12   Examine the drive assembly, and renew worn or damaged parts. Wash all parts in paraffin and dry off.

13   If the bushes allow excessive sideplay of the armature shaft, they should be renewed. Press the new bushes in and out, employing a shouldered mandrel which is a good fit in the bush bore. The bearings should stand in thin engine oil for 24 hours before fitting.

27 Starter motor, Lucas type M418G pre-engaged – removing, dismantling, reassembling and refitting

1   To remove, disconnect the battery, and remove the distributor as described in Chapter 4. Take out the motor top retaining bolt, disconnect the leads to the terminals, and remove the lower retaining bolt. Remove the starter.

2   To dismantle, disconnect the lower solenoid terminal marked STA, remove the nuts securing the solenoid unit, and take the solenoid from the drive end bracket whilst carefully disengaging the solenoid plunger and drive engagement lever.

3   Take off the cover band, and lift the brushes from their holders. Take out the through bolts at the commutator end.

4   Slacken the drive engagement lever pivot nut, and unscrew the pin. Hold the unit, solenoid housing uppermost, take the drive end bracket off, and remove the engaging lever. Take out the armature, and take off the commutator end bracket.

5   From the shaft, remove the thrustwasher and collar. Remove the retaining ring, followed by the drive assembly. Remove the retaining ring from the drive, and take off the collar, operating plate, and thrustwasher.

6   To reassemble, reverse the dismantling sequence. Lubricate all moving parts with a recommended grease.

7   To adjust the pinion travel, place a switch and 6 volt supply in series with the small solenoid terminal and the yoke. Switch on for only brief periods, to avoid overheating of the series winding. Close the switch. thus causing the drive assembly to move into the engaged position. Measure the dimension between the pinion and the shaft extension thrust collar, taking up slack in the linkage whilst measuring by pressing the pinion towards the armature. The dimension should be 0.005 to

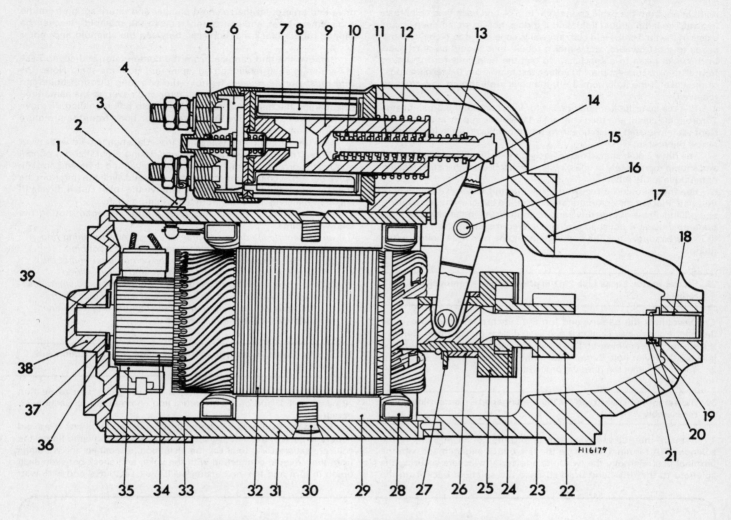

Fig 10.5 Starter motor, Lucas type M418 pre-engaged – exploded view (Sec 27)

1 Cover band	11 Inner engaging spring	21 Thrust collar starter drive	31 Yoke
2 Motor lead	12 Return spring	22 Pinion	32 Armature
3 STA terminal	13 Lost motion spring	23 Pinion bearing	33 Insulation strip
4 Solenoid battery terminal	14 Rubber moulding	24 Roller clutch action	34 Commutator
5 Contact assembly spring	15 Engaging lever	25 Drive sleeve	35 Brush
6 Contact assembly	16 Eccentric pin	26 Distance piece	36 Steel thrust washer
7 Hold-in winding	17 Fixing bracket	27 Drive operating plate	37 Fabric thrust washer
8 Pull-in winding	18 Fixing bracket bearing bush	28 Field winding	38 Commutator end bracket
9 Plunger	19 Thrust washer	29 Pole shoe	39 Commutator end bracket
10 Outer engaging spring	20 Jump ring	30 Pole shoe screw	bearing bush

0.015 in (0.13 to 0.4 mm). Adjust if necessary by freeing off the locknut on the lever pivot pin, and turning the pin, noting that the arrow on the head of the pivot pin should only be set between the arrows on the arc marked on the drive end bracket. Secure the pin with the locknut.

8 When the pinion travel is correct, the opening and closing of the starter switch contacts should be checked. Place a 10 volt supply from the small solenoid terminal to earth, the circuit to include a switch. Place a separate circuit, consisting of a 12 volt battery and test lamp, across the solenoid main terminals.

9 Insert a stop in the drive end bracket to restrict the pinion travel to that of the normal out-of-mesh clearance. Close the switch, very briefly, when the test lamp should light and indicate that the solenoid contact is closed. Switch off, remove the stop, and switch on again, holding the pinion assembly in the fully engaged position. Switch off, when the test lamp should go out, indicating that the solenoid contacts have opened.

10 Bench test the starter using heavy-gauge cables, with a switch and a 12 volt battery. The motor should run freely at 5800 to 6500 rpm.

28 Starter motor, Lucas type M418G pre-engaged – inspection and servicing

1 Check the brush lengths, and if they are approaching the specified minimum renew them as described in Section 26 paragraph 7. Service the commutator if necessary, as described in Section 26 paragraph 8.

2 Examine the armature. If conductors have lifted from the commutator, check the drive clutch (paragraph 5). If the armature shows signs of touching the pole shoes, this indicates a distorted shaft or worn bearings. Do not attempt to rectify damage to the armature. Test the insulation by connecting a 110 volt ac supply and test lamp from the shaft to each commutator segment in turn. The lamp should not light. To complete the armature check, test for short-circuited windings by using a growler, which will only be possessed by a specialist electrical firm. The only alternative to this is checking by substitution.

3 To test the field coils for continuity, connect a 12 volt test lamp

and battery from the cable connection to STA and each field coil brush in turn. The lamp should light, and if it does not do so, an open-circuit exists in the field coil. Field coil renewal is considered to be beyond the scope to most owners, and either a rebuilt unit should be purchased or the yoke taken to a specialist. To test the field coils for insulation from the yoke. connect the 110 volt ac test lamp from the terminal post to the yoke. If the light comes on, the coils are earthing and must be renewed.

4   Test the commutator end bracket for insulation of the brush boxes. Throroughly clean, and then connect a 110 volt ac supply and test lamp from each insulated brush box in turn to the bracket. If the lamp lights, renew the bracket.

5   The drive clutch should move freely on the splines without binding, and should rotate freely in one direction whilst providing instant take-up of the drive in the other.

6   Bearings should be renewed if they permit excessive sideplay of the shaft. Pull out the commutator end bearing by screwing a tap into it, and pulling. Press out the drive end bearing. Press in the new bearings, preferably using a polished and shouldered mandrel which is a close fit in the bearing. Soak the bearings in engine oil for 24 hours before fitting.

29   Starter motor, Lucas type 2M100 pre-engaged – removal and refitting

1   Disconnect the battery, and (on the synchromesh gearbox only) detach the clutch slave cylinder and keep it clear of the starter. Remove the starter top retaining bolt, remove the wiring to the solenoid, and take out the lower bolt. Remove the unit.

2   To refit, reverse the removal procedure.

30   Starter motor, Lucas type 2M100 pre-engaged – dismantling and reassembly

1   Remove the nut and washer securing the connecting link to the solenoid STA terminal, and ease the link out of engagement with the terminal post. Remove the two nuts and spring washers securing the solenoid to the drive end bracket. Ease the solenoid back from the

drive end bracket lift the solenoid plunger and return spring from the engagement lever, and completely remove the solenoid. Recover the shaped rubber block that is placed between the solenoid and motor body.

2   Remove the end cap seal from the commutator end cover. Ease the armature shaft retaining ring (spire nut) from the shaft. Note: *The ring must not be reused.* Remove the two long through bolts and spring washers. Detach the commutator end cover, at the same time disengaging the field brushes from the brush box moulding. Remove the thrustwasher. Remove the starter motor body from the armature and drive end assembly.

3   Ease the retaining ring (spire nut) from the engagement lever pivot pin. Note: *The ring must not be reused.* Using a parallel pin punch, remove the pivot pin from the engagement lever and drive end bracket. Move the thrust collar clear of the jump ring, and slide the ring from the shaft. Slide off the thrust collar, and remove the roller clutch drive and engagement lever assembly from the armature shaft.

4   To reassemble, reverse the dismantling sequence, noting the following points:

(a)   *Assemble the drive end bracket using a new retaining ring (spire nut) to secure the engagement lever pivot pin*

(b)   *Fit the internal thrustwasher to the commutator end of the armature shaft before the armature end cover is fitted*

(c)   *Fit a new retaining ring (spire nut) on the armature shaft. Push it on to give a maximum clearance of 0.010 in (0.254 mm) between the retaining ring and the bearing brush shoulder. This will be the armature endfloat.*

31   Starter motor, Lucas type 2M100 pre-engaged – inspection and servicing

1   For inspection and servicing of the brush gear, refer to Section 28 paragraph 1, and of the armature and commutator to Section 28, paragraph 2.

2   To test the field coils for continuity, connect a 12 volt test lamp and battery to each of the field brushes and the yoke. If the lamp lights, the coils are satisfactory. To check the insulation, disconnect the windings from their riveted connection with the yoke, and check between each brush in turn and the yoke using a 110 volt ac source and a 15 watt

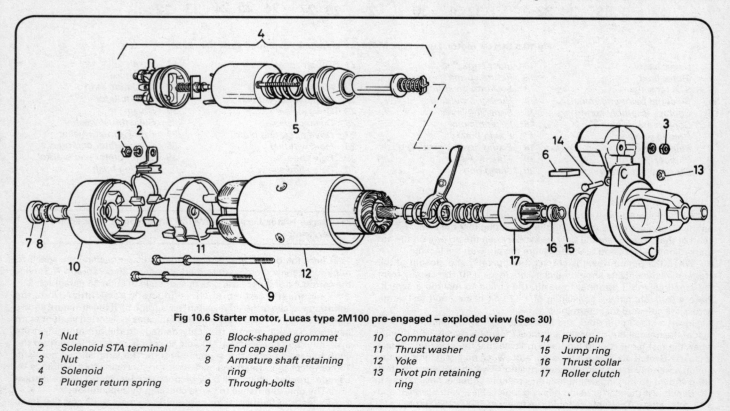

Fig 10.6 Starter motor, Lucas type 2M100 pre-engaged – exploded view (Sec 30)

1	Nut	6	Block-shaped grommet	10	Commutator end cover	14	Pivot pin
2	Solenoid STA terminal	7	End cap seal	11	Thrust washer	15	Jump ring
3	Nut	8	Armature shaft retaining	12	Yoke	16	Thrust collar
4	Solenoid		ring	13	Pivot pin retaining	17	Roller clutch
5	Plunger return spring	9	Through-bolts		ring		

test lamp. If the lamp lights, the coils are faulty. Field coil renewal is considered to be beyond the scope of most owners, and a specialist should be consulted or a rebuilt unit obtained.

3 Test the commutator end bracket for insulation of the brush springs. Connect a 110 volt ac source and test lamp from the end cover to each spring in turn. If the lamp lights, the insulation is unsatisfactory.

4 Refer to Section 28 paragraph 6 for details of bearing renewal, and to Section 28 paragraph 5 for the roller clutch drive.

5 The checking of lock torque and current, and of the function of the solenoid, involves the use of test equipment which most owners will not possess. Owners are advised to obtain specialist advice.

6 To renew the contacts in the solenoid (renew them only as a complete set), remove the screws holding the base assembly to the solenoid, and unsolder the coil connections from the cover terminals. Clamp the solenoid in a vice and remove the base assembly, fit the new base assembly and resolder the connections. Refit the securing screws.

32 Starter motor relay, Lucas model 6RA-33243 – removal, testing and refitting

1 To remove the relay when fitted, disconnect the batteries, and the wiring from the terminal blades on the relay. Remove the 2 screws securing the relay to the right-hand wing valance. To refit, reverse the removal procedure.

2 Testing and adjustment of this unit is felt to be outside the scope of the average owner. Owners are advised to consult an auto electrician, or to obtain a new unit.

33 Fuse block and fuses

Two-way fuse block

1 This block is fitted adjacent to the control box on the wing valance (photo). Fuse 1-2 protects items such as the horn and lights, which function whether the ignition is on or not. Fuse 3-4 protects the ignition system and items which only operate when the ignition is on, ie, the stoplights, fuel gauge, flasher unit, and wiper motor. On GT models with a heated rear window, there is a line fuse directly below the fuse box. Two spare 35 amp fuses are carried.

2 If a new fuse blows almost immediately, the cause must be established. Do not renew it again, or fit a fuse of a higher rating, until this has been done.

Four-way fuse block

3 GHN5 and GHD5 vehicles are fitted with a four-way fuse block. The fuses are 17 amp current rated, 35-amp blow rated. The general remarks given in paragraph 2 are applicable. One fuse protects the left-hand parking and tail lamps, the second the right-hand. The third covers ignition switch circuits such as stop and reverse lamps. The fourth protects items not wired through the ignition switch such

as horns, interior lights, and the brake pressure warning light. Just below the fuse box is a plastic container, holding a line fuse for the windscreen wiper and washer motors, the heater blower and the radio. On GT models the heated back window is also on this fuse. Behind the dash panel is another line fuse for the hazard warning flashers.

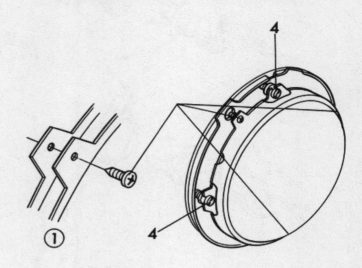

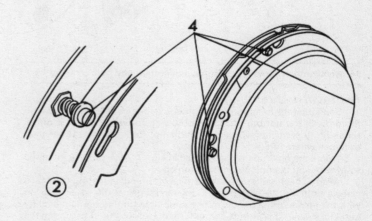

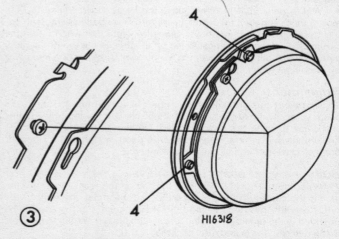

Fig 10.7 Headlamp beam setting and retaining screws – the various systems employed (Sec 34)

1	Removable screw	3	Captive retaining screw
2	Combined adjusting/ retaining screw	4	Beam-setting adjusting screws

33.1 Two-way fuse block (cover removed)

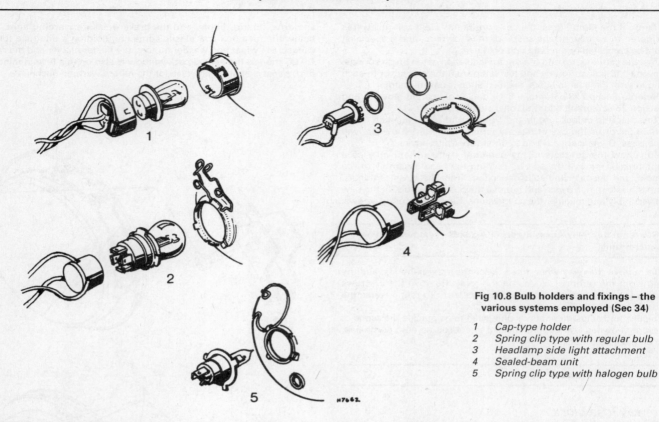

Fig 10.8 Bulb holders and fixings – the
various systems employed (Sec 34)

1   Cap-type holder
2   Spring clip type with regular bulb
3   Headlamp side light attachment
4   Sealed-beam unit
5   Spring clip type with halogen bulb

34 Headlamps – removal, refitting, adjustment and bulb renewal

Removal and refitting

1   Sealed beam headlights or lights with renewable bulbs may be
fitted. Ease the bottom of the chrome ring forward and lift it off its
retaining lugs at the top of the headlamp. Remove the rubber dust
excluder, where fitted.
2   Where the light unit is clamped as in Fig. 10.7 (1), remove the three
screws and lift the unit out of the lamp body.
3   Where the headlamp is held by combined adjustment/release
screws as in Fig. 10.7 (2), press in the lamp against the spring tension
with the palms of the hands, at the same time turning the unit slightly
anti-clockwise. This brings the enlarged area of the slots under the
heads of the screws. The rim will then pass over them.
4   Where the lamp is held by captive screws as shown in Fig. 10.7 (3),
loosen these and then follow the procedure described in paragraph 3.
5   To refit, reverse the removal sequence. Note that when fitting the
chrome ring it should be positioned on the lugs at the top of the lamp
body, with the cut-out in the rim at the bottom. Snap the ring into place
by pressing it down and in.

Adjustment

6   Carry out the procedure described in paragraph 1. Adjust the
beam vertically, by turning the adjusting screw at the top of the lamps
clockwise to raise the beam and anti-clockwise to lower it. Adjust
horizontally by turning the screws on the left or right-hand sides (or
both) clockwise or anti-clockwise as required.

Bulb or sealed beam unit renewal

7   Referring to Fig. 10.8 (1), press the cap on the rear of the reflector,
lift off the cap and remove the bulb. To refit, place the bulb in the
reflector with the notch in the bulb flange engaging the protrusion
provided in the reflector housing. Locate the lugs in the cap in the slots
in the reflector. Press and turn clockwise.
8   Referring to Fig. 10.8 (2), pull off the socket, disengage the spring
clip, and take out the bulb. Fit the new bulb, with the pip and slot
engaged, into the reflector. Bring down the clip, with the coils on the
bulb base, and engage the legs in the reflector lugs.
9   Referring to Fig. 10.8 (3), pull the holder from the reflector and
remove the bulb. Refit in reverse.

10   Where sealed beam units are fitted (Fig. 10.8 (4)), simply withdraw
the unit as described in paragraphs 1 to 4 (as appropriate) and pull the
connector plug from the rear of the unit. It will be noted that the lugs on
the sealed beam unit only permit fitting in one position.

35 Side and direction indicator lamps and bulbs – removal and refitting

Wing mounted type

1   Remove the screws, and take off the lens and sealing rubber
(photo). To remove the bulbs, rotate and pull out.
2   To remove the lamp bodies, disconnect the batteries and the lamp
leads at the nearest connector. Undo the two nuts behind the wing and
withdraw the body.
3   To refit, reverse the removal procedure.

35.1 An indicator lamp

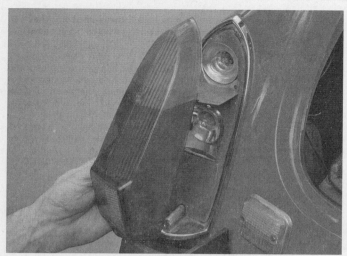

36.1 A tail, stop and rear indicator lamp

37.1 A number plate lamp, disassembled

Bumper mounted type (impact-absorbing bumpers)

4   Proceed as in paragraphs 1 and 2, but note that the lamp body is secured by two screws (photo). As the unit is pulled forward, disconnect the earth lead.

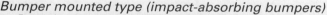

36 Tail, stop and rear direction indicator lamps and bulbs – removal and refitting

Earlier version

1   The tail and stoplights are combined and are of the double filament bulb type, the stoplight being considerably brighter than the tail light. To gain access to the bulbs, remove the rear light cover by undoing the screw at the bottom of the lens (photo).

2   To remove the lamp body, disconnect the batteries and the lamp leads at the nearest connector. Remove the lens (see paragraph 1), take out the three screws, and remove the lamp body.

3   To refit, reverse the removal procedure, ensuring that the sealing rubber is fitted correctly under the lens, and that the top end of the lens cover is placed over the upper lip on the lamp body before the screw is tightened.

Later version

4   The procedures in paragraphs 1, 2 and 3 apply, but the lamp body is secured by three nuts inside the boot. It is not necessary to remove the lens if the lamp body is to be removed.

37 Number plate lamps and bulbs – removal and refitting

Basic type

1   Two rear number plate lamps are fitted, of which various designs have been employed, one on each of the inside faces of the two overriders. Disconnect the batteries, and the leads to the lamps at the nearest snap connectors. Undo the 2 screws, noting the 2 nuts and distance pieces inside the overrider. Remove the lamp cover, the lens, washer, and plinth (photo). Remove the bulb.

2   To refit, reverse the removal procedure. Note that the thick edge of the distance piece is furthest away from the rear.

MGB (GHN4/5 and GHD4/5) for certain territories

3   Disconnect the battery, and either remove the two nuts and washers retaining the lamps to the bracket, or alternatively remove the bracket with the lamp. Disconnect the wiring at the relevant connectors and remove the lamp. Refit in reverse order.

Certain 1978 to 1979 models

4   Disconnect the battery, and the lamp wires at the nearest snap connectors. Unscrew the nuts and washers holding the lamp to the

number plate and remove the lamp and seal, feeding the wires through from the luggage compartment.

5   To refit, reverse the removal procedure.

38 Reverse lamps and bulbs – removal and refitting

1   Remove the two screws and washers holding the reverse lamp against the rear panel and pull off the lens and rubber seal (photo).

2   To remove the bulb, press it down towards the lower contact and pull clear.

3   To renew the bulb, fit one end into the lower contact. Press down and push the top in until it mates with the upper contact hole. Refit the seal, lens, screws and washers.

39 Front and rear side marker lamps (GHN4/5 and GHD4/5 vehicles for certain local and territorial requirements) – removal and refitting

1   To remove, disconnect the battery. Remove the 2 nuts and 4 washers which retain the lamp, partly remove it, and disconnect the feed wires at the harness connections.

2   To refit, reverse the removal procedure.

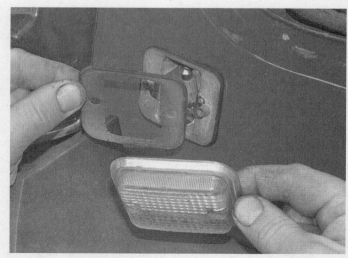

38.1 A reverse lamp, disassembled

40　Map, panel and warning lamps – removal and refitting

1　To renew the map lamp bulb, unscrew the lamp cover screws, take off the cover, and remove the bulb.
2　The panel and warning bulb holders are a push fit in their housings. and are accessible from under the facia panel. Bulbs are a normal bayonet fixing type.
3　To refit, reverse the removal procedure.

GHN4/5 and GHD4/5 vehicles, conforming to local and territorial requirements

4　To remove the brake failure warning lamp assembly, remove the speedometer and fuel gauge (Section 46, paragraphs 4 and 7), remove the wires from the rear of the lamp. release the spring clip, and take out the lamp. To refit, reverse the removal procedure.

GHN5 and GHD5 vehicles, conforming to local and territorial requirements (from model No 294251)

5　To remove the seat belt warning lamp, disconnect the battery, and remove the centre console (see Chapter 12). Remove the bulb holder from the lamp. Remove the lamp clip. Press the lamp from the console. Refit in reverse order.

Hazard warning lamp

6　To renew the hazard warning lamp, remove the centre console (see Chapter 12), and the bulb holder from the lamp. Unscrew the nut and take the lamp from the console. Refit in reverse order.

41　Courtesy lamp, 1978 to 79 models – removal and refitting

UK cars

1　Disconnect the battery and remove the centre console. Take out the bulb holder, release the two lamp retaining clips, and remove the lamp. To refit, reverse the procedure.

USA and Canada cars

2　Disconnect the battery, and pull the lamp body from the facia. Pull off the leads. Refit in reverse.

42　Flasher unit – checking

1　The unit is a small cylindrical metal container in the engine compartment, actuated by the direction indicator switch.
2　If the flasher unit fails to operate, or works very slowly or very rapidly, check the circuit before assuming the unit is faulty. Proceed as follows:

(a) *Examine the direction indicator bulbs and check the earthing of the bulb holders to the body*
(b) *If the flashers are working but the warning light has ceased to function, check the warning bulb*
(c) *Using the circuit diagram, check all the flasher circuit connections if a bulb is sound but does not work*
(d) *In the event of total direction indicator failure, check the relevant fuse*
(e) *With the ignition on, check that current is reaching the flasher unit by connecting a voltmeter between the plus or B terminal and earth. If this test is positive connect the plus or B terminal and the L terminal and operate the flasher switch. If the flasher bulb lights up the unit is defective and must be renewed.*

43　Fog lamp relay (fitted to early cars only)

The relay is removed by unscrewing the 2 screws and washers which retain it to the bulkhead in the engine compartment. The unit is sealed, and apart from checking the security of the terminals, no maintenance is required.

44　Hazard warning flasher unit and audible warning buzzer (GHN4/5 and GHD4/5 vehicles for certain local and territorial requirements) – removal and refitting

1　To remove the flasher unit and buzzer, disconnect the battery and remove the centre console (see Chapter 12). Take the flasher unit from the clip and remove the wires. Remove the nut or screw retaining the buzzer, and pull off the wires.
2　To refit, reverse the removal procedure.

45　Switches – removal and refitting

1　In all cases, disconnect the battery earth lead.

Early types – removal

2　To remove the ignition/starter switch, pull the connector from the switch, behind the facia. With a screwdriver remove the lockring and take out the switch. To separate the barrel from the body insert the key and turn the switch to on. Depress the barrel retaining plunger, and withdraw the barrel and key.
3　To remove the wiper, lighting and blower switches, pull the connectors from the switch, and undo the lockrings. Remove the switches from the facia.
4　To remove the panel and map-reading lamp switches, depress the spring-loaded plunger in the knob shanks and pull them off. Undo the lockrings and remove the switches from the facia.
5　To remove the direction indicator and headlamp flasher switch (GHN4 and GHD4 cars), remove the four screws holding the cowling together. Free the switch lead connectors and undo the two switch bracket screws. When refitting the switch and cowling, see that the locating peg on the cowling and the pin on the switch are aligned. If an early type switch is being renewed with one using spring-loaded metal paws and spring leaves, ensure that a square-headed trip stud is used with the height set at 1.177 to 1.187 in (29.9 to 30.45 mm) from the underside of the column.
6　To remove the dipswitch (GHN4 and GHD4 cars), remove the two screws securing the dipswitch to the front pedal box, take off the electrical connections, and remove the switch.
7　To remove the direction indicator/headlamp flasher/high-low beam/horn switch (GHN5 and GHD5 cars), proceed as described in paragraph 5.

Early types – refitting

8　To refit, reverse the removal procedures given.

GHN5 and GHD5 cars, from model No 258001 – removal

9　To remove the heater, wiper and lighting switches, remove the face level vents, as described in Chapter 12. Disconnect the connections to the switches, press in the retaining lugs (using tool 18G 1202 if available) and take out the heater and wiper switches. Remove the lighting switch by depressing the retaining lugs on one side, easing one side through the opening, and depressing the lugs on the other side. Take out the switch.
10　To remove the console switches, remove the console, as described in Chapter 12, and remove the switches by pressing in the four retaining lugs (use tool 18G 1202 if available).
11　To remove the ignition switch, proceed as follows. With the key at O, disconnect the switch wiring, remove the retaining screws, and remove the switch.
12　To remove the direction indicator/headlight flasher/low-high beam switch, remove the 4 retaining screws, and remove the switch cowl. Take the leads from the multi-connector block, unclip the block from the steering column, remove the screws from the switch, and remove the switch and retaining clip.

GHN5 and GHD5 cars, from model No 258001 – refitting

13　To refit, reverse the removal procedures given, but (referring to paragraph 12) ensure that the small tongue on the switch locates in the cutaway on the outer steering column.

GHN5 and GHD5 cars, from model No 410002 – removal

14　To remove the light switch, remove the 3 bolts retaining the steering column to the facia, and lower the column. Unscrew the 3 screws retaining the RH half of the steering column cowl and take it off. Remove the light switch leads, press down the clips, and remove the switch.

15 To remove the ignition/starter switch and steering lock, remove the 3 bolts retaining the steering column to the facia, and lower the column. Unscrew the 4 screws retaining the column cowl, and remove both halves. Disconnect the ignition wires at the multi-connector, take out the small retaining screw, and withdraw the switch assembly from the steering lock housing. Drill the heads of the shear bolts from the clamp plate, and free the lock assembly.

16 To remove the facia switches, remove the facia (see Chapter 12), disconnect the multi-connectors, depress the clips retaining the switch and remove.

17 To remove the panel lamp rheostat switch, remove the facia (see Chapter 12), disconnect the wires to the switch, push in the pin in the knob and withdraw the knob. Unscrew the retaining ring and remove the switch.

18 To remove the direction indicator/main beam/horn control switch. remove the steering column cowls (see paragraph 15) and disconnect the multi-plugs. Loosen the clamp screw and take off the switch. Remove the insulating tape to separate the switch leads. Drill out the

rivets securing the wipe/wash switch to the mounting plate, remove the screws, and separate the switch and plate.

19 To remove the wiper/washer switch, remove as described in paragraph 18.

20 To remove the handbrake warning switch, disconnect the battery, and remove the driving seat (see Chapter 12). Pull the carpet back, disconnect the wiring plug, remove the locknut locking the switch to the handbrake lever, and take out the switch.

GHN5 and GHD5 cars from model No 41002 – refitting

21 To refit the light switch, reverse the removal procedure.

22 To refit the ignition/starter switch and steering lock, locate the lock body centrally over the outer column slot, fit the clamp plate, but do not shear the bolt heads. Refit the switch, connect the wiring, and check the operation of the lock and switch. Tighten the shear bolts until they break. Reverse the remainder of the removal procedure.

23 To refit the facia switches, reverse the removal procedure.

24 To refit the panel lamp rheostat switch, reverse the removal procedure.

25 To refit the direction indicator/main beam/horn control switch,

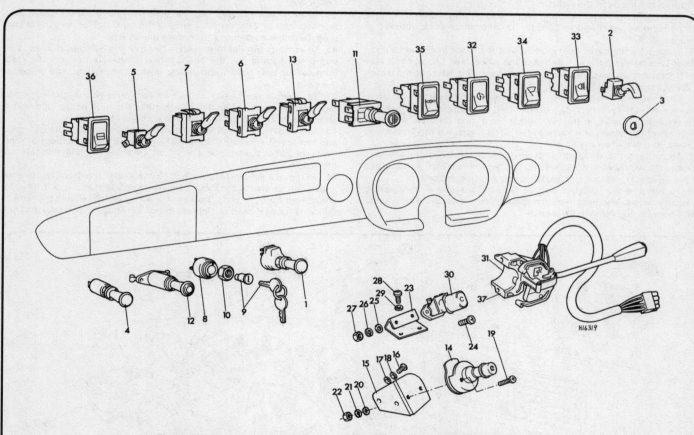

Fig 10.9 Facia and switch layout, RH drive vehicles up to model No 410 001 (Sec 45)

1 Panel light switch
2 Overdrive switch
3 Bezel
Cars up to and including early GHN5 and GHD5 models
4 Map light switch
5 Heater blower switch
6 Windscreen wiper switch
7 Windscreen wiper switch (Tourer)
8 Ignition/starter switch
9 Ignition switch lock and key
10 Locknut for ignition and starter switch

11 Light switch
12 Heated rear window switch (GT)
GHN3 and GHD3 models
13 Light switch
14 Headlight dip switch
15 to 22 Dipswitch bracket
RHD models up to and including GHN4 and GHD4 models
23 to 29 Dipswitch bracket
LHD models up to and including GHN4 and GHD4 cars
30 Headlight dipswitch

GHN4 and GHD4 models
31 Direction indicator/headlamp high and low beam/headlamp flasher/horn push switch
GHN5 and GHD5 from car number 258 001
32 Fog and spot light switch
33 Light switch
34 Windscreen wiper switch
35 Heater blower switch
36 Electrically heated rear window switch (GT)
37 Direction indicator/headlamp high and low beam/headlamp flasher switch

reverse the removal procedure. Check that the cancelling ring is free to rotate in the switch, that the lug on the inside diameter of the switch is located in the slot of the outer steering column, and that the striker dog on the nylon switch centre is both next to, and in line with, the direction indicator switch lever. If the cancelling ring is tight after the switch has been fitted, slacken the screws and reposition the top plate. Check that the steering wheel lugs engage easily with the cancelling ring.

26   To refit the wiper/washer switch, proceed as in paragraph 25.

27   For the handbrake warning switch, refit in reverse, adjusting the switch so that by pulling the handbrake lever up to the first notch, the warning light is operated.

GHN4/5 and GHD4/5 cars, conforming to local and territorial requirements – removal

28   To remove the heater blower switch, remove the heater air control by removing the knob and retaining nut, and releasing the control from the bracket. Remove the wires from the blower switch, and depress the inside retaining lugs (use tool 18G 1145 if available) and withdraw the inside of the switch.

29   To remove the lighting switch, remove the wires from the switch, depress the inside retaining lugs (use tool 18G 1145 if available) and withdraw the inside of the switch.

30   To remove the hazard warning switch and map light switch, remove the console as described in Chapter 12, and proceed as outlined in paragraph 29.

31   To remove the panel light switch, take the motif from the steering wheel boss, remove the nut, and then the wheel (see Chapter 11). Take out 3 screws from the LH switch cowl and remove it. Remove the wiring and the 2 screws, and take out the switch.

32   To remove the windscreen wiper/washer and overdrive switch, remove the LH switch cowl as described in paragraph 31, remove the retaining screws in the RH switch cowl, and remove the cowl. Disconnect the snap connectors in the wiring, remove the 2 retaining screws, and withdraw the switch.

33   To remove the direction indicator, horn and headlamp switch, remove the windscreen wiper/washer and overdrive switch as described in paragraph 32, remove the 2 screws, and remove the switch.

34   To remove the ignition switch, remove the complete steering column cowl as described in paragraph 32. Disconnect the wiring, undo the 4 screws, and remove the switch.

35   To remove the warning door switch (GHN5 and GHD5 vehicles only), remove the single screw and take out the switch. Remove the leads.

GHN4/5 and GHD4/5 cars, conforming to local and territorial requirements – refitting

36   To refit the heater blower switch, push the switch evenly through the aperture until held by the retainer lugs. Refit the wiring and the heater air control.

37   To refit the lighting switch, refer to paragraph 36 (excluding the reference to the heater air control).

38   To refit the hazard warning switch and map light switch, refer to paragraph 36 (excluding the reference to the heater air control). Refit the console.

39   To refit the panel light switch, windscreen wiper/washer and overdrive switch, direction indicator horn and headlamp switch, ignition switch and audible warning door switch reverse the removal sequences.

GHN5 and GHD5 cars, from model No 294 251, and conforming to local and territorial requirements – removal

40   To remove the hazard warning switch, remove the centre console, as described in Chapter 12. Remove the bulb holder and the wiring plug. Detach the retainer and remove the switch.

41   To remove the lighting switch, remove the 3 facia LH lower trim board screws and pull the board forward, releasing it from the clips. Remove the bulb holder and wiring, detach the retainer, and withdraw the switch.

42   To remove the heater blower switch, remove the glovebox and face level vents (see Chapter 12). Remove the bulb holder and wiring connections. Detach the retainer and withdraw the switch.

43   To remove the panel lamp rheostat switch, remove the glovebox and face level vents (see Chapter 12) and detach the switch connections. Press the pin in the knob and pull it off. Unscrew the ring, and take out the switch.

44   To remove the temperature and airflows rotary controls, remove the 3 securing screws in the facia LH lower trim board and pull it forward, releasing it from the clips. Take out the screw which secures the facia to the cross-tube LH bracket. Depress the switch knob pin and take the knob

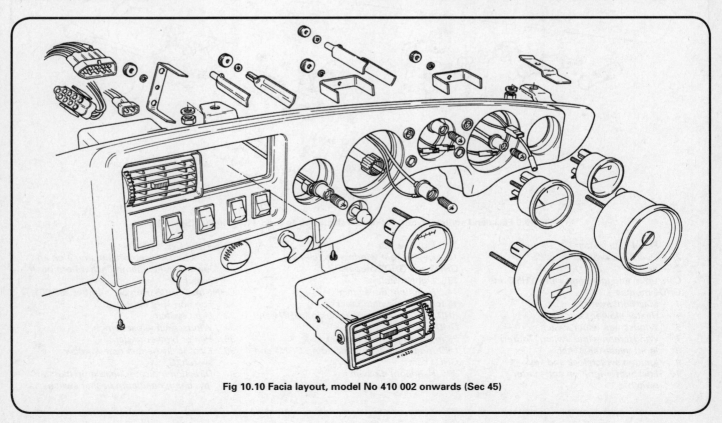

Fig 10.10 Facia layout, model No 410 002 onwards (Sec 45)

off. Take the bulb holder from the light box, and undo the rotary control retaining nut. Remove the nut with the spring and washer, and take the control from the facia. Unscrew the 3 nuts and washers to release the light box from the dial assembly, and remove the assembly.

GHN5 and GHD5 cars from model No 294 251, and conforming to local and territorial requirements – refitting

45 To refit, reverse the removal procedures given above.

1978 to 79 cars – removal

46 To remove the heater fan switch, free the clips which hold the switch in position. Pull off the connections and withdraw the switch.
47 To remove the rheostat switch, on USA and Canada cars, remove the LH lower facia panel (3 screws). Depress the knob plunger and take off the knob. Remove the switch retainer (use tool 18G 671 if available), remove the switch followed by the switch wires.
48 For the handbrake warning switch, remove as described in paragraph 20.

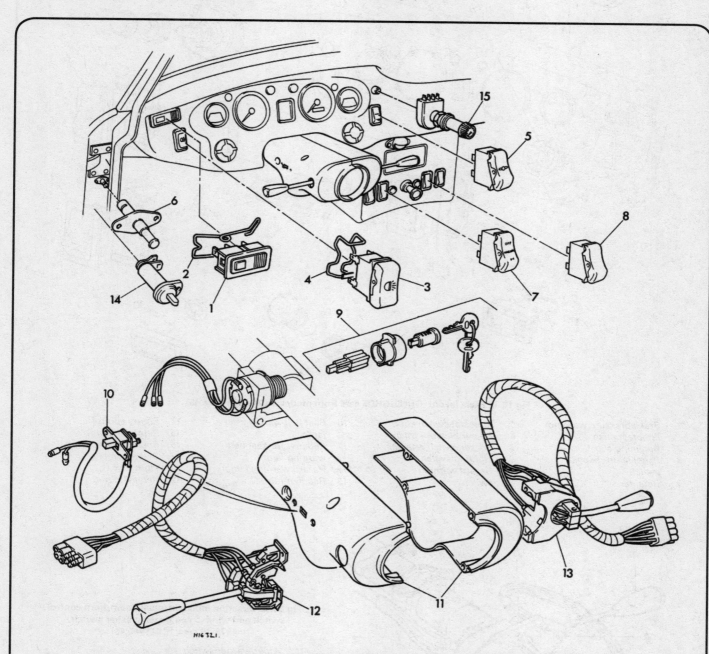

Fig 10.11 Facia layout, GHN5/GHN4 and GHD5/GHD4 cars conforming to local and territorial requirements (Sec 45)

1	Brake pressure warning light/ test push	
2	Retaining clip	
3	Lighting switch	
4	Retaining clip	
5	Heater blower switch	
6	Door switch – interior light	
7	Hazard warning switch	
8	Map light switch	
9	Ignition switch	
10	Panel light switch	
11	Steering column switch cowl	
12	Direction indicator/headlight flasher low/high beam/horn switch	
13	Windshield wiper/washer and overdrive switch	
14	Audible warning door switch	
15	Panel lamp rheostat switch	

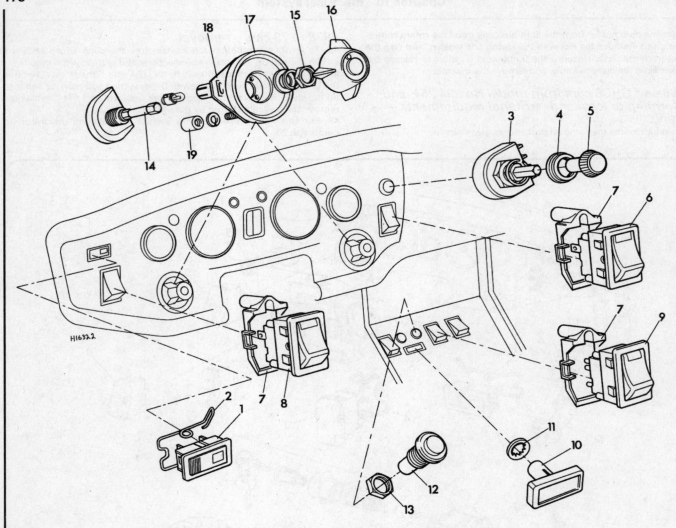

Fig 10.12 Facia layout, GHN5/GHD5 cars from model No 294 251 (Sec 45)

1	Brake pressure warning light test push	5	Rheostat switch knob
2	Retaining clip	6	Heater blower switch
3	Panel lamp rheostat switch	7	Rocker switch retainer
4	Retainer	8	Lighting switch
		9	Hazard warning switch
10	Seat belt warning lamp	14	Rotary control
11	Retainer for seat belt warning lamp	15	Retaining nut
12	Hazard warning lamp	16	Rotary control knob
13	Retainer nut	17	Dial assembly
		18	Light box
		19	Retaining nut

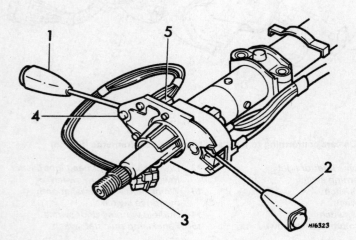

Fig 10.13 Direction indicator/main beam/horn control switch and windscreen wiper/washer switch – 1978-79 cars, RHD (Sec 45)

1 Wiper/washer switch
2 Direction indicator/main beam/horn control switch
3 Multi-plug
4 Wiper/washer switch screws
5 Clamp screw for direction indicator, etc, switch

49 To remove the hazard warning switch, on USA and Canada cars, remove the LH lower facia panel (3 screws). On UK cars, remove the face level vents (Chapter 12). Depress the clips securing the switch, remove it, and pull off the wires.

50 To remove the stoplight switch, disconnect the wires at the nearest connector, take off the locknut, and remove the switch.

51 To remove the direction indicator/main beam/horn control switch, remove the steering wheel (see Chapter 11), the cowling (see Chapter 11), and disconnect the wiring plugs. Remove the wire-retaining tape, and the 3 screws securing the wiper switch to the plate. Remove the clamp screw, followed by the switch.

52 For the windscreen wiper/washer switch, proceed as described in paragraph 51.

1978 to 79 cars – refitting

53 To refit the heater tan switch and rheostat switch, reverse the removal procedures

54 To refit the handbrake warning switch, proceed as described in paragraph 27.

55 To refit the hazard warning switch, reverse the removal procedure.

56 To refit the stoplight switch, reverse the removal procedure, ensuring that 1/8 in (3 mm) of free movement exists at the pedal before the pedal arm touches the switch.

57 To refit the direction indicator/main beam/horn control switch, reverse the removal procedure, ensuring that the switch lug is located in the steering column.

58 To refit the windscreen wiper/washer switch, proceed as described in paragraph 57.

---

46 Instruments – removal and refitting

Early cars
1 Refer to Chapter 12, Section 47.

GHN4/5 and GHD4/5 cars, conforming to local and territorial requirements – removal

2 To remove the tachometer, remove the lower LH facia panel cover, the 2 knurled tachometer retaining nuts, the earth cable and the brackets. Remove the instrument and disconnect the wiring.

3 To remove the oil pressure gauge, remove the tachometer (see paragraph 2), and the ignition warning lamp and holder. Remove the two retaining nuts, take out the instrument and disconnect the wiring.

4 To remove the speedometer, remove the heater air control knob and the control retaining nut, and release the control from the bracket. Release the trip recorder reset from the bracket by unscrewing the nut. Remove the speedometer knurled nuts and the holding brackets, and withdraw the instruments. Disconnect the drive cable.

5 To remove the temperature gauge, remove the heater air control (paragraph 4). Release the temperature gauge knurled nut, take out the gauge, and disconnect the wiring.

6 To remove the mixture (choke) control, remove the speedometer and temperature gauge (paragraphs 4 and 5), and release the choke inner cable at the carburettor. Free the cable from the gearbox cover clip, remove the retaining nut behind the facia, and withdraw the control.

7 To remove the fuel gauge, remove the knurled nut behind the gauge, take out the instrument, and pull off the wires.

GHN4/5 and GHD4/5 cars, conforming to local and territorial requirements – refitting

8 To refit, reverse the procedures given in paragraphs 2 to 7.

1978 to 79 cars – removal

9 To remove the tachometer (UK only), unscrew the 2 nuts, washers and brackets behind the instrument, and take it out. Disconnect the wiring, pull out the bulb holder, and withdraw the instrument.

10 To remove the tachometer (USA and Canada), remove the LH lower facia panel (3 screws). Press the instrument in and turn it clockwise 30 degrees, aligning the studs on the tachometer with the facia cut-outs. Remove the instrument, and disconnect the wires. Pull out the bulb holder, and remove the spring.

11 To remove the speedometer (UK), disconnect the speedometer cable by removing the knurled nut. Remove the 2 nuts, washers and brackets, and take out the instrument. Withdraw the bulb holder.

12 To remove the speedometer (USA and Canada), remove the LH lower facia panel (3 screws), and detach the speedometer cable from the instrument. Continue as in paragraph 10.

13 To remove the clock, remove the centre console (UK). Remove the speedometer (USA and Canada). Remove the 2 knurled nuts, the washers and the bridge piece from behind the instrument. Take out the clock, disconnect the wires, remove the bulb holder, and withdraw the instrument. Remove the clock seal.

14 To remove the oil pressure gauge, remove the LH lower facia panel by taking out the 3 screws (USA and Canada). Remove the RH face level vent (UK). Remove the 2 knurled nuts, washers, and the bridge piece from behind the instrument. Unscrew the pipe from the gauge, noting the sealing washer, withdraw the gauge, and pull out the bulb holder. Take out the gauge.

15 To remove the coolant temperature gauge, remove the speedometer as described in paragraph 12 (USA and Canada only). Pull out the bulb holder, remove the nut, washer and bridge piece from the gauge rear, and withdraw the gauge. Pull the wiring off, and remove the gauge.

16 To remove the fuel gauge, remove the LH lower facia panel by taking out the 3 screws (USA and Canada). Remove the nut, spring washer and bridge piece from the rear of the gauge, pull out the gauge, disconnect the wiring and remove the bulb holder.

1978 to 79 cars – refitting

17 To refit the tachometer (UK), reverse the removal procedure.

18 To refit the tachometer (USA and Canada), reverse the removal procedure, ensuring that the spring is fitted with the ends butted, and not overlapping. Engage the studs, push in the instrument, and rotate anticlockwise to lock.

19 To refit the speedometer, clock, oil pressure gauge, coolant temperature gauge, and fuel gauge, reverse the appropriate removal procedure.

---

47 Tachometer, impulse type – description and fault finding

1 The tachometer is very reliable and attention is not normally required. Voltage pulses from the coil are passed to the indicator head, where they are shown as engine rpm.

2 In the event of malfunction, check the wiring connections and the circuit for continuity (poor connections will give incorrect readings). Check that the pulse lead at the rear of the tachometer forms a symmetrical loop as shown in Fig. 10.14. It must not be tight against the plastic former.

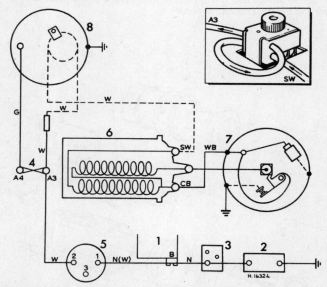

Fig 10.14 Impulse tachometer – wiring diagram, and pulse lead detail (Sec 47)

1	Control box	**Cable colour code**	W White
2	Batteries	B Black	Y Yellow
3	Starter solenoid	G Green	
4	A3-A4 fuse	LG Light Green	On cables having
5	Ignition switch	N Brown	two colour code
6	Ignition coil	O Orange	letters, the main
7	Distributor	P Purple	colour is denoted
8	Tachometer	R Red	first and the tracer
		U Blue	colour second

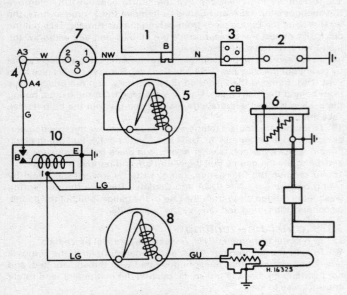

Fig 10.15 The voltage stabiliser circuit (Sec 48)

		Cable colour code	
1	Control box		
2	Batteries (12 volt)	B	Black
3	Starter solenoid	G	Green
4	Fuse (A3-A4)	LG	Light Green
5	Fuel gauge	N	Brown
6	Fuel tank unit	O	Orange
7	Ignition switch	P	Purple
8	Coolant temperature	R	Red
	gauge	U	Blue
9	Temperature sender	W	White
10	Voltage stabiliser	Y	Yellow

On cables having two colour code letters, the main colour is denoted first and the tracer colour second

48 Voltage stabiliser – checking

1   The bi-metallic voltage stabiliser ensures steady readings from the fuel and temperature gauges despite fluctuations in battery voltage. If the gauge readings are erratic, and particularly if they rise and fall with engine speed, the stabiliser may be suspect.

2   When checking for faults, first examine the wiring stabiliser, the gauges and their sender units. Connect a voltmeter to the stabiliser B terminal and earth and check that, with the ignition switched on. a reading of 12 volts is obtained with the engine stationary and 12 to 13 volts with the engine running at 1000 rpm.

3   Checking of the stabiliser output can only be done with a thermal ('hot wire') voltmeter. If such an instrument is available, connect it to the stabiliser I terminal and check that, after the ignition has been switched on for two minutes, a reading of 10 volts is obtained. The reading should not vary with engine speed.

4   If an ordinary voltmeter is connected to the stabiliser I terminal and earth, with the ignition on the meter reading should fluctuate between 12 to 13 volts and zero. The rate of fluctuation will depend upon input voltage. A steady reading of 12 to 13 volts or zero indicates a fault.

5   If the voltage stabiliser is faulty it must be renewed with the B and E terminals uppermost and not more than 20° from vertical. To remove, remove the LH lower facia panel by removing the three screws (USA and Canada only), disconnect the battery, and pull the wires from the stabiliser. Remove the screw, and hence the unit, which is located on the bulkhead behind the facia.

6   Do not check the gauges by short circuiting to earth but examine for continuity between the terminals with the wiring disconnected. If the transmitter is thought to be broken, disconnect the lead and check for continuity between the case and terminal.

49 Audible warning buzzer (when fitted) – removal and refitting

1   Disconnect the batteries and remove the centre console. Remove the wiring to the buzzer unit, take out the screw, and remove the unit. The unit is non-adjustable, and must be renewed if defective.

2   To refit, reverse the removal procedure.

50 Horn – removal, servicing and refitting

1   To remove, first disconnect the battery. Disconnect the horn wires and remove the mounting bolts.

2   If the horn works badly or fails completely, check for short circuits and loose connections. Check that the instrument is secure, and that there is nothing lying on the horn body. If the fault is not external, remove the cover and check the leads inside (early models). If these are sound, check the contacts which, if burnt or dirty, may be cleaned with a fine file. Clean finally with petrol. Test the current consumption of the horn which should be between 3 and 3 ½ amps.

3   To adjust, remove the cover screw, the cover, and retaining strap. Loosen the fixed contact locknut and turn the adjusting nut until the contacts just separate. Rotate the adjusting nut one turn anti-clockwise, and secure it with the locknut. Refit the cover and strap.

51 Cigar lighter – removal and refitting

1   Disconnect the battery. Remove the centre console (where applicable) as described in Chapter 12, and disconnect the wiring to the lighter. Gently press in the sides of the lamp cover and pull it from the lighter shell. Unscrew the shell from the switch base, and pull the base and glow ring from the front of the facia panel (or console).

2   To refit, reverse the removal procedure.

52 Windscreen wiper systems – maintenance

1   The gearbox and cable rack are lubricated during manufacture. No further lubrication is required. The wiper blades should be inspected frequently and renewed when necessary.

2   To remove and refit a wiper blade, lift the wiper arm away from the screen and remove the old blade by turning it in towards the arm and disengaging the arm from the slot in the blade. To fit a blade, slide the

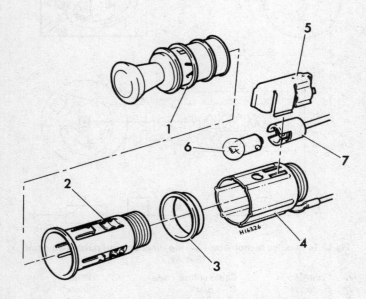

Fig 10.16 Cigar lighter – exploded view (Sec 51)

1	Pop-out heater	5	Lamp cover
2	Switch base	6	Bulb
3	Glow ring	7	Bulb holder
4	Shell		

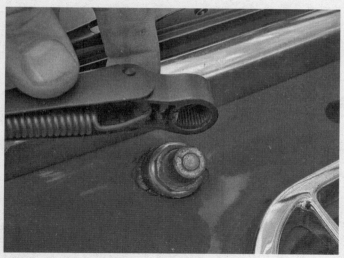

52.4 Wiper arm, push fit type

end of the wiper arm into the slotted spring fastening in the centre of the blade. Push the blade firmly onto the arm until the raised portion of the arm is fully home in the hole in the blade.

3 Before removing a wiper arm (early type), turn the wiper switch on and off to ensure that the arms are in their parked position. Pivot the arm back, and pull the head from the splined drive. To refit, position the arm in the parked position, and press the head onto the splined drive till the retaining clip clicks into place.

4 Some wiper arms (later type) have a screw clamp. To remove the arm, slacken the screw about two turns. Push in the screw, wriggle the arm on its spindle to free the locking wedge, and slide it off. To refit, tighten the screw, thus tightening the locking wedge. Other wiper arms are just a push pit on the spindle (photo).

53 Windscreen wiper systems – fault diagnosis and rectification

1 Should the wipers fail to park or park badly, check the limit switch on the gearbox cover. Loosen the four screws which retain the cover, and place the projection close to the rim of the limit switch in line with the groove in the cover. Rotate the switch anti-clockwise 25° and tighten the four screws retaining the cover. To park the wipers on the other side of the screen, rotate the limit switch 180° clockwise.

2 Should the wipers be inoperative, or only work slowly, check the motor current by connecting a 0 to 15 amp moving coil ammeter in the circuit and turning on the wiper switch. Check the current consumption against the Specifications. If no current is passing, check the fuse. If the fuse has blown renew it after having checked the wiring serviced by this fuse for short circuits. If the fuse is in good condition, check the wiper switch.

3 If the motor takes a high current check the wiper blades for freedom of movement If satisfactory, check the gearbox cover and gear assembly for damage. Measure the armature endfloat, and compare it with the Specifications. Reset the endfloat if necessary, by means of the adjusting screw. Check that friction in the connecting tubes caused by too small a curvature is not the cause of the high current consumption.

4 If the motor takes a low current, ensure that the battery is fully charged. Check the brush gear after removing the commutator end bracket and ensure that the brushes are bearing on the commutator. If not, check them for freedom of movement and if necessary renew the tension spring. Check the armature by substitution if it is suspect

5 If the two-speed type of motor does not function at high speed, check the switch connections; if these are in order, the third brush may be defective, and the motor must be dismantled as described in Section 55.

54 Windscreen wiper systems – removal and refitting

Type DR3A

1 Remove the wiper arms (see Section 52). Disconnect the wiring cables from the wiper motor and the outer cable from the gearbox housing. Remove the three screws which hold the bracket on which the combined wiper motor and gearbox is mounted under the passenger side of the facia. Remove the motor, gearbox, bracket and cable rack.

2 The wheelboxes are underneath the splined shafts over which the wiper arms fit. To remove the wheelboxes, release the rack casings by slackening the wheelbox cover screws. Remove the nut, brush, and washer from the base of the splines and pull the wheelboxes from under the facia.

3 To refit, reverse the removal procedure. Take care that the wheelboxes are correctly lined up to permit the rack to be fed easily back into engagement

Type 14W

4 Disconnect the battery, remove the wiper arms, and remove the right-hand facia panel (if fitted). Disconnect the leads to the motor, and unscrew the outer cable retaining nut from the motor housing. Take out the two fixing bolts, and withdraw the motor and gearbox assembly with the inner drive cable.

5 To remove the wheelboxes, remove the motor as described in paragraph 4. Loosen the cover plate screws on the wheelboxes and take out the cable casings. Remove the nut bush and washer from each wheelbox spindle, and withdraw them with their rear bushes from under the facia.

6 To refit reverse the removal procedure, taking care that the inner cable is properly engaged with the wheelbox gears.

7 It should be mentioned that, if only the motor is to be removed, the mechanism connecting it to the wiper arms can be uncoupled and left in place.

USA and Canada

8 After removing the motor and drive rack, remove the face level ventilators (see Chapter 12, Sections 58 and 59) before removing the wheelboxes.

55 Windscreen wiper systems – dismantling, inspection and reassembly

Type DR3A

1 To dismantle, undo the four screws holding the gearbox cover in place and remove it. Remove the two through bolts from the commutator end bracket. Pull out the wiring connector and free the bracket. Carefully remove the brush gear as a unit and withdraw the yoke.

2 Clean the commutator and brush gear. Fit new brushes if necessary. Check the resistance between adjacent segments of the commutator. This should be 0.34 to 0.41 ohms. Examine the internal wiring for deterioration, and renew where necessary.

3 The resistance of the field should be 12.8 to 14 ohms. A lower value indicates a probable short circuit, and the field coil should be renewed. Any gears with damaged teeth should also be renewed.

4 To reassemble, reverse the dismantling sequence. Lubricate the following items:

   (a) *Immerse the armature bearing in engine oil for 24 hours*
   (b) *Oil the armature bearings with engine oil*
   (c) *Soak the felt lubricator in the gearbox with engine oil*
   (d) *Grease the worm wheel bearings, cross head, guide channel, connecting rod, crankpin, worm, cable rack and wheelboxes, and final gear shaft*

Type 14W

5 Remove the four screws and the gearbox cover. Remove the circlip and flat washer securing the connecting rod and remove the rod, noting the additional washer underneath it. Remove the circlip and washer which secure the shaft and gear, remove burrs in the region of the circlip groove, and remove the gear, noting the dished washer beneath it.

6 Mark the yoke and gearbox to assist reassembly, take the two yoke fixing bolts out, and remove the yoke and armature. Do not allow metallic particles to be attracted to the pole piece. Remove the screws retaining the brush gear and terminal end switch assembly, and remove both items.

7 Examine the brushes, and renew the assembly if either the main brushes (diametrically opposite each other) are worn to 3/16 in (4.8 mm) or if the narrow section of the third brush is worn to the full brush width.

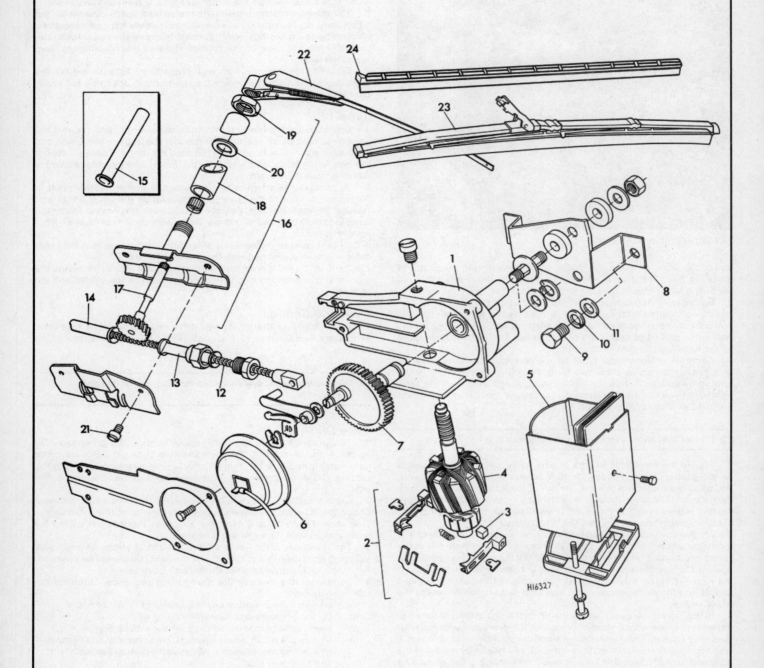

Fig 10.17 Windscreen wiper system, single-speed, Lucas type DR3A – exploded view (Sec 55)

1	Motor body	8	Bracket – wiper motor	14	Casing – wheelbox to wheelbox	19	Wheelbox nut
2	Brush gear	9	Screw			20	Washer (rubber)
3	Brush	10	Spring washer	15	Casing – wheelbox to extension	21	Cover screw
4	Armature	11	Plain washer			22	Wiper arm
5	Field coil	12	Crosshead and rack	16	Wheelbox	23	Wiper blade
6	Parking switch	13	Casing – motor to wheelbox	17	Spindle and gear	24	Rubber
7	Shaft and gear			18	Rubber tube		

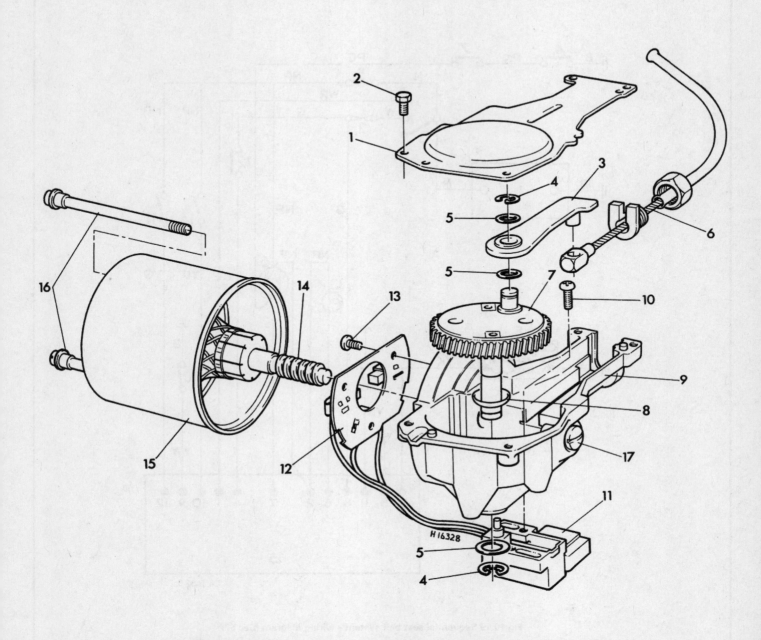

Fig 10.18 Windscreen wiper system, two-speed, Lucas type 14W – exploded view (Sec 55)

1 Gearbox cover	6 Flexible wiper drive	10 Limit switch screw	14 Armature
2 Screw for cover	7 Gear wheel with	11 Limit switch	15 Yoke
3 Connecting rod	crankpin	12 Brush gear	16 Bolts
4 Circlip	8 Dished washer	13 Screw for bushes	17 Thrust screw
5 Washers	9 Gearbox		

8   Renew the gear if damaged or worn.

9   To reassemble, reverse the dismantling procedure, noting the following:

   (a) Lubricate the bearing bushes, armature shaft bearing, gearshaft and pin, felt washer and wheelbox spindles.

   (b) Lubricate the gear wheel teeth, worm gear, connecting rod and pin, cross-head slide, cable rack, and wheelbox gears, using Ragosine Listate grease.

10   If a new armature is being fitted, the thrust screw should be slackened off to provide endfloat. Refit the armature and yoke,

tightening the yoke fixing bolts. Adjust the endfloat, using the thrust screw, to give the specified endfloat

---

56   Windscreen washer motor (if fitted) – removal and refitting

1   To remove, disconnect the battery and the wiring from the motor. Remove the water tubes. Take out the two pump mounting screws, and remove the pump.

2   To refit reverse the removal procedure.

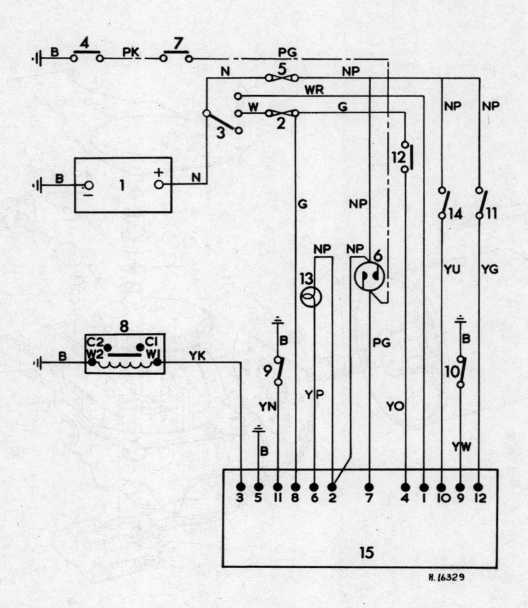

Fig 10.19 Sequential seat belt system – wiring diagram (Sec 57)

1	Battery	**Cable colour code**	
2	Fuse – 35 amp (connecting fusebox terminals 5 and 6)	B	Black
3	Ignition/starter key	G	Green
4	Ignition key switch	LG	Light Green
5	Line fuse – 500 milliamp	N	Brown
6	Warning buzzer	O	Orange
7	Warning buzzer door switch	P	Purple
8	Starter motor relay	R	Red
9	Driver's seat belt switch (normally closed)	U	Blue
10	Passenger's seat belt switch (normally closed)	W	White
11	Passenger's seat switch (normally open)	Y	Yellow
12	Gearbox switch (closed in gear)	On cables having two colour	
13	'Fasten belts' warning lamp	code letters, the main colour	
14	Driver's seat switch (normally open)	is denoted first and the tracer	
15	System control unit	colour secondw	

57 Sequential seat belt system (when fitted) – component removal and refitting

1   To remove the seat switch, disconnect the batteries, and take out the four bolts securing the seat. Disconnect the wiring, and remove the seat. Take off the clips to release the seat cover at the rear and one side of the seat detach the strapping from the front rear and one side, remove the hessian and take out the switch. To refit, reverse the procedure.

2   To remove the gearbox switch, disconnect the battery, and the wires to the switch on the gearbox remote control housing. Unscrew the switch. To refit, reverse the procedure.

3   To remove the seat belt switch disconnect the batteries, remove the bolt holding the belt to the floor tunnel, and pull off the connectors to the belt switch under the tunnel carpet. Pull back the buckle sleeve, prise off the belt switch cover, and release the switch by drilling off the rivetted ends of the rivets. Unsolder the wires. To refit, reverse the procedure.

4   To remove the control unit disconnect the battery, and detach the centre console (see Chapter 12) leaving the wires in position. Remove the nut to release the warning buzzer from the facia rail. and the two screws and nuts to release the control unit. Squeeze the 2 tags. and withdraw the wiring plug from the unit. To refit, reverse the removal procedure.

5   The test procedure is a complex one, and the owner is advised to consult an auto electrician. Before doing so, and assuming that the batteries are in good condition, check the 500-milliamp line fuse and the 35-amp fuse across fusebox terminals 5-6. The control unit should be checked by substitution.

6   To remove the alternative combined buzzer/timer module disconnect the battery and remove the centre console (see Chapter 12). Remove the buzzer/module securing screw. Depress the retaining lever and release the wiring plug. Remove the module. To refit, reverse the procedure.

58 Fault diagnosis – electrical system (general)

1   Faults peculiar to specific components have already been dealt with in previous Sections. In general, most electrical faults can be attributed to one of three causes:

    (a) *Failure of current supply (disconnected or broken wire, blown fuse, faulty switch etc)*

    (b) *Failure of earth return (component mountings loose or corroded, earth strap broken or loose)*

    (c) *Component failure*

2   Intermittent electrical faults are frequently due to loose or corroded connections, to wires chafing through their insulation (short-circuit) or cracking internally (open circuit). Bypass suspect wires and note if any improvement occurs.

3   Charging system defects may be due to nothing more than a slack drivebelt or a loose or dirty connection. Check these items before condemning the generator. Verify also that the problem is insufficient charging and not excessive discharging, perhaps due to a short-circuit or other malfunction discharging the battery whilst the car is not in use.

UK models up to approximately 1967
(dynamo, positive earth)

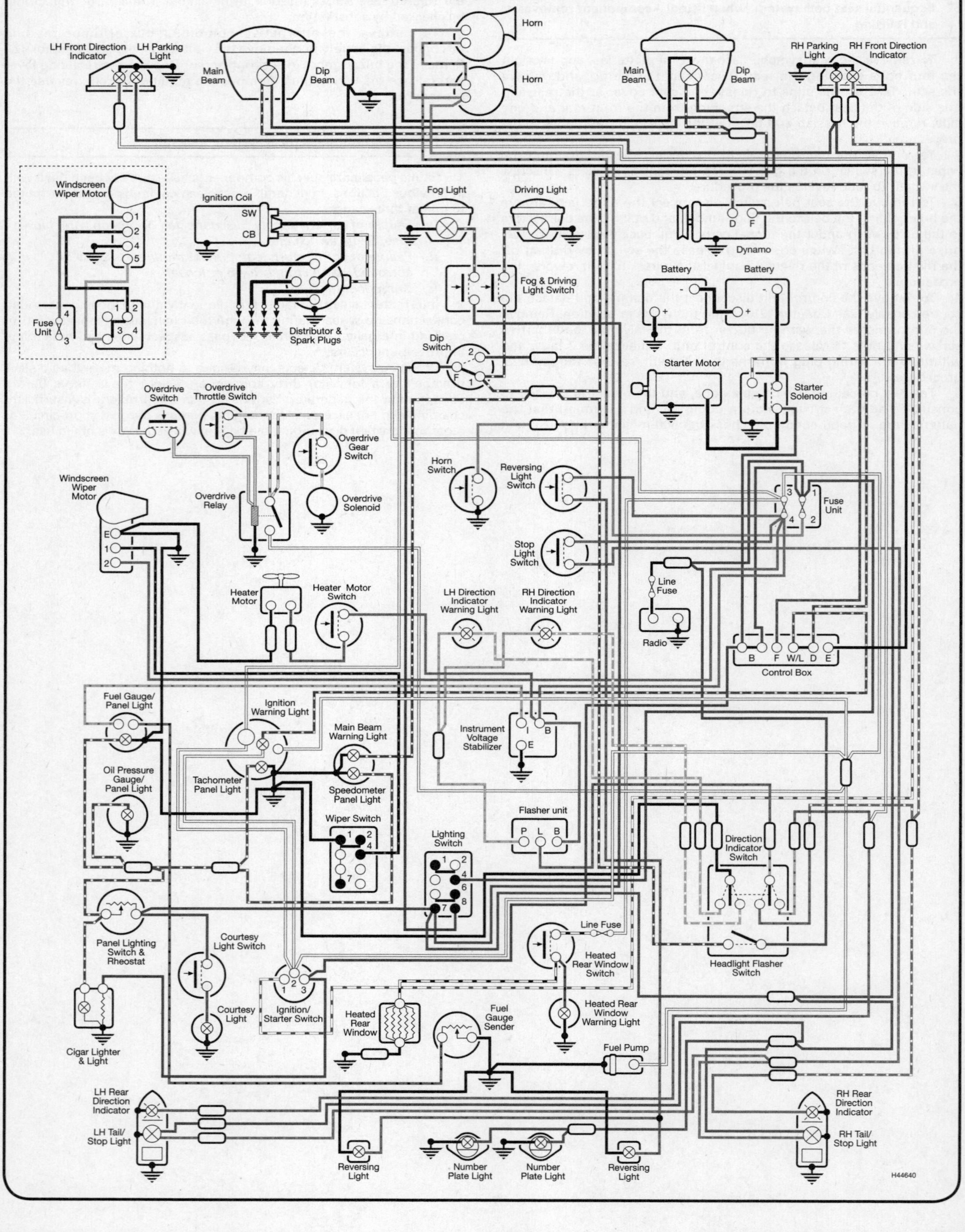

LH Front Direction Indicator
LH Parking Light
Main Beam
Dip Beam
Horn
Horn
Main Beam
Dip Beam
RH Parking Light
RH Front Direction Indicator

Windscreen Wiper Motor
1
2
4
5
Fuse Unit
4
3
1 2
3 4

Ignition Coil
SW
CB
Distributor & Spark Plugs

Fog Light
Driving Light
Fog & Driving Light Switch
Dip Switch
2
F 1

Dynamo
D F
Battery
Battery
- +
- +
Starter Motor
Starter Solenoid

Overdrive Switch
Overdrive Throttle Switch
Overdrive Gear Switch
Overdrive Solenoid
Overdrive Relay

Windscreen Wiper Motor
E
1
2

Heater Motor
Heater Motor Switch

Horn Switch
Reversing Light Switch
Stop Light Switch
LH Direction Indicator Warning Light
RH Direction Indicator Warning Light

Line Fuse
Radio

Fuse Unit
3 1
4 2

B F W/L D E
Control Box

Fuel Gauge/ Panel Light
Ignition Warning Light
Main Beam Warning Light
Instrument Voltage Stabilizer
I B
E

Oil Pressure Gauge/ Panel Light
Tachometer Panel Light
Speedometer Panel Light
Wiper Switch
1 2
4
7

Lighting Switch
1 2
4
6
8
7

Flasher unit
P L B

Direction Indicator Switch

Panel Lighting Switch & Rheostat
Courtesy Light Switch
Courtesy Light
Ignition/ Starter Switch
1 2 3

Heated Rear Window
Fuel Gauge Sender
Line Fuse
Heated Rear Window Switch
Heated Rear Window Warning Light
Fuel Pump
Headlight Flasher Switch

Cigar Lighter & Light

LH Rear Direction Indicator
LH Tail/ Stop Light
Reversing Light
Number Plate Light
Number Plate Light
Reversing Light
RH Rear Direction Indicator
RH Tail/ Stop Light

H44640

UK models from approximately 1967 to 1970
(alternator with separate regulator, negative earth)

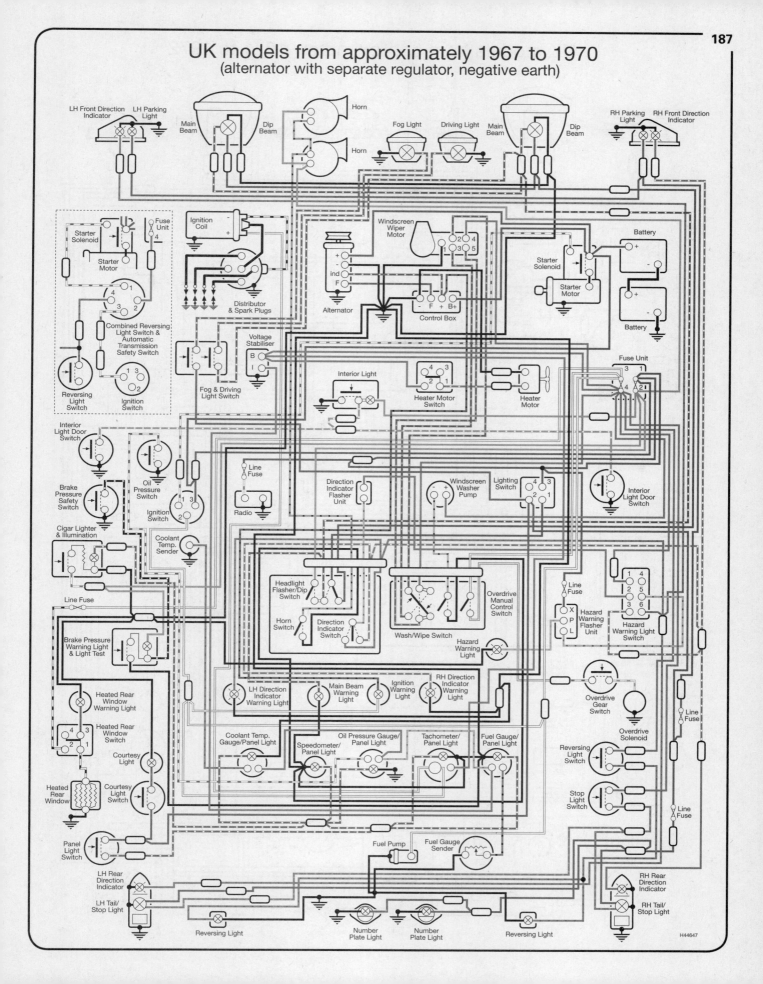

H44647

UK models from approximately 1971 to 1972

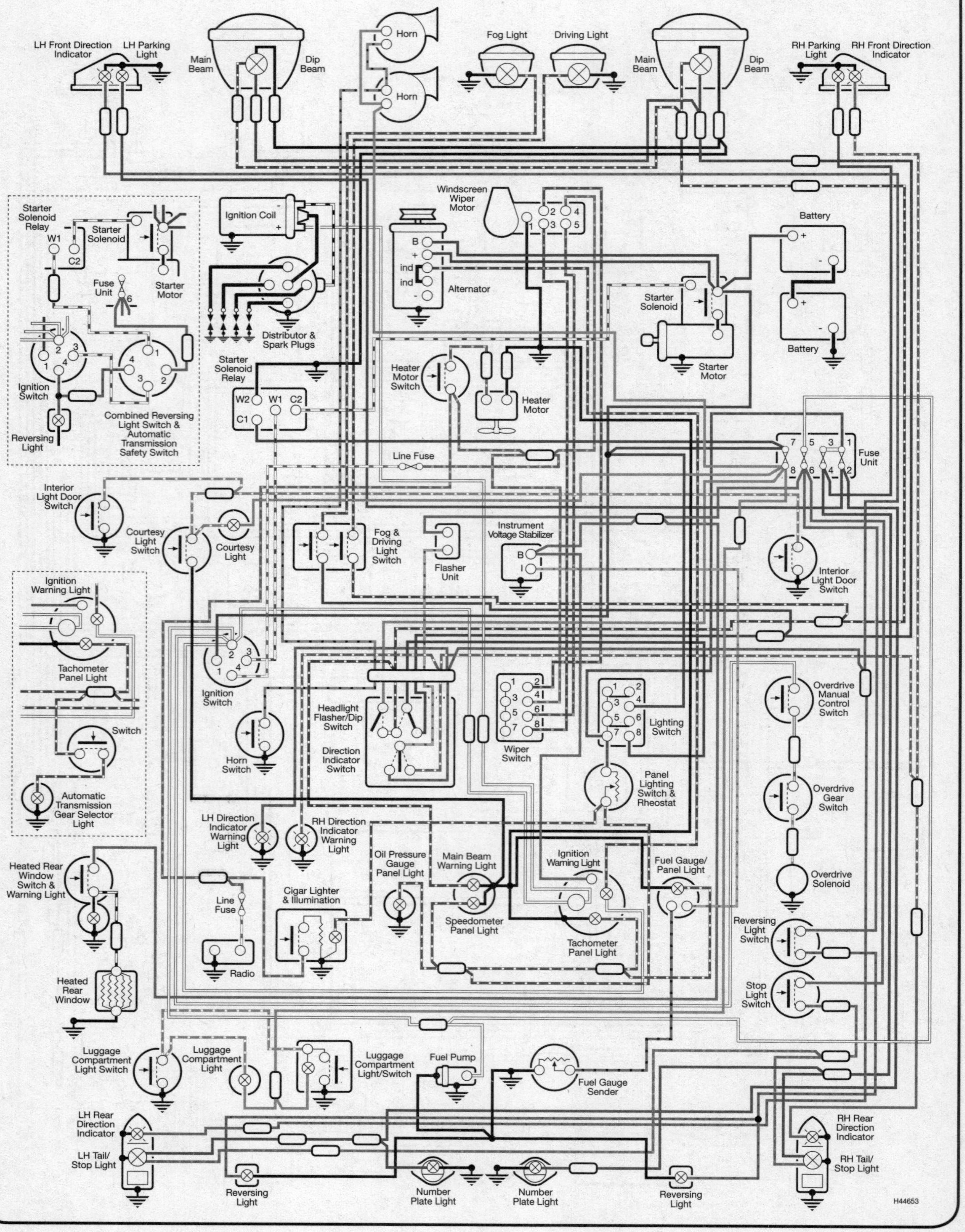

LH Front Direction Indicator

LH Parking Light

Main Beam

Dip Beam

Horn

Horn

Fog Light

Driving Light

Main Beam

Dip Beam

RH Parking Light

RH Front Direction Indicator

Starter Solenoid Relay

W1

C2

Starter Solenoid

Starter Motor

Fuse Unit

Ignition Switch

Reversing Light

Combined Reversing Light Switch & Automatic Transmission Safety Switch

Ignition Coil

Distributor & Spark Plugs

Starter Solenoid Relay

W2 W1 C2

C1

Windscreen Wiper Motor

Alternator

B
+
ind
ind
-

Heater Motor Switch

Heater Motor

Starter Solenoid

Starter Motor

Battery

+

-

+

Battery

Line Fuse

Fuse Unit

Interior Light Door Switch

Courtesy Light Switch

Courtesy Light

Fog & Driving Light Switch

Flasher Unit

Instrument Voltage Stabilizer

B

I

Interior Light Door Switch

Ignition Warning Light

Tachometer Panel Light

Switch

Automatic Transmission Gear Selector Light

Ignition Switch

Horn Switch

Headlight Flasher/Dip Switch

Direction Indicator Switch

Wiper Switch

Lighting Switch

Panel Lighting Switch & Rheostat

Overdrive Manual Control Switch

Overdrive Gear Switch

Overdrive Solenoid

Heated Rear Window Switch & Warning Light

Heated Rear Window

Line Fuse

Radio

Cigar Lighter & Illumination

LH Direction Indicator Warning Light

RH Direction Indicator Warning Light

Oil Pressure Gauge Panel Light

Main Beam Warning Light

Speedometer Panel Light

Ignition Warning Light

Tachometer Panel Light

Fuel Gauge/Panel Light

Reversing Light Switch

Stop Light Switch

Luggage Compartment Light Switch

Luggage Compartment Light

Luggage Compartment Light/Switch

Fuel Pump

Fuel Gauge Sender

LH Rear Direction Indicator

LH Tail/Stop Light

Reversing Light

Number Plate Light

Number Plate Light

Reversing Light

RH Rear Direction Indicator

RH Tail/Stop Light

H44653

UK models from approximately 1973 to 1974

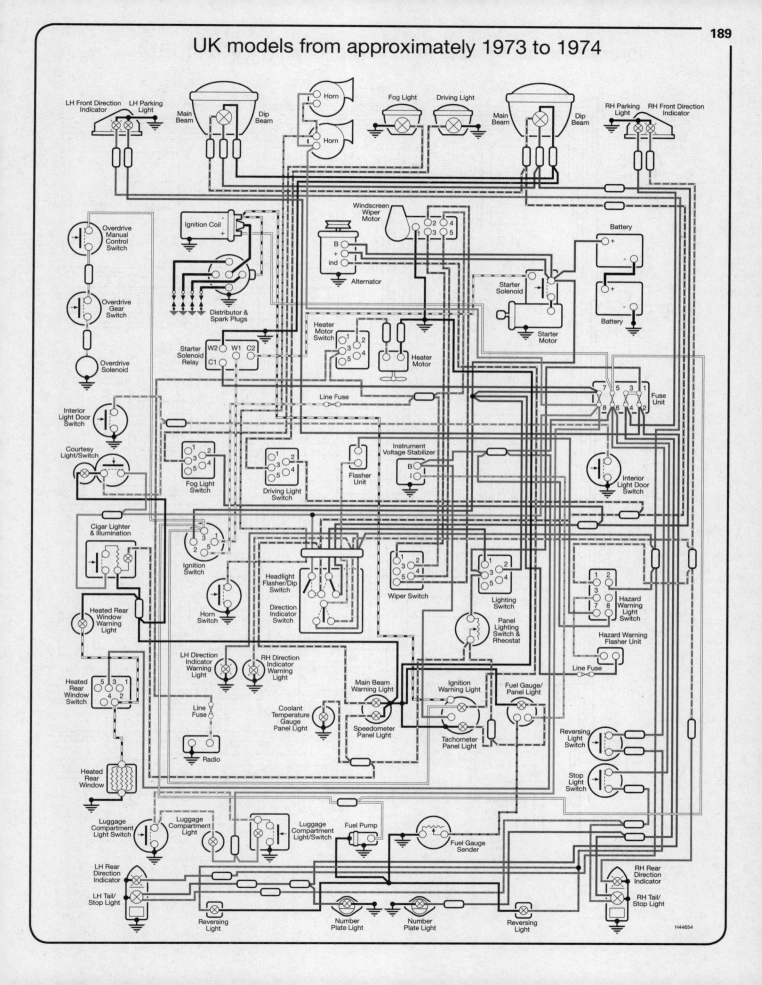

H44654

North American models from approximately 1973 to 1974

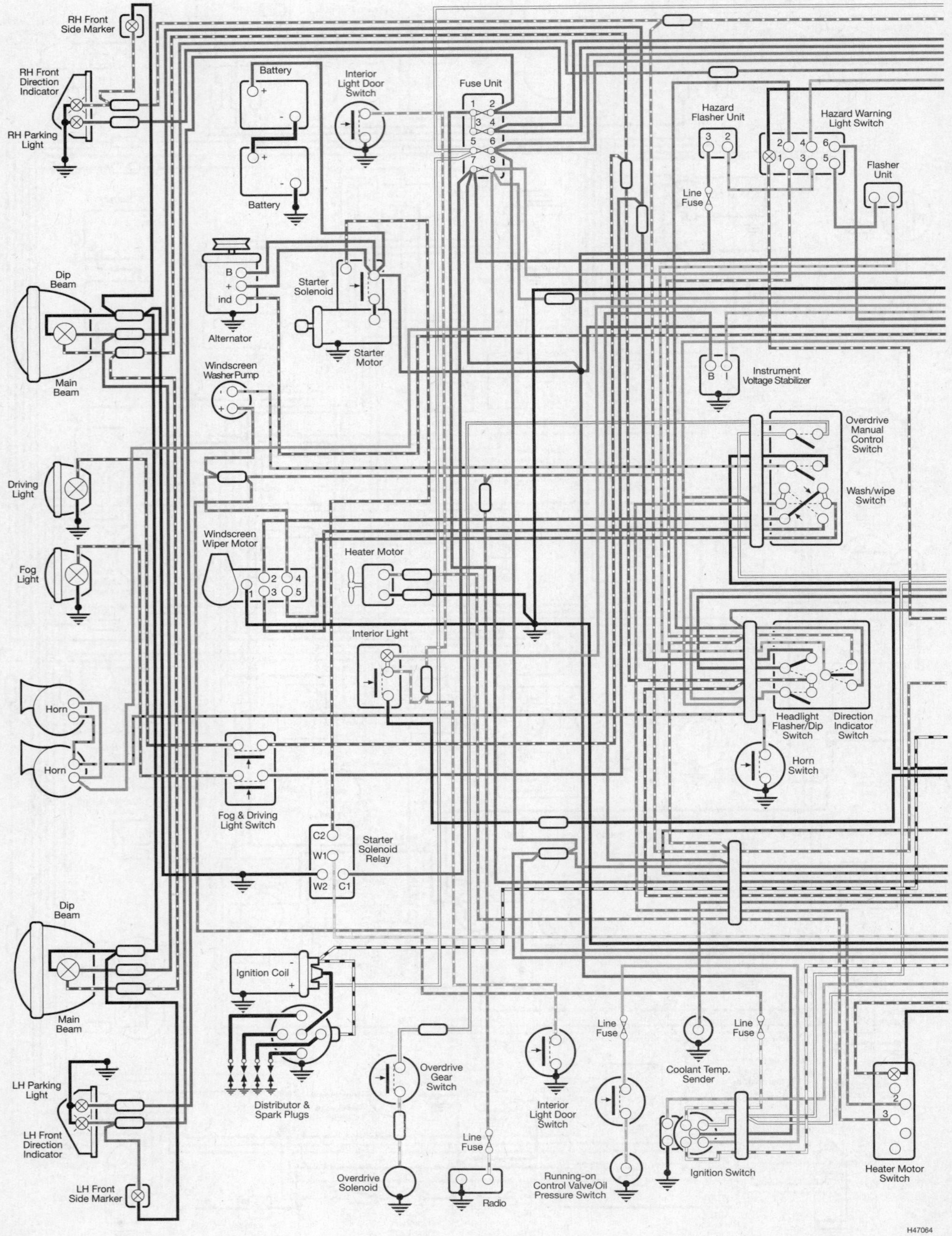
RH Front
Side Marker
RH Front
Direction
Indicator
RH Parking
Light
Battery
Battery
Interior
Light Door
Switch
Fuse Unit
1 2
3 4
5 6
7 8
Hazard
Flasher Unit
Line
Fuse
Hazard Warning
Light Switch
Flasher
Unit
B
+
ind
Alternator
Starter
Solenoid
Starter
Motor
Dip
Beam
Main
Beam
Windscreen
Washer Pump
Instrument
Voltage Stabilizer
Overdrive
Manual
Control
Switch
Wash/wipe
Switch
Driving
Light
Fog
Light
Windscreen
Wiper Motor
Heater Motor
Interior Light
Horn
Horn
Headlight
Flasher/Dip
Switch
Direction
Indicator
Switch
Horn
Switch
Fog & Driving
Light Switch
Starter
Solenoid
Relay
C2
W1
W2
C1
Dip
Beam
Main
Beam
Ignition Coil
LH Parking
Light
LH Front
Direction
Indicator
LH Front
Side Marker
Distributor &
Spark Plugs
Overdrive
Gear
Switch
Overdrive
Solenoid
Line
Fuse
Radio
Interior
Light Door
Switch
Line
Fuse
Running-on
Control Valve/Oil
Pressure Switch
Coolant Temp.
Sender
Line
Fuse
Ignition Switch
Heater Motor
Switch
H47064

North American models from approximately 1973 to 1974

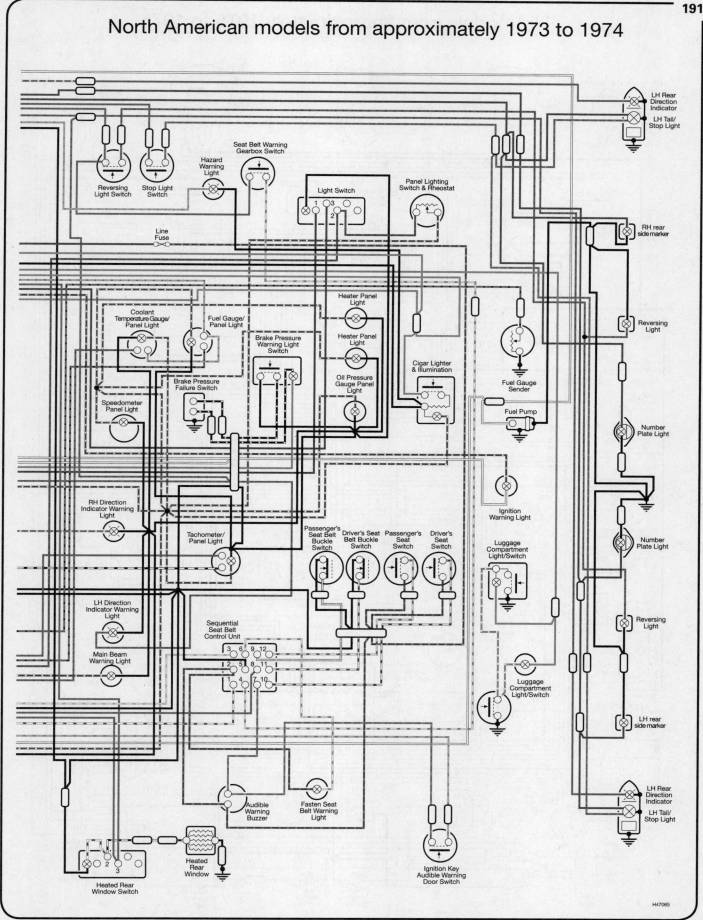

H47065

UK models from approximately 1975 to 1976

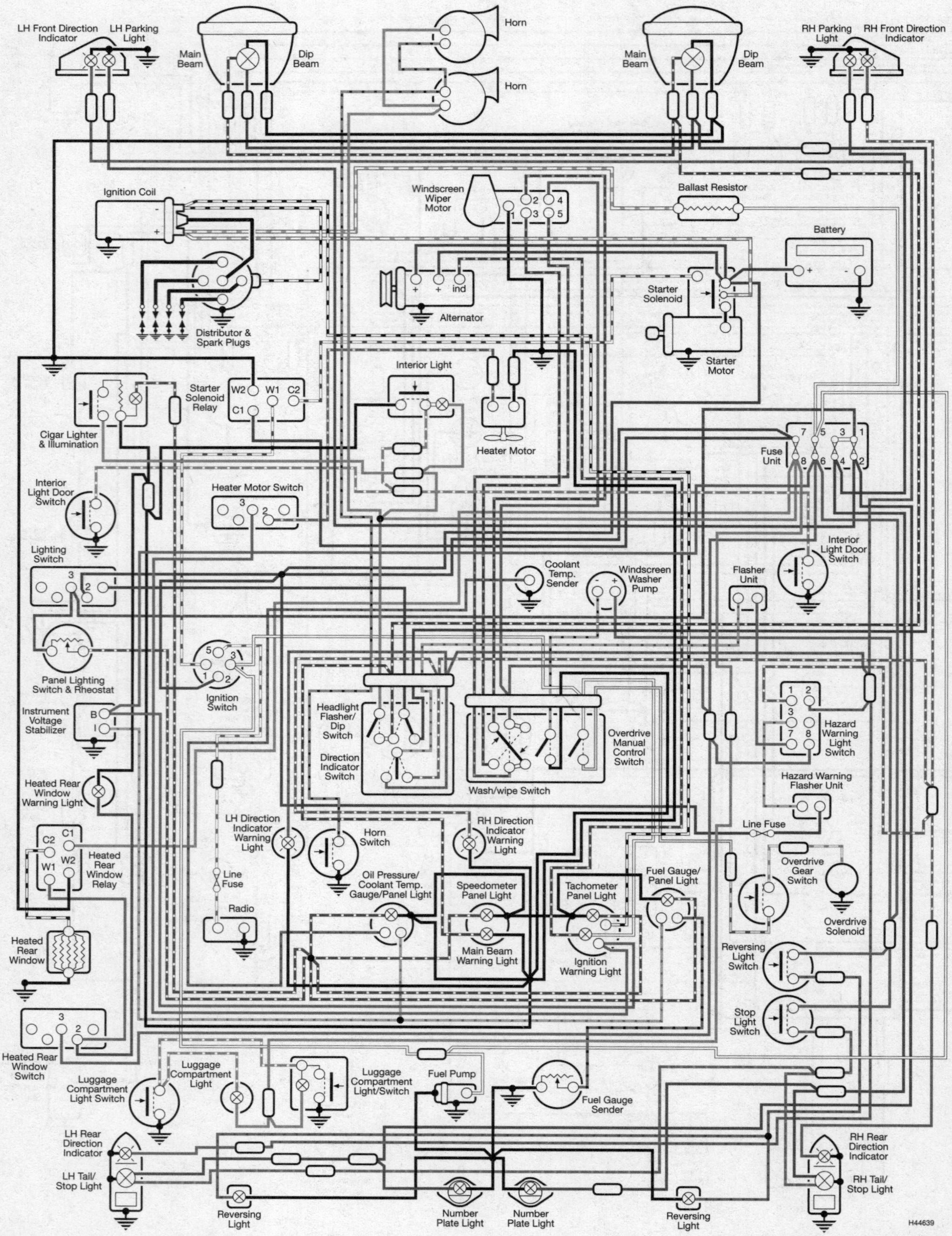

LH Front Direction Indicator

LH Parking Light

Main Beam

Dip Beam

Horn

Horn

Main Beam

Dip Beam

RH Parking Light

RH Front Direction Indicator

Ignition Coil

Windscreen Wiper Motor

Ballast Resistor

Battery

Starter Solenoid

Alternator

Starter Motor

Distributor & Spark Plugs

Interior Light

Heater Motor

Starter Solenoid Relay

W2 W1 C2

C1

Cigar Lighter & Illumination

Interior Light Door Switch

Lighting Switch

Heater Motor Switch

Fuse Unit

7 5 3 1

8 6 4 2

Interior Light Door Switch

Panel Lighting Switch & Rheostat

Coolant Temp. Sender

Windscreen Washer Pump

Flasher Unit

Instrument Voltage Stabilizer

B

I

Ignition Switch

Headlight Flasher/ Dip Switch

Direction Indicator Switch

Wash/wipe Switch

Overdrive Manual Control Switch

1 2

3

7 8

Hazard Warning Light Switch

Hazard Warning Flasher Unit

Heated Rear Window Warning Light

Line Fuse

Heated Rear Window Relay

C2

C1

W1 W2

LH Direction Indicator Warning Light

Line Fuse

Radio

Horn Switch

Oil Pressure/ Coolant Temp. Gauge/Panel Light

RH Direction Indicator Warning Light

Speedometer Panel Light

Main Beam Warning Light

Tachometer Panel Light

Ignition Warning Light

Fuel Gauge/ Panel Light

Overdrive Gear Switch

Overdrive Solenoid

Reversing Light Switch

Stop Light Switch

Heated Rear Window

Heated Rear Window Switch

3

2

Luggage Compartment Light Switch

Luggage Compartment Light

Luggage Compartment Light/Switch

Fuel Pump

Fuel Gauge Sender

LH Rear Direction Indicator

LH Tail/ Stop Light

Reversing Light

Number Plate Light

Number Plate Light

Reversing Light

RH Rear Direction Indicator

RH Tail/ Stop Light

H44639

UK models from approximately 1977

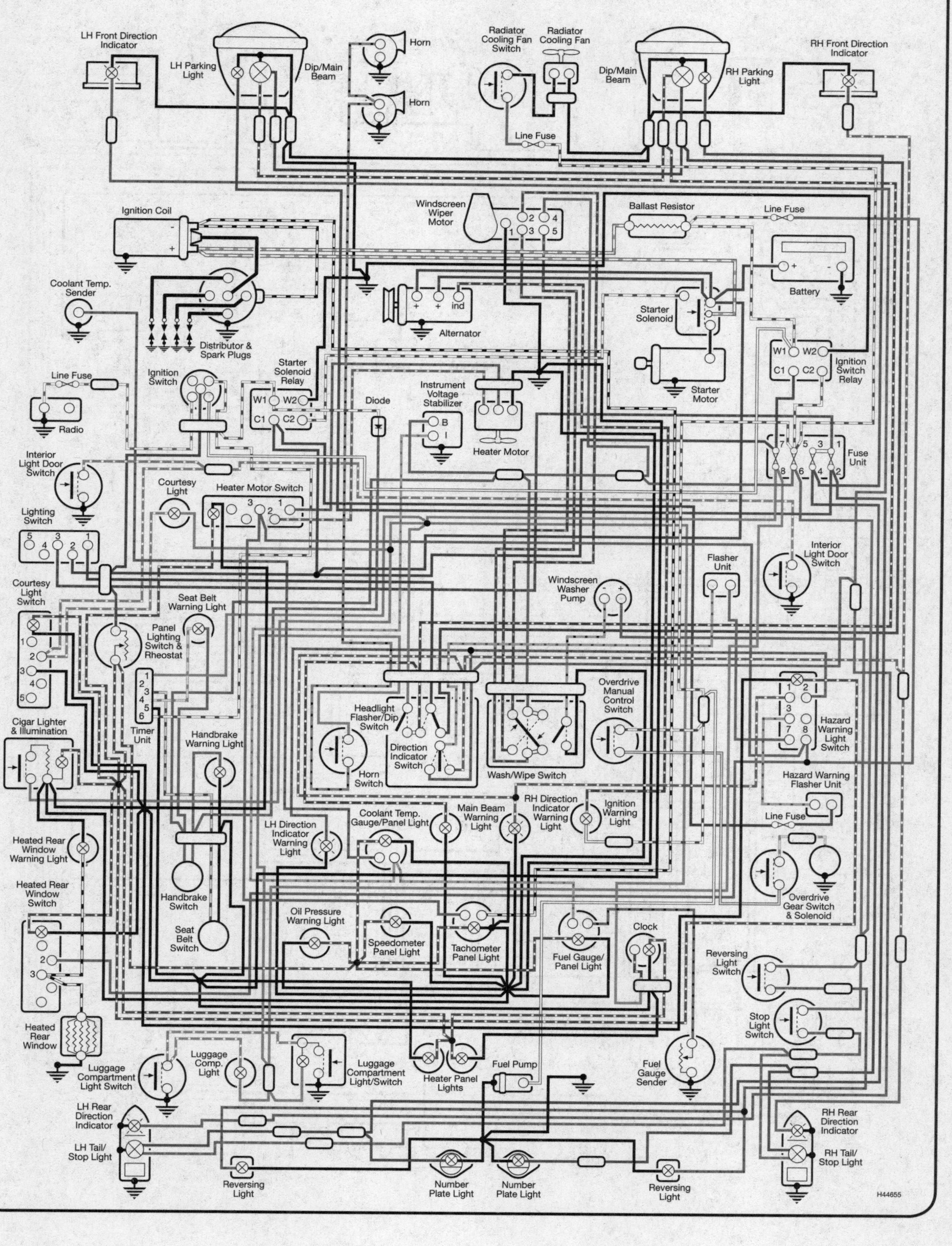

LH Front Direction Indicator
LH Parking Light
Horn
Dip/Main Beam
Horn
Radiator Cooling Fan Switch
Radiator Cooling Fan
Dip/Main Beam
RH Parking Light
RH Front Direction Indicator
Line Fuse

Ignition Coil
Windscreen Wiper Motor
Ballast Resistor
Line Fuse
Battery
Coolant Temp. Sender
Alternator
Starter Solenoid
Starter Motor
Distributor & Spark Plugs
W1 W2
C1 C2
Ignition Switch Relay
Line Fuse
Radio
Ignition Switch
Starter Solenoid Relay
W1 W2
C1 C2
Diode
Instrument Voltage Stabilizer
B
I
Heater Motor
7 5 3 1
8 6 4 2
Fuse Unit
Interior Light Door Switch
Lighting Switch
Courtesy Light
Heater Motor Switch
3 2 1
Flasher Unit
Interior Light Door Switch
Courtesy Light Switch
5 4 3 2 1
Panel Lighting Switch & Rheostat
Seat Belt Warning Light
1 2 3
4 5 6
Timer Unit
Windscreen Washer Pump
1 2
3
7 8
Hazard Warning Light Switch
Cigar Lighter & Illumination
Handbrake Warning Light
Headlight Flasher/Dip Switch
Direction Indicator Switch
Horn Switch
Overdrive Manual Control Switch
Wash/Wipe Switch
Hazard Warning Flasher Unit
Line Fuse
Heated Rear Window Warning Light
Heated Rear Window Switch
2
3
Handbrake Switch
Seat Belt Switch
Oil Pressure Warning Light
LH Direction Indicator Warning Light
Coolant Temp. Gauge/Panel Light
Main Beam Warning Light
RH Direction Indicator Warning Light
Ignition Warning Light
Overdrive Gear Switch & Solenoid
Speedometer Panel Light
Tachometer Panel Light
Fuel Gauge/Panel Light
Clock
Reversing Light Switch
Stop Light Switch
Heated Rear Window
Luggage Compartment Light Switch
Luggage Comp. Light
Luggage Compartment Light/Switch
Heater Panel Lights
Fuel Pump
Fuel Gauge Sender
LH Rear Direction Indicator
LH Tail/Stop Light
RH Rear Direction Indicator
RH Tail/Stop Light
Reversing Light
Number Plate Light
Number Plate Light
Reversing Light

H44655

Later North American models

LH Front Direction Indicator
LH Parking Light
LH Front Side Marker
Dip/Main Beam
Horn
Horn
Radiator Cooling Fan Switch
Radiator Cooling Fan
Radiator Cooling Fan
Dip/Main Beam
RH Parking Light
RH Front Direction Indicator
RH Front Side Marker
Line Fuse

Ignition Coil
Distributor Resistor
Ballast Resistor
Distributor & Spark Plugs
Coolant Temp. Sender
Running-on Control Valve/Oil Pressure Switch
Windscreen Wiper Motor
Alternator
Starter Solenoid
Starter Motor
Battery
Line Fuse

Line Fuse
Radio
Ignition Switch
Starter Solenoid Relay
Diode
Instrument Voltage Stabilizer
Heater Motor
W1 W2
C1 C2
Ignition Switch Relay
Fuse Unit

Interior Light Door Switch
Courtesy Light
Heater Motor Switch
Interior Light Door Switch
Flasher Unit

Lighting Switch

Panel Lighting Switch & Rheostat
Seat Belt Warning Light
Windscreen Washer Pump

Time Delay Buzzer
Diode
Service Interval Counter
Service Indicator Warning Light
Door Switch Buzzer
Inertia Switch
Handbrake Warning Light
Handbrake Switch
Seat Belt Switch
Headlight Flasher/Dip Switch
Direction Indicator Switch
Horn Switch
Wash/Wipe Switch
Hazard Warning Light Switch
Hazard Warning Light
Hazard Warning Flasher Unit
Line Fuse

Overdrive Gear/ TCSA Switch
Transmission Control Spark Advance Micro-switch
LH Direction Indicator Warning Light
Coolant Temp. Gauge/Panel Light
Main Beam Warning Light
RH Direction Indicator Warning Light
Ignition Warning Light
Reversing Light Switch
Induction Heater

Overdrive Manual Control Switch
Cigar Lighter & Illumination
Oil Pressure Warning Light
Speedometer Panel Light
Tachometer Panel Light
Fuel Gauge/ Panel Light
Clock
Stop Light Switch
Brake Pressure Failure Switch

Overdrive Solenoid
Transmission Control Spark Advance Solenoid
LH Rear Direction Indicator
LH Tail/ Stop Light
LH Rear Side Marker
Reversing Light
Luggage Comp. Light
Luggage Compartment Light Switch
Fuel Pump
Heater Panel Lights
Fuel Gauge Sender
Number Plate Light
Number Plate Light
Reversing Light
RH Rear Side Marker
RH Rear Direction Indicator
RH Tail/ Stop Light

H47066

Chapter 11   Suspension and Steering

Contents

Specifications

Front suspension

Type	Independent coil spring and wish bones
Coil spring free height:	
Early models (18G and 18GA)	9.9 in (251.5 mm)
Early models (18GB)	9.1 ± 0.06 in (231 ± 1.5 mm)
Tourer from model No 293446	10.20 ± 0.06 in (259.08 ± 1.5 mm)
GT from model No 296196	9.32 ± 0.06 in (237.0 ± 1.5 mm)
Camber angle	1° positive +¼° – 1¼° (static unloaded condition)
Castor angle	7° positive +¼° – 2° (static unloaded condition)
Kingpin inclination	8° positve +1° – ¾° (static unloaded condition)
Wheelbearing endfloat	0.002 to 0.004 in (0.05 to 0.10 mm)
Lubricant type	Multi-purpose lithium based grease

Rear suspension

Type	Semi-elliptical leaf springs. Anti-roll bar on later models
Number of spring leaves:	
Early models	5 plus bottom plate
Later models	6

Shock absorbers

Type	Hydraulic lever arm
Armcentres:	
Front	8 in (203.2 mm)
Rear	5¼ in (133 mm)
Damping fluid	Armstrong Super (Thin) Shock Absorber Fluid No 624 or any good-quality mineral oil to specification SAE 20W (this alternative is not suitable for low temperature operation)

Steering

Type	Rack and pinion
Turns lock-to-lock:	
Early models	2.93
Later models	3.57
Turning circle	32 ft (9.75 m)
Pinion endfloat	0.002 to 0.005 in (0.05 to 0.12 mm)
Damper endfloat	0.0005 to 0.003 in (0.012 to 0.076 mm) unloaded
Toe-in	1/16 to 3/32 in (1.5 to 2.3 mm)
Rack lubricant type/specification	Hypoid gear oil, viscosity SAE 90EP

Wheels

Type:
Early models .... Ventilated disc, 4-stud fixing, wire wheels optional
Later models .... Pressed spoked, 4-stud fixing, wire wheels optional
Rim size:
Disc wheels .... 4J x 14 or 5J x 14
Pressed spoked .... 5JFH x 14
Wire wheels .... 4½J x 14

Tyres (pay attention to the manufacturer's specifications)

Type:
Early models .... 5.60 x 14 tubed crossply
Later models .... 155 x 114 radial, 165 x 14 SP41 radial, 165 x 145 SP68 radial depending upon the model

Tyre pressures in lbf/in² (kgf/cm²) also consult vehicle handbook*:	Front	Rear
Tubed crossply	18 to 19 (1.3 to 1.34)	18 to 22 (1.3 to 1.55)
Radial	20 to 21 (1.4 to 1.5)	24 (1.7)

*For sustained speeds in excess of 90 mph (145 kph) increase the quoted pressures by 6 (0.42).
Increase pressures by 2 (0.14) if towing with loaded boot.

Torque wrench settings	lbf ft	Nm

Front suspension

	lbf ft	Nm
Shock absorber bolts	43 to 45	58 to 61
Anti-roll bar link nut	60	80
Spring pan nuts and screws	22	30
Bearing retaining nut	40 to 70	54 to 95
Crossmember to body	54 to 56	75 to 81

Steering

	lbf ft	Nm
Steering arm bolts	60 to 65	81 to 88
Steering rack fixings	30	41
Steering wheel nut:		
GHN4/5 and GHD4/5 models:		
9/16 in UNF	27 to 29	37 to 39
11/16 in UNF	41 to 43	56 to 58
GHN4/5 and GHD4/5 models conforming to certain local and territorial requirements:		
9/16 in UNF	27 to 29	37 to 39
All other nuts	36 to 38	49 to 52
All other models	41 to 43	56 to 58
Steering rack and pinion bearing nut	40	54
Steering tie-rod lock nut	33 to 38	45 to 52
Steering lever balljoint nut	34 to 35	46 to 48
Steering column universal joint bolt	20 to 22	27 to 30
Stiff nut to crossmember mounting bolt:		
GHN4/5 and GHD4/5 models	44 to 46	60 to 62
Swivel pin nut*	60	81

Roadwheels

	lbf ft	Nm
Securing nuts	60 to 65	81 to 88

*Further tighten if necessary to align split pin hole

1 General description

The independent front suspension, which can be removed from the car as a complete unit, has suspension units mounted one at each end of the crossmember assembly. Each suspension unit consists basically of a coil spring, a swivel axle unit, a lower wishbone assembly, and an upper assembly formed by the double arms of the shock absorber. The rear suspension is by semi-elliptic leaf springs which are rubber mounted. The spring shackles make use of rubber bushes.

The steering gear consists of a rack-and-pinion unit bolted to the crossmember, and connected to the steering levers by tie-rods.

2 Maintenance

1 At the recommended intervals, the six nipples on the front suspension (four only on early models) should be lubricated with grease, using a grease gun. A regular check on the security of all fixings is advised.

2 No lubrication is provided for on the rear suspension. Check the security of the nuts on the rear spring U-bolts at regular intervals. A regular check on the security and condition of the springs and other items is advised.

3 The lubricating nipple above the steering gearbox (below the car under the radiator on LHD models) should be wiped clean and then given ten strokes with the grease gun filled with the recommended lubricant at the specified intervals. Check the gaiters and their clips for damage and security. Check the security of the steering unit bolts, and all other steering joints and fixings.

4 The front and rear shock absorbers can be topped up by obtaining access as shown (Fig. 11.1 and photo). Clean thoroughly round the filler plug, remove it, and top up to the bottom of the filler plug hole using the recommended fluid. Do not allow the fluid to become too low, or air will enter the shock absorber and efficiency will be impaired. No adjustment is provided to the shock absorbers, and dismantling must not be attempted.

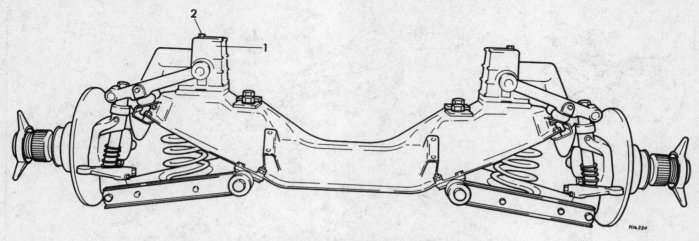

Fig. 11.1 The front suspension assembly (Sec 3)

1   *Hydraulic shock absorber*   2   *Shock absorber filler plug*

2.4 Access grommet for rear hydraulic shock absorbers, adjacent to the battery access apertures

3   Crossmember assembly, front suspension – removal and refitting

1   Loosen the front wheel nuts, jack up the front of the car, place supports under the side members (do not foul the crossmember securing nuts) and take off the wheels. Undo the nut and washer holding each anti-roll bar link to the wishbone. Remove the steering rack as described in Sections 23, 24 or 25.

2   Undo the union nuts and free the brake pipes from the flexible hoses and from the clips on the crossmember. Catch the brake fluid as it leaks away. Place a jack under the centre of the crossmember and raise it to take the weight. Referring to Fig. 11.2, undo the nuts and washers (7) from the tops of the support bolts (2), and lower and remove the crossmember complete with the front suspension from under the car. Remove the support bolts (2), mounting plates (5), and upper and lower rubber mounting pads (3, 4) from the crossmember, if necessary retaining them in position by inserting two 5 1/6 x 8 in (7.9 x 200 mm) long rods through the crossmember (later models only).

3   To refit, reverse the order of removal and bleed the brakes (see Chapter 9).

4   Crossmember assembly, front suspension – dismantling and reassembly

1   Remove the coil springs as described in Section 5, the hubs as described in Section 13, and the swivel axle and swivel pin as

described in Section 14. Remove the shock absorber bolts and thus the shock absorbers. Referring to Fig. 11.2, undo the nuts, bolts and spring washers (34, 35, 36) which hold the wishbone pivots (33) to the crossmember. Remove the wishbone arms. Remove the split pins and unscrew the castellated nuts (39) from each end of the wishbone pivots. Remove the washer (38), and bushes (37). Undo the nuts, bolts and spring washers (45, 43, 44) which hold the rebound buffer (40) to the crossmember.

2   Clean all the parts, and examine as described in Sections 5, 13 and 14. Renew all rubber bushes and seals and certainly those that are oil soaked, split, eccentric, or perished. Examine the holes in the wishbone arms and spring pans for ovality, and the swivel pin distance tubes for wear or scoring. Examine all the thrustwashers for wear or ridging and renew any whose faces are not flat and parallel.

3   To reassemble, reverse the dismantling sequence, but first temporarily assemble the distance tubes, thrustwashers, seal supports and seals in the bottom of the swivel pin. Check the endfloat which should be between 0.008 and 0.013 in (0.20 to 0.32 mm). If the endfloat is insufficient, the ends of the distance tube (25) are worn, and it should be renewed. If the endfloat is too large, and assuming that the faces of the thrustwashers (26) are in good condition, the thrust faces of the swivel pin will be worn and a new pin must be fitted. Ensure that the distance tube is a close sliding fit in the swivel pin bush (47). Renew the tube if corrosion or wear is evident. Ensure that the inner pivot of the lower wishbone arms is fully tightened before the coil spring is fitted.

5   Coil springs – removal, examination and refitting

1   If spring compressor part No 18G 693 is available, fit this on the lower wishbone arms and adjust it to take the weight of the spring. Remove the bolts securing the pan to the wishbone arms and unscrew the compressor to free the tension in the spring. Remove the pan and spring.

2   If the proper spring compressor is not available, employ a sturdy jack, preferably hydraulic. Loosen the wheel nuts, jack up the front of the car, place supports under each front side bodymember and remove the wheels. Where fitted, remove the anti-roll bar as described in Section 6. Place the jack under the front suspension pan (19 in Fig. 11.2) with a piece of wood interposed between the pan and the head of the jack. Raise the jack to partially compress the coil spring. With the weight partially removed from the wishbone arms (20) the four bolts, nuts, and spring washers (21, 22, 23, 24) which hold the spring pan to the arms can be removed and the jack slowly released. Take great care that the jack does not slip. As the jack is lowered, the coil spring and pan will come away.

3   Measure the spring length, and compare this with the Specifications. Renew both springs if noticeably different. To refit, reverse the removal process.

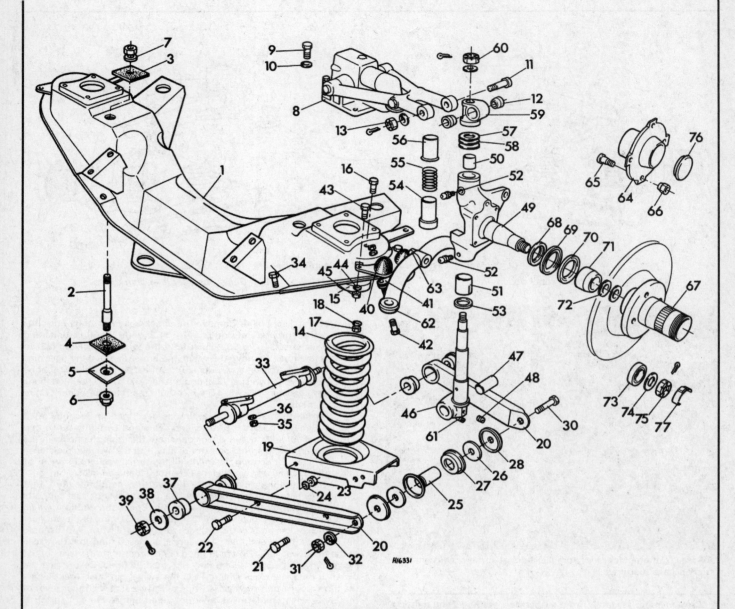

Fig. 11.2 The front suspension – exploded view (Sec 3)

1	Crossmember	20	Wishbone arm	41	Distance piece	61	Lubricator nipple
2	Bolt – crossmember to body	21	Screw – wishbone to pan	42	Bolt	62	Steering lever
3	Upper mounting pad (rubber)	22	Screw – wishbone to pan	43	Screw	63	Bolt for steering lever
4	Lower mounting pad (rubber)	23	Nut	44	Spring washer	64	Hub assembly (disc wheels fitted)
5	Plate	24	Washer	45	Nut	65	Wheel stud
6	Nut	25	Distance tube	46	Swivel pin	66	Wheel nut
7	Plain washer	26	Thrust washer	47	Bush for swivel pin	67	Hub assembly (wire wheels fitted)
8	Hydraulic shock absorber	27	Seal	48	Grub screw	68	Collar for oil seal
9	Bolt	28	Seal support	49	Swivel axle	69	Oil seal
10	Spring washer	30	Pivot bolt – wishbone to swivel pin	50	Swivel axle upper bush	70	Inner hub bearing
11	Fulcrum pin	31	Nut	51	Swivel axle lower bush	71	Bearing spacer
12	Bearing	32	Spring washer	52	Lubricator nipple	72	Shim – 0.003 in (0.076 mm)
13	Nut	33	Wishbone pivot	53	Cork ring	73	Outer hub bearing
14	Coil spring	34	Wishbone pivot retaining bolt	54	Lower dust excluder tube	74	Bearing retaining washer
15	Spigot for spring	35	Nut	55	Dust excluder tube	75	Bearing retaining nut
16	Screw	36	Washer	56	Upper dust excluder tube	76	Grease cup (disc wheel fitment)
17	Nut	37	Wishbone pivot bush	57	Thrust washer	77	Grease retainer (wire wheel fitment)
18	Washer	38	Washer	58	Floating thrust washer – 0.052 to 0.057 in (1.32 to 1.44 mm)		
19	Pan assembly	39	Nut	59	Trunnion		
		40	Rebound buffre	60	Nut for swivel axle		

6   Anti-roll bar (front) – removal and refitting

Sports Tourer and GT

1   On the Sports Tourer, raise and properly support the front of the car. Referring to Fig. 11.3, disconnect each end of the bar from the forked ends of links (4). Remove the screws securing the straps (6) and take away the bar. Examine the condition of the bearing rubbers (5) and the bushes (2), and renew if necessary. Press out the bush (2) if necessary, using a vice and a suitable diameter socket, with a piece of tubing placed to receive the emerging bush. To refit, reverse the removal procedure, positioning locating stops (14) 11 1/16 in (281 mm) from the centre-line of the bar to the inside face of each stop.

2   On the GT vehicle, proceed as in paragraph 1, but disconnect the links at the bottom wishbone and remove the links with the bar.

GHN5 and GHD5 cars from model No 410002

3   The layout is similar to that shown in Fig. 11.3. Raise the vehicle and support it securely, and disconnect the anti-roll bar from the links at the forked ends. Swing the bar down, and remove the bearing straps and bearings. Remove the bar. Check and renew any worn items as described in paragraph 1.

4   To refit, reverse the removal procedure, noting that the faces of the locators should each be 9 5/16 in (237 mm) from the centre of the bar. Note that it is essential for the bar to be fitted with the cranked ends downwards. Tighten all fixings to the specified torque.

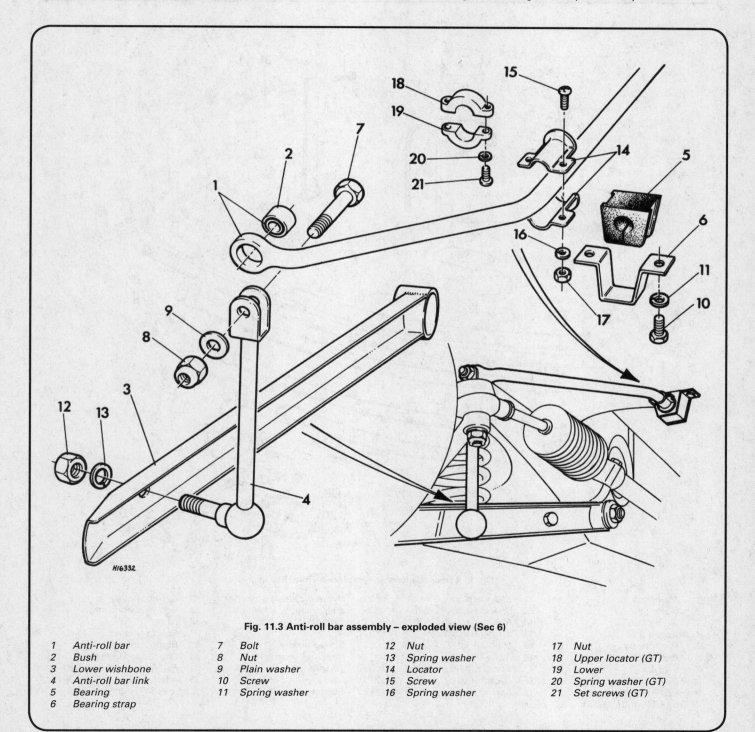

Fig. 11.3 Anti-roll bar assembly – exploded view (Sec 6)

1	Anti-roll bar	7	Bolt	12	Nut
2	Bush	8	Nut	13	Spring washer
3	Lower wishbone	9	Plain washer	14	Locator
4	Anti-roll bar link	10	Screw	15	Screw
5	Bearing	11	Spring washer	16	Spring washer
6	Bearing strap				

17	Nut
18	Upper locator (GT)
19	Lower
20	Spring washer (GT)
21	Set screws (GT)

7   Anti-roll bar (rear) – removal and refitting

1   Disconnect the leads and remove the battery.
2   Jack up the rear of the car and support it with axle stands.
3   Unscrew and remove the pivot bolts from the chassis, and the clamp nuts and bolts from the axle bracket.
4   Withdraw the anti-roll bar. If necessary prise the mounting rubbers from the bar, unbolt the locators and plastic washers, and unscrew the end fittings.
5   Examine the mountings and renew them if necessary.

6   Position the locators as described in Section 6 paragraph 4, and make sure that the end fittings are set parallel to the chassis brackets.
7   Refitting is a reversal of removal.

8   Rear springs – removal, dismantling, inspection and refitting

1   Loosen the wheel nuts, jack up the rear of the car, and place supports under the side members. Remove the jack and the wheels. Reposition the jack to take the weight of the axle casing. Referring to Fig. 11.4, undo the nut and washer holding the shock absorber arm link

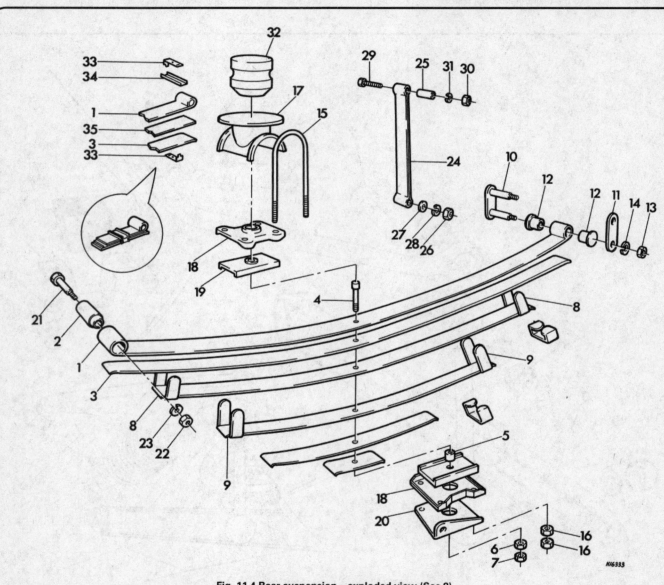

Fig. 11.4 Rear suspension – exploded view (Sec 8)

1	Main leaf	11	Shackle plate	20	Hydraulic shock absorber	28	Spring washer
2	Bush	12	Shackle rubber bush		attachment bracket	29	Bolt – rebound strap
3	Second leaf	13	Nut	21	Eyebolt	30	Nut
4	Centre bolt	14	Spring washer	22	Nut	31	Spring washer
5	Distance piece	15	U-bolt	23	Spring washer	32	Bump rubber
6	Nut	16	Nut	24	Rebound strap	33	Clip for second leaf*
7	Locknut	17	Bump rubber pedestal	25	Tube for rebound strap	34	Pad for second leaf clip*
8	Clip – third leaf	18	Locating pin	26	Nut	35	Interleaf strip 1-2, 2-3, 3-4*
9	Clip – fourth leaf	19	Spring seating pad	27	Plain washer		*Later vehicles only
10	Shackle and pin plate						

to the bracket (20) on the axle and free the rebound strap (24). At the rear of the spring remove the nuts and spring washers (13, 14) which hold the shackle plate (11) to the shackle pin plate (10). Tap each pin in turn, to push it out of the spring and bodyframe. At the front of the spring undo the nut and washer (22, 23) which hold the eyebolt (21) in place, and pull out the bolt. Undo the 8 locknuts and nuts (16) from the U-bolts (15), and lower the spring to the ground.

2   To dismantle the spring, place it in a vice so that all the leaves are clamped, but leaving access to the centre bolt (4). Straighten the ends of the clips (8) and (9). (On later models also release clips (33)). Remove the nuts from the centre bolt, and tap it out. Slowly release the leaves from the vice.

3   With a wire brush clean each leaf and inspect it for cracks. These are especially likely round the centre bolt holes. If the bushes in the front and rear eyes of the spring are to be renewed, press out the old ones, using a suitable drift and tube, in the vice. Press home the new bushes, using a suitable sized socket or tube.

4   To reassemble, paint each leaf with Shell Ensis 260 Fluid or equivalent. Align the leaves, compress them slowly in the vice, and refit the centre bolt and nuts, after having first rivetted new spring clips to leaves three and four. After compressing the leaves bend the spring clips over. Refit the spring assembly to the vehicle in reverse order of removal, ensuring that plates (18) and pads (19) are the correct way round.

9   Front shock absorbers – removal, testing and refitting

1   To remove a shock absorber, loosen the wheel nuts, jack up under the wishbone spring pan, and remove the wheel. Referring to Fig. 11.2, pull out the split pin, remove the castellated nut (13) and the spring washer, and gently tap the fulcrum pin (11) out of the link (59). Pull the hub unit and kingpin assembly away from the shock absorber arms, undo the four bolts and spring washers (9, 10) which hold the shock absorber to the bodyframe crossmember, and lift away the shock absorber unit. Keep the shock absorber upright to prevent air getting into the operating chambers. Ensure that the weight of the hub unit does not hang on the brake hose.

2   To refit, reverse the removal sequence and tighten all fixings to the specified torque.

3   To initially check the shock absorbers, bounce each corner of the vehicle and check for a uniform movement and resistance. If doubts exist, remove the shock absorber, secure it in a vice in the normal operating position, and move the lever arms up and down. Uniform resistance should be felt throughout the full stroke, but if not add fluid whilst working the arms through their full stroke to expel air. If no improvement is effected, the shock absorber must be discarded. If an excessive resistance exists, ie lever not movable by hand, seizure exists and a renewal is required. No dismantling of a shock absorber unit is permissible other than renewal of the lid gasket.

10   Rear shock absorbers – removal, testing and refitting

1   To remove, jack up and support the rear of the vehicle, or alternatively place it over a pit or ramp. Unscrew the nut and spring washer from the bolt which holds the shock absorber link to the bracket on the spring, remove the two nuts and spring washers from the bolts which hold the shock absorber to the bodyframe side member, and remove the shock absorber. Keep the shock absorber upright to prevent air getting into the operating chamber.

2   To refit, reverse the removal procedure, and secure all fixings to the specified torque.

3   To check shock absorber performance, proceed as described in Section 9. paragraph 3.

11   Front wheel alignment

The front wheel should toe-in by the amount given in the Specifications. Adjustment is effected by loosening the locknut on each tie-rod balljoint and the clips on the gaiters, and turning both tie-rods equally. Accurate alignment requires the correct equipment to be employed, and the work should be entrusted to specialists. No attempt should be made to use makeshift methods. Misalignment causes excessive tyre wear and undesirable steering characteristics.

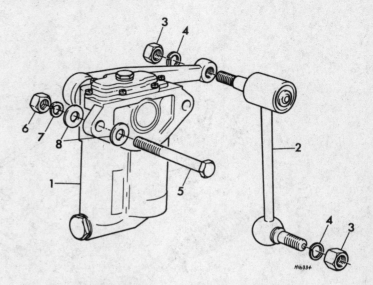

Fig. 11.5 Rear hydraulic shock absorber (Sec 10)

1	Body	5	Retaining bolt
2	Link	6	Nut
3	Nut	7	Spring washer
4	Washer	8	Plain washers

12   Tie-rod outer balljoint – removal and refitting

1   The balljoints cannot be repaired. To renew a joint, slacken the locknut (36) (Fig. 11.6), after marking the nut position on the tie-rod to ensure near accurate toe-in on reassembly. Free the shank of the joint from the steering arm, as described in Section 23, paragraph 2. Hold the tie-rod, and unscrew the balljoint from the rod.

2   To refit, reverse the removal procedure. Use a new self-locking nut on the balljoint. Note that on later models the hole for the balljoint shank in the steering arm is smaller than on early models. The plain washer fitted under the steering balljoint nut on early models should not be fitted on later models, which use a thicker securing nut. When early production cars are fitted with service steering levers, the plain washer must not be refitted. Tighten all nuts to the specified torque.

3   If difficulty is experienced in tightening the balljoint nut due to rotation of the shank, jack up underneath the joint until the shank is prevented from rotating, then tighten the nut.

13   Front hubs – description, removal, dismantling and refitting

1   The design of the front hubs varies in detail, depending upon whether disc wheels or wire wheels are fitted. Their construction can be seen from Fig. 11.2.

2   To remove a hub, slacken the roadwheel nuts, jack up the front of the car, support the underside, and remove the wheel. Remove the brake caliper as described in Chapter 9. Do not allow it to hang on the brake flexible hose. Referring to Fig. 11.2, withdraw the grease retainer (76) or (77), remove the split pin, and then the nut (75). Note that access to the split pin on wire-wheeled models is through the hole in the splines, using pointed-nosed pliers. The hub and brake disc will normally pull off quite easily, but it may be necessary to use a couple of tyre levers or strong screwdrivers in the absence of a proper hub puller. Take out the bearing retainer washer (74), the outer bearing (73), the shims (72), bearing spacer (71), inner bearing (70), oil seal (69) and oil seal collar (68). Do not remove the outer bearing race from the hub unless it is to be renewed. Clean the bearings and races in paraffin and examine them for grooving, flat spots, chips, pitting or other damage. Renew worn components. Tap out the outer bearing race if it is to be renewed.

3   If the races have been removed, refit them in the hub the correct way round. Pack each bearing with a high melting point grease. Fit the

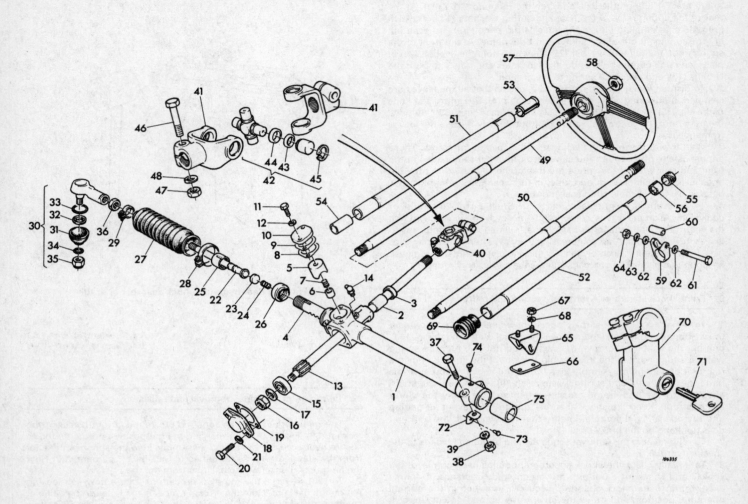

Fig. 11.6 The steering gear – exploded view (Sec 12)

1	Rack housing	21	Spring washer
2	Bush for rack pinion	22	Tie-rod
3	Oil seal	23	Ball seat
4	Rack	24	Spring
5	Yoke	25	Ballhousing
6	Damper pad	26	Ballhousing special
7	Damper spring		locknut
8	Damper plate shim	27	Gaiter
9	Damper plate joint	28	Inner clip
10	Damper cover	29	Outer clip
11	Bolt	30	Outer balljoint assembly
12	Spring washer	31	Boot
13	Pinion	32	Boot retainer
14	Lubricator nipple	33	Boot garter spring
15	Pinion bearing	34	Boot washer
16	Pinion bearing nut	35	Nut
17	Pinion bearing washer	36	Locknut
18	Pinion end cover	37	Rack retaining nut
19	Pinion end cover joint	38	Nut
20	Bolt	39	Spring washer

40	Universal joint	59	Steering column clamp
41	Yoke	60	Distance piece
42	Journal assembly	61	Bolt
43	Journal joint	62	Plain washer
44	Joint retainer	63	Spring washer
45	Circlip	64	Nut
46	Joint clamp bolt	65	Steering column bottom
47	Nut		bracket
48	Spring washer	66	Bracket blanking plate
49	Inner column assembly	67	Nut
50	Inner column assembly,	68	Spring washer
	RHD	69	Draght excluder
51	Column outer tube	70	Steering and ignition lock
52	Column outer tube, RHD	71	Key
53	Column upper bearing	72	Shim
54	Column lower bearing	73	Rivet
55	Felt bush*	74	Bush retaining screw
56	Retaining clip*	75	Rack housing bush
57	Steering wheel		*Used when a steering lock is
58	Steering wheel nut		fitted

collar to the axle. Fit the oil seal to the hub, filling the space between it and the inner bearing (70) with grease.

4   Assemble the hub onto the axle, fit the retaining washer and castellated nut, and tighten the nut until the bearings bind, thus ensuring that the outer races are pulled tightly against their locating flanges inside the hub. Remove the nut, washer, and outer bearing. Insert sufficient shims to give slightly excessive endfloat (shims are available in thicknesses of 0.003 in (0.076 mm), 0.005 in (0.127 mm)

and 0.010 in (0.254 mm) and then refit the bearing, washer and nut and tighten the latter securely.

5   Measure the endfloat with a dial gauge, and reduce the shims to give the correct endfloat reading. Check the measurement again to ensure it is correct and tighten the nut. This latitude is to allow the nut to be tightened sufficiently to line up the split pin hole in the hub with a cut-out in the castellated nut (75). Fit a new split pin and refit the hub cap.

14 Swivel axle and swivel pin (kingpin) assembly – removal, dismantling, reassembling and refitting

1 Loosen the wheel nuts, jack up the car, and remove the road wheel. Remove the hub together with the brake disc as described in Section 3. Disconnect the track rod end (see Section 23). Referring to Fig. 11.2, remove the steering lever bolts (63) from the swivel axle casting (49). Undo the four bolts and spring washers which hold the disc dust cover in place. Remove the coil spring as described in Section 5. Pull out the split pins from the castellated nuts (13, 31) which hold the fulcrum bolts (11, 30) to the top and bottom of the axle, undo the nuts, and carefully knock out the pins. Remove the split pin which holds the castellated nut (60). Undo the nut. Remove the bolt in the centre of the A shaped shock absorber arm. Prise each side of the shock absorber arm sufficiently apart to allow the removal of the axle and swivel pin. The top suspension link (50),steel and bronze thrustwashers (57, 58), axle casting (49), dust excluder tubes (54, 56), spring (55) and cork ring (53) can now be removed from the pin (46).
2 Clean the swivel axle and pin, and examine them carefully for wear. Place the foot of the pin in a vice and fit the axle. The latter should turn easily on the pin without rocking. If play is present, the parts should be entrusted to a main dealer, who will renew and line ream the bushes.
3 Examine the fulcrum pin bush (47), the distance tube (25), and the thrustwashers (26) for ridging and general wear. Renew any parts that are defective.
4 To reassemble, reverse the dismantling sequence. Use new rubber bushes and dust seals and do not forget the cork ring on the bottom of the kingpin. Lubricate the swivel pin bushes with grease before reassembly. After the castellated nut (60) has been tightened down, check for excessive tightness or vertical play between the stub axle and the kingpin. Remedy as necessary by altering the thickness of the thrustwashers (58) under the head of the top suspension link. The maximum permitted end play is 0.002 in (0.05 mm). Thrustwashers are available in the following thicknesses: 0.052 to 0.057 in (1.32 to 1.44 mm), 0.058 to 0.063 in (1.47 to 1 60 mm) and 0.064 to 0.069 in (1.62 to 1.75 mm).
5 Refitting is a reversal of removal.

15 Extra grease nipple – modification to early cars

1 An extra grease nipple is fitted to the swivel axle lower bush on later cars to improve lubrication at this point. Early cars can be modified as follows.
2 Dismantle and remove the axle castings as described in Section 14. With a No 3 drill (0.213 in) drill a hole in the axle at the position marked X in Fig. 11.7. The drilling is in the same place for both swivel axles, the right-hand drilling facing the rear and the left-hand drilling facing forward. Tap a thread ¼ in (6.35 mm) deep, using a ¼ in UNF tap. Ensure that the drilling fraze and swarf is removed from inside the bush. Fit a grease nipple (Part No UHN 400) to both axles. Grease the swivel pins before assembly.

16 Steering column cowl (1978-on) – removal and refitting

1 To remove the cowl. slacken the three screws securing the column to the toe-board, and the three screws securing the bracket on the column to the body, noting the packing washers. Remove the bracket screws, supporting the column whilst doing so. Disconnect the battery.
2 Remove the two screws holding the two halves of the cowl together, unscrew the right-hand screw and remove the cowl, and then the left-hand screw and cowl. Disconnect the lighting switch leads, depress the retaining clips, and extract the switch.
3 To refit, reverse the removal procedure. Note, however, that the toe-board screws should be tightened before the body clamp screws.

17 Steering column universal joint – removal, overhaul and refitting

1 Remove the bolts from each end of the universal joint (Fig. 11.6). Refer to the relevant Section of this Chapter, depending upon the model, and withdraw the steering column far enough to permit the universal joint to be pulled off.
2 Overhauling of the universal joint (on early models) is carried out exactly as for the joints on the propeller shaft, described in Chapter 7. It is not possible to overhaul the joint fitted to later models.
3 To refit, reverse the removal procedure. Ensure that the oval cut-outs in the splines of the inner steering column and the pinion shaft line up with the holes in the universal joints. Otherwise it will not be possible to refit the securing bolts. Carry out alignment procedures as specified in the relevant Section describing refitting of the steering column.

18 Steering wheel and hub – removal and refitting

1 There are variations of type, some wheels having the boss integrally manufactured, whilst others have a separate boss. Detail variations are commented upon in the paragraphs which follow. Whichever type is fitted, first disconnect the battery.
2 Where the wheel and boss are integral, place the roadwheels in the straight-ahead position. Remove the motif cap, either by removing the three grub screws from the side of the boss or alternatively prising out the motif cap. Mark the boss and steering column, to ensure correct refitting. Remove the wheel retaining nut, and pull off the wheel. To refit, reverse the removal process, ensuring where relevant that the tongues engage the slots of the cancelling trip. Tighten the nut to the specified torque. Note that where the wheel proves to be a very tight fit, it may be necessary to obtain the use of a puller.
3 On GHN and GHD5 cars, certain of the comments in paragraph 2 are applicable. However, the steering wheel and hub are separate items. Remove the motif, which is a press fit, and on later types remove the horn contact plunger. Lift the lockring tabs (integral with the lockring on early cars), remove the bolts, lockring and steering wheel. Slacken the hub nut, mark the hub and column, and remove the hub.
4 Refit in reverse order.

19 Steering column and bushes, basic type – removal and refitting

1 Referring to Fig. 11.6, undo the nut and bolt at the upper end of the universal joint (40). Disconnect the battery, and the wiring from the steering column lock (if fitted). Remove the four setscrews from the direction indicator cowling and remove the cowling and indicator mechanism. Undo the clamping bolts, nuts, spring and plain washers from the two brackets (59, 65), and remove the inner and outer columns together. To refit, reverse the removal procedure.
2 If there is any play in the steering column it will be necessary to fit new felt and nylon bushes between the inner and outer columns. These can be refitted after pulling out the inner column by means of the steering wheel. Prise out the felt bush and pull out the nylon bush. Before fitting a new felt bush soak it in graphite oil for 4 hours.
3 When refitting the column, carry out the alignment procedure described in Section 20, paragraph 4, to ensure a free condition at the universal joint.

20 Steering column, energy-absorbing type (GHN4/5 and GHD4/5 vehicles for certain local and territorial requirements) – removal and refitting

1 Disconnect the batteries and remove the carburettor air cleaners. Take out the upper pinch-bolt from the universal joint on the steering column, remove the lower panel from under the left-hand side of the facia, and disconnect the snap connectors in the wiring to the steering column. Remove the three bolts holding the steering column to the toeplates. Remove the bolts securing the column upper flange to the body brackets, noting the positions and quantities of the packing washers.
2 To refit, reverse the removal process. Tightly Tighten the top column securing bolts until the packing washers are just pinched, fit and fully tighten the toe-plate bolts, and tighten the upper fixing bolts, tighten the universal joint pinch bolt to the specified torque.

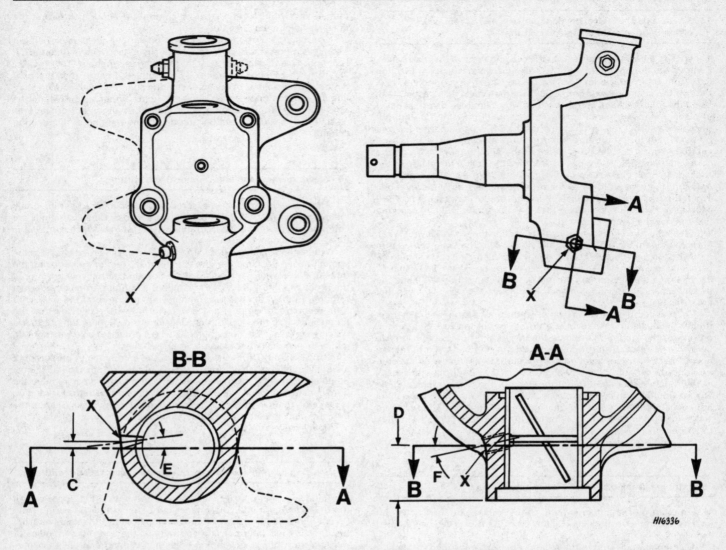

Fig. 11.7 Details of modifications required to early vehicles, to permit an additional lubricator nipple to be fitted to the swivel axle (Sec 15)

Dimension C = 1/16 in (1.6 mm)   Angle E = 6°
Dimension D = ¾ in (19 mm)   Angle F = 12°

3   It is essential that an alignment check is carried out if
 (a) The packing washers from the column upper mounting bracket
     are lost
 (b) If a new rack is fitted, or its shims lost
 (c) If a new column is fitted
4   Alignment is carried out by fitting the column and rack in position
without the universal joint, and then installing the alignment gauge
pointers (BL tool 18G 1140) on the pinion shaft of the rack and lower
end of the column.
5   Fit the toe-plate seal to the column, and put it in position in the
car. Fit one packing washer between each of the two upper column
fixing flanges and the body brackets, and fit the bolts, tightening only
enough just to pinch the packing washers. The column should be free
to slide forwards, backwards and sideways. Fit the three toe-plate bolts,
tightening them by hand only. Check that the bottom of the column is
free to slide about, and set it in the middle of the aperture. Now fit a
pointer to the end of the column. Fit the other pointer to the pinion
shaft; then fit the rack to the car (if necessary), and tighten its fixing
bolts. Slacken the screw on the column pointer until the points of
both gauges are on the same plane but not overlapping. The steering
column and rack assembly are correctly aligned when the gauges meet
exactly at their points (Fig. 11.8). Correct any horizontal misalignment
by moving the end of the steering column.

6   If any vertical misalignment exists between the gauge points,
proceed as follows:
 (a) Remove the rack fixing bolts
 (b) Add sufficient shims (shim thickness 0.020 in (0.508 mm) to
     correct the misalignment between the left-hand and right-hand
     mounting brackets and the crossmember mounting bosses. Do
     not rivet the shims to the bosses at this stage.
 (c) Refit and tighten the rack mounting bolts
 (d) Recheck the alignment of the gauge points
 (e) If the alignment is still unsatisfactory, adjust the shim thickness
 (f) When correct rivet the shims to the mounting bosses
Remove the rack assembly and take off the pointers from the pinion
and steering column.
7   Check that the steering column is in the straight-ahead position,
and fit the universal joint onto its splines with the pinch-bolt hole
aligned with the machined flat. Check that the rack is in the straight-
ahead position, and fit it to the car. Tighten the rack mounting bolts, and
the three toe-plate to steering column bolts. Tighten the two steering
column upper fixing bolts. Measure the gap between the column upper
mounting flange and the body bracket at the third bolt position. Fit
packing washers to the thickness of the gap, then fit and tighten the
bolt. Fit the two universal joint pinch-bolts and tighten them to the
specified torque.

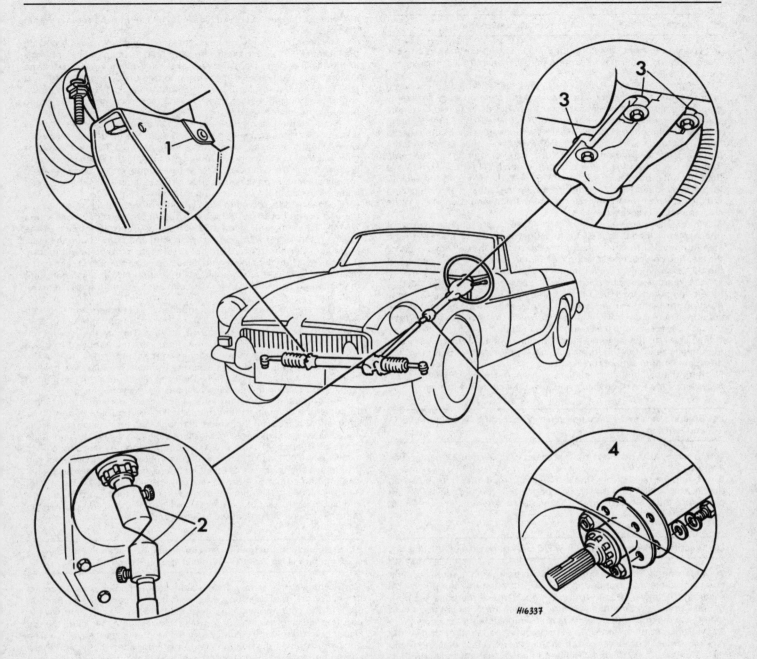

Fig. 11.8 Steering column and rack alignment (Sec 20)

1 Rack shims
2 Alignment gauge pointers (18G 11240)

3 Packing washers at brackets for column top
4 Toe-plate fixings

21 Steering column (GHN5 and GHD5 cars from model No 258001) – removal and refitting

1 With the steering in the straight-ahead position, disconnect the battery and mark the universal joint and inner steering column to ensure correct refitting. Remove the pinch-bolt and nut securing the universal joint to the column, disconnect the multi-connector block and the wiring from the ignition switch. Take out the bolts securing the upper and lower steering column clamps, and remove the column with the sealing tube, direction indicator and steering lock switch.

2 To refit, reverse the removal procedure, whilst ensuring that the steering column and rack remain in the straight-ahead position. Ensure that the alignment marks are correctly matched, and that the sealing tube is fitted to the column with the gaitered end towards the toe-board.

22 Steering column (1978 on) – removal and refitting

1 Remove the steering wheel as described in Section 18. Remove the upper pinch-bolt on the universal joint, disconnect the wiring at the connector, and whilst supporting the column remove the screws and packing washers retaining the column bracket to the body. Note the location and quantity of the packing washers.

2 Note that if a new steering column is to be fitted, the column must be aligned with the pinion as described in Section 20, paragraph 4 onwards.

23 Steering rack-and-pinion unit – removal and refitting

1   Loosen the front wheel securing nuts, jack up the front of the car, place supports under the coil spring pans between the wishbones and remove the frontwheels.

2   Referring to Fig. 11.6, loosen the nuts (35) and break the tapered joint between the balljoint assembly and the steering arm, preferably employing a proper balljoint extractor tool. Alternatively two hammers can be tried, one placed on one side of the tapered hole in the steering arm, whilst the other hammer strikes the opposite side of the tapered hole. This tends to momentarily distort the hole shape, and free the pin. Place the steering on left lock (RHD cars) or right lock (LHD cars). Remove the bolt at the lower end of the universal joint (41). Remove the four nuts, bolts and washers (37, 38, 39) which hold the rack to the crossmember. Note that the front bolts are fitted with self-locking nuts. Check and retain any packing shims between the rack and the cross-member brackets.

3   To refit, it is necessary to proceed in the proper sequence to prevent unacceptable loads, caused by misalignment, being placed on the steering gear. Correct alignment is achieved when the centre-lines of the steering column and steering rack pinion pass through the centre of the UJ spider when viewed from the top and the side.

4   Slacken the steering column bolts. Loosely assemble the steering rack to the bodyframe, and fit and bolt up the universal joint. Correctly position the joint, and tighten the clamp bolts at the bottom of the column. There may now be a gap between the rack bosses and the mounting brackets, and if so remove the securing bolts, fit the necessary shims, and refit the securing bolts. To ensure all is correct loosen and then finally retighten the lower column support bracket bolts. Tighten the upper column support bracket bolts.

5   Refit the balljoints to the steering arms, referring to Section 12 if necessary. Refit the roadwheels and lower the car to the ground.

24 Steering rack-and-pinion unit (energy absorbing type) – removal and refitting

1   To remove the rack assembly, proceed as in Section 23, paragraphs 1 and 2.

2   To refit the rack, reverse the dismantling procedure. Note, however, that if a new rack-and-pinion is being fitted, the proper alignment procedure must be carried out This being as described in Section 20, paragraph 4 onwards.

25 Steering rack-and-pinion unit (1978 on) – removal and refitting

1   Referring to Section 23, proceed as in paragraph 1, and break the taper pin joints as described in paragraph 2. Remove the pinch bolt securing the universal joint to the pinion. Remove the bolts securing the rack to the crossmember, noting that the front bolts are fitted with the nuts at the top. Withdraw the rack assembly forward and down.

2   To refit, set the steering wheel straight-ahead, and centralise the rack movement. Locate the pinion shaft in the universal joint and fit the rack. Tighten the rack fixings. Refit and tighten the universal joint nut, Refit and secure the balljoint nuts and the roadwheels. Have the front wheel alignment checked on proper equipment. Note also that where a new rack assembly is being fitted the proper alignment procedure must be carried out, as described in Section 20, paragraph 4.

26 Steering rack-and-pinion unit – dismantling, inspecting and reassembly

1   Remove the unit from the vehicle (Sections 23, 24 or 25). Referring to Fig. 11.6, place the rack housing between wooden clamps in a vice and mark the positions of the locknuts on the tie-rods (22) so that the toe-in will be approximately correct on reassembly. Slacken the locknuts and screw off the outer balljoints (30), holding the tie-rods with a wrench. Unscrew the clips holding the rubber gaiters (27) to the rack housing and tie-rod and catch the oil. Undo the bolts and spring washers which hold the pinion end cover (18) in place, and remove the cover and gasket (19). Undo the two bolts and spring washers which hold the damper plate in position and remove the shim and joint (8, 9) the yoke (5), spring (7) and the damper pad (6). The pinion shaft complete with bearing (15) and locknut (16) can now be removed from the housing.

2   The tie-rod balljoints are locked to slots in the rack ends by tabs on the locknuts (26), and to the ballhousing (25). Prise up the indentations in the locking rings from the rack and ballhousings, slack back the locking ring, and unscrew the housing to free the tie-rod (22), ball seat (23), and seat tension spring (24). Pull out the rack (4) from the pinion end of the housing. Before removing the rack housing bush (75) undo the retaining bush screw (74).

3   Examine the ball on the tie-rod (22) and the ball seat (23). Renew if worn. Clean the rack-and-pinion and examine the teeth. If they are worn, pitted or chipped, new items should be fitted. Renew the rubber gaiters if they are defective. Examine the bush in the rack and renew it if worn. Check the ball-bearing for excessive movement and renew it if wear is present. Peen the outer edge of the ballrace locknut into its slot in the pinion shaft if a new bearing is fitted.

4   To reassemble, press the bush (75) into place until it is flush against the end of the housing, drill the bush through the screw hole with a 7/64 in (2.7 mm) drill, clean all swarf away. Coat the threads of the retaining screw (74) with jointing compound and screw it into the hole. Make sure that the screw does not break right through into the bore. Push the rack into the pinion end of the housing assembly (1) and fit the pinion splined end first complete with bearing (15) and locknut. Refit the pinion end cover and seal. Use jointing compound to make an oil tight joint,

5   Lubricate the inner balljoint components and fit them, starting with the seat spring (24), ball seat (23), tie-rod (22) and ballhousing (25). Tighten the housing until no play is present. Tighten the locking nut (26). Test the inner balljoints by measuring the pull required to move them. using a spring balance attached to the tie-rod ends. A 2 to 4 lb (0.9 to 1.8 kg) pull should be necessary to move the rods. If a heavier pull is required, slacken off the ballhousing (25). Punch the locking nut (26) into the slots in the rack and ballhousing to secure the joints.

6   Refit the damper plunger (6) and associated parts in the housing. To adjust the damper tighten the cover (10) without the spring (7) or shims (8) in place until the pinion shaft only just turns when the rack is pulled sideways in its housing. Measure the gap between the underside of the damper cover (10), and its seating, using a feeler gauge. Add 0.0005 in to 0.003 in (0.013 mm to 0.076 mm) to the figure obtained and fit shims to the thickness of this total figure under the cover plate (10). Use jointing compound on the cover plate when finally assembling. Refit the gaiters (27), tighten both clips on one of them, turn the unit on end, and pour 1/3 pint of the specified oil in at the open end. Tighten the remaining gaiter clips. Refit the locknuts and track rod ends.

27 Steering lock and ignition/starter switch (GHN5 and GHD5 cars, from model No 258001) – removal and refitting

1   Disconnect the battery. Remove the steering column as described in Section 21, the steering wheel and hub as described in Section 18, and the column switch as described in Chapter 10. Remove the direction indicator switch trip from the inner column, and slide the top clamp bracket from the column. Turn the ignition key to position 1. The bolts which retain the column clamp plate are shear bolts, and these should be removed by drilling the heads until they come off. Unscrew the steering lock locating grub screw, and remove the steering lock and ignition starter switch.

2   To refit, reverse the removal procedure. Use new shear bolts, tightening them until they break off at the waisted point.

28 Steering lock and ignition/starter switch (1978 on) – removal and refitting

1   Disconnect the battery. Slacken the steering column and remove the right-hand cowl as described in Section 16, disconnect the multi-connector to the ignition switch, and remove the tape securing the cable to the column. Drill out the heads of the shear bolts from the clamp plate, and remove the lock assembly and plate. Remove the switch retaining screw, and remove the switch.

2   To refit, centralise the lock over the column slot and fit the clamp plate. Do not shear the new shear bolts yet. Reconnect the multi-connector, check for correct operation of the lock and switch, and then tighten the shear bolts until they break. Refit the cowl and secure the column fully.

29 Steering rack gaiter – removal and refitting

1 To remove a gaiter, remove the balljoint as described in Section 12, paragraph 1. Remove the locknut, noting its location. Remove the small clip, loosen the large clip, and pull off the gaiter, catching the oil which will come out of the rack.

2 To refit, reverse the removal procedure. Lubricate the gaiter contact area before refitting. Inject the correct grade of oil. Check the front wheel alignment

30 Wheels and tyres – maintenance

1 Whenever the roadwheels are removed it is sound advice to clean the inside of each wheel, to remove the accumulation of dirt and, in the case of the front ones, disc pad dust.

2 Wire wheels can be cleaned more easily by applying a grease solvent with a brush and then cleaning off with a high pressure hose or a stiff brush and clean water.

3 Check the general condition of the wheels for signs of rust and repaint if necessary.

4 Check the spokes for looseness, cracks or breakage. Loose spokes can be re-tensioned by tightening the adjustment nuts at the wheel rim with an open ended spanner. Only the loose spokes should be tightened, and the wheel should be checked for truth by a wheel specialist. Do not overtighten the spokes, and if loose spokes are found to be badly rusted, they must be renewed.

5 Examine the wheel stud holes. If they are elongated, or the dished recesses in which the nuts seat have worn, or become overcompressed, then the wheel will have to be renewed.

6 Likewise, badly buckled wheels must be renewed.

7 Clean and check the hub splines of spoke wheels. If showing signs of wear, have them checked and renewed if necessary.

8 Check the general condition of the tyres and pick out any embedded flints from the tread and check that the tread depth complies to the legal requirement. If the tread depth is 1.6 mm or less, the tyre must be renewed.

9 Periodical interchanging of the roadwheels may be worthwhile providing that the wheels are correctly balanced (independent of the car). The spare wheel should be interchanged also.

10 If the wheels have been balanced on the car, then they must not be interchanged, as the balance of the wheel, tyre and hub will be upset. The exact fitting position must be marked before removing a roadwheel so that it can be refitted to its balanced position.

11 Wheels should be balanced halfway through the life of a tyre to compensate for the loss of tread.

12 Ensure that the tyres, including the spare, are kept inflated to their recommended pressures. Tyre pressures are best checked when tyres are cold.

31 Fault diagnosis – steering and suspension

Before diagnosis faults from the table below, be sure that apparent steering or suspension faults are not caused by:
  (a) Impermissible mix of crossply and radial tyres
  (b) Incorrect or uneven tyre pressures
  (c) Brakes binding or pulling to one side
  (d) Bodyframe or rear axle misalignment

Symptom	Reason(s)
Steering vague, car wanders and floats at speed	Shock absorbers defective Wheel alignment incorrect Steering joints badly worn Wear or damage in steering mechanism
Steering stiff and heavy	Kingpins seized or unlubricated Steering rack unlubricated or maladjusted Wheel alignment incorrect Steering column misaligned
Wheel wobble and vibration	Wheel(s) unbalanced Wheel nuts loose Steering damper defective or maladjusted Steering balljoints worn Kingpins worn Shock absorbers defective
Tyre wear excessive or uneven	Wheel(s) unbalanced Wheel alignment incorrect Shock absorbers defective Misalignment due to accident damage

Chapter 12 Bodywork and fittings

Contents

1 General description

The combined body and underframe, of welded steel construction, is available in the Sports and GT versions. The Sports version is an open, two-door two-seater, with an occasional rear seat, whilst the GT has a more roomy closed coupe body, with fastback styling and a large rear door.

2 Maintenance – bodywork and underframe

The general condition of a vehicle's bodywork is the one thing that significantly affects its value. Maintenance is easy but needs to be regular. Neglect, particularly after minor damage, can lead quickly to further deterioration and costly repair bills. It is important also to keep watch on those parts of the vehicle not immediately visible, for instance the underside, inside all the wheel arches and the lower part of the engine compartment.

The basic maintenance routine for the bodywork is washing – preferably with a lot of water, from a hose. This will remove all the loose solids which may have stuck to the vehicle. It is important to flush these off in such a way as to prevent grit from scratching the finish. The wheel arches and underframe need washing in the same way to remove any accumulated mud which will retain moisture and tend to encourage rust. Paradoxically enough, the best time to clean the underframe and wheel arches is in wet weather when the mud is thoroughly wet and soft. In very wet weather the underframe is usually cleaned of large accumulations automatically and this is a good time for inspection.

Periodically, except on vehicles with a wax-based underbody protective coating, it is a good idea to have the whole of the underframe of the vehicle steam cleaned, engine compartment included, so that a thorough inspection can be carried out to see what minor repairs and renovations are necessary. Steam cleaning is available at many garages and is necessary for removal of the accumulation of oily grime which sometimes is allowed to become thick in certain areas. If steam cleaning facilities are not available, there are one or two excellent grease solvents available which can be brush applied. The dirt can then be simply hosed off. Note that these methods should not be used on vehicles with wax-based underbody protective coating or the coating will be removed. Such vehicles should be inspected annually, preferably just prior to winter, when the underbody should be washed down and any damage to the wax coating repaired. Ideally, a completely fresh coat should be applied. It would also be worth considering the use of such wax-based protection for injection into door panels, sills, box sections, etc, as an additional safeguard against rust damage where such protection is not provided by the vehicle manufacturer.

After washing paintwork, wipe off with a chamois leather to give an unspotted clear finish. A coat of clear protective wax polish will give added protection against chemical pollutants in the air. If the paintwork sheen has dulled or oxidised, use a cleaner/polisher combination to restore the brilliance of the shine. This requires a little effort, but such dulling is usually caused because regular washing has been neglected. Care needs to be taken with metallic paintwork, as special non-abrasive cleaner/polisher is required to avoid damage to the finish. Always check that the door and ventilator opening drain holes and pipes are completely clear so that water can be drained out. Bright work should be treated in the same way as paint work. Windscreens and windows can be kept clear of the smeary film which often appears by the use of a proprietary glass cleaner. Never use any form of wax or other body or chromium polish on glass.

3   Maintenance – upholstery and carpets

Mats and carpets should be brushed or vacuum cleaned regularly to keep them free of grit. If they are badly stained remove them from the vehicle for scrubbing or sponging and make quite sure they are dry before refitting. Seats and interior trim panels can be kept clean by wiping with a damp cloth. If they do become stained (which can be more apparent on light coloured upholstery) use a little liquid detergent and a soft nail brush to scour the grime out of the grain of the material. Do not forget to keep the headlining clean in the same way as the upholstery. When using liquid cleaners inside the vehicle do not over-wet the surfaces being cleaned. Excessive damp could get into the seams and padded interior causing stains, offensive odours or even rot. If the inside of the vehicle gets wet accidentally it is worthwhile taking some trouble to dry it out properly, particularly where carpets are involved. *Do not leave oil or electric heaters inside the vehicle for this purpose.*

4   Minor body damage – repair

Repair of minor scratches in bodywork

If the scratch is very superficial, and does not penetrate to the metal of the bodywork, repair is very simple. Lightly rub the area of the scratch with a paintwork renovator, or a very fine cutting paste, to remove loose paint from the scratch and to clear the surrounding bodywork of wax polish. Rinse the area with clean water.

Apply touch-up paint or a paint film to the scratch using a fine paint brush; continue to apply fine layers of paint until the surface of the paint in the scratch is level with the surrounding paintwork. Allow the new paint at least two weeks to harden; then blend it into the surrounding paintwork by rubbing the scratch area with a paintwork renovator or a very fine cutting paste. Finally, apply wax polish.

Where the scratch has penetrated right through to the metal of the bodywork, causing the metal to rust, a different repair technique is required. Remove any loose rust from the bottom of the scratch with a penknife, then apply rust inhibiting paint to prevent the formation of rust in the future. Using a rubber or nylon applicator fill the scratch with bodystopper paste. If required, this paste can be mixed with cellulose thinners, to provide a very thin paste which is ideal for filling narrow scratches. Before the stopper-paste in the scratch hardens, wrap a piece of smooth cotton rag around the top of a finger. Dip the finger in cellulose thinners, and then quickly sweep it across the surface of the stopper-paste in the scratch; this will ensure that the surface of the stopper-paste is slightly hollowed. The scratch can now be painted over as described earlier in this Section.

Repair of dents in bodywork

When deep denting of the vehicle's bodywork has taken place, the first task is to pull the dent out, until the affected bodywork almost attains its original shape. There is little point in trying to restore the original shape completely, as the metal in the damaged area will have stretched on impact and cannot be reshaped fully to its original contour. It is better to bring the level of the dent up to a point which is about 1/8 in (3 mm) below the level of the surrounding bodywork. In cases where the dent is very shallow anyway, it is not worth trying to pull it out at all. If the underside of the dent is accessible, it can be hammered out gently from behind, using a mallet with a wooden or plastic head.

Whilst doing this, hold a suitable block of wood firmly against the outside of the panel to absorb the impact from the hammer blows and thus prevent a large area of the bodywork from being 'belled-out'.

Should the dent be in a section of the bodywork which has a double skin or some other factor making it inaccessible from behind, a different technique is called for. Drill several small holes through the metal inside the area – particularly in the deeper section. Then screw long self-tapping screws into the holes just sufficiently for them to gain a good purchase in the metal. Now the dent can be pulled out by pulling on the protruding heads of the screws with a pair of pliers.

The next stage of the repair is the removal of the paint from the damaged area, and from an inch or so of the surrounding 'sound' bodywork. This is accomplished most easily by using a wire brush or abrasive pad on a power drill, although it can be done just as effectively by hand using sheets of abrasive paper. To complete the preparation for filling, score the surface of the bare metal with a screwdriver or the tang of a file, or alternatively, drill small holes in the affected area. This will provide a really good 'key' for the filler paste.

To complete the repair see the Section on filling and re-spraying.

Repair of rust holes or gashes in bodywork

Remove all paint from the affected area and from an inch or so of the surrounding 'sound' bodywork, using an abrasive pad or a wire brush on a power drill. If these are not available a few sheets of abrasive paper will do the job just as effectively. With the paint removed you will be able to gauge the severity of the corrosion and therefore decide whether to renew the whole panel (if this is possible) or to repair the affected area. New body panels are not as expensive as most people think and it is often quicker and more satisfactory to fit a new panel than to attempt to repair large areas of corrosion.

Remove all fittings from the affected area except those which will act as a guide to the original shape of the damaged bodywork (eg headlamp shells etc) Then, using tin snips or a hacksaw blade, remove all loose metal and any other metal badly affected by corrosion. Hammer the edges of the hole inwards in order to create a slight depression for the filler paste.

Wire brush the affected area to remove the powdery rust from the surface of the remaining metal. Paint the affected area with rust inhibiting paint; if the back of the rusted area is accessible treat this also.

Before filling can take place it will be necessary to block the hole in some way. This can be achieved by the use of aluminium or plastic mesh, or aluminium tape.

Aluminium or plastic mesh or glass fibre matting is probably the best material to use for a large hole. Cut a piece to the approximate size and shape of the hole to be filled, then position it in the hole so that its edges are below the level of the surrounding bodywork. It can be retained in position by several blobs of filler paste around its periphery.

Aluminium tape should be used for small or very narrow holes. Pull a piece off the roll and trim it to the approximate size and shape required, then pull off the backing paper (if used) and stick the tape over the hole; it can be overlapped if the thickness of one piece is insufficient. Burnish down the edges of the tape with the handle of a screwdriver or similar, to ensure that the tape is securely attached to the metal underneath.

Bodywork repairs – filling and re-spraying

Before using this Section, see the Sections on dent, deep scratch, rust holes and gash repairs.

Many types of bodyfiller are available, but generally speaking those proprietary kits which contain a tin of filler paste and a tube of resin hardener are best for this type of repair which can be used directly from the tube. A wide, flexible plastic or nylon applicator will be found invaluable for imparting a smooth and well contoured finish to the surface of the filler.

Mix up a little filler on a clean piece of card or board – measure the hardener carefully (follow the maker's instructions on the pack) otherwise the filler will set too rapidly or too slowly. Alternatively, some products can be used straight from the tube without mixing, but daylight is required to cure it. Using the applicator apply the filler paste to the prepared area; draw the applicator across the surface of the filler to achieve the correct contour and to level the filler surface. As soon as a contour that approximates to the correct one is achieved, stop working the paste – if you carry on too long the paste will become sticky and begin to 'pick up' on the applicator. Continue to add thin layers of filler paste at twenty-minute intervals until the level of the filler is just proud of the surrounding bodywork.

Once the filler has hardened, excess can be removed using a metal plane or file. From then on, progressively finer grades of abrasive paper should be used, starting with a 40 grade production paper and finishing with 400 grade wet-and-dry paper. Always wrap the abrasive paper around a flat rubber, cork, or wooden block – otherwise the surface of the filler will not be completely flat. During the smoothing of the filler surface the wet-and-dry paper should be periodically rinsed in water. This will ensure that a very smooth finish is imparted to the filler at the final stage.

At this stage the 'dent' should be surrounded by a ring of bare metal, which in turn should be encircled by the finely 'feathered' edge of the good paintwork. Rinse the repair area with clean water, until all of the dust produced by the rubbing-down operation has gone.

Spray the whole repair area with a light coat of primer – this will show up any imperfections in the surface of the filler. Repair these imperfections with fresh filler paste or bodystopper, and once more smooth the surface with abrasive paper. If bodystopper is used, it can be mixed with cellulose thinners to form a really thin paste which is ideal for filling small holes. Repeat this spray and repair procedure until you are satisfied that the surface of the filled and the feathered edge of the paintwork are perfect. Clean the repair area with clean water and allow to dry fully.

The repair area is now ready for final spraying. Paint spraying must be carried out in a warm, dry, windless and dust free atmosphere. This condition can be created artificially if you have access to a large indoor working area, but if you are forced to work in the open, you will have to pick your day very carefully. If you are working indoors, dousing the floor in the work area with water will help to settle the dust which would otherwise be in the atmosphere. If the repair area is confined to one body panel, mask off the surrounding panels; this will help to minimise the effects of a slight mis-match in paint colours. Bodywork fittings (eg chrome strips, door handles etc) will also need to be masked off. Use genuine masking tape and several thicknesses of newspaper for the masking operations.

Before commencing to spray, agitate the aerosol can thoroughly, then spray a test area (an old tin, or similar) until the technique is mastered. Cover the repair area with a thick coat of primer; the thickness should be built up using several thin layers of paint rather than one thick one. Using 400 grade wet-and-dry paper, rub down the surface of the primer until it is really smooth. While doing this, the work area should be thoroughly doused with water, and the wet-and-dry paper periodically rinsed in water. Allow to dry before spraying on more paint.

Spray on the top coat, again building up the thickness by using several thin layers of paint. Start spraying at the top of the repair area and then work downwards, with a side-to-side motion, until the whole repair area and about 2 inches of the surrounding original paintwork is covered. Remove all masking material 10 to 15 minutes after spraying on the final coat of paint.

Allow the new paint at least two weeks to harden, then, using a paintwork renovator or a very fine cutting paste, blend the edges of the paint into the existing paintwork. Finally, apply wax polish.

5 Major body damage – repair

Where serious damage or considerable corrosion has occurred, the welding of the new panels which will be required is best left to specialists. In the case of impact damage, the bodyshell alignment should be checked on the jigs made for this purpose and normally held by a main dealer. A misaligned vehicle is dangerous; not only will the handling be poor, but severe stresses may also be placed upon certain parts of the vehicle which can cause abnormal wear or complete failure. Tyre wear may also be excessive.

6 Bonnet and bonnet lock – removal and refitting

1   Open the bonnet support it on the stay, then place a piece of rag under each bottom corner to prevent damage to the paintwork. Loosen and remove the two nuts and washers on each side which hold the bonnet to the hinge. Remove the bolts and lift the bonnet off.
2   When refitting the bonnet, use the outlines in the paint on the hinges as alignment marks to ensure that the bonnet will fit squarely. Close the bonnet to check the alignment, before finally tightening the nuts.
3   To remove the bonnet lock assembly, raise the bonnet, loosen the locknut on the bonnet pin, and remove the pin, thimble and spring.

Remove the three bolts which hold the safety catch in place on the bonnet, and lift off the catch.
4   Undo the two bolts which hold the safety catch bracket to the bonnet lock platform and remove the bracket. Undo the bonnet lock control cable clamp screw and withdraw the cable from the bonnet lockplate. Remove the locating cup and bonnet lockfrom the platform by undoing the three retaining bolts (photo).
5   Refit all bonnet lock parts in the reverse order to removal. Note, however, that the safety catch, bonnet lock and bonnet should all be correctly aligned before the bolts are finally tightened. It may be necessary to adjust the latch pin to obtain smooth closure of the bonnet

7 Front grille (except GHN5 and GHD5 models) – removal refitting

1   Remove the three screws in the grille top steady brackets (photo). At the bottom, remove the three grille-to-radiator duct panel bolts, and withdraw the grille. Remove the steady brackets, motif and rubber buffers, if necessary.
2   To refit, reverse the removal procedures.

8 Front grille (GHN5 and GHD5 models, up to vehicle No 294250) – removal and refitting

1   Remove the three screws to the bonnet lock platform, and the two self-tapping screws retaining the outer surround. Ease the three rubber plugs out, and unscrew the screws revealed.
2   To refit, reverse the removal procedure.

9 Front grille and grille panels (GHN5 and GHD5 models, from vehicle No 294251) – removal and refitting

1   Remove the three screws securing the grille brackets to the bonnet lock platform, and the three screws holding the bottom of the grille to the radiator duct panel. Remove the grille.
2   To remove the panels, remove the twelve screws and clips, thereby releasing the right and left-hand panels.
3   To reassemble, place the grille panels into position, ensuring that the grille panel thin slats are V-shaped when viewed from the front, and secure with the clips and screws. Refit the remaining parts in the reverse order.

10 Front bumper unit (early models) – removal and refitting

1   Undo the two screws which hold the steady bracket to the bumper and the nuts and bolts holding the bumper spring blade to the body. Pull the front bumper forward and remove it (see Fig. 12.1).
2   To remove the overriders (where fitted), remove the nuts, washers and distance pieces which secure them to the bar.
3   To refit, reverse the removal procedure.

6.4 The bonnet locating cup and lock

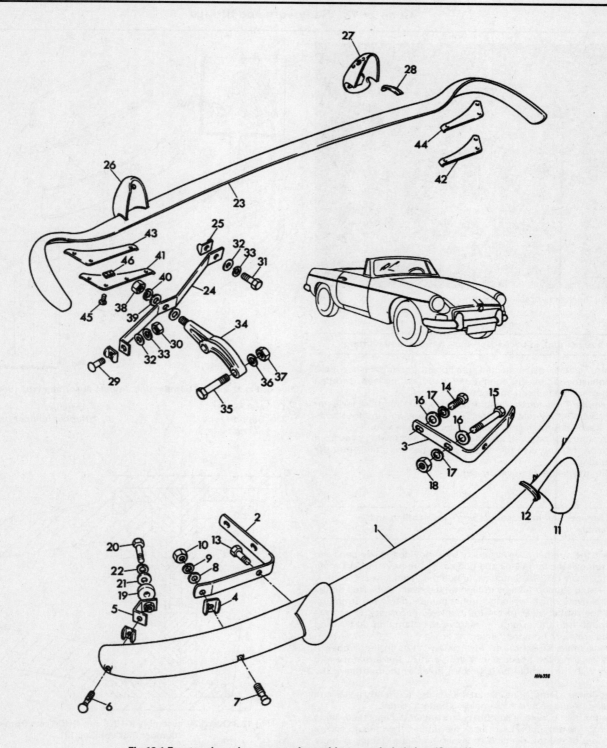

Fig 12.1 Front and rear bumpers and overriders – exploded view (Sec 10)

1	Front bumper assembly	13	Bolt	24	Spring bar	35	Bolt
2	RH spring bar	14	Screw	25	Distance washer	36	Spring washer
3	LH spring bar	15	Bolt	26	RH overrider	37	Nut
4	Distance washer	16	Plain washer	27	LH overrider	38	Nut
5	Steady bracket	17	Spring washer	28	Moulding	39	Plain washer
6	Bolt	18	Nut	29	Bolt	40	Spring washer
7	Bolt	19	Rubber pad	30	Nut	41	RH filler
8	Plain washer	20	Screw	31	Bolt	42	LH filler
9	Spring washer	21	Plain washer	32	Plain washer	43	RH filler
10	Nut	22	Spring washer	33	Spring washer	44	LH filler
11	Front overrider	23	Rear bumper bar	34	Bumper mounting	45	Screw
12	Moulding		assembly		bracket	46	Spring nut

7.1 Remove the steady bracket screws

11 Front bumper unit, impact-absorbing – removal and refitting

1   With the battery disconnected, unclip the parking/flasher lamp wiring connectors under the bonnet and withdraw the leads through the rubber grommet to hang under the front wings.

2   Remove the four nuts and eight washers from the bumper inner mountings where they join the chassis members, and the four bolts and eight washers from the bumper to outer spring location.

3   Remove the bumper unit, together with the two towing eyes from the outer springs, and also the spacer plates (where fitted) from the inner mountings.

4   To refit, reverse the removal procedure.

12 Front bumper unit impact-absorbing – dismantling and reassembly

1   Remove the number plate assembly by removing the two bolts and washers, remove the lamp lens and bodies, and remove the MG motif (see Fig. 12.2). On 1978/1979 models, unbolt the towing eyes.

2   Remove the support tube by drilling off the rivet heads. Drill off the heads of the rivets which retain the rubber bumper bar to the armature, and lever the rubber clear of the top rivets as necessary. Punch the rivets through into the armature, remove the clamping plates, and remove the armature from the rubber.

3   To reassemble, check the fit of the new rivets in the rubber, if necessary clearing the holes with a drill, and fit the armature into the rubber with the number plate bracket holes to the bottom of the assembly.

4   Fit the lower clamp plate, insert the centre and end rivets, and secure them. Fit and secure the remaining bottom rivets.

5   Fit the top clamp plate, insert the centre and end rivets, then clamp the rubber to the armature. Lever back the rubber, then fit and secure the remainder of the top rivets. If necessary, refit the clamps close to the area being levered.

6   Rivet the support tube in place. Refit the remaining items in reverse order, ensuring that the drainage holes in the lenses are downwards.

13 Front bumper and overriders (GHN5 and GHD5 models, from vehicle No 339095) – removal and refitting

1   Remove the bolts at each end of the bumper, noting the rubber pad. Remove the nuts and bolts which secure the bumper springs to the body sections. Remove the bumper assembly.

2   Remove the dome-headed bolts and nuts, noting the small distance pieces (outer bolts) and medium distance pieces (inner bolts). Remove the two overrider securing bolts, and remove the overrider assemblies,

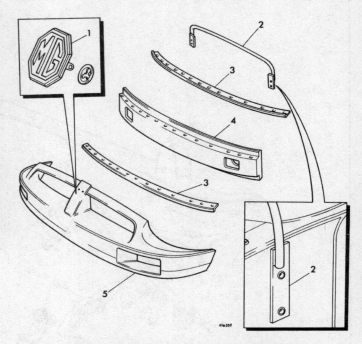

Fig 12.2 Front bumper unit, impact-absorbing type (Sec 12)

1	MG motif	4	Armature
2	Support tube	5	Rubber bumper bar
3	Clamp plate		

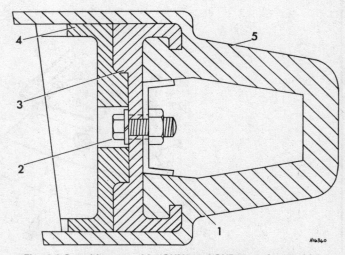

Fig 12.3 Overrider assembly (GHN5 and GHD5 cars from vehicle number 339095) (Sec 13)

1	Clamping bracket	4	Support casting
2	Clamping bracket bolt	5	Overrider
3	Mounting bracket		

noting the two large distance pieces. Remove the nut and bolt securing the lashing bracket to the distance spring.

3   To dismantle the overrider assembly, mark the overrider clamp bracket and mounting bracket at the top, to facilitate reassembly. Remove the clamping bracket securing screws and remove the bracket. Slide the mounting bracket from the overrider.

4   To refit, reverse the removal sequence. Ensure that parts are refitted in the correct places, as some are handed.

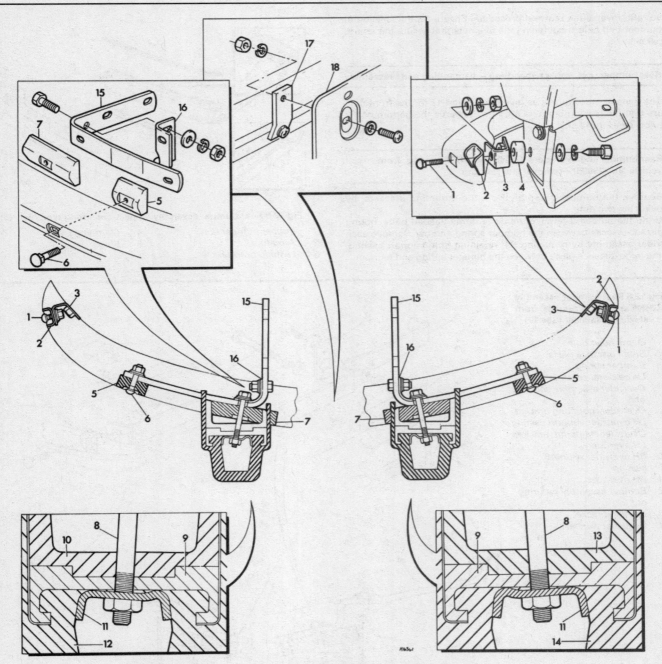

Fig 12.4 Front bumper assembly (GHN5 and GHD5 models, from car No 339095) (Sec 13)

1	Small dome head bolt	7	Large distance piece	13	LH overrider support casing
2	Small distance piece	8	Overrider assembly securing bolt	14	LH overrider
3	Steady bracket	9	Overrider mounting bracket	15	Bumper spring
4	Rubber pad	10	RH overrider support casting	16	Lashing bracket
5	Medium distance piece	11	Overrider clamping bracket	17	Number plate support bracket
6	Long dome head bolt	12	RH overrider	18	Number plate

14 Rear bumper unit (early models) – removal and refitting

1 Disconnect the leads to the two number plate lamps, remove the nuts and washers which hold the bumper bar spring to the mounting brackets, and pull the bumper bar away (see Fig. 12.1). To remove the bar from the mounting bracket, undo the nuts and washers which hold them together.

2 To refit, reverse the removal procedure. Check that the bumper is straight and that the number plate lights are working.

15 Rear bumper unit, impact-absorbing – removal and refitting

1 Remove the nuts, washers and spacers at each rear wing location. Bend back the rubber at each wing and disconnect the side fixing bracket and spacer at each side.

2 From inside the boot, remove the three nuts and six washers securing the bumper unit to the rear panel. Under the rear panel, support the bumper and remove the two nuts and four washers that secure the bumper to the body. Remove the bumper.

3 To refit, reverse the removal procedure. Ensure central location of the bumper unit before tightening the five nuts that secure the unit to the panel.

16 Rear bumper unit, impact-absorbing – dismantling and reassembly

The general procedure is as given in Section 12 for the front unit. Ensure that the lashing brackets are fitted towards the bottom of the assembly (see Fig. 12.5).

17 Rear bumper and overriders (GHN5 and GHD5 models, from vehicle No 339095) – removal and refitting

1 Remove the bumper assembly from the mounting brackets, by removing the two nuts.
2 Undo the nuts and remove the three dome-headed bolts, noting the distance pieces between the bumper spring and bar. Remove each overrider assembly by removing the retaining bolt, support casting, and the large distance piece between the bumper spring and bar.

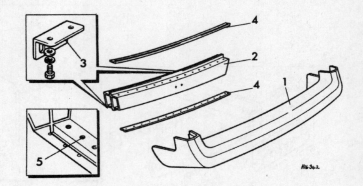

Fig 12.5 Rear bumper assembly, impact-absorbing type (Sec 16)

1	Rubber bumper bar	4	Clamping plates
2	Armature	5	Rivets
3	Lashing bracket		

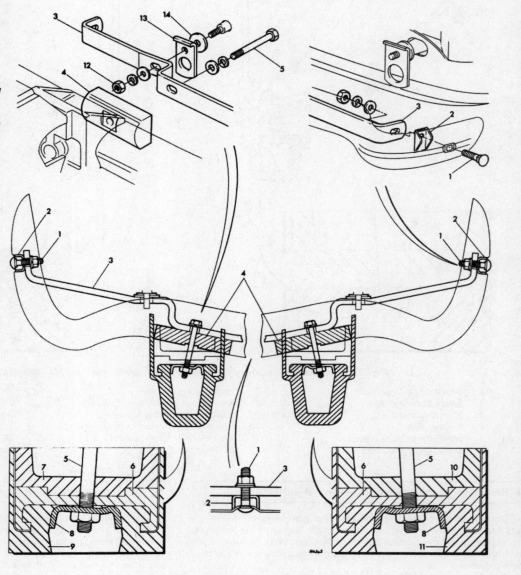

Fig 12.6 Rear bumper assembly (GHN5 and GHD5 models, from vehicle No 339095) (Sec 17)

1 Dome head bolt
2 Small distance piece
3 Bumper spring
4 Large distance piece
5 Overrider assembly securing bolt
6 Overrider mounting bracket
7 LH overrider support casting
8 Overrider clamping bracket
9 LH overrider
10 RH overrider support casting
11 RH overrider
12 Bumper assembly securing nut
13 Lashing bracket
14 Large flat washer

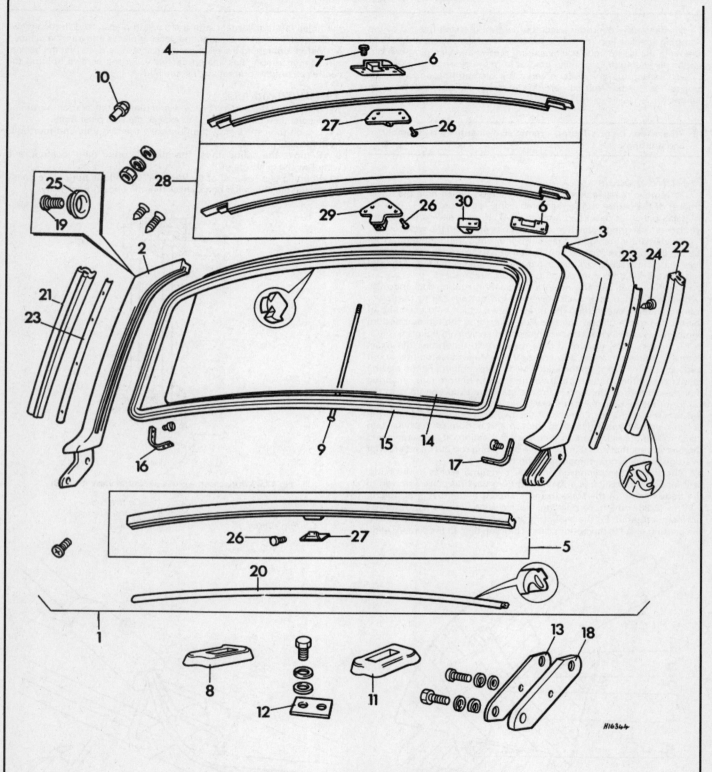

Fig 12.7 Windscreen and surrounds – exploded view (Sec 18)

1	Windscreen assembly	9	Centre rod	17	Bottom LH reinforcement	24	Rivet retainer
2	RH pillar	10	Nut	18	Outer packing plate	25	Dot fastener
3	LH pillar	11	LH grommet	19	Rivet	26	Rivet
4	Top rail assembly, type 1	12	Centre bracket	20	Seal	27	Upper bracket
5	Bottom rail assembly	13	Inner packing plate	21	RH seal	28	Top rail assembly, type 2
6	Hood fastener bracket	14	Windscreen	22	LH seal	29	Upper bracket
7	Rivet	15	Glazing rubber	23	Pillar seal retainer	30	Bracket
8	RH grommet	16	Bottom RH reinforcement				

3 Dismantle the overrider assembly by first marking the top of the clamping bracket and mounting bracket (to assist reassembly), then removing the clamping bracket securing screws and clamping bracket, and finally sliding the mounting bracket from the overrider.

4 To reassemble and refit, reverse the dismantling and removal procedures. Ensure that all parts are correctly refitted, as some are handed.

18 Windscreen (Sports Tourer) – removal, dismantling, reassembly and refitting

Pre-1978 models

1 To remove the screen, undo the two screws which hold the lower bracket of the centre windscreen stabilising rod to the body. Take off the facia panel, as described in Section 47, to gain access to the four windscreen securing bolts. Remove the bolts and then the windscreen.

2 To dismantle the windscreen surround, undo the domed nut from the top of the centre rod and pull the rod down through the top bracket. Take the plain washer, spring washer and flat nut off the top of the rod and pull the rod down and out of the bottom bracket.

3 Carefully, pull out the bottom rail sealing rubber and undo the two screws which hold each corner of the bottom rail to the lower reinforcement pieces. Undo the three screws which hold each end of the top rail to the pillars. The two side pillars and the top and bottom windscreen rails can now be carefully eased away from the glass.

4 To reassemble, employ a tape measure to determine the exact centre of the windscreen, top and bottom. Mark these points, about one inch (25 mm) in from the edges, with a wax crayon. Fit the glazing rubber round the windscreen, then the top and bottom rails, ensuring that the centres of the bracket for the stabilising rod line up with the centre of the screen. Temporarily fit the centre stabilising rod to hold the two rails together. Fit each of the two side pillars starting at the bottom, and alternately tapping the top and bottom of the pillar into place. When the pillars are in their correct location, fit the screws and the bottom weather seal. Firmly fix the stabilising rod but on no account overtighten the centre domed securing nut.

5 The foot of each windscreen pillar rests in a recess in the body, at the bottom of which is a metal and fibre packing piece screwed to the body. The fit of the screen can be altered by removing or adding 0.09 in (2.38 mm) fibre packing pieces. However, no alteration is normally required. Fit the sealing grommet to the windscreen pillars, the packing piece to the bottom centre bracket, then fit the screen. Align the holes in the pillar feet with the packing pieces, and fit the screws (with special washers) through the packing pieces and into the pillars.

6 Before tightening the pillar securing screws, ensure that the bottom rail sealing rubber has seated correctly. Fit the screws holding the centre rod bottom bracket against the body.

1978/1979 models

7 Disconnect the battery, unscrew and remove the interior mirror and sun visors, then move the facia to expose the side pillar bolts.

8 Unbolt the centre stay, then unscrew the two nuts and four bolts from the side pillars.

9 Remove the shims under the pillars, noting their location, and withdraw the windscreen.

10 Refitting is a reversal of the removal procedure, but before finally tightening the side pillar bolts, check that the hood fits correctly.

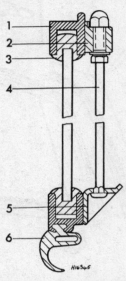

Fig 12.8 Windscreen – cross-sectional view (Sec 18)

1	Top rail	4	Centre rod
2	Centre rod upper bracket	5	Bottom bracket
3	Glazing rubber	6	Seal

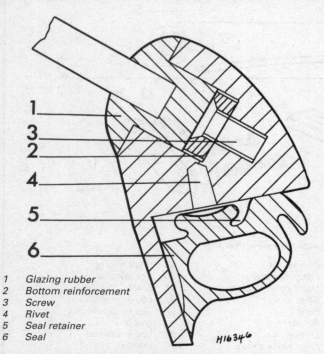

1 Glazing rubber
2 Bottom reinforcement
3 Screw
4 Rivet
5 Seal retainer
6 Seal

Fig 12.9 Windscreen side pillar – cross-sectional view (Sec 18)

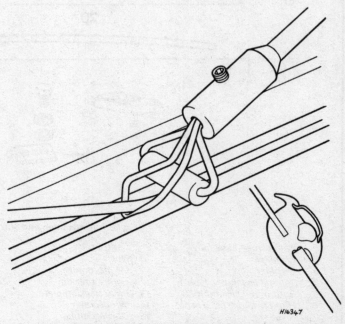

Fig 12.10 Special tool in use, feeding the locking filler strip into the rubber surround (Sec 18)

19 Windscreen and tailgate window (GT models) – removal and refitting

1   The windscreen and the tailgate window are removed in virtually the same way, the only differences being that for the front screen, the screen wiper arms should be removed, and a blanket placed on the bonnet.

2   Carefully, pull out the finisher strip. Locate the two ends of the locking filler strip near the centre of the glass, prise out one end and, carefully, pull it from the rubber surround.

3   From inside the car, press out a corner of the glass together with the rubber surround; pull the surround rubber from the metal edge of the body aperture. Lift away the screen.

4   If the front glass was broken, it is essential that the demister ducts and tubing are separated from the heater box and all glass particles carefully cleaned out. Failure to do this may result in particles being discharged into the face of the driver when the blower motor is switched on. Clear any glass from the channel in the surround rubber. Renew the surround if it has become cut, or if it has otherwise deteriorated, to prevent water leaks.

5   Position the sealing rubber over the metal edge of the body aperture. Lubricate the rubber channel into which the glass fits with soap and water and fit the glass to the bottom portion of the channelling. Employing a small, blunt screwdriver with the end bent over at 180°, insert this under the lip of the rubber channel starting at one of the bottom corners. Lift the lip of the rubber over the glass, working gradually all round.

6   Generously lubricate the strip of rubber locking filler with soap and water and force it into the outside channel of the surround rubber, ensuring that the thicker section of the strip is fitted towards the glass. After fitting, cut off the ends of the strip, leaving an overlap of 0.25 in (6.35 mm) so that the ends of the rubber butt against each other under pressure.

20 Electrically heated rear window (GT models) – removal and refitting

1   Remove the rear upper quarter trim panels, one on either side of the car. and separate the snap connectors in the wires which carry the current to the rear window. Remove the window as described in Section 19, and draw the wires for the heating element through the holes in the body and rubber surround.

2   To refit, reverse the removal sequence. Refit the heater wires through the surround and body before fitting the window.

21 Quarter-light (early Sports Tourer models) – removal and refitting

Remove the door trim pad, as described in Section 29. Remove the lower end of the door glass front channel from the bracket on the door. Remove the screws adjacent to the sleeve nuts. Remove the sleeve nuts. Wind the window down as far as possible, and remove the quarter-light from the top of the door. To refit, reverse the removal procedure.

22 Quarter-light (later models) – removal and refitting

Remove the door trim pad as described in Section 30. Remove the door glass assembly as described in Section 40. Remove the screws and nuts retaining the quarter-light top to the door, the quarter-light steady screws, and the screws holding the door glass front channel to the door bottom. Lift away the quarter-light assembly. To refit, reverse the removal procedure.

23 Quarter-light (1978/1979 models) – removal and refitting

1   Remove the door trim pad as described in Section 31. Remove the door glass and regulator as described in Section 41. Ease the two plastic caps out, and remove the washers and bolts securing the quarter-light to the door front edge.

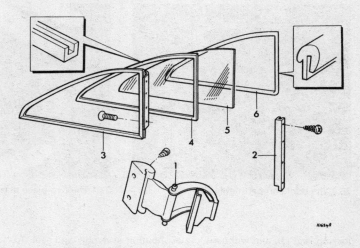

Fig 12.11 The quarter-light fitted to GT models (Sec 24)

1	Toggle catch	4	Glazing rubber
2	Hinge	5	Glass
3	Frame	6	Sealing rubber

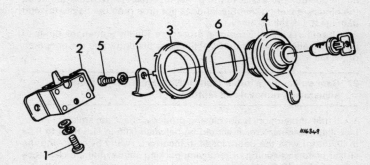

Fig 12.12 Boot compartment or tailgate lock – exploded view (Sec 25)

1	Locking securing screws	5	Lock barrel retaining
2	Lock		screw
3	Pushbutton retaining ring	6	Pushbutton assembly seal
4	Pushbutton assembly	7	Operating lever

2   Remove the two washers, nuts and locating plates which retain the quarter-light assembly to the door top edge, and the bolt which secures the bottom of the door glass front channel. Tilt the quarter-light assembly, removing the bottom bracket from the channel, and lift out the assembly.

3   Refitting is a reversal of the removal procedure.

24 Rear quarter-light (GT models) – removal and refitting

To remove this, take out the screws retaining the window catch to the body. Ease away the door seal at the door pillar, in front of the quarter-light, and remove the screws retaining the finishing strip. Remove the screws retaining the hinges to the door pillar, and lift away the quarter-light. To refit, reverse the removal sequence.

25 Boot compartment or tailgate lock – removal and refitting

1   Never, under any circumstances, close the boot lid when the lock is being removed.

2   Remove the lock cover (GT models). Remove the screws securing the lock to the lid, and remove the lock. Refer to Fig. 12.12, remove the

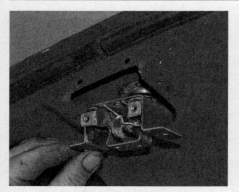

25.2 The boot compartment lock

31.1 The two-piece plastic bezel

32.1 The screws securing the hinge to the door

locking ring (3), and withdraw the pushbutton assembly and seal. To dismantle further, remove the screw (6), insert the key, and withdraw the barrel. To refit, reverse the removal procedure (photo).

26 Boot lid (Sports Tourer models) – removal and refitting

1   To remove the boot lid open the lid, erect the lid stay, and mark the hinge positions to assist refitting. Remove the screws from the lid to the hinges, ensuring that the lid does not drop onto the paintwork and damage it. Lift the lid away.
2   To refit, reverse the removal procedure. Finally tighten the hinge to lid screws after checking the fit of the lid in the body, and the operation of the latch.

27 Door striker plate (other than GHN4/5 and GHD4/5 models) – adjustment, removal and refitting

1   If one of the doors is not closing properly, check the striker plate-to-lockplate clearance which should be between 0.06 in (1.6 mm) to 0.03 in (0.8 mm) with the door closed. If incorrect, rectify by removing the striker plate and adding or removing packing shims until the clearance is correct Fig. 12.13 refers.
2   When removing the striker plate, mark round it with a pencil to aid refitting. Undo the screws, and lift off the striker plate and backing shims.
3   Adjust the striker plate by adding or removing packing pieces, and by moving it horizontally and longitudinally until the door closes easily without lifting, dropping or rattling. Tighten the screws firmly when the correct position has been found, and check, by opening and closing the door by the inside and outside handles, and by locking and opening the door using the key and inside handle.

28 Door striker plate (GHN4/5 and GHD4/5 models) – adjusting, removal and refitting

1   With the door closed, check that there is a 0.03 to 0.06 in (0.8 to 1.6 mm) clearance between the striker and latch faces. Adjustment, if required, is obtained by removing the striker plate retaining screws (item 11 in Fig. 12.14), and adding or removing shims behind the plate.
2   With the screws slackened to permit the striker to move, but sufficiently tight to allow the door to he fully closed, press the door inwards or pull outwards so that it aligns correctly with the body. Do not slam the door during adjustments. With the door open. mark round the striker with a pencil to position it. With the striker at right angles to the hinge axis, tighten the securing screws.
3   Open and close the door. The striker can be further adjusted in the vertical plane if the door has dropped or lifted by slackening the screws. When the door is fully closed, there should be a small amount of movement visible when the door is pressed against the seal.

29 Door trim pad (early Sports Tourer models) – removal and refitting

Remove the interior door handle, door pull, window winder handle and locking knob, by removing their fixing screws and washers. Remove

the screws securing the trim pad and waist rail ends, then lift off the trim pad to expose the waist rail centre screw, and remove the screw together with the rail. Pull off the stuck-down door liner if necessary. To refit, reverse the removal process.

30 Door trim pad (later models) – removal and refitting

Remove the interior door handle, door pull and window winder handle, by removing their fixing screws and washers. Remove the screws securing the waist rail and trim pad, and lift away both items. Pull off the stuck-down door liner if necessary. To refit, reverse the removal process.

31 Door trim pad and interior handles (GHN4/5 and GHD4/5 models) – removal and refitting

1   Disconnect the battery, and, with the window closed, remove the window winder handle and the door pull or armrest (whichever is fitted), by removing the fixing screws and washers. Remove the two-piece plastic bezel from the interior door control, by pulling one half upwards and the other half down, causing them to pull apart at the sides where they overlap (photo).
2   Unscrew the waist rail screws and remove the rail, unclip or unscrew the trim pad from the door, disconnect the speaker wires (if applicable) and remove the trim pad. Pull off the stuck-down door liner if necessary.
3   To refit, reverse the removal procedure.

32 Doors and hinges – removal and refitting

Front doors

1   Remove the trim pad as described in the relevant Section. Remove the three screws securing each hinge to the door, and lift the door away (photo).
2   To remove a hinge, undo the six screws inside the front wing which retain the splash panel. Remove the hinge bracket nuts, followed by the four screws holding the hinge bracket to the body. Remove the hinge and bracket assembly.
3   To refit, reverse the removal procedure. Before finally tightening the hinge screws, ensure that proper positioning and closing of the door has been achieved. Adjust the door position if necessary.

Tail door (GT models)

4   To remove the tail door, disconnect the battery, remove the luggage compartment lamp, prise out the roof trim pad, and disconnect the wires to the heated rear window.
5   Unscrew and remove the nuts to release the stays, remove the hinge screws, and withdraw the tail door.
6   Refitting is a reversal of the removal procedure, but align the door in the aperture before finally tightening the hinge screws.

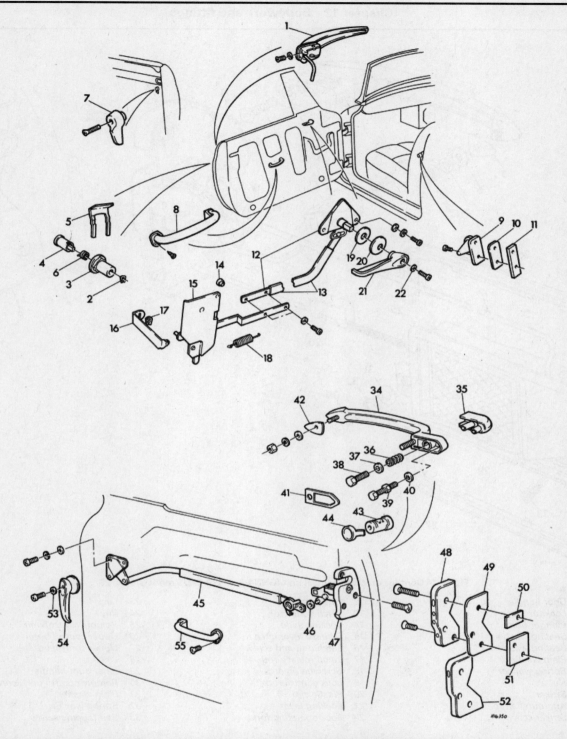

Fig 12.13 Exterior door handle, and handle locking mechanism (all except GHN4/5 and GHD4/5 models). Items 1 to 22 apply to early Sports Tourer only (Sec 27)

1	Outer door handle	13	Anti-rattle sleeve	35	Pushbutton	46	Anti-rattle washer
2	Spring clip	14	Outside door handle	36	Spring	47	Lock
3	Lock housing		buffer	37	Shakeproof washer	48	Striker
4	Lock barrel	15	Lock	38	Set screw	49	Shim – 0.003in or 0.006 in
5	Lock retaining clip	16	Operating link	39	Set screw with locknut		(0.08 mm or 0.16 mm)
6	Self-centring spring	17	Spring clip	40	Shakeproof washer	50	Tapping plate (upper)
7	Inner locking knob	18	Tension spring	41	Fibre washer	51	Tapping plate (lower)
8	Door pull	19	Fibre washer	42	Fibre washer	52	Striker lock
9	Striker	20	Finisher	43	Lock barrel	53	Spring washer
10	Packing	21	Inner door handle	44	Retaining clip	54	Inner door handle
11	Tapping plate	22	Spring washer	45	Remote control link	55	Door pull
12	Remote control lock	34	Outer door handle				

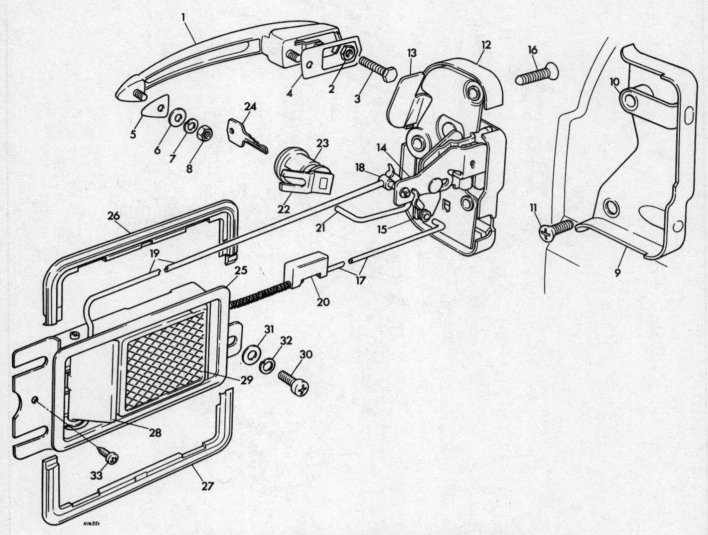

Fig 12.14 Door lock remote control unit (GHN4/5 and GHD4/5 models) (Sec 28)

1	Door handle	12	Latch unit	23	Lock
2	Locknut	13	Latch contactor	24	Key
3	Plunger bolt	14	Locking slide	25	Remote control unit
4	Sealing washer	15	Release lever latch	26	Upper control bezel
5	Sealing washer	16	Latch unit and screw	27	Upper control bezel
6	Plain washer	17	Latch release rod	28	Latch
7	Spring washer	18	Screwed pivot	29	Inner door handle
8	Nut	19	Lock control rod	30	Remote control unit screw
9	Striker	20	Plastic clip	31	Plain washer
10	Anti-burst strap	21	Locking lever	32	Spring washer
11	Striker screw	22	Lock operating fork	33	Self-tapping screw

33 Key-operated lock (all models) – removal and refitting

1   To remove the lock on early Sports Tourers, refer to Section 35, paragraphs 1 and 2.

2   To remove the lock on later Sports Tourer and GT models, close the window and remove the door trim pad as described in Section 30 or 31. From inside the door, compress the legs of the spring retainer and pull out the barrel assembly from the outside.

3   Refit in the reverse order, ensuring that the lock barrel operating fork is facing the door hinges.

4   On GHN4/5 and GHD4/5 cars, remove the remote control unit as described in Section 44. paragraph 1. From inside the door, compress the retaining collar legs and withdraw the lock barrel from the outside.

Refit in the reverse order, ensuring that the lock barrel operating fork is facing the door hinges.

34 Door handles, exterior – removal and refitting

1   On early models, remove the screws securing the handle. Remove the handle (see Fig. 12.13).

2   On later models, remove the trim pad, then raise the window to obtain access to nuts and washers securing the handle, and hence remove the handle (see Fig. 12.13).

3   To refit, reverse the removal procedure. Ensure that a minimum gap of 0.03 in (0.8 mm) exists between the contact point on the lock and the adjustable bolt on the pushbutton. Adjust as necessary.

35 Door locks (early Sports Tourer models) – removal and refitting

1   Remove the door trim pad, as described in Section 29, and the door glass assembly as described in Section 39. Disconnect the remote control link by removing the screws in the linking bar, remove the three screws securing the lock and withdraw the mechanism (see Fig. 12.13).
2   Remove the two screws which secure the outside door handle, and free the handle. Slide the retaining clip (5) from lock housing (3) inside the door, and withdraw the barrel and coupling link. Undo the four screws holding the lock to the door, and remove the lock.
3   To refit, reverse the removal procedure. Correctly adjust the remote control mechanism, using the elongated holes provided in the panel. Lubricate, and check all functions. Note that a minimum gap of 0.03 in (0.8 mm) must be provided between the contact point on the lock and the adjustable bolt on the pushbutton. Adjust as necessary.

36 Door locks (later models) – removal and refitting

Remove the door trim pad, as described in Section 30. Remove the C-clip holding the remote control link to the door lock, and remove the link. Remove lock (47) by removing the securing screws (see Fig. 12.13). Ensure that the latch is in the open position when the lock is fitted, and that the locking lever is engaged with the lock operating fork. Check for correct functioning. Lubricate all parts.

37 Door locks (GHN4/5 and GHD4/5 models) – removal and refitting

1   Remove the door trim pad, as described in Section 31. Unclip the retainers, and detach the remote control rods from the lock; take out the three screws from the lock, and remove it. Fig. 12.14 refers.
2   Refit in the reverse sequence, ensuring that the locking lever (21) is engaged with the lock operating fork (22). Lubricate, and check all functions.

38 Door glass regulator – removal and refitting

Remove the trim pad, as described in Sections 29, 30 or 31, depending on model. Remove the regulator and regulator extension securing screws, release the window regulator arc from the bottom of the door glass, lift the glass, and remove the regulator assembly through the door panel aperture. To refit, reverse the removal procedure. (Figs. 12.15, 12.16 and 12.17 refer).

39 Door windows (early Sports Tourer models) – removal and refitting

Remove the door trim as described in Section 29, and the fixings at the top and bottom of the rear door glass channel (see Fig. 12.15) with the glass in the high position. Release the regulator and regulator extension fixings, slide the regulator arms forward to disengage the studs from the door glass lower channel, and lift the glass out. To refit, reverse the removal procedure.

40 Door windows (later models) – removal and refitting

1   Remove the door trim pad as described in Section 30, and, referring to Fig. 12.16, remove the regulator bolts (4) and extension screws (5). Pull the regulator arc from the bottom of the door glass, lift the glass window up manually, and take the regulator and extension assembly out through the door panel aperture.
2   Remove the nut retaining the window rear guide channel to the door, and lift out the glass. To refit, reverse the removal procedure.

41 Door windows (1978/1979 models) – removal and refitting

1   Remove the door trim pad as described in Section 31. Remove the regulator arm stop, the four regulator screws, and the three regulator

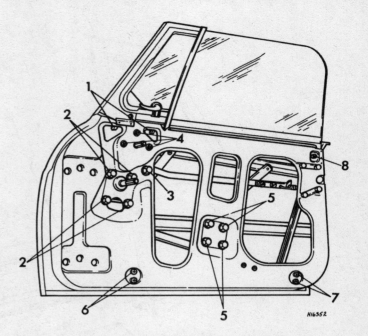

Fig 12.15 Door interior with trim removed – early Sports Tourer (Sec 38)

1   Ventilator securing nuts
2   Regulator securing bolts
3   Regulator arm stop
4   Door lock remote control securing screws
5   Regulator extension securing set screws
6   Front door glass mounting bracket securing screws
7   Rear door glass mounting bracket securing screws
8   Door glass channel securing screws

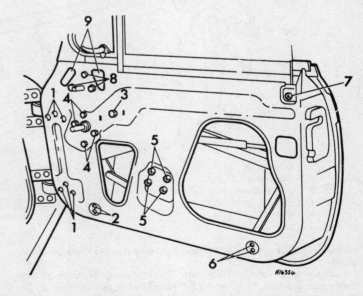

Fig 12.16 Door interior with trim removed – later models (Sec 38)

1   Door hinge securing screws
2   Front glass mounting bracket screws
3   Regulator arm stop
4   Regulator securing screws
5   Regulator extension screws
6   Rear glass mounting bracket screws
7   Door glass channel screws
8   Lock remote control screws
9   Ventilator screws

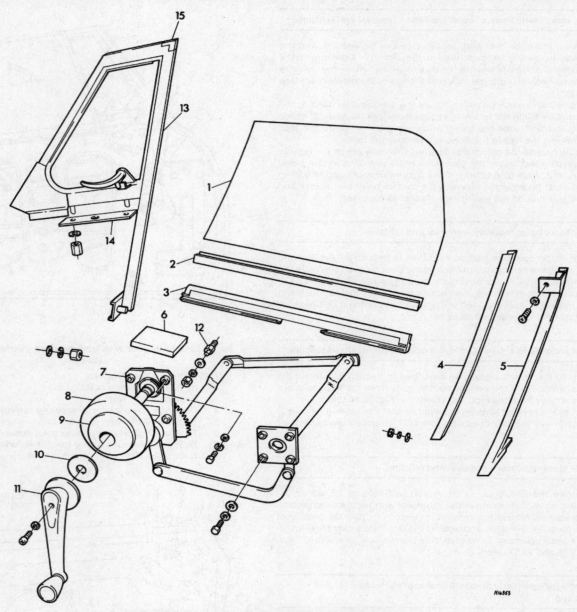

Fig 12.17 Window and window winding mechanism (Sec 38)

1	Door glass	6	Buffer	11	Handle and finisher
2	Glazing channel	7	Regulator	12	Stop
3	Lower channel	8	Pad	13	Ventilator
4	Flexible channel	9	Escutcheon	14	Seating plate
5	Channel	10	Fibre washer	15	Rubber capping

extension securing screws. Remove the regulator arc from the door glass.

2   Lift the glass, and withdraw the regulator assembly through the door panel aperture. Remove the nut retaining the window rear guide channel to the door, and lift out the glass. If necessary, remove the regulator channel and rubber protector from the glass. To refit, reverse the removal procedure.

42 Door lock remote control unit (early Sports Tourer models) – removal and refitting

To remove the remote control unit, proceed as described in Section 35, paragraph 1.

43 Door lock remote control unit (later models and GT models) – removal and refitting

1   Remove the door trim pad (see Section 30), remove the C-clip, and detach the link (45) from the lock (Fig. 12.13). Remove the remote control unit screws.

2   Remove the rubber capping (15) and stop (12) (Fig. 12.17). Raise the windows and disengage the studs from the channel.

3   Remove the securing screws at the back of the front window channel, wedge the glass in the up position, and remove the window regulator screws.

4   Press the regulator and front channel towards the outer door panel, bring the remote control unit down between the regulator and inner panel. Withdraw it through the large aperture.

5   To refit, reverse the removal sequence. Adjust the remote control unit by means of the elongated holes, to place the spring-loaded lever of the remote control link just in contact with the spring.

44 Door lock remote control unit (GHN4/5 and GHD4/5 models) – removal and refitting

1   Remove the door trim pad, as described in Section 31. Referring to Fig. 12.14, detach rods (17) and (19) from the latch unit (12). Remove the screws (33), and on later cars screw (30). Withdraw the rod (19) from the top of latch (28), and withdraw the remote control unit complete with rod (17).
2   To refit, reverse the removal sequence. Adjust as described in Section 45.

45 Door lock remote control unit (GHN4/5 and GHD4/5 models) – adjustment

1   Remove the door trim pad as described in Section 31. and wind the window right up.
2   Loosen the remote control unit retaining screws, and move the unit towards the latch, without compressing the rod spring, until the latch release lever (15) contacts the stop. Fig. 12.14 refers. Tighten the control unit screws, filing out the slots as required if insufficient adjustment exists.
3   With the latch release lever in the closed position, check that the striker is released by operating the door handle before the handle has reached the full extent of movement. Refit the self-tapping screw.
4   Refer to Fig. 12.14. Adjust the lock control by placing the latch release lever in the closed position and the locking latch (28) rearwards also to the closed position. Adjust the screwed end pivot (18) until it will pass freely into the locking slide (14). Clip the pivot into place. Check for proper operation. Lubricate the linkages inside the door with grease, and apply a little thin oil in the keyholes.

46 Anti-burst door units (GHN5 and GHD5 models, from vehicle No 294251) – removal and refitting

To remove the anti-burst plate, remove the two screws which secure it to the door pillar. To remove the anti-burst pin, remove the door trim as described in Section 31, remove the nut and washer, and remove the pin. To refit, reverse the removal sequence.

47 Facia panel, instruments and controls (early models) – removal and refitting

1   Disconnect the batteries, drain the cooling system, and remove the union which holds the temperature gauge sender unit to the cylinder head.
2   Take off the speaker panel surround after undoing the retaining screws. Lower the steering column after freeing the steering column upper fixing bracket.
3   Press in the plungers in the shanks of the heater control knobs and pull them off. Undo the nuts which hold the heater controls in place and pull out the controls from behind the facia panel.
4   Undo the choke cable nut behind the facia. Free the cable from the air cleaner bracket and pull out the inner and outer cables. Undo the union nut holding the oil pressure pipe in place. Undo the nut on the screenwasher pump, and remove the pump from the dashboard.
5   Remove the screw and nut holding the steady bracket to the glovebox attachment, the nuts and washers holding the top of the facia to the body, and the two screws which hold the bottom of the centre panel to the speaker panel. Pull the facia panel forward until sufficient access to the rear of the panel is obtained.
6   Label the warning lamps and electrical connections to ensure correct refitting and pull out or disconnect as applicable. Disconnect the

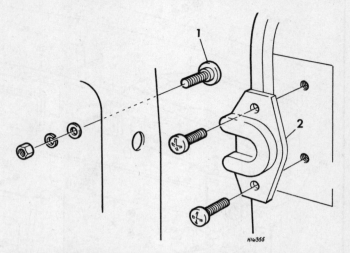

Fig 12.18 Anti-burst door units (GHN5 and GHD5 models, from vehicle No 294251) (Sec 46)

1   Door pin   2   Plate

cables from the rev counter and speedometer, and pull the temperature gauge capillary tube through from the engine compartment.
7   Lift the facia panel from the car and remove the instruments by undoing their securing straps. Remove the remaining knobs and switches as described in Chapter 10.
8   Refit in the reverse order. Top up the cooling system and test all switches and instruments for correct functioning.

48 Facia (GHN5 and GHD5 models, from vehicle No 410002) – removal and refitting

1   Disconnect the battery, and remove the centre console (see Section 56).
2   Extract the face level vents (see Section 58 or 59) and remove the three upper securing nuts from the facia with washers and brackets. Remove the four lower retaining screws. Remove the steering column-to-facia support rail bolts, and lower the column.
3   Remove the screw, nut and bracket from the rear of the glovebox. Lower the facia unit to clear the upper fixing studs and then withdraw the unit. Detach the various facia components, and remove the facia panel completely.
4   To refit the facia, reverse the removal procedure.

49 Facia (GHN4/5 and GHD4/5 models for certain territories) – removal and refitting

1   Disconnect the battery, remove the lower facia panels by removing the three retaining screws, and disconnect the choke cable at the carburettors. Remove the heater air and temperature control knobs, by unscrewing the securing nuts and disengaging the controls from the respective brackets. Remove the two fixing screws from the lower edge of the facia.
2   Remove the tachometer knurled fixing nuts, remove the earth wire and retaining brackets, disconnect the wiring and remove the tachometer.
3   Remove the six nuts from the facia top fixing studs, and the screws securing each end of the facia trim from behind the facia. Unscrew the nut on the trip recorder reset knob, and disengage the reset knob from the bracket. Remove the speedometer drive cable from the instrument.
4   Pull the facia away, disengaging the top fixing studs, and lift it clear of the steering column switch. Remove the switch wiring, identifying as necessary to ensure correct refitting. Withdraw the choke control cable. Remove the facia with the instruments and switches.
5   To refit, reverse the removal procedure.

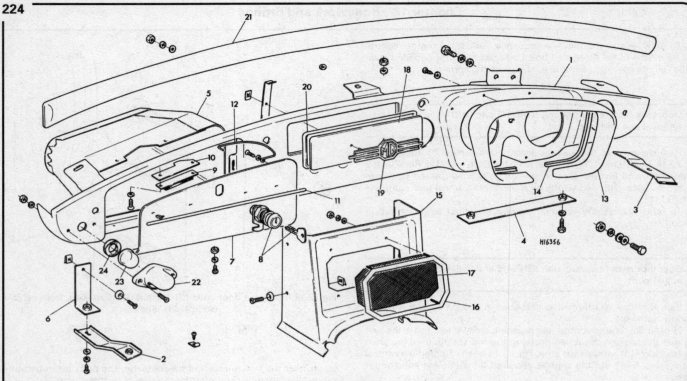

Fig 12.19 Facia, early vehicles – exploded view (Sec 47)

1	Facia panel	8	Lock	14	Hood finisher	19	MG motif
2	Steady bracket	9	Lid buffer	15	Speaker panel	20	Radio aperture bezel
3	Facia fixing plate	10	Lock catch	16	Speaker panel bezel	21	Crash roll assembly
4	Facia fixing plate	11	Lid finisher	17	Speaker grille	22	Map light cover
5	Glovebox	12	Check arm	18	Radio aperture blanking	23	Map light glass
6	Glovebox bracket	13	Instrument hood		plate	24	Seating gasket
7	Glovebox lid assembly						

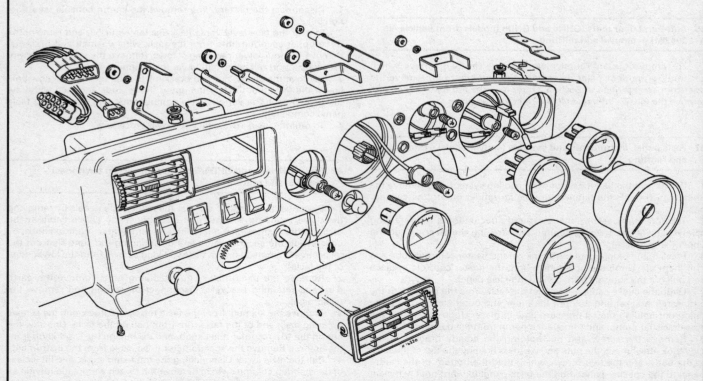

Fig 12.20 Facia (GHN5 and GHD5 models, from vehicle No 410002) (Sec 48)

50 Facia (1978 and 1979 models) – removal and refitting

USA and Canada

1 Disconnect the battery, remove the facia lower panels, and disconnect the facia harness connection at the multi-plug. Remove the console to one side, sufficiently to give access to the facia centre fixing screws (see Section 56).
2 Withdraw the three lower fixing screws in the facia, remove the vents (see Section 58 or 59) and the tachometer (see Chapter 10). Remove the six upper fixing screws in the facia.
3 Disconnect the speedometer cable and the oil pressure gauge pipe, and withdraw the facia.
4 To refit, reverse the removal sequence.

UK

5 Disconnect the battery and remove the centre console to one side.
6 Remove the glovebox and disconnect the face level vent hoses. Remove the vents by lifting one corner, positioning the locating tag on the aperture, and withdrawing the vents.
7 Remove the three upper nuts, washers and brackets, and the lower fixing screws.
8 Unbolt and lower the steering column from the support rail, noting the location and quantity of packing washers.
9 Move the facia downwards and forwards and disconnect the various instruments and cables.
10 Withdraw the facia from the car.
11 Refitting is a reversal of the removal procedure but adjust the choke cable as described in Chapter 3.

51 Glovebox and lid (GHN5 and GHD5 models, from vehicle No 258001) – removal and refitting

Remove the screws retaining each end of the lid stay, the catch, and the glovebox. Remove the glovebox. Remove the lid if necessary by removing screws and nuts. To refit, reverse the removal sequence.

52 Glovebox and lid (later UK models) – removal and refitting

Removal and refitting is largely as described in Section 51.

53 Glovebox and lid (USA and Canada models) – removal and refitting

To remove the glovebox, remove the lid catch securing screws and the glovebox securing screws. Withdraw the glovebox. Remove the screws and nuts securing the lid, and remove it. To refit, reverse the removal sequence.

54 Seats, front (and rear on GT models only) – removal and refitting

1 Where a seat belt warning system is fitted, disconnect the battery. To remove a front seat, free the seat catch and push it right back to expose the seat front securing screws. Remove the screws, and then push the seat completely forward. Remove the rear screws. Disconnect the seat belt warning cables, where relevant. Lift out the seat, and slide it from the runners. Retain any spacers used.
2 To remove the rear seat assembly (GT models), unlock the squab and remove it forward to the horizontal. Raise the boot carpet. Remove the screws which secure the hinges to the floor, and lift out the seat assembly.
3 To refit, reverse the removal sequence. Check for freedom of movement of the front seats, before finally tightening the runners.

55 Console (with hinged armrest) – removal and refitting

1 Disconnect the battery, remove the gear lever knob and locknut, and remove the four screws securing the retaining ring. Lift the armrest,

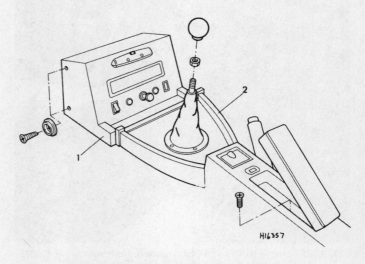

Fig 12.21 Console with hinged armrest (Sec 55)

1 *Console*   2 *Armrest assembly*

remove the screw underneath, and withdraw the armrest assembly, complete with gear lever boot and ring.
2 Remove the four console screws, pull it away, disconnect the wiring, and remove the console.
3 To refit, reverse the removal sequence.

56 Console (GHN5 and GHD5 models, from vehicle No 410002) – removal and refitting

1 With the battery disconnected first remove the gaiter retaining ring by unscrewing the securing screws. Remove the armrest by hinging upwards, removing the securing screw, and lifting it over the gaiter and gear lever.
2 Undo the four screws and move the console rearwards. Remove the heater control knobs by pressing in the retaining clips, using a pin through the knob holes. The heater control securing nut can now be removed and the controls withdrawn.
3 Remove the clock, warning lights, and bulb holders from the heater controls, disconnect the clock wires, and take the clock (where fitted) from the console by removing the two knurled nuts and retaining bracket. Remove the wires from the cigar lighter (USA models only).
4 Remove the console warning lights, and the nuts retaining the light boxes and illumination dial. Remove the console.
5 To refit, reverse the removal sequence.

57 Console (GHN4/5 and GHD4/5 models for certain territories) – removal and refitting

Disconnect the battery, remove the four screws, remove the ashtray if fitted, turn the carpet back and pull the console away. Disconnect the wiring and remove the console. To refit, reverse the removal procedure.

58 Face level air vents (early models) – removal and refitting

1 Disconnect the ducting from the back of the vents, which are themselves located by tags on the inside of the facia panel. To remove a vent, depress the bottom tag, partly withdraw the vent so that the tag rests on the vent aperture of the facia panel, and depress the top location tag. Remove the vent complete with packing.

Fig 12.22 Console (GHN5 and GHD5 models, from vehicle No 41002) (Sec 56)

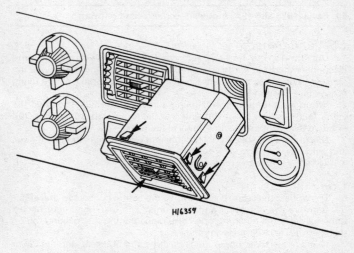

Fig 12.23 Face level vents, showing the locating tags (arrowed) (Sec 58)

2   To refit, reverse the removal sequence. Note that the round corners of the vent are level with the serrated wheel registers of the facia recess. Both vents are marked right- or left-hand on their flaps.

59   Face level air vents (GHN5 and GHD5 models, from vehicle No 258001) – removal and refitting

1   Remove the glovebox as described in Section 51. Disconnect the ducting from the back of the vents, remove the two screws securing the escutcheon assembly strap, and withdraw the vents and escutcheon. Remove the vents from the escutcheon panel by depressing the location tags with a small screwdriver.
2   To refit, reverse the removal sequence. Note that the vents are marked left- and right-hand. Ensure that the round corners of the vents (next to the serrated wheel) correspond with the round corners in the escutcheon, and that the complete escutcheon assembly is refitted with the serrated wheels uppermost.

60   Seat belts (early type) – fitting details

1   Secure one side of the belt to the rear wheel arch on early cars by removing the two domed nuts and plain washers from the fixing studs, fitting the bracket on the seat belt over the studs, and fitting the plain washers, spring washers, and domed nuts.
2   Secure one side of the belt to the rear wheel arch (on later cars) by removing the plastic cap from the fixing boss, fitting a spring washer to the short 7/16 in bolt, and inserting the bolt through the middle hole in the bracket on the belt. Secure the bracket to the boss. With the alternative type of belt, place the short 7/16 in bolt through the belt bracket, followed by the spring washer, and then the distance piece with the small diameter end towards the bolt head. Secure the bracket to the boss.
3   To secure the lower side of the belt to the sill, find the fixing point by feeling through the trim and cutting it away to give access to the hole. Fit the bracket on the belt to one of the 7/16 in bolts, followed by a waved washer and the distance piece with the smaller diameter towards the bolt head. Screw the assembled bracket into the hole in the sill.
4   To secure the other side of the lap strap to the propeller shaft tunnel, remove the plug from the fixing point on the opposite side of the tunnel to the seat for which the belt is being fitted. Place the remaining 7/16 in bolt in the hole in the bracket of the short belt. followed by the waved washer and distance piece with the smaller diameter end facing the bolt head. Position the assembled bolt through a hole in the propeller shaft tunnel and fit the spring washer and nut to the bolt from inside the tunnel. On later cars, an exposed fixing boss is positioned on the tunnel to which the short belt can be fitted.
5   It is advised that belts should be fitted in all versions of the MGB.

61   Seat belts (later type) – removal and refitting

1   To remove, take out the bolt securing the belt to the sill, retaining the anti-rattle spring. Raise the reel cover, and take out the retaining bolt. Where relevant, raise the carpet and disconnect the locking device wiring. Take out the bolt, spacer and anti-rattle washer securing the locking device. (Fig. 12.25 refers).
2   Refitting is a reversal of the removal procedure.

62   Seat belts (GHN4/5 and GHD4/5 models for certain territories) – removal and refitting

1   To remove the short belt, raise the carpet next to the tunnel and disconnect the seat belt wiring. Remove the belt by removing the bolt with the spacer. Remove the reel and the long belt by removing the

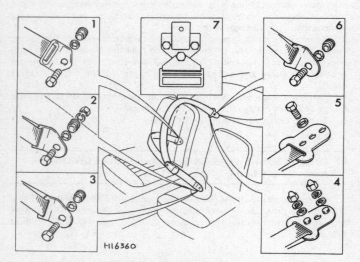

Fig 12.24 The various seat belt fixings (Sec 60)

1   Sill
2   Driveshaft tunnel (early cars)
3   Driveshaft tunnel (later cars)
4   Wheel arch (early cars)
5   Wheel arch (later cars)
6   Wheel arch, second type belt (later cars)
7   Stowage clip

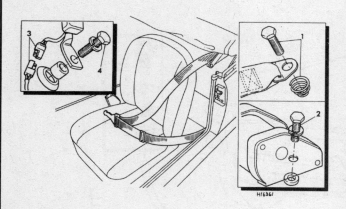

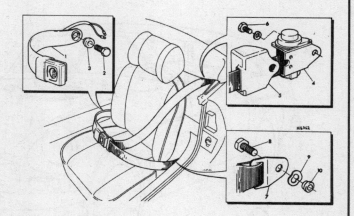

Fig 12.26 Seat belts (GHN4/5 and GHD4/5 vehicles for certain territories) (Sec 62)

1	Short belt	6	Retaining bolt
2	Retaining bolt	7	Seat belt sill mounting
3	Spacer	8	Retaining bolt
4	Seat belt reel	9	Anti-rattle washer
5	Cover for reel	10	Spacer

Fig 12.25 Seat belts (later type) (Sec 61)

1 Bolt anti-rattle spring, securing the bolt to the sill
2 Bolt and washer, retaining the reel
3 Wiring connector (USA and Canada)
4 Bolt, spacer and anti-rattle washer, securing the locker device

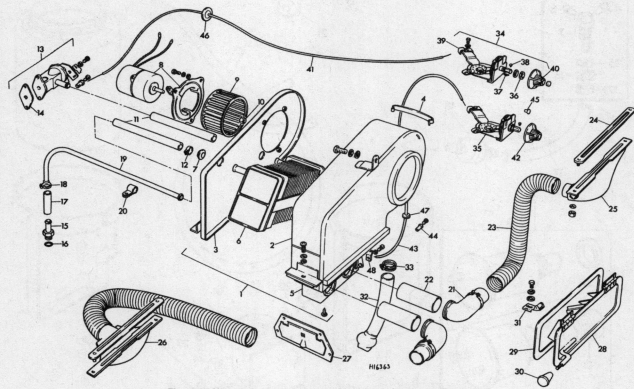

Fig 12.27 Heater and blower motor assembly (early cars) (Sec 63)

1	Heater assembly	14	Water valve gasket	26	LH demister nozzle	37	Knob clip
2	Cover	15	Water union	27	Heater outlet door	38	Knob pin
3	Motor side cover	16	Union washer	28	Fresh air vent door	39	Cable clamp
4	Cover clip	17	Water hose (2 in x ½ in)	29	Door seal	40	Heat knob
5	Outlet duct	18	Hose clip	30	Door knob	41	Heat control cable
6	Radiator	19	Water return pipe	31	Fresh air bent door spring	42	Air knob
7	Washer for radiator pipe	20	Clip to inlet manifold	32	Drain and dust valve	43	Air control cable
8	Motor end mounting plate	21	Demister elbow		assembly tube	44	Trunnion
9	Runner	22	Connecting tube	33	Tube assembly clip	45	Heater control rivet
10	Collet nut	23	Demister air hose	34	Heat control	46	Heater cable grommet
11	Water hose (8½ in x ½ in)	24	Demister escutcheon	35	Air control	47	Air cable grommet
12	Hose clip	25	RH demister nozzle	36	Locknut	48	Cable clamp
13	Water valve assembly						

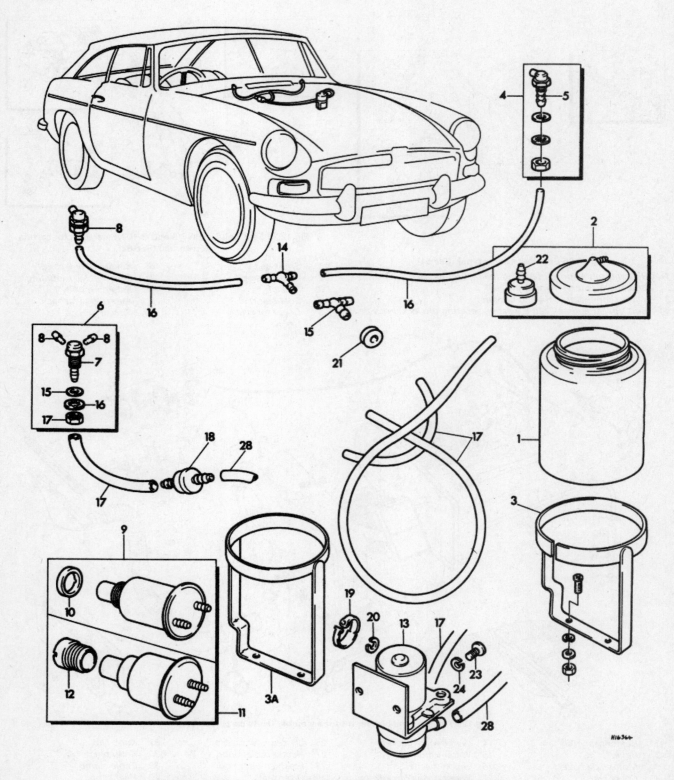

Fig 12.28 Windscreen washer system (early, hand-operated type) (Sec 66)

1 Container
2 Cap assembly
3 Container carrier
4 Jet assembly (single)
5 Jet
6 Jet assembly (twin)
7 Adaptor
8 Nozzle
9 Washer pump
10 Pump locking ring
11 Washer pump (alternative type)
12 Pump locking ring
13 Pump assembly (USA)
14 3-way connector
15 3-way connector (alternative design)
16 Tubing
17 Tubing, pump to 3-way connector
18 Line valve
19 Strap
20 Circlip
21 Grommet
22 Bottle valve

securing bolt from the sill. Unscrew the bolt from the rear wheel arch to release the reel.

2   To refit, reassemble in revere order (Fig. 12.26 refers).

63   Heater and blower motor assembly (early models) – removal, dismantling and refitting

1   To remove the blower motor, disconnect the batteries, disconnect the snap connectors to the blower motor, and remove the three screws which hold the motor mounting plate. Remove the plate and motor.

2   To remove the heater assembly, disconnect the battery and the snap connectors in the motor leads. Drain the cooling system and take the heater hoses from the heater. Remove the screws which secure the heater to the bulkhead, then remove the control console or speaker panel, loosen the clips on the demister tubes, and take away one of the demister tube elbows. Remove the tube plate, and withdraw the fibre demister tubes.

3   On early models, remove the overdrive vacuum switch. Remove the heater air control from the facia, and disconnect the cable. Free the air control cable to the heater from the clip. Lift out the heater assembly.

4   To dismantle, remove the clips and take off the front panel, together with the motor and matrix. Take the matrix from the plate, remove the motor by removing the securing screws, and disconnect the air control cable.

5   To refit, reverse the removal sequence. Take care to re-route the air control cable correctly, checking the function before refitting the demister tubes and speaker panel.

64   Heater, heater matrix and airflow cable (GHN5 and GHD5 models, from vehicle No 410002) – removal, dismantling and refitting

1   Disconnect the battery terminals and drain the cooling system. Detach the heater wires from the multi-connector plug and unclip the washer motor wires from the clip on the heater motor unit. On USA and Canada vehicles, detach the clip securing the engine breather hose. Loosen the hose clips and detach the heater hoses. Unscrew the heater unit securing screws. Detach the clips securing the washer tube and speedometer cable (on USA and Canada vehicles). From inside the car, remove the centre console sufficiently to disconnect the temperature control cable to the heater. Detach the demister tubes from the heater, and withdraw the heater unit from the car.

2   To refit, reverse the removal procedure. Feed the temperature control cable through the bulkhead slot before fitting the heater unit.

3   To remove the matrix, remove the heater unit, empty any remaining coolant out, and take off the heater casing retaining clips. Lift the casing side over the matrix outlets (note the fan motor wires, still connected). Remove the matrix from the main casing, and take the packing foam from the matrix. To refit, reverse the removal procedure.

4   To remove the airflow control cable, remove the heater unit or on later models, remove the centre console, loosen the outer cable retaining bracket and the inner cable trunnion screw, and withdraw

the cable from the bracket on the flap. To refit, reverse the removal procedure.

65   Heater water valve, fan motor, controls and temperature control cable (GHN5 and GHD5 models, from vehicle No 410002) – removal and refitting

1   To remove the water valve from the cylinder head, drain the cooling system and remove the heater hose from the valve. Loosen the trunnion on the heater temperature control inner cable, and the retaining bracket screw on the outer cable. Withdraw the cable, remove the valve securing bolts, and remove the valve and washer. To refit, reverse the removal procedure.

2   To remove the fan motor, disconnect the battery and the wires from the motor terminals. Remove the three securing screws and take the fan motor from the casing. Remove the fan retaining clip and then the fan. To refit, reverse the removal procedure.

3   To remove the heater controls, remove the console (see Section 56), and remove the heater control knob, by pressing in the retainer clip using a small pin through the knob hole. Remove the nut securing the heater control, and withdraw it. Loosen the outer cable bracket screw and the inner cable trunnion, and withdraw the control from the cable. To refit, reverse the removal procedure.

4   To remove the temperature control cable, loosen the outer cable bracket screw on the water valve, loosen the inner cable trunnion screw, and take the cable from the water valve. Withdraw the centre console (see Section 56) and, on the heater temperature control, loosen the outer cable bracket screw and the inner cable trunnion screw. Remove the cable from the control, feed it through the bulkhead, and remove it from the vehicle. To refit, reverse the removal procedure.

66   Windscreen washer system

Early type

1   In this system, a simple pump draws water from the reservoir and pumps it along a pipe to the jets. If there is water in the reservoir and the system does not operate, disconnect the pipe from the jets and retest. If the system now operates, the jets are blocked and should be cleared with a pin. If no water comes down the pipe, check for kinks or breaks. Finally, if the system still does not operate, remove the pump from the dashboard and check by attaching a piece of pipe to it and placing this in water. If the system still doesn't operate, renew the pump.

Later type

2   An electric pump is fitted (see Chapter 10). In the event of failure, a check can be made as described in paragraph 1, but instead of removing the pump, simply detach the outlet pipe and operate the pump to ensure that water is pumped out. If this does not happen, and if the supply to the pump is adequate and not choked, the pump must be renewed.

General repair procedures

Whenever servicing, repair or overhaul work is carried out on the car or its components, observe the following procedures and instructions. This will assist in carrying out the operation efficiently and to a professional standard of workmanship.

Joint mating faces and gaskets

When separating components at their mating faces, never insert screwdrivers or similar implements into the joint between the faces in order to prise them apart. This can cause severe damage which results in oil leaks, coolant leaks, etc upon reassembly. Separation is usually achieved by tapping along the joint with a soft-faced hammer in order to break the seal. However, note that this method may not be suitable where dowels are used for component location.

Where a gasket is used between the mating faces of two components, a new one must be fitted on reassembly; fit it dry unless otherwise stated in the repair procedure. Make sure that the mating faces are clean and dry, with all traces of old gasket removed. When cleaning a joint face, use a tool which is unlikely to score or damage the face, and remove any burrs or nicks with an oilstone or fine file.

Make sure that tapped holes are cleaned with a pipe cleaner, and keep them free of jointing compound, if this is being used, unless specifically instructed otherwise.

Ensure that all orifices, channels or pipes are clear, and blow through them, preferably using compressed air.

Oil seals

Oil seals can be removed by levering them out with a wide flat-bladed screwdriver or similar implement. Alternatively, a number of self-tapping screws may be screwed into the seal, and these used as a purchase for pliers or some similar device in order to pull the seal free.

Whenever an oil seal is removed from its working location, either individually or as part of an assembly, it should be renewed.

The very fine sealing lip of the seal is easily damaged, and will not seal if the surface it contacts is not completely clean and free from scratches, nicks or grooves. If the original sealing surface of the component cannot be restored, and the manufacturer has not made provision for slight relocation of the seal relative to the sealing surface, the component should be renewed.

Protect the lips of the seal from any surface which may damage them in the course of fitting. Use tape or a conical sleeve where possible. Where indicated, lubricate the seal lips with oil before fitting and, on dual-lipped seals, fill the space between the lips with grease.

Unless otherwise stated, oil seals must be fitted with their sealing lips toward the lubricant to be sealed.

Use a tubular drift or block of wood of the appropriate size to install the seal and, if the seal housing is shouldered, drive the seal down to the shoulder. If the seal housing is unshouldered, the seal should be fitted with its face flush with the housing top face (unless otherwise instructed).

Screw threads and fastenings

Seized nuts, bolts and screws are quite a common occurrence where corrosion has set in, and the use of penetrating oil or releasing fluid will often overcome this problem if the offending item is soaked for a while before attempting to release it. The use of an impact driver may also provide a means of releasing such stubborn fastening devices, when used in conjunction with the appropriate screwdriver bit or socket. If none of these methods works, it may be necessary to resort to the careful application of heat, or the use of a hacksaw or nut splitter device. Before resorting to extreme methods, check that you are not dealing with a left-hand thread!

Studs are usually removed by locking two nuts together on the threaded part, and then using a spanner on the lower nut to unscrew the stud. Studs or bolts which have broken off below the surface of the component in which they are mounted can sometimes be removed using a stud extractor.

Always ensure that a blind tapped hole is completely free from oil, grease, water or other fluid before installing the bolt or stud. Failure to do this could cause the housing to crack due to the hydraulic action of the bolt or stud as it is screwed in.

For some screw fastenings, notably cylinder head bolts or nuts, torque wrench settings are no longer specified for the latter stages of tightening, "angle-tightening" being called up instead. Typically, a fairly low torque wrench setting will be applied to the bolts/ nuts in the correct sequence, followed by one or more stages of tightening through specified angles.

When checking or retightening a nut or bolt to a specified torque setting, slacken the nut or bolt by a quarter of a turn, and then retighten to the specified setting. However, this should not be attempted where angular tightening has been used.

Locknuts, locktabs and washers

Any fastening which will rotate against a component or housing during tightening should always have a washer between it and the relevant component or housing.

Spring or split washers should always be renewed when they are used to lock a critical component such as a big-end bearing retaining bolt or nut. Locktabs which are folded over to retain a nut or bolt should always be renewed.

Self-locking nuts can be re-used in non-critical areas, providing resistance can be felt when the locking portion passes over the bolt or stud thread. However, it should be noted that self-locking stiffnuts tend to lose their effectiveness after long periods of use, and should then be renewed as a matter of course.

Split pins must always be replaced with new ones of the correct size for the hole.

When thread-locking compound is found on the threads of a fastener which is to be re-used, it should be cleaned off with a wire brush and solvent, and fresh compound applied on reassembly.

Special tools

Some repair procedures in this manual entail the use of special tools such as a press, two or three-legged pullers, spring compressors, etc. Wherever possible, suitable readily-available alternatives to the manufacturer's special tools are described, and are shown in use. In some instances, where no alternative is possible, it has been necessary to resort to the use of a manufacturer's tool, and this has been done for reasons of safety as well as the efficient completion of the repair operation. Unless you are highly-skilled and have a thorough understanding of the procedures described, never attempt to bypass the use of any special tool when the procedure described specifies its use. Not only is there a very great risk of personal injury, but expensive damage could be caused to the components involved.

Environmental considerations

When disposing of used engine oil, brake fluid, antifreeze, etc, give due consideration to any detrimental environmental effects. Do not, for instance, pour any of the above liquids down drains into the general sewage system, or onto the ground to soak away, as this is likely to pollute your local environment. Many local council refuse tips provide a facility for waste oil disposal, as do some garages. You can find your nearest disposal point by calling the Environment Agency on 03708 506 506 or by visiting www.oilbankline.org.uk.

Note: It is illegal and anti-social to dump oil down the drain. To find the location of your local oil recycling bank, call 03708 506 506 or visit www.oilbankline.org.uk.

MOT Test Checks

This is a guide to getting your vehicle through the MOT test. Obviously it will not be possible to examine the vehicle to the same standard as the professional MOT tester. However, working through the following checks will enable you to identify any problem areas before submitting the vehicle for the test.

It has only been possible to summarise the test requirements here, based on the regulations in force at the time of printing. Test standards are becoming increasingly stringent, although there are some exemptions for older vehicles.

An assistant will be needed to help carry out some of these checks.

The checks have been sub-divided into four categories, as follows:

1 Checks carried out **FROM THE DRIVER'S SEAT**

2 Checks carried out **WITH THE VEHICLE ON THE GROUND**

3 Checks carried out **WITH THE VEHICLE RAISED AND THE WHEELS FREE TO TURN**

4 Checks carried out on **YOUR VEHICLE'S EXHAUST EMISSION SYSTEM**

---

1 Checks carried out **FROM THE DRIVER'S SEAT**

Handbrake
☐ Test the operation of the handbrake. Excessive travel (too many clicks) indicates incorrect brake or cable adjustment.
☐ Check that the handbrake cannot be released by tapping the lever sideways. Check the security of the lever mountings.

Footbrake
☐ Depress the brake pedal and check that it does not creep down to the floor, indicating a master cylinder fault. Release the pedal, wait a few seconds, then depress it again. If the pedal travels nearly to the floor before firm resistance is felt, brake adjustment or repair is necessary. If the pedal feels spongy, there is air in the hydraulic system which must be removed by bleeding.

☐ Check that the brake pedal is secure and in good condition. Check also for signs of fluid leaks on the pedal, floor or carpets, which would indicate failed seals in the brake master cylinder.
☐ Check the servo unit (when applicable) by operating the brake pedal several times, then keeping the pedal depressed and starting the engine. As the engine starts, the pedal will move down slightly. If not, the vacuum hose or the servo itself may be faulty.

Steering wheel and column
☐ Examine the steering wheel for fractures or looseness of the hub, spokes or rim.
☐ Move the steering wheel from side to side and then up and down. Check that the steering wheel is not loose on the column, indicating wear or a loose retaining nut. Continue moving the steering wheel as before, but also turn it slightly from left to right.
☐ Check that the steering wheel is not loose on the column, and that there is no abnormal

movement of the steering wheel, indicating wear in the column support bearings or couplings.

Windscreen, mirrors and sunvisor
☐ The windscreen must be free of cracks or other significant damage within the driver's field of view. (Small stone chips are acceptable.) Rear view mirrors must be secure, intact, and capable of being adjusted.

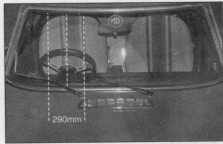

☐ The driver's sunvisor must be capable of being stored in the "up" position.

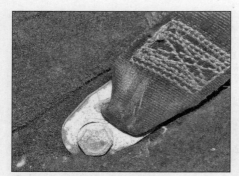

Seat belts and seats

Note: *The following checks are applicable to all seat belts, front and rear.*

☐ Examine the webbing of all the belts (including rear belts if fitted) for cuts, serious fraying or deterioration. Fasten and unfasten each belt to check the buckles. If applicable, check the retracting mechanism. Check the security of all seat belt mountings accessible from inside the vehicle.

☐ Seat belts with pre-tensioners, once activated, have a "flag" or similar showing on the seat belt stalk. This, in itself, is not a reason for test failure.

☐ The front seats themselves must be securely attached and the backrests must lock in the upright position.

Doors

☐ Both front doors must be able to be opened and closed from outside and inside, and must latch securely when closed.

2 Checks carried out WITH THE VEHICLE ON THE GROUND

Vehicle identification

☐ Number plates must be in good condition, secure and legible, with letters and numbers correctly spaced.

☐ The VIN plate and/or homologation plate must be legible.

Electrical equipment

☐ Switch on the ignition and check the operation of the horn.

☐ Check the windscreen washers and wipers, examining the wiper blades; renew damaged or perished blades. Also check the operation of the stop-lights.

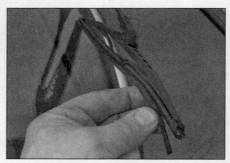

☐ Check the operation of the sidelights and number plate lights. The lenses and reflectors must be secure, clean and undamaged.

☐ Check the operation and alignment of the headlights. The headlight reflectors must not be tarnished and the lenses must be undamaged.

☐ Switch on the ignition and check the operation of the direction indicators (including the instrument panel tell-tale) and the hazard warning lights. Operation of the sidelights and stop-lights must not affect the indicators - if it does, the cause is usually a bad earth at the rear light cluster.

☐ Check the operation of the rear foglight(s), including the warning light on the instrument panel or in the switch.

Footbrake

☐ Examine the master cylinder, brake pipes and servo unit for leaks, loose mountings, corrosion or other damage.

☐ The fluid reservoir must be secure and the fluid level must be topped up.

☐ Inspect both front brake flexible hoses for cracks or deterioration of the rubber. Turn the steering from lock to lock, and ensure that the hoses do not contact the wheel, tyre, or any part of the steering or suspension mechanism. With the brake pedal firmly depressed, check the hoses for bulges or leaks under pressure.

Steering and suspension

☐ Have your assistant turn the steering wheel from side to side slightly, up to the point where the steering gear just begins to transmit this movement to the roadwheels. Check for excessive free play between the steering wheel and the steering gear, indicating wear or insecurity of the steering column joints, the column-to-steering gear coupling, or the steering gear itself.

☐ Have your assistant turn the steering wheel more vigorously in each direction, so that the roadwheels just begin to turn. As this is done, examine all the steering joints, linkages, fittings and attachments. Renew any component that shows signs of wear or damage.

☐ Check that the vehicle is standing level, and at approximately the correct ride height.

Shock absorbers

☐ Depress each corner of the vehicle in turn, then release it. The vehicle should rise and then settle in its normal position. If the vehicle continues to rise and fall, the shock absorber is defective. A shock absorber which has seized will also cause the vehicle to fail.

Exhaust system
☐ Start the engine. With your assistant holding a rag over the tailpipe, check the entire system for leaks. Repair or renew leaking sections.

3 Checks carried out WITH THE VEHICLE RAISED AND THE WHEELS FREE TO TURN

Jack up the front and rear of the vehicle, and securely support it on axle stands. Position the stands clear of the suspension assemblies. Ensure that the wheels are clear of the ground and that the steering can be turned from lock to lock.

Steering mechanism
☐ Have your assistant turn the steering from lock to lock. Check that the steering turns smoothly, and that no part of the steering mechanism, including a wheel or tyre, fouls any brake hose or pipe or any part of the body structure.

☐ Examine the steering rack rubber gaiters for damage or insecurity of the retaining clips. If power steering is fitted, check for signs of damage or leakage of the fluid hoses, pipes or connections. Also check for excessive stiffness or binding of the steering, a missing split pin or locking device, or severe corrosion of the body structure within 30 cm of any steering component attachment point.

Front and rear suspension and wheel bearings
☐ Starting at the front right-hand side, grasp the roadwheel at the 3 o'clock and 9 o'clock positions and rock gently but firmly. Check for free play or insecurity at the wheel bearings, suspension balljoints, or suspension mount-ings, pivots and attachments.

☐ Now grasp the wheel at the 12 o'clock and 6 o'clock positions and repeat the previous inspection. Spin the wheel, and check for roughness or tightness of the front wheel bearing.

☐ If excess free play is suspected at a component pivot point, this can be confirmed by using a large screwdriver or similar tool and levering between the mounting and the component attachment. This will confirm whether the wear is in the pivot bush, its retaining bolt, or in the mounting itself (the bolt holes can often become elongated).

☐ Carry out all the above checks at the other front wheel, and then at both rear wheels.

Springs and shock absorbers
☐ Examine the suspension struts (when applicable) for serious fluid leakage, corrosion, or damage to the casing. Also check the security of the mounting points.

☐ If coil springs are fitted, check that the spring ends locate in their seats, and that the spring is not corroded, cracked or broken.

☐ If leaf springs are fitted, check that all leaves are intact, that the axle is securely attached to each spring, and that there is no deterioration of the spring eye mountings, bushes, and shackles.

☐ The same general checks apply to vehicles fitted with other suspension types, such as torsion bars, hydraulic displacer units, etc. Ensure that all mountings and attachments are secure, that there are no signs of excessive wear, corrosion or damage, and (on hydraulic types) that there are no fluid leaks or damaged pipes.

☐ Inspect the shock absorbers for signs of serious fluid leakage. Check for wear of the mounting bushes or attachments, or damage to the body of the unit.

Braking system
☐ If possible without dismantling, check brake pad wear and disc condition. Ensure that the friction lining material has not worn excessively, (A) and that the discs are not fractured, pitted, scored or badly worn (B).

☐ Examine all the rigid brake pipes underneath the vehicle, and the flexible hose(s) at the rear. Look for corrosion, chafing or insecurity of the pipes, and for signs of bulging under pressure, chafing, splits or deterioration of the flexible hoses.

☐ Look for signs of fluid leaks at the brake calipers or on the brake backplates. Repair or renew leaking components.

☐ Slowly spin each wheel, while your assistant depresses and releases the footbrake. Ensure that each brake is operating and does not bind when the pedal is released.

☐ Examine the handbrake mechanism, checking for frayed or broken cables, excessive

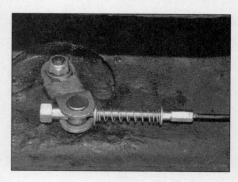

corrosion, or wear or insecurity of the linkage. Check that the mechanism works on each relevant wheel, and releases fully, without binding.

☐ It is not possible to test brake efficiency without special equipment, but a road test can be carried out later to check that the vehicle pulls up in a straight line.

Fuel and exhaust systems

☐ Inspect the fuel tank (including the filler cap), fuel pipes, hoses and unions. All components must be secure and free from leaks.

☐ Examine the exhaust system over its entire length, checking for any damaged, broken or missing mountings, security of the retaining clamps and rust or corrosion.

Wheels and tyres

☐ Examine the sidewalls and tread area of each tyre in turn. Check for cuts, tears, lumps, bulges, separation of the tread, and exposure of the ply or cord due to wear or damage. Check that the tyre bead is correctly seated on the wheel rim, that the valve is sound and properly seated, and that the wheel is not distorted or damaged.

☐ Check that the tyres are of the correct size for the vehicle, that they are of the same size and type on each axle, and that the pressures are correct.

☐ Check the tyre tread depth. The legal minimum at the time of writing is 1.6 mm over at least three-quarters of the tread width. Abnormal tread wear may indicate incorrect front wheel alignment.

Body corrosion

☐ Check the condition of the entire vehicle structure for signs of corrosion in load-bearing areas. (These include chassis box sections, side sills, cross-members, pillars, and all suspension, steering, braking system and seat belt mountings and anchorages.) Any corrosion which has seriously reduced the thickness of a load-bearing area is likely to cause the vehicle to fail. In this case professional repairs are likely to be needed.

☐ Damage or corrosion which causes sharp or otherwise dangerous edges to be exposed will also cause the vehicle to fail.

4 Checks carried out on YOUR VEHICLE'S EXHAUST EMISSION SYSTEM

Petrol models

☐ The engine should be warmed up, and running well (ignition system in good order, air filter element clean, etc).

☐ Before testing, run the engine at around 2500 rpm for 20 seconds. Let the engine drop to idle, and watch for smoke from the exhaust. If the idle speed is too high, or if dense blue or black smoke emerges for more than 5 seconds, the vehicle will fail. Typically, blue smoke signifies oil burning (engine wear); black smoke means unburnt fuel (dirty air cleaner element, or other fuel system fault).

☐ An exhaust gas analyser for measuring carbon monoxide (CO) and hydrocarbons (HC) is now needed. If one cannot be hired or borrowed, have a local garage perform the check.

CO emissions (mixture)

☐ The MOT tester has access to the CO limits for all vehicles. The CO level is measured at idle speed, and at 'fast idle' (2500 to 3000 rpm). The following limits are given as a general guide:

Vehicles registered before 1st August 1975 – Visual check only

Vehicles registered between 1st August 1975 and 31st July 1986 – Less than or equal to 4.5% CO

☐ If the CO level is too high, this may point to poor maintenance (in particular, a blocked air cleaner element) or carburettor maladjustment (mixture too rich, float level incorrect or float needle valve leaking).

HC emissions

☐ The MOT tester has access to HC limits for all vehicles. The HC level is measured at 'fast idle' (2500 to 3000 rpm). The following limits are given as a general guide:

Vehicles registered before 1st August 1975 – Visual check only

Vehicles registered between 1st August 1975 and 31st July 1986 – Less than or equal to 1200 ppm

☐ Excessive HC emissions are typically caused by oil being burnt (worn engine), or by a blocked crankcase ventilation system ('breather'). If the engine oil is old and thin, an oil change may help.

Index

Preserving Our Motoring Heritage

The Model J Duesenberg Derham Tourster. Only eight of these magnificent cars were ever built – this is the only example to be found outside the United States of America.

Almost every car you have ever loved, loathed or desired is gathered under one roof at the Haynes International Motor Museum. Over 400 immaculately presented cars and motorcycles represent every aspect of our motoring heritage, from elegant reminders of bygone days, such as the superb Model J Duesenberg to curiosities like the bug-eyed Heinkel Cabin-Cruiser. There are also many old friends and familiar family favorites. Perhaps you remember the 1959 Ford Popular that you did your courting in? The magnificent 'Red Collection' is a spectacle of classic sports cars including AC, Alfa Romeo, Austin Healey, Ferrari, Lamborghini, Maserati, MG, Riley, Porsche and Triumph.

A Perfect Day Out

Each and every vehicle at the Haynes International Motor Museum has played its part in the history and culture of motoring. Today, they make a wonderful spectacle and a great day out for all the family. Bring the kids, bring Mum and Dad, but above all bring your camera to capture those golden memories forever. You will also find an impressive array of motoring memorabilia, history of the penny arcade from the point of view motoring and one of the most extensive transport book shops in Britain. The Haynes Café serves everything from a cup of tea to wholesome, home-made meals or if you prefer, you can enjoy the large picnic area nestled in the beautiful rural surrounding of Somerset.

John Haynes O.B.E., Founder and Chairman of the museum.

Michael Schumacher's 1996, Ferrari, Formula 1 Type F310, designed by John Bernard

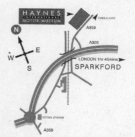

The Museum is situated on the A359 Yeovil to Frome road at Sparkford, just off the A303 in Somerset. It is about 40 miles south of Bristol, and 25 minutes drive from the M5, J25 at Taunton.

Open every day (except 24th, 25th, 26th December & 1st January).
1st October to 31st March, 10:00am-4:30pm and 1st April to 30th September, 9:30am-5:30pm
(Summer holidays open until 6pm).

Special rates available for schools and coach parties. Charitable Trust No. 292048.